NATIONS OF THE MODERN WORLD

ARGENTINA	H. S. Ferns
AUSTRALIA	O. H. K. Spate
CEYLON	S. A. Pakeman
CYPRUS	H. D. Purcell
MODERN EGYPT	Tom Little
ENGLAND	John Bowle
FINLAND	W. R. Mead
EAST GERMANY	David Childs
WEST GERMANY	Michael Balfour
MODERN GREECE	John Campbell and Philip Sherrard
MODERN INDIA	Sir Percival Griffiths
MODERN IRAN	Peter Avery
ITALY	Muriel Grindrod
JAPAN	Sir Esler Dening
KENYA	A. Marshall MacPhee
LIBYA	John Wright
MALAYSIA	J. M. Gullick
MOROCCO	Mark I. Cohen and Lorna Hahn
NEW ZEALAND	James W. Rowe and Margaret A. Rowe
NIGERIA	Sir Rex Niven
PAKISTAN	Ian Stephens
SOUTH AFRICA	John Cope
SUDAN REPUBLIC	K. D. D. Henderson
TURKEY	Geoffrey Lewis
THE UNITED STATES OF AMERICA	H. C. Allen
YUGOSLAVIA	Muriel Heppell and F. B. Singleton

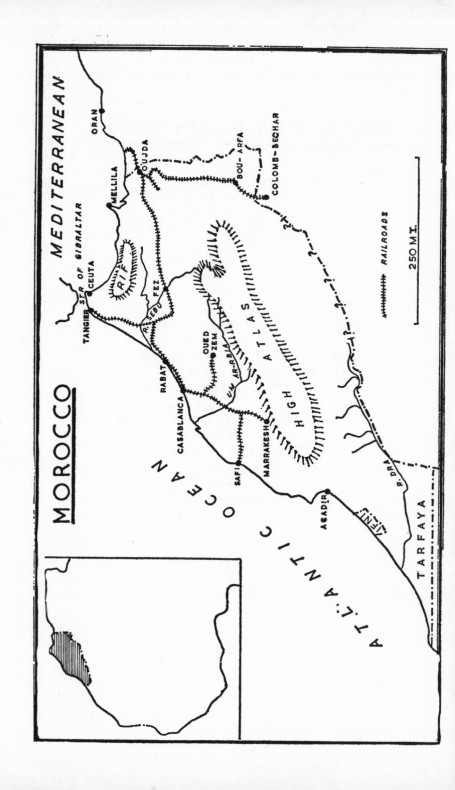

MOROCCO

OLD LAND, NEW NATION

by

Mark I. Cohen

and

Lorna Hahn

FREDERICK A. PRAEGER, *Publishers*

New York • Washington • London

FREDERICK A. PRAEGER, Publishers
111 Fourth Avenue, New York, N.Y. 10003, U.S.A.
5, Cromwell Place, London S.W. 7, England

Published in the United States of America in 1966
by Frederick A. Praeger, Inc., Publishers

Second printing, 1969

© 1966 by Frederick A. Praeger, Inc.

Library of Congress Catalog Card Number: 65-14062

Printed in the United States of America

Preface

THIS BOOK was written to acquaint persons seriously interested in newly independent countries with one of the more perplexing members of this emerging "third world."

A multi-party monarchy in an age and area of one-party republics, ruled in an authoritarian yet often haphazard manner by a government that has tended to be cautious at home but aggressive abroad, Morocco is a bundle of apparent paradoxes that defies many of the stereotypes usually applied to "developing" nations. To make the reader aware of the features peculiar to Morocco, to recreate the atmosphere that spawned them, and to expound the existing political system, we have approached the subject both descriptively and analytically. To facilitate comparison with, and perhaps some comprehension of, other "new" countries, moreover, we have tried wherever feasible to cite problems and cause-effect relationships that, *mutatis mutandis*, could occur elsewhere.

Our task has been complicated by the scarcity of reliable documentary materials on Morocco. Ministries of the Moroccan Government and political party headquarters sporadically issue various information bulletins, but even the ministries often lack adequate data and statistics. The partisan flavor of newspapers in Morocco, combined with the reluctance of Moroccan officials to answer questions by journalists, makes full and accurate reporting even more complicated. In many cases, then, we have been forced to rely upon private sources of information and to make our own estimates of a situation.

Another and somewhat different dilemma stemmed from our desire to be thorough, yet to avoid restating material that has already been amply presented elsewhere, particularly in the case of recent books and monographs that focus in great detail on specific aspects of Moroccan political or economic development. We have therefore compromised by trying to be brief when treading ground that reputable scholars have already covered.

A final problem was that of transliterating Arabic words in a manner that would cause the reader as little confusion as possible. French, Spanish, and English all have their own preferred renditions for many names and places, but even within one language there is no uniform or generally accepted method of transcription. Furthermore, many Moroccans wish to have their names spelled arbitrarily despite conflicts with the preferences of Western linguists or with the spellings generally chosen by other Moroccans or other Arabs. For the sake of simplicity, if sometimes at the cost of consistency, we have therefore spelled proper names and terms as they usually appear and, in the case of living persons, as they prefer to see them. Many names and terms appear as they do in French publications, since the bulk of literature on North Africa is written in French and since French is the first and preferred Western tongue of most Moroccans. However, widely accepted English spellings of such names as Tangier and Koran are employed.

Since this book was independently conceived and produced, it is free of obligation to any government, or foundation, or institution. We do, however, wish to thank the many persons in Morocco, France, and the United States who directly or indirectly provided us with useful information or acted as sounding boards for our ideas.

M. I. C.
L. H.

New York and Washington,
Summer, 1965

Contents

Part One

Old Land

Introduction

O N MARCH 2, 1956, seven minutes of formal negotiation in the Salon d'Horloge of the French Foreign Ministry terminated forty-four years of French rule over nine-tenths of Morocco. Under the newsreel lights and to the grinding of cameras, Christian Pineau, Foreign Minister of the French Government, and Si M'Barek Bekkai, Premier of Morocco's new transitional government, initialed an agreement that affirmed:

> As a result of Moroccan advances on the path of progress, the Treaty of Fez of March 30, 1912, no longer corresponds to the necessities of modern life and can no longer govern Franco-Moroccan relations. In consequence, the Government of the French Republic solemnly affirms its recognition of the independence of Morocco, which in particular implies its right to diplomatic representation and the maintenance of armed forces, as well as its desire to respect and have respected the integrity of Moroccan territory, guaranteed by international treaties. The negotiations that have just begun in Paris between Morocco and France, sovereign and equal states, have as their object the conclusion of new agreements that will define the interdependence of the two countries in the fields in which their interests are in common; that will thus organize their cooperation on the basis of liberty and equality, notably in matters of defense, external relations, economy, and culture; and that will guarantee the rights and freedoms of the French settled in Morocco and of the Moroccans settled in France, subject to respect for the sovereignty of the two states.

On April 7, Si Bekkai completed his government's first major task by signing with the Spanish Foreign Minister, Martín-Artajo, an agreement that ended Spanish control over the northern zone of the Sherifian Empire. Officially independent—albeit within a framework of "interdependence"—and nominally unified, Morocco thus became the first country of French North Africa to take its proper place in the family of nations.

Unlike many newly independent nations, Morocco achieved her freedom, not through a long period of friendly negotiation, but mainly by force. For Morocco, the price of liberty was two and a half years of revolt climaxing a generation of nationalist activities, at the height of which more than 100,000 French troops and security forces were pitted against the small but effective Moroccan Liberation Army and several urban terrorist groups. In further and even more significant contrast to the many members of the *tiers monde* that owe their national tongues, their national boundaries, and their very identities to Europe, this Muslim country on the northwest coast of Africa had enjoyed a more or less "national" existence since ancient times.

Chapter 1

Morocco from Antiquity to
the Twentieth Century

BOUNDED ON the north by the Mediterranean Sea, on the west
by the Atlantic Ocean, on the east by Algeria, and on the
south by the as yet undefined boundaries of the Sahara,
Morocco is often described as a "cold country with a hot sun" or as
having a "Mediterranean climate modified by the Atlantic." Her
coast is favored with temperate weather and only two seasons: a
long dry summer and a brief rainy winter. In the interior, however,
where temperatures may drop far below freezing or rise to over
100° F., the climate varies as sharply as the geography. In northern
Morocco, in the center of the coastal massifs running from the
Straits of Gibraltar to the Moulouya River, lie the Rif Mountains,
still the center of fierce resistance to outside control. South from
the Rif for about 375 miles along the Atlantic coast stretch the
plains and plateaus of western Morocco, region of most of the sizable towns and cities. These plains terminate in the foothills of the
Great Atlas, a vast mountain range that includes the High Atlas,
running east-northeast from the Atlantic coast to Algeria and
towering to more than 13,000 feet in the southwest; the Middle
Atlas, branching off from the High Atlas in a northeasterly direction; and the Anti-Atlas, extending southeast between the High
Atlas and the Sahara. The rock-strewn desert of the pre-Sahara in
southern Morocco leads into the Beni Snassene Massif, the plains
of Oudjda and Triffa, and the vast steppes and plateaus of eastern
Morocco, which are geographically an extension of Algeria. This

varied terrain has played a major role throughout the centuries in shaping Morocco's people, their way of life, and their politics.

A. Ancient Morocco

The original inhabitants of Morocco, as of all North Africa, were the people who are referred to in the West as Berbers, but who call themselves *imazaghen* (free men). The Berbers of Morocco are considered a "white race"; speaking, though hardly ever writing, a basically Hamito-Semitic language, they developed three major dialects: Rif, Atlas, and Shleuh. When they first began to till the soil and tend their flocks, in the Neolithic period, the patriarchal families of earlier nomadic times gradually developed a wider social structure: the *igh* (clan), or group of families living in a cluster; the *arrem* (village), composed of several *ighs*; the *kabila* (tribe), consisting of several villages; and sometimes the *thakebilt*, or federation of several tribes. The three principal divisions of Berber tribes were the Masmuda, the Zeneta, and the Sanhaja. Even today, the tribal unit commands the basic loyalty of many Berbers.

The strength of blood ties and the scarcity of arable land made the Berbers socialistic in economic and social affairs. Grazing land, for example, was under the communal ownership of a tribe or village; maintaining irrigation ditches was a collective responsibility. This same land scarcity, together with the proximity of other tribes, also led to constant intertribal strife. A state of war often existed between tribes for several generations until one of the feuding parties was exterminated, a condition that caused serious difficulties for the rulers of Morocco.

Although willing to share much of their property, the Berbers jealously guarded their individual rights, and their political organization tended to be democratic. Democracy was expressed mainly through the *djemaa* (tribal council), composed of all the adult males in the tribe, which decided all matters relating to justice and war. While the age of majority varied with different tribes, with the advent of Islam, a male was generally regarded as adult after he had reached the age of puberty. *Temmam* (magistrates or overseers) were occasionally appointed as *ad hoc* executives, but the Berbers disliked personal power and preferred decision by assembly.

While dynasties have come and gone, this basic Berber political structure has changed little since ancient, even prehistoric, times. Other aspects of Berber life, however, were modified considerably by Morocco's many invaders. Yet, save for some occasional intermarriage with the Harratin, a Negroid people who inhabited the edge of the Sahara, and some trading contacts with Phoenicians who settled at Lixus (Larache) as early as 1101 B.C., the Berbers remained virtually free of foreign influences until the fifth century B.C. (A few authorities claim that some Jews reached Morocco at the time of Nebuchadnezzar, in the seventh century B.C. It is more widely believed, however, that the first Jews arrived after the destruction of the Temple in Jerusalem, A.D. 70. These early arrivals obtained some Berber converts before the arrival of Islam.)

Between 475 and 450 B.C., the Carthaginian admiral Hanno became Morocco's first colonizer, establishing settlements at Rusaddir (now called Melilla) and Tingis (modern Tangier). Rome's conquest of Carthage eventually led its legions to Morocco, and, A.D. 42, Suetonius Paulinus founded the Roman province of Mauritania Tingitana, which embraced the present sites of Tangier, Ceuta, Fez, and Rabat, with Tingis as its capital. Roman influence was extended throughout Morocco by alliances with many of the tribal chieftains, but Rome was unable to extend direct control beyond the northern province. As one Roman captain was reputed to have said, "These people can be conquered but not subjugated." Centuries later, France was to reach the same conclusion. Within the Roman orbit, however, the Berbers assimilated Roman custom, dress, and even language. The stamp of Roman civilization is, in fact, still visible in Moroccan architecture and language: the *ksar* of the oasis keeps the general outline of the Roman *castra* (camp), and most of the terms relating to agriculture in the modern Berber vocabulary are of Latin origin.

Rome fell, A.D. 155, but her influence in Morocco continued to be strong for another 200 years. The Vandals, the Germanic people who had sacked Rome and overrun the fallen Roman Empire, arrived in North Africa in the fifth century. They occupied Morocco without resistance but held the country only a short time and made no change in its organization. Shortly thereafter, the Byzantines occupied Tangier and Ceuta, but never penetrated farther into Morocco. It was at this point that Christianity, first introduced by the Romans in the third century A.D., took hold most strongly.

Although these invasions were not without some lasting effects on the indigenous Berbers, the roles of these Mediterranean cultures in Morocco were in large part obliterated by the advent of Islam. Prior to that event, the Berbers had absorbed some foreign customs, but particularism had remained their characteristic quality. It was Islam that first gave to the Berber tribes some political unity and continuity, as well as a great religion and a way of life.

B. Islam Comes to Morocco

In A.D. 683, Okba bin Nafi and his Arab army reached the shores of the Atlantic in a conquering drive undertaken on behalf of the Umayyads of Damascus. Many of the Berbers promptly succumbed to the invaders and to their offer of a life of looting, conquest, and the Koran. Only twenty-eight years later, Spain was invaded by a Muslim army led by a Berber—Tarik bin Ziyad, the man for whom Gibraltar (literally *jebel tarik*, or Mount Tarik) was named. Tarik's army, which included 20,000 recently converted Berbers, swept to the Pyrenees and beyond and was finally halted at Tours, near Poitiers, in 732 by Charles Martel.

During these fifty years, the majority of Berbers in Morocco resisted conversion to Islam and, even more, assimilation by Arabic culture. Even those who did adopt the new creed were dissatisfied with the domination of the country by a small number of Arab officials and soldiers. The Arab rule, which soon proved to be as poorly organized as it was tyrannical, aroused bitter objections, culminating in the Kharijite revolt of 739. For the cause of Kharijism, which proclaimed the equality of all believers in opposition to Arab domination, Muslim Berbers crushed the Eastern armies and drove them from the country. Its political purpose of freeing Islam from foreign domination satisfied, Kharijism was gradually replaced in Morocco by the Sunni orthodoxy.*

* Kharijism deviates from orthodox Islam by maintaining that the Caliphate (the office whose holder is the authoritative head of the Islamic community and also guardian of the faith) is open to any believer whom the faithful consider suitable—rather than only a relative of the prophet Muhammad. Its followers insist that he who commits a great sin can no longer be a believer, thus rejecting the generally accepted doctrine of justification by faith. On this latter point, the Kharijites are adamant and consider all Muslims who disagree as heretics. Today, the sect, whose following is small, is found principally in eastern Arabia.

Sunnism is the form of orthodox Islamic belief held by most Muslims. In addition to regarding the Koran and the Hadith (the tradition of extra-Koranic sayings of Muhammad) as sources of the Sharia (Islamic law), the Sunnis adhere to the Sunna (customs and examples) of the Prophet and of the Muslim community. On this point (and two others), the major schism in Islam has resulted.

The Shiite sect refuses to acknowledge the Sunna and insists that the Caliphate can pass only through Muhammad's descendants. They also believe that the Imams (literally "prayer leaders") are divinely inspired and can interpret the Koran—a power Sunnis deny even to caliphs. There are today some 325 million Sunnis, living from Morocco to Pakistan, and 20 million Shiites, principally in India and Iran.

The new religion was from the first interpreted differently by the mountain folk, desert tribesmen, and rural farmers on the one hand and city dwellers on the other. The latter were able to assimilate the classic Islamic theological and social patterns of the Middle East, but the former adopted the name more than the content of Islam. In most areas, their culture retained its traditional pagan beliefs—such as credence in the evil eye, the value of curses, the protective and vindictive power of saints, and the djinn (invisible creatures of the other world)—under the veneer of a few Islamic formalities. As time passed, this "folk Islam" of the *bled* (countryside) approached the classic Islam of the cities, but a clear distinction between the two still remains today.

The uprising of the Berbers against their Arab overlords marked the first time that these people had united beyond the tribal level, but it did not denote the end of their pronounced particularism. Until the twentieth century, Morocco was constantly torn by struggles between its separate elements, and only a strong individual was able to hold the state together. Unfortunately, the energies of each dynasty were expended more on erecting an empire than on creating state unity, with the result that the central government required periodic rebuilding.

C. Morocco's Early Kingdoms

Morocco owes its emergence as a state to the first of these great leaders, Sherif Maulay Idris.* In 788, Maulay Idris fled to Morocco for refuge from Harun al-Rashid, Caliph of Baghdad, a descendant of Muhammad's uncle, who had been waging war against the lineal descendants of the Prophet in order to eliminate potential rivals. Settling in Volubilis, where he was welcomed by a recently converted Berber tribe, Maulay Idris used to great advantage his *baraka* (the beneficial influence that emanates from all sherifs), piety, wisdom, and learning, and was soon acclaimed its chief. He promptly welded the other Berber tribes of the area into a confederation and then set out to conquer other sections of the country.

Maulay Idris advanced as far east as Tlemcen—which today lies in Algeria, just across the border from Oudjda—and as far south

---

* Muhammad had among his titles that of Sherif of Mecca, and the appellation Sherif has been given to all those descended from him through his daughter Fatima and her husband Ali. Morocco has been ruled by three dynasties claiming this title (Idrisid, Saadian, and the present-day Alawite), thus the designation of Sherifian Empire which the country bore until 1956.

as the present site of Marrakesh. But when word of his successes reached al-Rashid, the Caliph dispatched an assassin to Volubilis. Sniffing a bottle of poisoned perfume, al-Rashid's potential rival and first King of Morocco passed into history in 791. Maulay Idris was buried at the site of the present-day holy city of Maulay Idris (from which, until recently, nonbelievers were barred).

The Idrisid dynasty continued through a son born to Kensa, Maulay Idris' Berber concubine. An intelligent and capable administrator, Maulay Idris II moved his capital to Fez, which had been founded by his father in 789, and extended his domain while stabilizing its government. In fact, he organized Morocco's first true *makhzen*, or central government, an Arabic concept that was alien to Berber traditions. The royal armies did not control all of present-day Morocco, but they did cover most of the northern portion. Upon Maulay Idris II's death in 829, however, the kingdom was divided among his sons, who soon lost all their territory except Fez and the Rif to independent tribes.

By 920, the political domain of the Idrisid had vanished, but their cultural contributions left a permanent mark on Morocco. Islam, its oriental civilization, and the Arabic language were diffused throughout the realm from its great new center, Fez, where the renowned Karouine university had been founded in 859. It was not until the eleventh century, however, that Morocco became predominantly Arab, and then only as a result of the most important of the Arabic invasions. A great influx of 200,000 families of the Beni Hillal tribe, which had its origin in what is now Yemen, was responsible for this principal infusion of Arabic blood. The Arabs, who generally settled in the lowlands and built many of the nation's cities, immediately intermarried with the Berbers in these areas; eventually, the only pure Berbers remaining were those residing in the four great mountain regions.

Most of the century and a quarter following the downfall of the Idrisid was marred by political disunity and religious strife until, early in the eleventh century, the Almoravids began a conquest of the Sahara. Members of the Sanhaja Berber tribes, the Almoravids lived mostly in the northern part of present-day Mauritania. Thanks to the camel, however, which had recently been introduced from the East, they had successfully penetrated south as far as what is today Senegal. In the course of that advance, they became Muslims and in turn imposed Islam on many Negro tribes. In 1053, the Almoravids halted their southward drive to stop the Zeneta Berber tribes, who were venturing from the east into the oasis area for the first time. Turning north, they swept through the Sous and, crossing the Atlas, drove on to the Atlantic. Under the leadership of Yusuf bin Tashfin, they founded the city of Marrakesh in 1062 as the first Almoravid capital. By 1082, the Zeneta Berbers had been brought completely under their rule; northern and southern Morocco were unified for the first time.

In answer to an appeal from the Moors * of Andalusia, who were menaced by Christians to the north, Yusuf bin Tashfin then led his forces into Spain, eventually conquering its southern region. Under Ali bin Yusuf, son of Yusuf bin Tashfin, the Almoravids adopted much of the Christian Andalusian culture and governmental organization and even integrated a Christian militia into their military structure. At the same time, however, they championed Muslim orthodoxy to the point of crushing the last vestiges of Shiite and Kharijite heresies in Morocco. It was this lack of religious tolerance that finally led the Masmuda tribes under Ibn Tumart to rebel in 1125, causing the Almoravids' eventual downfall. Ibn Tumart's initial rebellion failed, but a later effort of his leading general, Abd al-Mumin, a Zeneta, succeeded. The fall of Marrakesh in 1147 marked the end of the country's first great empire and the beginning of the Almohad dynasty.

Under the Almoravids and Almohads, Morocco and the Moors enjoyed their greatest glory. It is said that, at that period, most of the Moors could read and write, while the nobles of Charlemagne's court were still learning to spell their names. Scholars at Cordova enjoyed the resources of seventeen great libraries, one of which contained more than 400,000 volumes, and the city was dotted with luxurious baths at a time when washing was still considered a dangerous custom at Oxford.

The first Almohad thrust was eastward, reaching as far as Tripoli, where it finally checked the Hillalian advance. Then, like his predecessors before him, Abd al-Mumin answered the call of Andalusian emirs and invaded Spain, soon stretching his empire as far north as Castile. In 1170, the primacy of Andalusia was accentuated when the Almohad capital was moved to Seville; a period of peace and prosperity ensued. The third Almohad monarch, Abu Yusuf Yakub

---

* "Moor," a term commonly used to identify collectively the people of the Maghrib, originated in the name of the Roman province Mauritania Tingitana. The word is also used in reference to the Arabized peoples of southern Spain. The terms North Africa, Maghrib (meaning "West" in Arabic), and Barbary have been used interchangeably here to designate the same general geographic area—including modern Morocco, Algeria, and Tunisia.

Mansur (1184–99) constructed the Giralda minaret in Seville, the Koutoubia in Marrakesh, and Hassan's Tower in Rabat—three of Islam's greatest landmarks still standing. Almohad power and wealth reached its peak under his reign, but its decline was imminent.

When the armies of Muhammed al-Nasir, fourth Almohad leader (1199–1213), were defeated at Las Navas de Tolosa in northern Andalusia in 1212 by King Alfonso VIII, the Almohads withdrew from the European continent, leaving only the Kingdom of Granada under Moorish rule. Military, political, and moral decadence followed; the decline was climaxed in 1270 by the death of the last Almohad sovereign, who was killed in battle by the Beni Merin.

The Beni Merin Berber tribes, nomads who gave their name to a breed of sheep and the woolen fabric merino, ruled Morocco during her final period of glory. The Merinid period saw an official return to Sunnism and the initial appearance of a new Islamic movement, Sufism. Its practitioners do not form a separate Islamic sect but concentrate on an aspect not common to any of the other three sects—asceticism—and are concerned primarily with the worship of saints, postulated on the references in the Koran to the "friends of Allah," whom He had chosen as governors of His kingdom.* Sufism appealed greatly to the Berbers. At the same time, the *Ikhwan* (religious brotherhoods), which were to become the chief corporate institution of folk Islam, were established in Morocco. Founded by mystics and appealing to emotionalism, the brotherhoods were to play a political role after the middle of the nineteenth century, when they came to exert a reactionary influence on Moroccan life.

The major policies of the new dynasty, which returned the capital to Fez, differed little from those of its predecessor: holy war in Spain, imperialism in Barbary, and coexistence with the area's Arabs. Strangely enough, the failure of the first two was partial but not debilitating, while the success of the third was complete but eventually fatal to the Berber dynasties. By the middle of the fourteenth century, the Merinids began a slow decline to decadence from which they never recovered, and the country sank into a morass from which, despite several attempts at rescue, it was not to emerge before the twentieth century.

---

* One of the most famous groups of Sufis are the Marilawiya, or Whirling Dervishes, whose name is derived from their ritual dance, which induces religious ecstasy and so, it is thought, brings the dancer in closer communion with God.

D. European Encroachment

Morocco reacted to the onset of European colonialism in the fifteenth century by isolating herself, and she thus succumbed not only to growing anarchy but to stagnation as well. Misgovernment, disorder, and detachment from the intellectual, scientific, and social advances that were revolutionizing the Western world enfeebled Morocco and left her ill prepared to combat European encroachment. The culmination of this decline was still 500 years distant when the Beni Wattasi entered on the Moroccan scene, but critical forces were then set in motion. The Wattasi, who were Zeneta Berbers, acted as regents to the last ruler of the Merinid dynasty, Abu Said Uthman III (1420–72). After his demise, a Wattasi chief, Muhammad al-Shaykh, was proclaimed Sultan in 1475.

The fifteenth century witnessed the end of Moorish power in Spain, as well as the beginning of European colonization in Morocco. In 1492, Granada fell to the united Catholic power of Isabella of Aragon and Ferdinand of Castile, and Andalusian Moors and Spanish Jews fled together to Morocco. In the meantime, the Portuguese had established settlements along the Barbary coast: Ceuta in 1415, Arzila and Tangier in 1471. New fortresses were built by the invaders at Santa Cruz de Aguer (Agadir) in 1505, Safi in 1508, Azemmour in 1513, and Mazagan in 1514. The Portuguese raided as far as the very gates of Marrakesh, but, for the most part, they confined themselves to their control of the coastal strip. The Wattasi were helpless before this Christian onslaught.

In reaction to the weakness of the Wattasi and the strength of the Portuguese, a new movement sprang up in the valley of the Dra, in southern Morocco, led by an Arab tribe that was soon to provide Morocco's second Sherifian dynasty. Under the cry of *jihad* (holy war), xenophobic Saadian sherifs defeated the ruling Wattasi and launched a full-scale attack against the Portuguese. Between 1541 and 1550, all the Portuguese footholds in Morocco except Mazagan, Ceuta, and Tangier were retaken, and, for a time, the Christian menace was checked.

The Saadians had come to the Dra from Arabia in the thirteenth century, reputedly because the people had requested the pleasure of their Sherifian company in order to assure good date crops. After settling near Zagora, the Saadians had embarked on a policy of political expediency that belied their ostensible religious fanaticism. To achieve a position of strength against the Wattasi, they had signed truces with the Portuguese early in the sixteenth century. Then, after turning against the Portuguese, they allied themselves with Spain in eastern Barbary in order to combat the advancing Ottoman Turks. This unholy alliance lasted as long as the Saadian dynasty maintained control in Morocco, and it successfully prevented Ottoman intervention in Morocco.

In 1578, following the historic "Battle of the Three Kings" (King Sebastian of Portugal; his temporary ally, Maulay Muhammad Mutawakkil, dethroned monarch of Morocco; and Maulay Abd al-Malik, reigning Sultan of Morocco), the most famous of the Saadian monarchs won the throne. Known as "the Victorious" and "the Golden," al-Mansur provided Morocco with twenty-five years of stability and prosperity. He maintained good relations with the European powers and, with an army of foreign mercenaries, successfully invaded *Afrique noire*. Reaching as far south as Timbuctu, his army returned laden with black slaves and yellow gold. After the death of al-Mansur, the Saadian dynasty began its decline, and the country returned to anarchy.

To add to its problems of foreign intrigue and domestic turmoil, Morocco began to suffer from the exploits of the "Barbary pirates." These pirates were mostly "Moriscos," the last to depart from Muslim Spain, expelled by Philip III between 1609 and 1614. They settled principally in Salé (hence the term "Sallee rovers") and Tetuán and proceeded immediately to terrorize shipping in that area. The success of their activities, which included kidnaping sailors and women for ransom and slavery, as well as plundering cargoes, soon increased the determination of the European powers to subjugate Morocco, but the pirates controlled the coastal waters for two centuries before they were defeated.

The third, and present-day, Sherifian dynasty sprang up in the Tafilalt region of Morocco. These descendants of the Prophet, whose family name, Alawite, was derived from the Prophet's son-in-law, Ali, had come to the Tafilalt from Arabia at the end of the twelfth century. Upon the disintegration of the Saadian Empire, Maulay Rashid, an adventurous Alawite leader, began a series of conquests in eastern Morocco, using the title of Sultan. In 1666, Maulay Rashid captured Fez, and, five years later, all Morocco lay at his feet. This first Alawite monarch died, however, before he was able to realize the benefits of his achievements.

Upon the death of Rashid in 1672, his brother, Maulay Ismail, was named Sultan of Morocco. Maulay Ismail, the most infamous ruler the country has known, was the son of a Negro concubine of his father, Maulay al-Sharif, who had been governor of Meknes.

With an army of perhaps 50,000 Negro troops, Maulay Ismail ruled the country with an iron hand for fifty-five years, earning the title of "the Bloodthirsty" as a result of his execution of some 36,000 foes. In addition to women, Maulay Ismail had two con-suming interests—horses and building: the royal stable at Meknes was three miles long and contained 12,000 horses. Maulay Ismail did not achieve his goal of recreating a Versailles at Meknes, but some remarkable structures remain as evidence of his intentions. This cold-blooded and mentally deranged despot was nevertheless an extremely able soldier, administrator, and politician, who con-solidated the country and restored relative tranquility and some prosperity.

Maulay Ismail's attempts to extend the empire, however, were not equally successful. He was unable to defeat the Turks in Al-geria; the Spanish retained Ceuta and Melilla, which they had taken in 1580 and 1579, respectively; and the Portuguese held on to Mazagan. He did succeed, however, in capturing Mehdia and Larache from the Spanish and in reoccupying Tangier. (England had received Tangier in 1662 as part of the dowry of Catherine of Braganza upon her marriage to King Charles II, but constant pres-sure from Maulay Ismail's forces, plus lack of money, caused the British to evacuate the city in 1684.) Commercial relations with Europe, initiated in the fifteenth century, were continued, but Maulay Ismail was an inveterate xenophobe and attempted to minimize contact to matters of economic necessity. In 1727, Mau-lay Ismail died, and Morocco was thrown into thirty years of anarchy under the nominal rule of various Alawite pretenders.

During these years of the mid-eighteenth century, the "system of protection" which played a significant role in the later European intervention in Morocco was established. The right of foreign diplomatic and consular officials in backward, non-Christian coun-tries to extend protection to their nationals and to favored natives was then an important feature of extraterritorial jurisdiction and was so recognized in international law. In Morocco, these capitu-latory rights were initially significant only in Tangier, where diplo-matic missions and foreign trade contacts were maintained. (The limitation of diplomatic missions to Tangier was designed to keep Fez, the capital, free of foreign influences.) Subsequently, however, their abuse became so widespread that the internal authority of the nation was considerably strained.

In 1757, peace was restored by Sidi Muhammed bin Abdullah, and, for the next sixty-five years, Morocco enjoyed relative stabil-ity in her foreign relations by reason of her self-imposed isolation.

Europe was preoccupied with the French Revolution and then with Bonaparte; the Turks were on their way out of Barbary; and the pirates were at last being checked by European naval power. Mazagan was evacuated by Portugal in 1769; only Spain, with Ceuta and Melilla, retained any control in Morocco. This was the country's opportunity to solve its internal problems, to escape the Middle Ages and establish a foothold in modern times, but the traditional problem of tribal independence could not be solved, and the central government remained generally corrupt, inefficient, oppressive, and hated. The Sultans spent most of their time seeking tribute and taxes by means of the sword. From then until 1934, the existence of a *bled es-siba* (countryside in which the *makhzen* had no control) remained an incontestable fact. At times, the *bled es-siba* covered approximately one-half of Morocco's territory and embraced one-third of its population. The *bled el-makhzen* grew progressively more impoverished and the royal army more impotent. An attempt was made to counter the prevailing Sufism and the local chauvinism it fostered, but it met with little success. The opportunity for reform thus was lost; and as the nineteenth century began, Morocco remained a medieval country.

By the time Maulay Abd al-Rahman succeeded to the throne in 1822, Europe was once again casting longing glances at the land mass to its south. To Moroccans, the question of foreign intervention in their country appeared only a matter of time, degree, and parties. Alawite foreign policy was designed principally to gain time while playing off the great powers against one another. Such efforts as were made to face internal problems came too late.

Sultan Abd al-Rahman achieved a significant domestic reform by governing the country through a system of *caids* (tribal chiefs), thereby relieving some of the central makhzen's burden. He also signed a treaty whereby the British were assured a preponderance of Moroccan trade, but he launched an untimely attack in Algeria against the French, who had begun to occupy Algerian territory in 1830, and in 1844, Marshal Thomas Bugeaud easily defeated the Moroccan armies in the Battle of Isly. Abd al-Rahman was succeeded by his son, Sidi Muhammad bin Abd al-Rahman, in 1859. The new Sultan showed military judgment little better than his father's by declaring war on Spain after an incident at Ceuta. The Spaniards were quickly victorious and in 1859 obtained a large indemnity and Tetuán for their trouble.

During this period, both France and Spain undertook concentrated efforts to gain control over Morocco. France's key motives were economic ones, combined with her sense of a *mission civili-*

satrice and a desire to protect her Algerian interests. For Spain, it was a question of imagined "manifest destiny." France led the way with a well-designed financial, diplomatic, and military offensive.

In 1871, the Sultan, Sidi Muhammad, fully aware of the intentions of certain European powers, approached the American consul general in Rabat with the proposal that the United States take Morocco under its protection. The American Government replied that, while the United States would regret any attempt on the part of foreign powers to dismember the Empire of Morocco and would agree to use its friendly offices to prevent such an act, it must nevertheless decline His Majesty's offer to confer upon the United States a protectorate over his dominions. This refusal did not affect the friendly relations inaugurated between the two countries nearly a hundred years before.*

After 1873, Morocco accepted enormous foreign loans, particularly from France, but the money was wasted—due to a combination of ignorance and corruption and the archaic system under which national and palace finances were merged. Taxes were increased to meet interest payments, but the tax collectors put a major portion of their receipts into their own purses. The loans thus weakened rather than strengthened the country. The Sultan's personal prestige diminished, his government grew weaker, and he became increasingly dependent on those whose domination he sought to avoid.

---

* In 1787, the United States Congress successfully persuaded Morocco to intervene with the Barbary pirates on behalf of the United States. Earlier that year, Morocco had accorded diplomatic recognition to and entered into a treaty of friendship with the young American republic. The treaty gave the United States a most-favored-nation status in Morocco, guaranteed the security of American citizens and commerce, and accorded the United States consular jurisdiction over disputes between Americans (including American protégés, or natives under American protection). Two years later, George Washington expressed America's gratitude to the Sultan in a now famous letter.

The 1787 treaty was renewed in 1836 by a Treaty of Meknes and is, in large part, still in effect today, forming the basis of the present relations between the two states. In 1819, Morocco gave the United States title to its first real estate on foreign soil—a building in Tangier that still houses the American Consulate in that city. The original relationship was broadened, in accordance with America's most-favored-nation status, when, in 1859, comprehensive rights obtained by the United Kingdom were extended to the U.S. From then on, American consular courts in Morocco had jurisdiction, not only over disputes between Americans in Morocco, but also over disputes between American and Moroccans in which the former were defendants.

The text of George Washington's letter to the Sultan is found below, Appendix A.

At this point, the European powers were trying to solve the "Moroccan question" with a view to obviating conflict among themselves, rather than with the purpose of restoring the internal peace of Morocco or strengthening the central authority of the makhzen. The principal desire was to find a modus vivendi whereby each could pursue its commercial interests in Africa without arousing the jealousy and mistrust of its neighbors. At first, this approach was multilateral, but eventually it was resolved by dividing the colonial spoils.

A conference of Morocco and eleven interested powers, including the United States, held at Madrid in 1880, was the first step toward foreign regulation of Moroccan affairs. The resulting Madrid Convention recognized the application in commercial affairs of the most-favored-nation clause to all participating powers, but also limited the right of foreign states to extend diplomatic protection to Moroccan nationals. The economic provision was the first step in creating an "open-door" policy in Morocco; the Act of Algeciras twenty-six years later achieved this aim.

In 1894, the Sultan, Maulay Hassan, became ill and died during a military expedition in the bled; one of his sons, the fourteen-year-old Maulay Abd al-Aziz, was proclaimed the new Sultan in Rabat. Maulay Abd al-Aziz subsequently tried to reform the national finances by instituting a *tertib* (agricultural levy) as a single tax and providing for more regular collection methods, but his personal expenditures all but offset his governmental program. (Surrounded by European advisers and adventurers, the Sultan purchased absurd quantities of such items as bicycles, cameras, and phonographs. He is reported to have ordered 500 perambulators after seeing one for the first time.)

In 1900, France and Italy agreed that France would renounce any designs on Tripolitania, while Italy would give France a free hand in Morocco. This was the first of a series of horse-trading agreements that was to lead directly to the establishment of the French Protectorate in Morocco twelve years later. On April 8, 1904, an agreement signed between France and England provided that the latter would refrain from intervention in Morocco's internal affairs in return for France's removal from Egypt and agreement to the internationalization of Tangier. (The neutralization of Tangier, lying directly across the straits from England's strategic base at Gibraltar, had long been a prime objective of British foreign policy.) In a secret clause to the agreement, Great Britain further recognized France's right to see to the tranquillity of Morocco and to assist all military, administrative, and financial reforms that Morocco might require. The reference to reforms was particularly significant, as it amounted to a British endorsement of a French protectorate. On October 3, 1904, Spain and France signed a secret treaty whereby Spain adhered to the terms of the Anglo-French treaty and France in turn agreed to give Spain a zone of influence in Morocco "if the authority of the Sultan could no longer be maintained."

The powers, however, had reckoned without Germany. Alarmed at the prospect that the open door might be slammed shut, Kaiser Wilhelm II visited Tangier on March 31, 1905, and made a belligerent speech demanding that the sovereignty of the Sultan and the liberty of Morocco be maintained. In the hope of resolving the resulting international tensions without going to war or losing face, he urged the Sultan to call a conference of all interested powers.

Anxious for his own reasons to avoid war at this time, President Theodore Roosevelt supported the proposal, and England and France felt constrained to agree to it as well. The conference began at Algeciras, Spain, on January 16, 1906, with representatives present from Morocco and the other states that had attended the Madrid conference in 1880. The parties admitted the need for reforms that would produce order, peace, and prosperity in Morocco and agreed to base their discussions on three principles: the Sultan's sovereignty and independence, the territorial integrity of his empire, and equal economic rights for all the powers represented in Morocco. The agreement finally reached on April 7 not only defined a program of essential reforms; it also recognized France's special position and gave her a large part of the control in a new Moroccan state bank, responsibility for training the Moroccan army (to be jointly controlled by Spain and France), and a share with Spain in policing Moroccan ports. Backed by virtually all the powers at the conference table except Austria and Germany, France had won a clean diplomatic victory.

When it was learned that the Sultan had adhered to the Act of Algeciras on June 18, the resentment against him and the European powers which was latent in the Moroccan bled burst forth. Taza tribes under Bu Hamara, the "pretender" to the Sultan's throne, increased their attacks against the royal armies. Further trouble was presented by Raisuli, a chieftain of the Rif region who specialized in kidnaping important persons and then releasing them for large ransoms. Among his victims were the London *Times* correspondent Walter Harris, the Scottish "caid" Sir Harry Maclean, and the wealthy American Ion Perdicaris.* Raisuli was so successful at his trade that the Sultan decided that, since he could not defeat the brigand, he would join him. In 1904, he therefore authorized Raisuli to administer, in behalf of the central government, the area he had formerly terrorized. As an "official," Raisuli was so despotic that he was finally outlawed in 1907. Nevertheless, he was able to continue his infamous career for many years thereafter.

In 1907, as the general lawlessness spread, several prominent Frenchmen were assassinated in various parts of Morocco, and France ordered her army in Algeria to occupy the border town of Oudjda. Another force was landed near present-day Casablanca, and France undertook to pacify the entire surrounding province of Chaouia. Popular sentiment against the Sultan, which reached its peak in 1908, encouraged a *coup* by his brother Maulay Hafid, Khalifa of Marrakesh. Maulay Hafid, with the support of Si Madin el-Glaoui, a Berber chieftain in Marrakesh, proclaimed himself Sultan and marched on the capital at Fez. Maulay Abd al-Aziz first fled to Rabat, then marched on Marrakesh, but he was deserted by his troops. His fourteen years on the throne ended when he abdicated and sought French protection in Tangier.

In the next few years, events moved rapidly. In 1909, Germany reluctantly recognized France's special interest in Morocco. Meanwhile, on the pretext of putting down revolts of tribes in the Rif, Spain slowly began to occupy the zone of influence France had promised her in 1904. Bu Hamara was captured, but Fez was still besieged by rebels. France was poised, but Germany had a last card to play. On July 1, 1911, the German gunboat *Panther* appeared in Agadir harbor "in order to protect German interests." War seemed imminent, but Britain again supported France, and Germany settled for another concession: in return for a slice of the French

* Maclean, a British soldier, had been transferred on loan by his regiment stationed in Gibraltar to the makhzen as instructor of the Sherifian army. He served Maulay Hassan and his two sons in that capacity and, in addition, was a popular and influential figure in the royal court.

The kidnaping of Perdicaris, a resident of Tangier, led to the dispatch of an American naval squadron to that city and President Roosevelt's famous warning to the Sultan: "Perdicaris alive or Raisuli dead." Perdicaris was released unharmed, but only when the bandit chief received a $70,000 ransom in return. The incident was somewhat ironic, since Perdicaris had, unknown to Roosevelt at first, renounced his American citizenship. The Secretary of State informed Roosevelt of this fact, but Roosevelt felt he could not draw back without losing face. Perdicaris thus continued to be identified as an American. See Barbara W. Tuchman, "Perdicaris Alive or Raisuli Dead," *American Heritage*, X, No. 5 (1959), 118–22.

Congo, Germany recognized France's right to occupy, with agreement of the Sherifian Government, any point in Morocco where maintenance of order might render such action necessary, and to represent the Sultan in foreign relations. France was further permitted to control Sherifian finances and ensure payment of foreign debts, while respecting the provisions for economic equality set forth by the Act of Algeciras.

At this point, France declared that both the European community in Fez and the Sultan himself were threatened with annihilation by anarchistic elements. According to French sources, Maulay Hafid asked for France's help, and she had no alternative but to go to the rescue. Once in the capital, the French negotiated with the government, and on March 30, 1912, the Sultan and a French representative, Eugène Regnault, signed the historic Treaty of Fez. This document established a protectorate—a contractual link between two states whereby the weaker cedes to the stronger some of its foreign and domestic rights in exchange for defense against internal or external attacks and for assistance in the development of its institutions and the safeguarding of its interests.

Years later, Moroccan nationalists told a different story about the events immediately preceding the Treaty of Fez. According to their version, France stirred up tribesmen such as Bu Hamara against the Sultan and even provided them with the arms necessary to wage a rebellion. Warning against anarchy, the French then proclaimed their apprehension concerning the lives of Europeans in Morocco and when, in fact, a few Europeans were killed, rushed large numbers of troops into the country—thus setting the stage to force Maulay Hafid to sign the treaty creating the Protectorate.

Whether this version is more accurate than the French is difficult to say. Subsequent events seem to prove that certain French statesmen were capable of such chicanery. On the other hand, the Moroccan nationalists were equally capable of distorting facts in order to help their cause. Whether France was the prime mover or not, there seems little doubt that the Sherifian Government exercised only slight control over Morocco in 1912.

The Treaty of Fez specifically permitted France to inaugurate in Morocco such internal reforms as she wished, although the Muslim faith and its official status, and respect for the traditional prestige of the Sultan, were to be safeguarded; to occupy the country militarily when necessary for the maintenance of order and the security of commerce; and to exercise police supervision. The treaty also permitted France to consolidate the Moroccan debt, to organize tax collections, and to approve loans or public concessions.

Finally, French diplomatic and consular agents were to represent and protect Moroccan subjects and interests abroad. France, in turn, pledged herself to lend constant support to His Sherifian Majesty against all the dangers that might threaten his person or throne or endanger the tranquillity of his state.

The Sultan, as the repository of sovereignty, remained the head of the government. He continued to promulgate all measures, but only upon the previous decisions of the French Government, represented in Morocco by a Resident General who directed the Protectorate's administrative services, controlled the military and security forces, and legislated directly on certain matters.

Article 1 of the Treaty of Fez required France to reach an understanding with Spain regarding the interests the latter derived from her geographical position and territorial possessions on the Moroccan coast. Actually, the two had already secretly reached such an agreement in 1904, when Madrid agreed to recognize the Sultan as sovereign and, as a protecting power, to assume responsibility for instituting governmental reforms in her own zone of Morocco. Under this agreement, Spain's share of Morocco amounted to about 10 per cent of the Sherifian Empire, all within the bled es-siba, and it included a native population of approximately 500,000. Spanish Morocco consisted of two noncontiguous sections: the northern section was delineated approximately by the 35th Parallel—from Alcazarquivir to Mechra-Saf-Saf, excluding the city and immediate surroundings of Tangier; the southern section, comprising more than half the area of the Spanish zone, lay south of the Dra and north of the Spanish province of Saguia el Hamra.

Most nations had recognized the Spanish zone as an independent protectorate, but the United States and France were notable dissenters. Article 26 of the Franco-Spanish agreement, however, had cast some doubt on the French position by providing that international agreements concluded by the Sultan would not extend to Spanish Morocco except with the previous consent of the King of Spain. Both countries, in fact, had operated on the principle of separate protectorates. When, on November 27, 1912, France and Spain formally ratified the 1904 accord, Morocco was effectively divided in two—and thrust into the twentieth century. Only a reassertion of central authority could prepare Morocco to enter the modern world; the Protectorate was to be the means to that end.

Chapter 2

The French Protectorate and the Rise of Moroccan Nationalism: 1912–52

A. *Social and Economic Conditions in 1912*

IN 1912, Morocco extended over approximately 170,000 square miles of land and contained perhaps 4 million inhabitants.* The majority of the native Muslim population was by then composed of varying mixtures of Arab and Berber (and, to a lesser extent, negroid and Andalusian) stock, but there were still significant numbers of pure Berbers living in the mountain regions. (As late as 1949, according to French estimates, 22 per cent of Morocco's native population spoke only Berber, and another 14 per cent claimed Berber as their mother tongue.) The French subsequently tried to dramatize and even intensify the differences between Berbers and Arabs, but actually the distinction had become one less of race than of location. The characteristics the French usually attributed to Berbers—independence, fierceness, loyalty, and bravery—applied generally to the rural population, whether they were Arabized or pure Berber; those traits the French associated

---

* Total area and population estimates for Morocco in the early twentieth century vary. French officials claimed that the country was inhabited by 3 to 3.5 million persons, but nationalists subsequently pointed to inadequate census facilities (particularly in unpacified areas) and to French political designs, and alleged that this figure was as much as 500 per cent too low. The *Encyclopaedia Britannica* (1911 edition) made a vague estimate of between 5 and 10 million.

with Arabs—religious orthodoxy, materialism, intellectualism, and laziness—were more characteristic of city dwellers, who were usually of mixed racial backgrounds.

Morocco's indigenous Jewish population numbered about 100,-000 persons, more than half of whom lived in the larger cities and engaged primarily in commerce, the crafts, and the professions. Although a number had attained considerable wealth, most were in the lower middle class. The majority spoke some Hebrew, but their basic tongue was usually a mixture of Arabic and Spanish or Berber, depending on their locale.

Historically, Morocco's Jews had been officially treated as equals of the Muslim population, although they were not citizens but rather *dimihi* (guests or wards of the Sultan under his personal protection). This tolerance stemmed from the Muslim belief that the Old and New Testaments were earlier, authentic, but imperfect revelations of God, and from the Koran passage declaring, "The people of the book who believe in God, the day of judgment, and the future life will not be punished, nor need they fear." The Jews thus retained the right to practice their religion and engage in their trades, as well as to have their own schools and courts. Despite official and Islamic injunctions, however, they were subjected to many personal discriminations and indignities. In addition to being required to live in *mellahs* (special sections), Moroccan Jews, according to early Western observers, were obliged to pay the *jeziya* (poll tax on non-Muslims); wear black skullcaps rather than the traditional Moroccan headgear; dismount from their mules on passing a Muslim; walk barefoot through the Muslim quarter; and refrain from carrying arms or using a Moorish bath. Nevertheless, the vast majority of Moroccan Jews lived lives no better and no worse than their compatriots and, since the fourteenth century, had led a relatively untroubled existence compared with that of European Jewry.

Morocco had no native Christians in 1912, but she did play host to 6,000 Europeans who professed that faith. For centuries, Christians had been treated mercilessly by xenophobic Moroccan rulers and slave-trading pirates, although tolerance toward them, as toward Jews, was traditional Muslim policy. As late as the mid-nineteenth century, European travelers could not penetrate inland Morocco except in disguise, although the few who engaged in diplomacy and trade were able to move freely in coastal cities. In 1912, four-fifths of the Europeans in Morocco lived in Tangier. Fez and Marrakesh had the only other foreign population of note, while Casablanca—then a fishing village called Anfa with but

4,000 inhabitants—had only 60 Europeans. There were also several Christian missions in Morocco, engaged less in proselytizing than in charitable work, since attempts at conversion were futile at best and dangerous at worst.

In 1912, most Moroccans lived in the country, making a living as tillers and herders, using the methods their ancestors had employed for centuries. Moroccan farmers sowed by hand, used wooden plows drawn by camels and donkeys, harvested with a sickle, and threshed grain by having mules tread over it. Only a part of the total land area was cultivated, and even the better arable land was misused. Fertilizer was unknown; when the soil was exhausted, the farmer merely moved to another locality. Although yields per acre were poor, in years when the weather was favorable Morocco produced enough food to be self-sufficient.

There were four types of land tenure in Morocco: the *melk*, or individually owned land; the makhzen, or state, domains; land owned collectively by tribes or villages and worked for the general interest, including *gish* land, granted to tribes in return for military service provided by its members, and *naiba* land, granted in return for tribute to the makhzen; and the *habous*, or lands held by the state for religious foundations. Farmers were also classified in four categories: *khammas*, or tenant farmers, composing 69 per cent; *fellahs*, or landowners, 20 per cent; wage laborers, 1 per cent; and large landowners, 10 per cent. *Khamma* means "five" in Arabic, indicating that these tenant farmers were paid one-fifth of their harvest for their services. Farmers included many semi-nomads, who cultivated land during the winter and roamed with their flocks in the summer.

The breeding of livestock, often favored over farming because it permitted mobility in a world full of dangers from both men and weather, stressed quantity over quality. Selective breeding was unknown, and Moroccan herders seldom stored sufficient feed in winter for use during the dry summer and failed to provide adequate shelter for their animals. Thus, cattle were periodically decimated by drought and disease. In areas seldom blessed by rain, fruit-growing was favored over farming and breeding. There were orchards of almonds, oranges, peaches, figs, lemons, apricots, olives, and dates.

While the climate is the key regulator of the flora in any country, the Moroccans themselves played a significant role in diminishing the country's once vast forests. By 1912, most of the country's trees had been cut down, and there was no program of conservation to keep this great natural resource at even minimum strength.

Still, there were eucalyptus, acacia, mimosa, date palms, cypress, pine, juniper, beech, oak, fruit, thuja, and cedar trees, and the only argan trees in the world. The fruit of the argan tree is not edible by humans, but is heartily devoured by goats, which climb the branches for it, and camels, which merely lift their heads to enjoy the meal. In the summer, the countryside was brown, with the exception of the prickly-pear cactuses, which were used as fences to protect crops and houses; animals were forced to search among the stones for dried vegetation. With the rains, however, Morocco bloomed with wild flowers. By spring, the land was carpeted with iris, daffodil, anemone, poppy, bougainvillaea, poinsettia, carnation, hibiscus, rose, and jasmine.

Lions and elephants had long disappeared from the Moroccan scene by 1912, but there was still much small game, in addition to fox, jackal, panther, and antelope. Two animals had been imported from the East: the barb horse, developed by the Arabs, and the Bactrian camel. (Moroccans never used the dromedary, or one-humped camel, which is bred for speed rather than reliable desert service.) The camel (with his head high reputedly because he knows the hundred names of Allah) was found not only in the desert but on farms, pulling the plows with a donkey or cow by its side. The donkey or mule, however, was the real workhorse of Morocco: in the field, as transportation, or for odd jobs around the farmhouse. Last but not least in Morocco's indigenous menagerie was the stork. This bird is the subject of many Moroccan stories; it is considered good luck if a stork rests on one's house, according to a tale that relates how a Sultan, who had laughed at a pilgrim who came to pay him homage, was turned into a stork by Allah in His wrath. His descendants, still storks, recognize the true faith and settle only on the homes of true believers.

Rural habitations in Morocco varied, depending on the locality and the occupation of the dweller. In northern Morocco, most people lived in tents made of camel- or goat-skin. These were waterproof and strong; the bottom of the tent purposely did not touch the ground, as the breeze was welcome in summer and straw could be used to close the gap in winter. The tent was particularly well suited to Morocco's nomadic herders, whose tents often had, in addition to the family's living quarters, two compartments reserved for livestock. A clan's tents were usually grouped in a circle, called a *douar*, with the doors facing inward. When the animals were not kept in the tents themselves, they were herded in the center of the douar during the night, and the tent door was located so that they could be watched. In addition to tents, *noual-*

las, which are mud-and-reed huts, were popular. They were also portable, though not so easily transported as the tent. Finally, there were huts made of sun-dried brick or dry untrimmed stone, with reed or mud roofs. There were no windows in these huts, but only holes for guns, and they usually had only one room.

In southern Morocco, the majestic *ksar* was the common living structure. These large, many-storied edifices built of mud and straw usually housed several scores of families, and sometimes even more. The ksars were surrounded by high, crenellated walls and had strong gates and numerous towers. They were self-sufficient units; the granary and other stores, as well as the animals, were kept within their walls; they were, in fact, fortified villages. Additional protection was afforded by the color of their brick, which blended into the earth around them and made a natural camouflage.

The towns were centers for Morocco's artisan production, its trade, and its religion. Artisans produced leather goods, carpets, pottery, textiles, metalware, and many other items of practical and ornamental value. There was little industry other than a few flour mills. Commercial fishing was of little economic importance, as Moroccan boats were oar-propelled, and the catch was sufficient only to supply coastal areas. Although the country's mineral wealth was legendary, and copper, salt, lead, antimony, and iron had been mined in quantity for centuries, there was no attempt at large-scale exploitation of mineral resources.

Domestic commerce was carried on by sale or barter at small stores or at *souks* (markets); Morocco's foreign trade was conducted through eight port cities—the largest being Mogador, which handled as much as 2[?]0,000 metric tons a year. Every district of Morocco had a souk within a day's "walk, shop, and return." Often, its site was unmarked, and it was simply known that on a particular day of the week the market would regularly be held. Some Moroccan towns are even named after the day on which they hold their souks, such as Settat, which means "six" in Arabic, and Souk el Arba, or "Souk of Wednesday." Everything was traded at the souk. In addition to grain and animals and the produce derived from both, there was a large variety of handicrafts and clothing. Services were also offered. Much administrative work was carried on, including valuation of brides and donkeys. The souk also served as a general meeting place for friends. There were barbers, bloodletters, cobblers, medicine men, professional mendicants, dentists—with false teeth piled before them—water-carriers, whose bells scare away the devil, and countless entertainers—acrobats, snake charmers, dancing boys, and fortunetellers.

Contemporary European visitors described Moroccan cities as dirty, tumble-down places with the crudest of sanitary arrangements. Narrow, dark lanes provided access to crowded homes and stores, and the latter were usually walled in for protection. Even in Tangier, paved alleys were riddled with holes. Homes were made of plaster and were often in disrepair. There were a few small, grated windows. From the outside, only the door generally indicated the wealth of the inhabitants: a massive door with a heavy brass knocker and large round-headed nails was an indication of relative affluence. Inside the better homes were center courtyards with fountains, long and narrow rooms with divans lined against the walls, brocaded cushions on the divans, carpets on the tiled floors, and hand-carved designs on the wooden ceilings. The poorer homes were bare except for a brazier, a few bowls and glasses, a teapot, a brass tray, and a *pouf* (a large low cushion used as a seat). Members of the family slept on rush mats or carpets, with rough blanket or sheepskin covers. These items increased in quantity and quality as the individual standard of living rose, and they would then be supplemented by low tables and all types of Western furniture and household items.

In the cities, as in the bled, the Moroccan diet consisted primarily of wheat, semolina, chicken, goat's and cow's milk, sugar, tea, olive oil, eggs, citrus fruits, dates, figs, and salt. Only the more affluent ate meat or vegetables regularly. Favorite dishes included *mechoui*, a quarter of lamb roasted or grilled; *pastella*, a pigeon pie covered with pastry; *harcra*, a thick spicy soup of lentils or chick peas; and chicken flavored with saffron and honey. The peasant thrived on *cous-cous* (a semolina dish) and mint tea. Food was served in a common dish, the first three fingers of the right hand being used to carry morsels to the mouth.

Steamship service linked Morocco to ports on the Mediterranean and elsewhere, but internal transportation was primitive. To travel inland, it was necessary to go by horse, camel, or donkey—and in caravans, for protection against the numerous brigands who roamed the countryside and busied themselves taking captives for ransom. One European visitor in Morocco told of the eight-day journey from Tangier to Fez (215 miles), which was as expensive as it was dangerous: no provisions could be obtained en route except an occasional chicken or sheep, and protection fees, extracted by brigands, guaranteed no feeling of security. There were no modern roads and few bridges, no inland water transportation, and no railroad. While the early Sherifian mail system was much criticized, several European countries maintained post offices in Tangier with

service along the coast. Other communication was rudimentary; there were few inland telephone and power lines. Telegraph cables, however, extended under the Mediterranean to Europe.

The country was scourged by epidemic and endemic diseases, with the plague, cholera, typhus, smallpox, and malaria regularly ravaging the population. Health services were primitive at best: the doctors were holy men; black magic was their science and talismans their remedies. In particular, broth of unborn puppy was recommended for the symptoms of tuberculosis; every lock in the house was opened in case of an asthma attack; camel fat was swallowed for whooping cough; and dates from Mecca or sand from a particular saint's grave were other remedies. Bloodletting was a general practice, but "doctors" also provided other services, prescribing fox saliva as a love potion and jackal's liver to keep sentries awake. Epilepsy was considered contagious, and those showing its signs were shunned. The insane, the blind, and the crippled were considered affected by the hand of God and so at least were not mistreated.

Traditionally, charity was considered the responsibility of the patriarchal family, but begging was sanctioned when relatives were too poor to give aid. Islam demands generosity to beggars, but there were no social welfare organizations other than the *habous*, the ancient Islamic institution of public charities.

Slavery was still prevalent, and women were little more than chattel. Their inferiority was due to Islamic teaching, and to custom. The Koran states that "men are in charge of women, because Allah hath made the one of them excel the other," and it limits the property rights of the fairer sex. It nevertheless enjoins men to treat their women well, and Muhammad limited the number of wives for each man to four (though concubines were without limit) and decreed that all wives must be treated equally. Historically, Moroccan women received no education other than studying the Koran and did no work other than in the home or in the fields, where they often worked harder than their menfolk. Girls traditionally donned the veil at puberty and often were married by their parents' arrangement in their early teens. Divorce could be obtained almost at the husband's will. Berber women, however, did not wear the veil, and they enjoyed a greater equality in the home than their Arab sisters. Both Berber and Arabized women wore the *djellaba* (a hooded cloak) and baggy trousers or a *haik* (sheet wrapped around the body) as their principal apparel. A woman's social position was reflected more in her jewelry than her clothes, and henna, a red flower dye, was often used to decorate the feet and hands. Moorish men traditionally wore the djellaba, *babouches* (pointed backless slippers), and a red fez or a *rizza* (white turban). The *burnoose*, a cloaklike outer garment, was usually the sign of wealth or position. The heads of young children were shaved clean except for a lock of hair—by which God could aid them if they stumbled on the difficult road to heaven.

Education, like so many other facets of Moroccan life, was principally religious. All Koranic schools in Morocco were administered by a *Naib* (assistant) of the Grand Vizier. State primary education, offered in about a thousand schools, consisted almost entirely of the study of the Koran, with only incidental attention to the Arabic language and some elementary mathematics. In the city schools, a little logic, history, and Islamic law were taught. The average teacher, a man chosen by the community for his piety rather than his erudition and who was paid not with money but with gifts, recited verses from the Koran while his pupils, usually sitting around him on straw mats on the floor, repeated his words in chorus. These schools were intended to instill the religious and ethical principles of Islam in the young and thus provide them with moral support against an encroaching world of scientific concepts to which they were not adapted.

Advanced education was offered at the Karouine university at Fez to more than a thousand students, some of whom came from far corners of the Muslim world: the Karouine was famous for the preparation it offered professors, judges in religious courts, and mosque officials. The Karouine's curriculum, like the schools', also consisted of religious and scholastic subjects taught according to the formulas of medieval pedagogy, with stress on the laws and rituals of the Koran, Islamic literature, history, and philosophy. Some attention was given to mathematics, astronomy, logic, and syntax. Extracurricular activities were not offered, nor were examinations given, but students were required to show considerable ability in order to continue the courses of study, which varied from three to nine, occasionally twelve, years. Instruction at the Karouine was by lecture, and professors were distinguished by the step of the platform from which they spoke, the highest rank speaking from the fifth step. There was no tuition fee, and rooms in the *medersa*, or living quarters, were free, but a student's family often made substantial sacrifices to provide living expenses. Some students subsisted on the one free loaf of bread dispensed each day.

Moroccan Jews had their own Talmudic schools, which likewise dispensed traditional instruction of a basically religious nature. In addition, schools opened by the Universal Jewish Alliance attempted to offer a modern education in the French language after 1862.

B. *Government and Law Prior to the Protectorate*

The Government of Morocco in 1912 was a theocracy under the temporal and spiritual rule of the Sultan. As a representative of the Prophet, the Sultan was both Imam (spiritual leader) and Amir al-Muminin (Prince of Believers). An absolute monarch, he held the supreme legislative, executive, and judicial powers of the nation in his hands. The absence of a religious hierarchy and the importance of the religious law, which he applied, increased his temporal authority. His power was limited somewhat, however, by the Sharia (the "divine law" of the Prophet) and by the *ulema* (theologians), who interpreted the Sharia, defined doctrine, and appointed the Sultan's successor. Actually, the Sultan's effectiveness was directly related to his military strength and ability as a leader.

The line distinguishing the bled es-siba from the bled el-makhzen was fluid, continually shifting as tribes gave or withheld their allegiance to the central government. Hence, the Sultan spent much of his time in campaigns of pacification and tax collection, known as *harka* (literally, "the burning"). His troops were composed of soldiers, who inherited their place in the Sultan's forces, mercenaries, and men acquired from the tribes in return for land tenure. They were never more than semi-organized and had no standard equipment.

Morocco did not have branches of government in the Western sense, nor was there any demarcation between judicial and administrative functions. The makhzen was divided into two broad services, those of court and of state. The former consisted of the offices of Caid el-Mechouar, who was master of ceremonies and chief of protocol for the palace and also responsible for guarding it, and the *Hajib* (chamberlain), who was charged with internal management of the palace and for keeping the seal that was affixed to all official documents issued by the Sultan. The latter consisted of a central ministry and regional governments. A central ministry, responsible for carrying out all royal decisions and ensuring the satisfactory working of the departments, was headed by a Chief Vizier (Prime Minister), who could issue executive orders (known as Vizierial decrees) and who was also Minister of the Interior, with direct authority over the regional administrators. There were also Viziers for Foreign Affairs, War, Finance, and Justice.

On a local level, royal authority was exercised through the caids and djemaas in rural areas, and by the pashas in urban areas. The caids and pashas were appointed by the Sultan and were in turn assisted by sheiks or *khalifas* (administrators) and *mokkadem* (police). The tasks of these local administrators were to maintain order, levy military recruits, exact taxes, judge petty crimes and commercial cases, and execute and administer the Sultan's *dahirs* (legislative decrees). As officeholders were badly paid by the government, their remuneration came principally from "presents" (that is, bribes and extortions). The Sultan also had four special khalifas in Fez, Tetuán, Marrakesh, and the Tafilalt Oasis, and a *mendoub* in Tangier, who served as his religious and secular assistants. The mendoub was also the Sultan's official representative to the foreign embassies located in his city.

In 1912, four different systems of jurisprudence were in use in the country. In the bled el-makhzen, all Islamic religious questions and matters of personal status (including inheritance, marriage, divorce, and nonregistered realty issues) were judged, according to the divine Sharia, in religious courts, whose officers (*cadis*), often trained at the Karouine, were appointed by the Sultan. All other matters in this region were subject to makhzen law, which was synonymous with the will of the Sultan. Original jurisdiction in all civil and commercial cases, and in criminal cases involving a maximum punishment of less than two years' imprisonment, rested with the caids and pashas. Procedure in their courts was informal, and decisions, which were based on a combination of traditional law and nonjudicial influence, were often inconsistent. Appeals could be taken to a High Sherifian Tribunal (which also had original jurisdiction in criminal cases beyond the caid's or pasha's scope). There was no jury trial in makhzen courts, and judges were seldom trained adequately in the law. Sometimes, the pasha or caid delegated his authority to hold court to a more qualified deputy. Fines in criminal cases were not fixed by law, and, as the judges retained a large part for themselves, they were usually substantial.

In the bled es-siba, the Sharia was applied, but, instead of makhzen law, there was a juridical system of Berber customary law, which was the expression of tribal will. It was based on the principle of justice by arbitration, and the parties to the dispute historically had the right to choose their arbitrator. If the parties could not agree on one, the djemaa was given the power to do so. Gradually, the rule of the djemaa grew to such importance that the parties often asked it outright to decide the issue. Penal cases, however, remained subject to the jurisdiction of the caid, if there was one in the area.

An interesting part of Berber justice was the punishments inflicted under it. The usual punishment in Berber criminal law was a fine; imprisonment was never imposed, as the Berbers hated physical restraint above all else; the most serious punishment was banishment from the tribe. Arabized punishment was often more insidious. Capital punishment was seldom inflicted, even for murder, except "by accident," but the variety of cruelties imposed as punishment was limited solely by the ingenuity of its administrators. (One was the leather-glove torture, which was disappearing at the end of the nineteenth century. A lump of quicklime was placed in a man's hand, which was then forcibly kept closed. Death was frequently the result, but sometimes the victim was lucky enough to escape with only the loss of his hand.)

Another religious law was the Jewish Talmudic code, which in Morocco was interpreted according to the Sephardic traditions of Mediterranean Jewry. Its jurisdiction, exercised through rabbinical courts, was limited to disputes concerning religious matters, personal status, and inheritances. A High Rabbinical Tribunal in Rabat heard appeals.

In addition to these four indigenous systems of jurisprudence, there existed capitulatory law, under which foreign consuls had jurisdiction over their own citizens and over a few *protégés* (Moroccan citizens under their special protection), in accordance with international treaties. The law applied by the consuls included certain makhzen decrees, their own legislative and common law, the rules of equity, and ministerial regulations. Citizens of countries with no such extraterritorial rights were subject solely to makhzen law.

Though administrative problems were serious, the most critical facing Morocco before the Protectorate was finance. Since the Prophet had opposed organized secular taxation as demoralizing, the only original Islamic taxes were voluntary and given as charity. The *zekkat* (a sort of tithe) on agricultural produce, which was collected by the cadis, were thus given by the people from a sense of religious duty. Later, Moroccan governments instituted compulsory taxes, including the *jeziya* (a poll tax on non-Muslims), *kharaj* (land tax imposed on conquered peoples for the right to till their old land), *mokus* (gate and market dues), and, finally, a customs duty.

As the Sultan's purse was not separated from governmental resources, the special means used to supplement the former must be noted in any discussion of the latter. The Sultan was, in fact, enriched by the *mona*, or gifts from his caids, and the *hadiya*, gifts presented to him by the faithful on important religious holidays. Later, a percentage of the loot of the Barbary pirates considerably enhanced the royal coffers.

In the final analysis, total government revenue at any given time depended on the strength of the Sultan. By 1912, his ability to collect funds was almost nil, and the yields were correspondingly insignificant. Furthermore, officials had misappropriated so much that the government was almost bankrupt. Officials of the Protectorates charged with improving Morocco's government and administration were thus confronted with an enormous task.

C. The French Protectorate

French Morocco's first Resident General was the renowned Marshal Louis Lyautey. A brilliant soldier, a great statesman, and an idealist, he was to acquire fame as the "royalist who presented a republic with an empire." A graduate of St Cyr, he had served as a cavalry officer, later as staff and command officer, in Indochina, Madagascar, and Algeria, and he was already an experienced colonial administrator when he arrived in Morroco. Aristocratic and authoritarian, Lyautey was also sympathetic, in the finest sense of the word. His conception of the Protectorate, based on the treaty terms outlining the Resident's duties, his own beliefs concerning colonial issues, and the Moroccan situation as he saw it, was defined and dominated by the principle of supervision rather than direct administration. He believed that the Protectorate meant that Morocco would retain her own institutions and govern and administer her affairs in her own way, except for the control of a European power in the areas of external representation, general administration of the army, and the financing and guiding of the country's economic development. Furthermore, Lyautey believed the Protectorate was a transient arrangement whose success would eventually render it unnecessary. In return for her assistance, France would receive military and economic advantages, particularly in natural resources, a foreign market, manpower, and a strategic position; above all, she would enjoy the grand sense of accomplishment in her *mission civilisatrice*.

Lyautey faced three fundamental problems: pacifying the country, rebuilding central authority, and creating a sound, modern economy. In the first task, he achieved some immediate success, engaging in the process the services of the leading Atlas chieftain, Si Thami el-Glaoui, who was to become the chief native bulwark of the French Protectorate.*

By 1914, the French had pacified all of central Morocco between Fez and Marrakesh nearly up to the Moulouya River; the connection of Fez to Oudjda through Taza had been achieved; and resisting tribes had been driven from the plains into the mountains.

In the course of overcoming wartime disturbances in the Spanish-protected Rif, often fomented by German agents, and the great Rif rebellion launched by Abd el-Krim in 1921 and carried into French territory in 1925, Lyautey pacified most of French Morocco. (Abd el-Krim, of the Khatibi family, born in 1882, an educated and fanatical chieftain, had had early successes with the 50,000 troops he led against the Spanish forces. In 1923, he declared himself ruler of an independent Rif Republic. However, the ill-advised invasion of French Morocco placed him against two fronts and more than 300,000 soldiers.) Following Abd el-Krim's surrender and the termination of the Rif War in 1926 (Abd el-Krim was exiled to Réunion Island), it remained only for Lyautey's successors to pacify the southern end of the Middle Atlas, the Sous, and the Dra valleys. This final phase proceeded slowly, as the French Protectorate wisely concentrated first on consolidation. There were few difficulties with the larger towns, and many rural tribes made a hasty settlement in the face of superior military force or appealing prospects set forth by the government. For more than 20 years, however, almost constant warfare was waged with one or more tribes, all of which swore allegiance to the French

* In 1912, al-Hiba, a mystic from the Sous region, occupied Marrakesh and proclaimed himself Sultan. Lyautey sent an expeditionary force to the southern capital to engage the rebel, and el-Glaoui, the Pasha of Marrakesh, decided to lend him his support. This shrewd feudal lord, who commanded an estimated 100,000 Berber warriors, thus first endeared himself to his French friends.

El-Glaoui, born in 1878, was known popularly as the "Black Panther" and "Lord of the Atlas." His family had been chieftains for more than 200 years, and his oldest brother was Grand Vizier under Maulay Hafid. El-Glaoui had a number of sons, including Hassan, a talented painter; Si Sadek, Khalifa of Marrakesh; and Si Brahim, who ran the family estate. (Another son was killed in the Italian campaign during World War II.)

Under the Protectorate, el-Glaoui's already heavy purse became legendary, and, before he died, his personal wealth was estimated at more than $50 million. The sources of his wealth were numerous and included mining concessions, control of fish canneries, the world's largest estate of date and olive trees, import tax rebates, and a cut on the income of Marrakesh's several thousand prostitutes.

Protectorate only after being subdued on the battlefield at the cost of many lives. It was not until 1934 that the entire French zone came under effective Protectorate control.

Despite his early emphasis on military force, however, Lyautey clearly realized that successful pacification of Morocco could only be achieved in conjunction with judicious government. His motto was, "Show force only to avoid its use," and he wisely observed that "Opponents of today are associates of tomorrow." Thus, after his initial efforts, his military program called for limited control over occupied regions, together with efforts to revitalize the other areas, and ententes with several Great Atlas caids. This administrative policy was carried out most successfully by the men of his Bureau of Native Affairs, at the very edge of French-occupied territory. Working through native chiefs, these skillful and dedicated men, whose marked characteristics were dignity and respect, slowly overcame native opposition and eventually achieved native cooperation with the new regime.

Although Lyautey was a soldier by profession, he devoted most of his energies to extending Sherifian authority throughout the country and to building the national economy. Scrupulously carrying out France's pledge to safeguard the Muslim religion and enhance the prestige of the new Sultan Moulay Youssef, he simultaneously strengthened other Moroccan political institutions and resisted the pressures from Paris to assimilate French Morocco into France.

The principal organ of the Sultan's government under the Protectorate remained the makhzen. It was renovated, however, for the new regime. The functions of the Vizier of Foreign Affairs devolved upon the Resident General and those of the Vizier of War on the commanding general of the French troops, who was often the Resident General. The Vizier of Justice retained control over the Sharia law courts, but the Vizier of Finance's powers were assumed by the Resident General's Director of Sherifian Finance. A new vizierial position was created for the officer responsible for the management of the habous. While the central ministry was thus streamlined to meet the demands and responsibilities of the new regime, local administration remained basically intact but became subservient to the French will. Makhzen and local officials were chosen by the Sultan from a list presented to him by the French authorities.

In addition to the makhzen, the Protectorate availed itself of two other central governmental services: its own and the Neo-Sherifian departments. The former, acting solely in the name of

France, were actually agencies of the Residency, among the most important being the Department of Sherifian Affairs, which supervised the central makhzen and drew up its budget, and the Department of the Interior, which assumed the duties of the Grand Vizier as Minister of the Interior. The Department of Sherifian Affairs was headed by the Councilor of the Sherifian Government, who by the nature of his task was one of the most important men in the Protectorate government. The eight Neo-Sherifian directorates included: Finance, Health and Youth, Education, Mining, Agricultural Production and Supply, Transportation and Communications, Public Works, Commerce and Industry, and Labor. This structure provided a great duplication and complexity of administration in which order and direction could be provided only by the Resident General himself.

On the working level, the Neo-Sherifian services were linked to the makhzen by delegates charged with an information and liaison mission. This mission was a mere façade, however, as there was no requirement that the Directors contact the Viziers on any matter. A measure of reform in 1947 established a Council of Viziers and Directors that theoretically had legislative and administrative duties; it was composed of the Viziers and delegates, the Secretary General of the Protectorate, the Councilor of the Sherifian Government, and the Directors—in all, fourteen Moroccans and seventeen Frenchmen. The Grand Vizier was President of the Council, and the Secretary General was Vice President. The Council was theoretically to be consulted on all questions of general interest, but in practice it was ignored.

The only truly representative element in the central organization was the Government Council, which advised the government on economic and social matters. It actually carried very little weight. Originally created in 1919, it underwent various changes in structure and scope over the years. By 1955, it included two sections of three "colleges" each. The colleges met jointly and the sections separately twice each year. The first and second colleges of both the French and Moroccan sections represented agricultural and commercial-industrial interests, respectively. Members of the local French Chambers of Commerce and Agriculture—corporate semi-official bodies—elected representatives to their respective colleges. The representatives of the third college of the French section were elected by French residents of Morocco who were not members of either the Chamber of Agriculture or the Chamber of Commerce; they were regarded as representatives of the consumer viewpoint. All French residents thus formed the electorate for the

French section, though often only no more than 30 per cent voted. Women were enfranchised, and fathers were allowed extra votes when they had four or more children. Members of Moroccan sections were appointed by the administration until 1947; thereafter, the first and second colleges were elected by the Moroccan Chambers of Commerce and of Agriculture. The third Moroccan college, however, continued to be named by municipal commissions and the Resident General. For this section, even after 1947, there were only 150,000 eligible Moroccan voters out of a Moroccan population of 9 million. In addition to the Muslims in the third college of the Moroccan section, there were six Jewish representatives, elected by certain Jewish committees in the country.

French settlers in Morocco, *qua* citizens of France, were represented in France in a very limited manner. They had no representation in the French National Assembly and although a council in Morocco selected six nominees for three Senate seats, only a few of these Moroccan choices were ever elected. Thus, the settlers were forced to exert political influence on Paris leaders directly or through quasi-political or economic organizations. In many instances, the former method was utilized, but the French Chambers of Commerce, Industry, and Agriculture in Morocco were also a constant source of heavy pressure. French bureaucrats in the Protectorate administration provided another real force. The most vocal group was the agricultural lobby in Morocco, but the most powerful was a financial lobby in France known as the Comité du Maroc. As a group, French labor in Morocco had little influence. In addition to these economic groups, several political groups and veterans' and other patriotic organizations engaged in political activity. These were quite vocal, but they never exerted an influence on Paris comparable to that of the economic interests.

D. Spanish Morocco

Spain administered its zone of Morocco under the nominal authority of the Sultan's Khalifa in Tetuán, the capital, and had the same right as the French to carry out reforms. The Sultan continued to name the Khalifa, but only by selecting one of two names presented by Spanish authorities. A separate makhzen in the Spanish zone administered functions closely related to Muslim and traditional ways of life. Direct control of other matters was from the first assumed by a Spanish administration headed by a High Commissioner, who, after the Spanish Civil War, was named by decree of the Spanish Council of Ministers. He held the rank of Minister; if he was the highest military officer in the area, he also commanded the Spanish forces, which, after the 1920's, numbered perhaps 60,000, some 80 per cent of whom were Muslim. Under the Franco regime, the High Commissioner was required to consult the Generalissimo on all matters of foreign relations, finance, and general policy. His independence of action in other fields depended on his relations with Franco.

The High Commissioner was the supreme legislative authority, as well as the executive chief of state. All legislation required formal validation by the official seal of the Khalifa as the Sultan's representative, but the Khalifa's power to oppose drafts submitted to him by the Spanish administration was only theoretical. Furthermore, the High Commissioner could issue ordinances for administrative control without the formality of his seal.

The execution of local policy was the responsibility of an *interventor* (district commissioner), who was subordinate to the Director of Native Affairs. A district commissioner's office was established in almost all of the sixty-odd tribal territories of the zone, and the post was usually filled by an army officer; the Franco regime in particular believed that soldiers were best suited for the job. The local native administration, headed by caids and pashas, was utilized in much the same manner as in the French zone.

Under Franco, the only political party in Spanish Morocco was the Falange. Spanish settlers had no true representation either in Morocco or in Spain. However, a few Spanish Protectorate bureaucrats and military officers were disproportionately influential in Madrid. The Communist Party in Spanish Morocco was completely suppressed and did not even have a clandestine organization, although several hundred Communists took up residence in the Spanish zone after the Spanish Civil War.

The Franco-Spanish Treaty of 1912 authorized Spain to set up its own judicial system in its zone of Morocco. The Hispanic-Khalifian Court that was established adopted the legal code in force in Spain at the beginning of the twentieth century, with modifications to meet local conditions. This system operated on three levels: tribunals of peace, courts of the first instance, and a court of appeals. There was no right to trial by jury, but, in nonpolitical cases, individual rights were generally observed. These courts had jurisdiction in cases where either party was a foreigner. Aside from the Hispanic-Khalifian courts, the indigenous legal systems resembled those in the French zone.

E.   The Beginnings of Moroccan Nationalism

As the first step in rebuilding the national economy and creating a modern infrastructure, Lyautey completed the country's first modern seaport, Casablanca. A national transportation and communications system was then developed; modern health, sanitation, and educational facilities were inaugurated; judicial and financial reforms were instituted. Except in the field of education, Lyautey's material efforts were ably continued by his successors and ultimately constituted an important legacy to Morocco. These French efforts were a fulfillment of the Protectorate pledge, but, in addition, they created an excellent commercial and industrial climate for French enterprise, providing the basic facilities required by the growing European community dedicated to modern ways of life.

Lyautey had attempted to keep native life free of alien influence, and in one step toward that end, he had forbidden the French to build in the *medinas* (native towns), thereby maintaining them as entities distinct from the *ville nouvelle*, as the European section of each city was to be known. He also tried to limit French colonization on the land, as he feared that the growth of a powerful settler group would lead to the formation of a privileged class determined to attain direct political domination.

Unfortunately, financial and, later, political considerations excluded the great majority of the Moroccan population from any significant benefit from the material gains acquired by the Europeans, except in the matter of public health. Furthermore, Lyautey's view of the Protectorate was not shared by his successors, their subordinates, their rapidly growing number of constituents in Morocco, or their friends in France.* To the majority of the Frenchmen with a vested interest in Morocco, the country became principally the source of their own livelihood—or, in numerous cases, their wealth. The natives were *sales arabes*, to be kept in their place while Frenchmen administered and developed the country as they saw fit. Therefore, although the standard of living

* In 1931, there were 172,000 Europeans (most of them French) living in French Morocco. This figure grew to 420,000 (plus 50,000 Algerians of French nationality) by 1955. The number of civil servants in the French Protectorate grew steadily, reaching 41,450 in 1950 (of whom about 33 per cent were regular or auxiliary police); roughly 40 per cent were Moroccans, who were generally employed as servants and guards. In the highest ranks, 90 per cent were French; in the second level, 80 per cent; in the third, 70 per cent; and of the lowest, 4 per cent. The makhzen employed another 1,500 Moroccans, including 300 pashas and caids and 500 palace guards.

for some Moroccans improved under the Protectorate, there was a critical failure to provide adequate opportunities for self-development and, most important, personal dignity.

The modernization of Morocco was an amazing French accomplishment, but it was also to be a major cause of France's ultimate defeat. The traditions and tribal ties of a significant part of the Moroccan people were broken, while the impact of Western technology and ideology increased population pressures, altered patterns of living and thinking, and generated dissatisfaction with the social, economic, and political order. Younger Moroccans—especially those of the urban middle class, who were the principal witnesses of the French methods—resented the fact that French activities generally benefited Frenchmen, while Moroccans often suffered discrimination. The intellectuals, in particular, complained that, although the Treaty of Fez did not in principle violate the Act of Algeciras and the guarantee of Moroccan sovereignty, France's gradual assumption of direct control over the country proceeded steadily, thwarting the political development of the native population. After Lyautey's retirement in 1926, all hope that France might prepare Morocco for self-government was, in fact, lost.

The result was the birth of Moroccan nationalism. Confined at first to small elite groups, Moroccan nationalism in its infancy manifested itself mainly in protests and agitation, in insistence on traditional ways of life in the face of French efforts at assimilation, and in a reform religious movement (salafiya) that preached a return to Islamic fundamentals and was directed against the French alliance with the religious brotherhoods. As Moroccan frustrations and ambitions grew, moreover, so did popular support of political organizations and the scope of their activities.

Moderate nationalists, mainly businessmen and intellectuals, originally hoped that the French would make evolutionary changes, and they warned the Resident General that the alternative was extremism. Most colons * opposed any concession to the nationalists, advocating their suppression; their voices echoed loudly in Paris. At first, the French reacted to Moroccan nationalism with a policy of divide and rule, playing off the tribes against the Sultan

* The word colon was originally reserved for the French who settled on farms, as contrasted to the more numerous city-dwellers. During the period 1953–55, "colon" came to connote the die-hard element of French settlers and fonctionnaires of the city and bled. The word will be used hereafter (except in Chapter 6) in this latter sense, being concisely descriptive of an otherwise heterogeneous group.

and the Berbers against the Arabs. Next, they attempted to minimize the growing nationalist movement, instead of seeking to resolve the issues that created it and reach an entente with its leaders.
Finally, the official reaction was suppression and violence, which
did more to unify the Moroccan people than nationalism itself.

⌐ The most important fountainheads of Moroccan nationalist protest were the student groups founded in 1926 by Allal al-Fassi in
Fez and by Ahmed Balafrej in Rabat. Al-Fassi was an ambitious
twenty-year-old Karouine Professor of Islamic Studies; he spoke
little French but was a spellbinding orator, poet, and philosopher
in Arabic. Balafrej was an eighteen-year-old student trained in
Paris. Al-Fassi and Balafrej differed greatly in orientation and personality, but they agreed on the need for cooperation between
their respective organizations, the Students' Union and the Supporters of Truth. An informal collaboration of these two groups
began in 1927 and shortly thereafter became the basis for the
Moroccan League and, subsequently, the Committee for National
Action, which included representatives from the capital of the
Spanish zone, Tetuán, and from groups in other major cities.
There was little political activity, however, until the Residency,
through the Sultan, promulgated the now famous Berber Dahir
of May 16, 1930.

The Berber Dahir, which gave official national recognition to
Berber customary law in those areas where it existed, aroused great
opposition in Morocco and other Arab states because it formally
divided the country, thus tending to weaken the Sultan's authority
and strengthen French control. Although designed to help the
Protectorate, it had the opposite effect, attracting Berbers as well
as Arabs to the nationalist cause and uniting in protest some of
the most Westernized and most traditional elements in the country. Prominent individuals in all circles were outraged at what
they described as an infringement of the Sultan's authority in his
dual capacity as religious and secular head of state.

The Berber Dahir furnished the nationalist leaders with a rallying cry, an awareness that many ordinary Moroccans could be ral-
lied against French actions, and the sympathy of many Arab
leaders and French liberals. As a result, nationalist activities quickly
multiplied.

In 1930, the Syrian Pan-Arab leader Chekib Arslan visited
Tetuán, where he met Allal al-Fassi and Mohammed Hassan
Ouazzani, a Sorbonne student from Fez, who became his secretary.
Pan-Arabism became progressively stronger in Morocco, particu-
larly in the Spanish zone, where Arab culture was venerated, where

students considered Cairo a polestar, and where access to French schools was forbidden. The activity of Moroccan nationalists from the French zone remained centered, by contrast, in Paris, where several French Socialists assisted Balafrej in launching the French-language paper *El Maghreb* and also contributed to the weekly *L'Action du Peuple*, launched in Fez by Ouazzani. At the same time, contacts were strengthened with other North African students in Paris. This was facilitated by the fact that Balafrej had helped to found there the Association of North African Muslim Students in 1927.

Within Morocco, nationalist activities evolved from lecturing and propagandizing to forming auxiliaries such as alumni associations and Boy Scout troops, opening free schools, and organizing demonstrations in favor of the new Sultan, Mohammed V.

In 1927, when Sultan Moulay Youssef (successor to his brother Moulay Hafid) had died, the French chose as his successor his fourth son—eighteen-year-old Sidi Mohammed Ben Youssef—known officially as Mohammed V. This eighteenth monarch of the Alawite dynasty had been educated along traditional lines by a pro-French tutor, but he had also learned the French language and was well read in several modern subjects, particularly history. Pious, with a dignified appearance that seemed to embody wisdom and moderation, he usually wore his djellaba over Western clothes and a *tarbouche* (a fez creased like a fedora). (A handsome and gentle man, Mohammed V eventually acquired two wives and forty or fifty concubines. He was the devoted father of six children, five of whom were borne by his elder wife. The younger wife—a servant girl seventeen years his junior, given to him by el-Glaoui as a gift in later years—bore his youngest child in 1954.)

Mohammed V had been selected by the French ahead of his older brothers because he was believed to be more docile and amenable to the wishes of the Residency. Protectorate officials pampered the young monarch with women and pomp in an effort to keep him a contented and tranquil potentate. But Moroccan nationalists hoped to make of him a national symbol, and they wanted to win him to their cause. They achieved some success on the first count, largely through annual Throne Day celebrations initiated on November 18, 1933, but little on the second. Finding their publications and meetings banned, and seeing a further threat to sovereignty in Paris' transfer of the Protectorate administration to the Ministry for France Overseas in February, 1934, they decided to take more direct, although still moderate, action.

The result was the creation in Fez of a Moroccan Action Committee (Comité d'Action Marocaine, CAM), which, on December 1, 1934, presented to the French Foreign Minister in Paris and to the Resident General and the Sultan in Rabat a Plan for Moroccan Reforms. Calling for strict application of the Treaty of Fez and abolition of all direct French administration, the CAM also demanded administrative and judicial unity for Morocco; Moroccan participation in numerous departments of the administration; a curb on the powers then in the hands of the caids and pashas; creation of local governing and economic assemblies and of a national council consisting of Muslim and Jewish Moroccan representatives; more civil liberties; improved educational facilities; a halt to expropriation of native lands; and prohibition of further French colonization. The comprehensive plan did not suggest that the Protectorate be ended, however, an idea that would have antagonized most sections of French political opinion and to which few Moroccans themselves were as yet committed.

Although the French Government ignored the plan and dismissed its sponsors as representing no one but themselves, nationalists continued their efforts to arouse the country. On October 25, 1936, the CAM held its first nationalist congress, with Allal al-Fassi presiding. The following spring, it evolved into the Watani (National Party for the Realization of the Plan for Reforms); al-Fassi was President and Balafrej Secretary General. Ouazzani, disgruntled at not being offered the presidency, founded the small, rival Popular Movement.

Nationalist activities were developing simultaneously in Spanish Morocco. Abd el-Khalek Torres, who was in contact with al-Fassi, formed the Islah (National Reform Party) in Tetuán in 1936. Mekki El Naciri, a CAM alumnus from the French zone, took refuge in Tetuán and, after quarreling with Torres, founded the Wahda (Moroccan Unity Party) in the same year. The Islah's few cadres consisted almost entirely of intellectuals and students; there was no significant Muslim middle class in Spanish Morocco, and the rural population was too tradition-bound, with too few Western contacts to be interested in national politics as such. Nevertheless, its contacts with the Arab world and the general tolerance of the Franco regime toward it permitted the Islah to play an important auxiliary role in subsequent years.

In July and October, 1937, the Watani instigated disturbances in several French Moroccan cities, whereupon the Resident General, Auguste Noguès, banned all the new nationalist groups and exiled al-Fassi to Gabon, in French Equatorial Africa. Ouazzani was placed under house arrest in the Atlas Mountains; Balafrej, who was in France at the time, was refused permission to re-enter his country; others sought refuge in Spanish Morocco. Noguès then followed political suppression with social reform, inaugurating a pattern that was to become common in the following years. New schools and hospitals were built, and certain administrative posts were opened to Moroccans, but the question of the Sultan's authority was virtually ignored. In the years immediately preceding the outbreak of World War II, Morocco was tranquil.

When France fell, in 1940, French Morocco gave its adherence to the Vichy government, and General Noguès was named Commander in Chief of the Vichy North African Army. The Moroccans themselves, on the other hand, did not acquiesce in this surrender; neither, despite some individual instances of collaboration, did they assist the Axis against the Free French. The Sultan, who had initially backed the Allied cause, was naturally cool to the Vichy regime and stoutly opposed the adoption of its racial laws in his country, maintaining that the Jews of Morocco were loyal subjects of his realm who could not be discriminated against. This attitude won Mohammed V a decoration as Companion of the Resistance from General de Gaulle, when the Allies finally landed in North Africa and retook Morocco, after a brief resistance, in November, 1942. The Sultan had refused Noguès' orders to leave Rabat for a more secure position inland, remaining to greet the Allied forces. Noguès was shortly thereafter relieved of his duties in Rabat.

In the Spanish zone, there was considerable local support for the Axis, due mainly to Franco's promises of reforms following an Allied defeat, but there was little in the way of organized activities. Franco had reportedly sought large territorial concessions in Africa, including French Morocco, in return for entering the war on the side of the Axis.

French Morocco's subsequent contribution to the war effort was the service of 83,000 *goumiers* (Berber infantrymen) in the Free French Army; they fought with distinction in the Italian campaign.

F. The Nationalist Movement Gathers Momentum

Gabriel Puaux, the new Resident General in French Morocco, permitted Balafrej to return to the country, and nationalist hopes of effecting the principles of self-government outlined in the Atlantic Charter were raised high. These hopes were intensified following the Sultan's meeting with President Roosevelt and Prime

Minister Winston Churchill at Casablanca, in January, 1943, when Roosevelt told His Majesty:

> Why does Morocco, inhabited by Moroccans, belong to France? Anything must be better than to live under French colonial rule . . . When we've won this war, I will work with all my might to see to it that the United States is not wheedled into the position of accepting any plan that will further France's imperialistic ambitions.*

Roosevelt's promise was hardly "the source of all our troubles," as some colons later claimed. But this statement, so at variance with previous United States policy to negotiate with Morocco through the recognized French authorities, doubtless encouraged the Sultan to take a second look at his attitude toward Moroccan nationalism, which had heretofore been lukewarm. Furthermore, it encouraged the nationalists to proceed with plans for a new and more ambitious political organization.

In December, 1943, Balafrej integrated veterans of the Watani and the Popular Movement with new nationalist recruits in the Istiqlal (Independence Party), the first political movement with a mass base that Morocco had yet produced. Although al-Fassi was still in exile, Balafrej permitted the widely popular *doyen* of Moroccan nationalism to be named President; he himself assumed the post of Secretary General.

On January 14, 1944, after informing the Sultan of their plans, leaders of the new party presented Puaux and the Allied powers with a manifesto. For the first time, a demand was included for "the independence, unity, and territorial integrity of Morocco and the establishment of a democratic regime guaranteeing the rights of all elements and classes of Moroccan society." The Allies made no reply to this manifesto, while Puaux responded with more suppression and arrests and once again exiled Balafrej, this time to Corsica.

This period of suppression benefited the Istiqlal in many ways, for it permitted younger nationalists such as Abderrahmin Bouabid, a brilliant lawyer, and Mehdi Ben Barka, a dynamic intellectual, to gain leadership experience and to circulate petitions abroad and propaganda at home; it also caused the leaders to organize a disciplined yet flexible party structure. Largely due to the organizational skills of Ben Barka, who served as Balafrej's assistant, a pyramidal hierarchy was formed on the model of Communist parties and many effective nationalist movements. Personal and

* Elliott Roosevelt, *As He Saw It* (New York, 1946), pp. 115–16.

ideological differences among various individuals, as well as poor communications and discipline within the party, limited the Istiqlal's effectiveness for several years and almost caused its destruction during a period of crisis. Its new organizational framework, however, permitted it steadily to enlarge its cadres, organize the urban masses and some rural adherents, and plan for clandestine operations. Both these deficiencies and assets were extremely important in the postwar years.

In March, 1946, Erik Labonne became Resident General of French Morocco and immediately permitted all the exiled nationalist leaders to return to the country, including al-Fassi, who had been exiled for nine years and was now permitted to reside in Tangier. He even arranged and held talks with them in hopes of forestalling serious trouble with the nationalist movement, and he subsequently initiated various reforms—establishing the Council of Viziers and Directors in 1947; permitting the election of representatives to the Moroccan colleges in the Government Council in 1948; opening more junior administrative posts to Moroccans; and sponsoring a plan to bring 10,000 Moroccan children a year into the school system.

Opposed by the colons for going too far and by the nationalists for not going far enough, the Labonne reforms ended by causing a serious split in nationalist ranks. The extreme element, led by the uncompromising al-Fassi and the astute diplomat Balafrej, favored an appeal to Arab countries and the United States for help in gaining immediate independence. Under Ouazzani's leadership, the group favoring gentler measures urged cooperation with the French in hopes of obtaining independence gradually. In the end, the latter group left the Istiqlal and established the Shourra, or PDI (Democratic Party for Independence).

The postwar period also saw the first offer by the Moroccan Communist Party to aid the nationalist groups in their struggle toward a "common end." The offer was categorically rejected by all factions, and the Communist Party never played a significant role in Moroccan Protectorate politics. Its strategy, however, is worth noting.

As far back as 1920, Stalin had said that Communism favored separating Morocco from France, as the "liberation of oppressed countries from imperialism" would undermine the position of world capitalism and strengthen that of the Communist revolution. In 1936, Léon Sultan, a Frenchman, had formed a French Communist Party regional committee in Morocco, which in 1943 became the theoretically autonomous Moroccan Communist Party

(MCP). The change in title, designed to broaden the Party's appeal among Moroccans, was followed by the establishment in the bled of *amicales* (mutual interest associations), reminiscent of the Party's "rural friendship leagues" in Indochina. To become a party of the masses, as it desired, and not merely a small group of hardcore fanatics, the MCP felt it must expand into the countryside where the majority of the population lived. In addition to the urban cells and *amicales*, several fronts were set up, including Friends of Democracy, the Union of Moroccan Women, and the barely disguised France-U.S.S.R.

By 1946, however, the MCP had abandoned its hope of organizing the countryside and had turned its attention to the urban trade unions, which were just beginning to admit Moroccan members. Infiltrating the largest organization, the General Union of Confederated Moroccan Syndicates, the Moroccan Communists, like their Continental comrades in the mother union, captured several key posts and controlled the organization for a few years. This could greatly have increased the MCP's influence, particularly since Moroccans were forbidden to form their own unions, but several factors checked its popularity and prevented the nationalists from making common cause with it.

Despite its claimed autonomy, the MCP was regarded as subservient to the French Communist Party, which in turn took orders from Moscow. Communist parties in "colonized" areas were supposed to be subservient to the parties in the colonizing country; the Philippine Communist Party, for example, took orders from the American Communist Party in the interwar period. Furthermore, the membership and leadership of the Moroccan Communist Party were at first predominantly European. After the death of Léon Sultan in 1945 and his replacement by Ali Yata, a Muslim of Algerian descent and French citizenship, Moroccan membership and influence in the Party steadily increased. Nevertheless, several Frenchmen continued to play key roles, although behind the scenes. Protectorate officials periodically attempted to discipline these men, but Communist pressure on the government in Paris was usually sufficient to prevent their permanent removal from the scene.

In addition to the taint of its foreign associations, the MCP, following the directive of the French Communist Party (PCF), had failed to advocate Moroccan independence until 1946. The PCF opposed independence for French colonies and protectorates simply because of its desire to maintain control of the Communist movement in these areas; it thus alienated many individuals who were nationalists first and Communists or Marxists only second. In 1946, however, Mohammed V consented to receive a Communist delegation, and support of the MCP was at its peak. Thereafter, the Party declined in importance, its membership dropping from 10,000 (including 800 Europeans) in 1946 to 7,000 (including 700 Europeans) in 1952.

The MCP decline was due to the fact that bona-fide nationalists had long since pre-empted direction of the growing Pan-Arab and Moroccan nationalist movements. Their position was further strengthened by two important events in 1947. One was a visit made by Mohammed V to Tangier on April 10, the first journey of a Moroccan monarch to the international city since 1898. The Sultan had originally prepared a mild speech to give in Tangier with vague references to nationalist aspirations and some praise for French accomplishments, but on the eve of the speech, a brawl in Rabat's "reserve quarter" (red-light district), in which several scores of Moroccans were killed by French soldiers, so enraged him that he altered his prepared text. Declaring his solidarity with the newly formed Arab League, he omitted even the customary professions of friendship and gratitude to France. In addition, he said:

> Morocco took an active part in the last war, offering her sons and her resources until final victory was achieved. Today, as all people claim those rights compatible with modern times, it is just that the Moroccan people obtain their lawful rights and realize their legitimate aspirations, which are the same for all peoples. Morocco ardently desires to regain her rights.

The Sultan's speech was interpreted by the Istiqlal as a plea for independence; it was in any case Mohammed V's first public support of the nationalist cause.

The following month, in Cairo, a North African Liberation Committee was formed under the joint direction of al-Fassi, who had left Tangier; Torres; and the elderly Abd el-Krim, who had returned from exile.* Together with other North African national-

* Abd el-Krim, the same "Lion of the Rif" who had almost defeated Protectorate forces in the early 1920's, had escaped in 1947 from an Australian ship carrying him from Réunion Island to the French Riviera, where France had offered him a more comfortable exile. He disembarked at Port Said, allegedly with the complicity of Egypt's King Farouk, and was given a twelve-room villa in Kubleh, a garden suburb of Cairo, as guest of the Egyptian Government. Abd el-Krim worked with the Liberation Committee until 1952, when, due to friction with the other leaders and his inability to attract a following or wield any personal influence outside the Rif, he temporarily gave up his political activities.

ists (Habib Bourguiba among them), they began to plan concerted domestic and, particularly, diplomatic action designed to oust the French from the Maghrib. Although it was some time before the Committee produced concrete results, the "Tangier Speech" had immediate repercussions. France responded by replacing the moderate Labonne with General Alphonse Pierre Juin, who was determined to squelch the nationalists by intimidating their most important supporter, Mohammed V. There followed three years of conflict between the two men and their adherents.

In October, 1950, the Sultan visited Paris in an unsuccessful effort to improve the rapidly deteriorating Moroccan situation. Two months later, two of the eleven newly elected Istiqlal representatives on the Government Council made their report on the Protectorate budget. Ahmed Lyazidi, President of the Federation of Moroccan Chambers of Commerce and Industry and a major figure in the Istiqlal, remarked:

> We should be betraying the mandate given us if we did not say that the budget, as conceived and applied, is incapable of assuring the development of the Moroccan people. Our criticisms are not directed against the experts who have drafted it but against the policy to which they are forced to conform. It is therefore the Protectorate regime as such that we question.

His colleague Mohammed Laghzaoui, President of the Moroccan Chamber of Commerce and Industry at Fez, added: "In actual fact, it is the European colony, with its increasing command of the key sectors of the Moroccan economy, that profits directly and mainly from the infrastructure of ports, road and rail networks, water power, etc. Moroccans benefit from them also, but only in a secondary sense." The infuriated Resident General immediately expelled both men from the Council, whereupon the other nine Istiqlal men withdrew in protest.

A showdown occurred in February, 1951, when el-Glaoui, encouraged by Juin, provocatively referred to Mohammed V as a "Sultan of the Istiqlal . . . leading the Empire to disaster." When the Sultan called el-Glaoui to the palace to discuss this attack, the latter reiterated his charge and was henceforth forbidden the palace. The French press pictured el-Glaoui as the wronged but righteous defender of Muslim ethics and religion, and the Sultan became the subject of imaginative and ruthless stories circulated by his enemies. Juin, in the meantime, demanded that the Sultan dismiss his nationalist advisers, repudiate both the Istiqlal and the

Communists (who had never really had his ear), and agree to sign the sixty-eight dahirs drawn up by Juin and heretofore ignored. To enforce these demands, Juin utilized el-Glaoui's services, on whose command 300,000 Berber tribesmen marched toward Fez and Rabat and camped outside the cities, awaiting further orders. The Sultan accepted French President Auriol's advice to cooperate in order to avoid bloodshed. He dismissed his Istiqlal advisers, repudiated Communism, and criticized "certain parties that obstruct progress," but he did not mention the nationalist groups directly.

The Sultan let it be known, however, that he had capitulated under duress, and he thereby strengthened the very opposition the Resident General had sought to curb. Juin wished immediately to depose him, despite his concessions, but the government in Paris instead replaced Juin. General Augustin Guillaume was named the new Resident General, the Berber warriors returned home, and the nationalists, who had never before consolidated their energies, collectively picked up the gauntlet Juin had hurled.

When the smoke of the "Throne Plot" had cleared, representatives of the Istiqlal and PDI in the French zone and of the Islah and Wahda in the Spanish zone met in Tangier with a recently arrived spokesman for the Arab League and signed a pact of unity. Partly at the Arab League's urging, the party representatives promised to support Morocco's complete independence and to oppose further negotiations with France prior to the granting of such independence, flatly rejecting an unofficial French proposal to incorporate Morocco fully into the French Union.

On November 18, 1952, in what was to be his last Throne Speech for several years, the Sultan uttered an eleventh-hour plea for the solution of the rapidly deteriorating situation and for Franco-Moroccan cooperation based on mutual friendship and respect. No response came from the Residency or from Paris. Then, on December 7, blood flowed in Morocco, and the violent phase of the struggle for independence began.

When news of the assassination of Ferhat Hashed (a widely respected Tunisian leader and Arab nationalist, who was believed to have been killed by Tunisian police) reached Casablanca on December 7, 1952, Moroccan nationalists seized the opportunity to call a protest solidarity strike against French policies throughout North Africa. All Moroccan shopkeepers closed their stores and opposed action by the French police designed to force their reopening. In the Carrières Centrales (workers' quarters), Istiqlal militants resisted the police violently, and the latter opened fire to restore order. The next day, surly mobs roamed the streets, and a group of natives moved toward a local police station. The police, either fearing attack or wishing to end the demonstration, fired into the crowd. The riots then began in earnest. *La Vigie*, a conservative French daily in Casablanca, featured a story that two European women had been raped and knifed by Moroccans on this occasion. Although it was later proved false and retracted, this story provoked the Europeans, who had previously exerted their influence quietly but effectively, to counterattack. Under the leadership of men such as Casablanca's Chef de Région, Philippe Boniface, they indicated they were as willing to resort to violence to achieve their aims as the most extreme of the nationalist elements.

On December 9, the official French report said that seven Europeans and thirty-three Moroccans had been killed during the two days; nationalist estimates ranged as high as 500 casualties. The true figure, as usual in incidents of this nature, fell somewhere in between. Both sides felt that they had reason to stretch the truth, and they never hesitated to do so.

As an immediate result of the December riots, the French outlawed the Istiqlal, which had perhaps 80,000 members at the time, and the Moroccan Communist Party and arrested or exiled leading nationalists and even sympathetic Frenchmen in Morocco. (In Paris, Frenchmen who were vocal against the Protectorate's hardening policy included the writer Pierre Parent; members of the French Maghrib Committee, a political group led by François Mauriac; several prominent Catholic leaders, foremost among them Robert Barrat, General Secretary of the Circle of Catholic Intellectuals, and Father Ignace Lepp.) The PDI (about 6,500 members) was not banned, however, in order to keep a door open to negotiations. Subsequently, allegations were made that the riots were an Istiqlal-Communist–inspired plot against the government, a charge reflecting France's concern over the imminent United Nations debate on the Moroccan question. Morocco's case was to be presented to the U.N. by Arab countries at the behest of Balafrej and other nationalists who had recently established a Moroccan Liberation Office in New York. France was therefore particularly anxious to keep United States public opinion in line during the first critical period of world reaction.

At the seventh session of the General Assembly in the fall of 1952, thirteen Arab and Asian nations introduced a resolution on Morocco that, in weakened form, was passed by a vote of forty-five to three, with eleven abstentions. The resolution expressed confidence in France's intentions, hope that negotiations would continue, and an appeal to both parties to conduct their relations in accordance with the spirit of the U.N. Charter. This represented but a slight advance over the action taken at the sixth session of the General Assembly in 1951, when Egypt attempted to place on the agenda a complaint that France's actions in Morocco violated the principles of the Charter and contravened the Declaration of Human Rights. Bowing to France's contention that it was not accountable to the Assembly, the steering committee tabled the motion. Only at the eighth session in 1953 did the Assembly pass an emasculated resolution urging that the right of the Moroccan people to free and democratic political institutions be insured.

In the spring of 1953, French Resident General Guillaume, Marshal Juin, and el-Glaoui made plans to rid Morocco of its by now free-spoken Sultan. In the summer, el-Glaoui, Moulay Idris, leader of a "puppet" party (the Democratic Party of Free Men), and Sherif Abdelhai el-Kittani, head of the Kittanya brotherhood, one of Morocco's *ikhwan*, took an oath not to rest until the enemies of the faith were removed from the steps of the throne. El-Kittani was motivated by hatred of the royal family, to which he attributed the death of an elder brother. The ulema at Fez issued a statement anathematizing the conspirators, but the French press proclaimed that the people were solidly behind them. General Guillaume then asked the Sultan to approve the dahirs he had thus far refused to sign, one of which provided for elected city councils with equal French-Moroccan representation, a measure that would have instituted co-sovereignty of France and Morocco and violated the Treaty of Fez. When the Sultan, despite threats of dire consequences, refused to sign, his days were numbered.

On August 16, 1953, Mohammed V issued a last futile communique to his people, expressing the hope that the French Government would rectify a situation that could lead only to further bloodshed. But when el-Glaoui circulated a petition among the caids and pashas calling for the Sultan's actual deposition, more than 75 per cent of the almost 350 French-selected officials signed, despite the ulema's objections. At this point, General Guillaume, prodded by Premier Laniel's government in Paris, tried to arrest the revolt he had helped set in motion; his subordinates, however, notably Boniface, pressed el-Glaoui to stand fast and did not carry out the pro-Sultan orders sent from Paris by Foreign Minister Bidault. The day before, el-Glaoui had proclaimed Moulay Ben Arafa, an aging cousin of Mohammed V, as the Imam, the country's true commander of the faithful. The French, facing the unpleasant choice between supporting el-Glaoui, the colons, and their

friends or carrying out the Protectorate treaty obligations to defend
the Sultan against all dangers, reluctantly accepted the former
alternative. Persuasion and threats convinced the ulema of Fez
and recalcitrant caids and pashas to change their minds; only one
pasha, M'Barek Bekkai of Sefrou (an oft-decorated major in the
French Army during World War II), stood firm. The ulema, with
only two dissenting votes, then proclaimed Moulay Ben Arafa as
Sultan, and Mohammed Ben Youssef was whisked away from Rabat
by Protectorate officials in the middle of the night of August 21.
Still in his pajamas, he was flown with his two wives, five children,
and eight concubines to Corsica, whence he was later transferred
to Madagascar. El-Glaoui reportedly remarked that "now he could
die happy," and Si Bekkai, in protest, exiled himself from Morocco.

Not only Moroccan nationalists, but most French officials in
Paris realized that the deposition of the Sultan had violated the
Treaty of Fez. Furthermore, many of the French sensed that, in
the words of Talleyrand, the move "is worse than a crime, it is a
blunder." In truth, the deposition was to accomplish in two years
what the nationalists, whether quarreling among themselves or
cooperating, had never been able to bring about: it was to rally
tribesman and farmer, bourgeois and laborer, to a successful,
nationwide effort to restore Morocco's rightful ruler and to gain
Morocco's independence.

Chapter 3

The Final Struggle for Independence: 1953–55

THE REPLACEMENT of Mohammed V by his cousin, the docile Moulay Ben Arafa, transformed the former into a national hero-martyr and irreparably damaged the French Protectorate administration in Morocco. This was due in part to the fact that Moulay Ben Arafa was a nonentity who was generally regarded as a puppet and usurper. Seven months after Ben Arafa assumed the throne, two attempts were made on his life. Thereafter his major preoccupation became attempting to stay alive. Nationalists of every persuasion immediately grasped the political value of the French "infamy" and proceeded to organize around the symbol of the throne a campaign that soon led to a reign of terror. Concluding then that only complete suppression and, ultimately, counterterror would preserve their vested interests, the more reactionary colons and their supporters in France began to take matters in their own hands. French Government influence and control over both groups progressively weakened; grounds for compromise vanished; and prospects for eventual reconcilation between all elements were gravely jeopardized. The events of this strife-ridden period merit considerable attention, not only because they precipitated Morocco's sudden acquisition of independence, but also because they are related to many of Morocco's post-independence difficulties.

Resistance to the French Protectorate that developed after Mohammed V's deposition did not begin as a concerted effort

organized either by the Istiqlal or a united nationalist front. The
Istiqlal, badly crippled since the mass arrests in December, 1952,
continued to function during 1953 due largely to a hastily formed
Provisional Executive Committee in Casablanca. This committee,
however, had little or no control over the various urban terrorist
groups that sprang up independently, although it did at least
establish liaison with most terrorist elements. Veteran Istiqlal
leaders who had previously opposed the use of force when younger
militants had advocated it thus found themselves obliged to support extremist activities in order to keep the party united and to
secure its position as chief spokesman for Moroccan nationalism.

At first, terroristic activities were directed against Moroccan
collaborators with the French regime and Muslims who violated
nationalist directives—a familiar tactic intended to deprive the
Protectorate of its native support and weld the country into one
army of resistance. Killing was supplemented by destruction of
telephone lines, burning of crops, forest fires, and boycotts of
French goods such as bread, cigarettes, sugar, and textiles, and of
French stores, cafés, and movies. In an average week, there were
five fatal and eighteen other shootings, ten bombings, two acts
of arson, and one train sabotage. Shops were closed as a control
measure and as a protest on days of "national mourning" (former
holidays). Even Mouloud, the Prophet's birthday, was now considered an occasion for grieving rather than rejoicing, since the
celebrations would be led by a Sultan imposed by the French.
Finally, Coca-Cola, a popular drink, was banned by the nationalists, who believed that privation sharpened the fighting spirit, and
who also desired to impress upon the people, through further enforced hardships, the gravity of their plight.

This policy of resistance had noticeable effects on the Moroccan
economy by mid-1955. Moroccan imports from France were down
about 10 per cent from the pre-1953 figures; the number of new
corporations per year had dwindled from a high of 753 in 1951 to
375 in 1954, while the number of companies going out of business
increased from 50 to 130 in the same period. Furthermore, in
1954–55, the number of tourists was 27 per cent below the preceding season.

Equally militant words accompanied and encouraged the action.
Although their use of the press was limited by strict French censorship and the illiteracy of most of their followers, and although
they had no radio outlet, Moroccan nationalists received substantial propaganda assistance from outside sources. Radio Cairo, the
xenophobic voice of Pan-Arabism, exhorted Moroccans that "blood

must flow in the fight for the cause of Allah"; Radio Damascus joined the Cairo chorus. Radio Budapest gratuitously denounced colonialism and supported nationalist aspirations in thirty-minute short-wave broadcasts three times daily.

The immediate French reaction was an attempt to suppress completely all nationalist activities within Morocco. In addition to reinforcing the existing curbs on personal liberties in accordance with the state-of-siege laws (passed in 1914 and never repealed), arrests were made on the flimsiest of charges; trials, when held, were before military tribunals. While a decree guaranteed to French settlers the same civil rights they enjoyed in France, the siege laws were the basis for the increasing suppression of Moroccan civil liberties after 1930. Under this authority, newspapers often appeared with blank columns due to last-minute deletions—until 1951, when a system was inaugurated that, instead, imposed fines and imprisonment for editors who printed "seditious" matter. Freedom of speech was generally curtailed. Meetings were restricted by a ruling requiring forty hours' notice and the disclosure of full information to the authorities. All organizations, even the Boy Scouts, were closely regulated or prohibited. Freedom of movement was limited by the daily demarcation of "zones of insecurity," entry into which required a military permit. Finally, search without warrant was authorized. These restrictive measures were accompanied by propaganda disseminated through Radio Maroc, the government-owned (and only) station in French Morocco, and several daily French-language newspapers.

Arrests of suspected nationalists totaled several hundred each week, according to official reports, but the nationalists alleged that the figures were often much greater. In addition to those suspected of terrorism, all Moroccans found in the European section of a city without a proper identity card were arrested. In an effort to eradicate the memory of the deposed Sultan, anyone discovered harboring his photograph was seized. Finally, any action that could possibly result in disturbing the public order was considered criminal.

Trials of Moroccan nationalists were usually closed to the public, though a few were staged for the masses as show trials. Serious offenses usually brought stiff sentences, including death. Minor cases did not go to trial but were handled by administrative decision and entailed varying terms of imprisonment. In Meknes, in August, 1954, for example, a religious professor and the notary of a Muslim court each received a sentence of three months' imprisonment, $400 fine, five years' banishment from the city, and a ten-year prohibition on practicing their profession—all this for the vague crime of committing "acts tending to disturb the public order." In September, 1954, fifty-one Moroccans who had been held under investigation for twenty-one months on charges of conspiracy against national security were released due to insufficient evidence. A trial in Oudjda opened with the revelation that fourteen of the forty-five suspects had died during a sixteen-hour imprisonment in an unventilated room eight feet by five.

In French papers—*L'Écho du Maroc* of Rabat, *Le Courrier* of Fez, *Le Petit Marocain* and *La Vigie* of Casablanca—editorializing was common, and headlines were occasionally unsupported or even contradicted by the stories that followed. Furthermore, these newspapers often had difficulty in coordinating reports of terrorist acts. On one occasion when a train had been derailed, one paper stated that there was no indication of sabotage, while another noted that a section of track had been removed. Only *Maroc-Presse* of Casablanca offered objective reporting and an editorial stance that could be considered enlightened.*

After a wave of terrorism turned against the Europeans in May, 1954, Premier Pierre Mendès-France took the positive steps of creating a Ministry of Tunisian and Moroccan Affairs and of replacing Resident General Guillaume with Francis Lacoste, a career diplomat. . ʾuming office on June 14, Lacoste promised to implement the reform pledges that France had made at the time of Ben Arafa's enthronement—promises to end royal absolutism, grant new civil liberties, end martial law, establish a new labor charter, found a new parliamentary system, and end the performance of both executive and judicial functions by caids. Actually, steps were taken only toward the first goal, a meaningless gesture, since the Sultan was now without power. The ceremony of the *heyda* (allegiance) and the formality of prostration before the Sultan were abolished, and the title "His Majesty" suppressed. In addition, the Protectorate announced that the Sultan would no longer be allowed to impede progress by refusing to give his approval to French-drafted dahirs.

* *Maroc-Presse* was owned by a French syndicate and actually administered by one of the owners' sons. In 1955, it was bought by Jacques Lemaigre-Dubreuil, a French war hero, publisher, and friend of Edgar Faure, who had encouraged him to buy the paper as an organ for the expression of moderate and reformist views. Throughout the following turbulent years, the paper continued to defend these ideas. *Maroc-Presse* finally went out of business, though, at the end of April, 1957, its editors explaining that between the Arabic press and the right-wing French press, there was no longer any place for an independent French-language journal in Morocco.

As soon as Lacoste announced his program, the nationalists ordered a hiatus in the terrorist campaign, but when the promised reforms were not forthcoming, violence flared again. On August 8, the eve of the important feast of Aid El Kebir (honoring Abraham's offer to sacrifice his son Ismael to God), the biggest outbreak occurred in Port Lyautey. The medina shops closed on nationalist orders, the French police commanded the merchants to reopen for business, and mobs immediately gathered to demonstrate in protest. The police then shot "at the feet" of the crowd in order to maintain control; five Frenchmen and many Moroccans died—the French said thirty, but nearly 300 fresh graves were counted the next day.

When the shooting in Port Lyautey was over, a *ratissage* (literally, "raking-in") commenced, a procedure designed to inculcate obedience by a show of force. French troops surrounded the medina, systematically broke into every home, and herded some 20,000 men to the town's sheep market. A gantlet was formed and the Moroccans were thrust into it, their hands on their heads. With truncheons, fists, and boots, they were thoroughly beaten and then separated into two groups; into one group went some 6,000 men suspected of having participated in the riots the day before—they were loaded into trucks and carted off to jail; others were released, with advice from the pasha to resume their peaceful way of life on penalty of a recurrence of punishment. In the European quarter that evening, French men and women lined the streets to cheer the military forces. An investigation of the Port Lyautey police department was later ordered by the Residency, but no action was ever announced.

In Fez, the Sultan's Black Guard, with French complicity, violated the holy sanctuary of Maulay Idris and seized the fifty ulema who had sought refuge there. The ulema's crime had been to address a letter to Lacoste asking for the return of Mohammed V. After being held incommunicado in Rabat for a month, the ulema were released.

Following the August outbreaks, the Protectorate intensified its restrictive measures. This, however, only led to increased violence —sometimes ordered by the nationalists, sometimes spontaneous— and to the subsequent formation of vigilante groups organized by the most reactionary colon organization, the Présence Française. To offset this despicable group, seventy-five men, including the editor of *Maroc-Presse*, Henri Sartout, and the President of the Meknes Bar Association, formed an organization in June, 1954, called Conscience Française, which urged President René Coty to initiate reforms in Morocco and to condemn counterterrorism as well as terrorism. (Conscience Française astutely observed that the only effective guarantee of French presence in Morocco was the consent of the Moroccan people.) Chapters of the French Socialist Party and the centrist Mouvement Républicain Populaire (MRP) in Morocco also urged settlement of the dynasty question, and the French section of the Government Council urged reforms and denigrated the Présence Française. These voices, however, were seldom listened to, much less heeded.

By September, most Europeans were arming, despite the fact that it was a crime to carry a concealed weapon. Groups such as the Veterans of the French Expeditionary Forces in Italy appeared "to safeguard and defend Morocco," warning that "we hope we shall not have to substitute ourselves for official action." "Five nationalists will die," they promised, "for every European killed." The Organization for Anti-Terrorist Defense asked the Residency for the arrest of anyone who provided funds to Moroccan terrorist groups. "If not," they added, "let us do the work, and be assured that we can do it without charge." Hiring Spanish, Corsican, and French thugs to do their dirty work, these organizations first attacked nationalist Moroccans and, later, sympathetic Frenchmen.

A side effect of the renewed terrorism in August was the initial violence against Moroccan Jews. During the late summer and fall of 1954, Moroccan Jews increasingly became the victims of hatred. Jewish homes and schools were burned and shops were pillaged; there were Jewish casualties in almost every mass disturbance, despite the official Jewish policy of noninvolvement in the Franco-Moroccan dispute. In part, Muslim resentment of the Jewish position led to the difficulties. In particular, the Jews' frequent refusal to close shop on days of mourning led Muslims to suspect them of pro-French sentiment. However, the at least equally significant reason for the attacks was Muslim frustration when French troops prevented them from venting their rage against their real enemies—the French populace and particularly those involved in the counterterrorist activities.

In September, Lacoste went again to Paris and returned this time with a plan that called for the right of Moroccans eventually to have unions, for an economic-recovery program, and for a governmental reorganization to transfer the Grand Vizier's legislative powers to a six-man council of three Frenchmen and three Moroccans. The plan did not, however, recognize the nationalist insistence that the return of Mohammed V precede any agreements on other topics and ignored the demand for a guarantee of civil liberties.

The nationalists' intransigence was not only a response to the inadequacies of the reform program, which skirted all major political issues, but also a product of their deep-seated distrust of French intentions. The reaction in Paris to the Moroccan terrorist campaign, coupled with the situation then confronting France in Tunisia and Indochina, persuaded many Moroccans that violence was the only language France understood and that continued resistance would bring ultimate victory. However, although some Moroccans regarded any French concession as an indication of France's increasing willingness to negotiate, others thought this merely indicated a disposition to allow the United Nations to adopt another meaningless resolution. Since France was certain of rallying Western support for her position there on a showdown vote, she felt that some discussion before the General Assembly might placate impatience or more violent criticism of her policies.

By October, 1954, the only result of Lacoste's reform program was an increase in agricultural wages from fifty-two to sixty-five cents per day. When Si Bekkai, at that time residing in France in self-imposed exile, demanded a new treaty between France and Morocco, as well as the return of Mohammed V, el-Glaoui went to Paris himself to stem the growing tide in favor of reconsidering the throne question. Meanwhile, the French Government sent Dr. Dubois Roquebert, the former Sultan's personal physician, to Madagascar to offer the monarch a refuge in France in return for his formal abdication and cooperation in ending the violence unleashed in his name. The Sultan rejected the offer, and the year ended with the Residency's release of several nationalists—including Ben Barka, who had been under virtual house arrest in southern Morocco since December, 1952—and the revelation that Sultan Moulay Ben Arafa had purchased property in Tangier as a possible refuge.

A. The Last Year of the Protectorate

As 1955 dawned in Morocco, the country was left with little law and less order. In January, following a serious skirmish in Rabat's reserve quarter, the Residency closed the section and its equivalent in Casablanca on the ground that they had become terrorist refuges and centers for vice. When no progressive action was forthcoming on more important issues, the Istiqlal decided unilaterally to create a Moroccan trade union. This step not only would demonstrate nationalist ability to act in defiance of France, but would also facilitate cooperation with trade unions in other countries that were sympathetic to the cause of Moroccan independence. Accordingly, the Istiqlal helped Mahjoub Ben Seddik and Taieb Bouazza, former members of the central committee of the General Union of Confederated Moroccan Syndicates to sponsor a Committee of Free Trade Unions and to contact the International Confederation of Free Trade Unions. In March, these men surreptitiously formed the Union of Moroccan Workers (UMT), which grew steadily while France debated the question of recognizing it.

At the end of February, Pierre July, who had just been appointed Minister of State for Tunisian and Moroccan Affairs by the new French Premier, Edgar Faure, set forth a program calling for a more significant role for Moroccans in the trade-union movement, repression of terror, administrative reorganization, and more public offices for Moroccans. He added, however, that "there is no throne question in Morocco," a sentiment that Premier Faure confirmed. These words might have been more convincing if France's last large segment of native Moroccan support had not begun to crumble: a rumored dissidence plot in "friendly" Berber territory caused great uncertainty as to the Berbers' loyalty to el-Glaoui and to France, while French collaborators in the cities were also reportedly restive. Furthermore, the Conscience Française was stepping up its attack on the Protectorate, going as far as to suggest the possibility of counter-counterterrorism.

April and May witnessed more and more talk, but no actual implementation of reform; various individuals journeyed to Madagascar to ascertain the ex-Sultan's views. On the return of his attorneys, Weil and Izard (the former an intimate of Premier Faure), from a "business" trip to see Mohammed V, the two lawyers would say only that they had noted Mohammed V's pro-French feelings and his desire to abstain from political activity, and that they were of the opinion that the ex-Sultan and his family should be returned to France. A few weeks later, *Paris Match* gave a somewhat different version, saying that the deposed Sultan would not renounce his rights and did not wish to sponsor any operation he was not able to control.

Then, on May 19, the Protectorate raised tension in Moroccan cities to a new height by announcing that the Pasha of Casablanca had recommended that all merchants who had closed their shops on orders from the Moroccan terrorists be sent back to their homes in the bled. The measure, which would have affected no more than a few hundred persons, was stated to be part of a plan to reduce congestion in the country's largest city. The nationalists responded by appealing to all Moroccan shopkeepers in the coastal cities to close their stores and by sending out tracts, signed with a crudely drawn pistol, advising that "he who does not obey condemns himself to death." When most merchants chose the more prudent alternative, business in the cities came to an abrupt halt.

Several days later, in Paris, Pierre July finally acknowledged that there was after all a throne question but described it as a purely Moroccan problem—thus adhering to the fantasy that France had taken no part in deposing Mohammed Ben Youssef. He also blandly declared that France's only concern was the political problem posed by Franco-Moroccan relations; that terrorism was confined to Casablanca alone; and that economic conditions in Morocco were satisfactory.

These brave words were quickly belied, however, by evidence that the merchant strike had assumed critical proportions. The closing of shops and the rising tempo of terroristic activities spread to all cities in the country, affecting building construction and the entertainment industry most seriously. By June, the medinas of Casablanca, Port Lyautey, Rabat, Salé, Fez, and Oudjda were practically devoid of commercial activity, and Muslim and Jewish shops in the European sections were also affected. When the police in Fez forced a number of shopkeepers to open their doors, the merchants abandoned their stores. Some business was still done through the back door, but the volume was insignificant. Nationalist discipline was rigorous, and any Moroccan caught violating orders was assassinated or his shop burned. Although the Residency and the Moroccan Chamber of Commerce appealed to merchants to reopen their shops and although it was announced that the Pasha would reconsider the decision expelling recalcitrant merchants, the time for compromise was past. The strike continued.

At this point, Pierre July compromised by suggesting that Moulay Ben Arafa be replaced by a regency council. (He reiterated, however, the French Government's opposition to the return of Mohammed Ben Youssef, even to France.) A regency council as an interim measure was not unacceptable to moderate nationalists: Si Bekkai had already advocated the creation of such a body as a step to remove the accumulated passions and symbolism from

the throne question and clear the path to reform, and had hinted
that a regency council might be satisfactory to Mohammed V,
whose acceptance would be indispensable to its establishment.
Si Bekkai was sure that the agreement of all political parties to
the council could be guaranteed, but he insisted that it was first
of all essential that the former Sultan be returned to France,
then:

> Once this problem is solved, full negotiations may be undertaken. It
> is necessary that a truly representative Moroccan government then
> be constituted. We are not thinking of internal autonomy; Morocco
> intends to recover its time-honored independence. The time of colo-
> nial empire has irreparably passed, as Edgar Faure himself admitted
> before the National Assembly. We want to break the bonds of de-
> pendency that have been imposed upon us by force, and we hope to
> substitute therefor the bond of voluntary association. I know per-
> fectly well that in these times, even more than in the past, the con-
> cept of independence is relative and that it is wiser to speak of inter-
> dependence. French interests will be safeguarded, but the Moroccans
> will be masters of their destinies. I end by saying that we hope to see
> France as she really is, and not as certain people misrepresent her.*

Continued *immobilisme* in Paris, however, was not matched
in Morocco. The attempted assassination of Jacques Reitzer, a
prominent Casablanca industrialist and member of the Conscience
Française, was followed by the murder of Jacques Lemaigre-
Dubreuil, the publisher and principal stockholder of *Maroc-Presse*,
by counterterrorists who opposed his long advocacy of reform
and independence for Morocco. The bullets that killed him were
the type used by Casablanca's police force. Thousands of Moroccans attended Lemaigre-Dubreuil's funeral.

Finally aroused by this widely publicized political crime against
a distinguished French citizen, the French Government sent
Robert Wybot, director of the French counterintelligence agency,
from Paris to investigate. Pierre July roundly condemned the
counterterrorists, but the Présence Française coldly replied that
all victims are equal in terrorism and that it would not be intimi-
dated. The group remarked that July was expressing an emotion
apparently not aroused by the daily murders of Frenchmen in
Morocco; by holding counterterrorists responsible for the crimes,
they said, he was leveling a collective accusation against the French
in Morocco in an attempt to justify his own position.

---

* *Maroc-Presse*, June 7, 1955.

B. *"Last Chance" for the French*

On July 15, 1955, when Wybot returned to Paris, he submitted a report that led to the arrest of several leading counterterrorists in Morocco, including a former Casablanca police inspector. Two days later, Lacoste was summoned to Paris and, shortly thereafter, was replaced by the extremely capable and dedicated diplomat Gilbert Grandval. Premier Faure also declared the government's intention to grant a measure of home rule in Morocco and to return to the "real concept of the Protectorate," not to be confused with "direct government" of a country. Broad economic, social, and political reforms, based on five principles, were to be carried out: no compromise on the matter of the French "presence" in Morocco; abolition of direct French administration; creation of modern institutions; real interdependence between the two countries; and immediate re-establishment of order, with wide delegation of power to local authorities. A measure announced a week later, providing that Moroccans would henceforth be recruited for certain jobs in the public administration without having to show a diploma and without having to take examinations following the five-year apprenticeship, bolstered the hope that France might actually make the needed concessions instead of merely changing administrators again. A reorganization of the Moroccan section of the Government Council to give it real, although limited powers, and some form of local elections were foreseen as the steps the Protectorate would take next. However, strikes and violent demonstrations by colons against the arrest of several Europeans charged with counterterrorism soon dimmed this hope. Grandval was dubbed the "Man of the Last Chance" by all those who still favored some form of Franco-Moroccan cooperation.

His chance was unfortunately slim and short-lived. After sounding out informal opinion in France—where General de Gaulle had advocated a federal link between Morocco and France and a policy of service rather than exploitation, in recognition of waxing Moroccan nationalism and waning French strength—Grandval arrived in Rabat on July 7. His obvious desire to implement the reform program he had brought with him won him the confidence of the nationalists, and, two days later, they ordered all stores operated by Muslim merchants to end their crippling fifty-day strike. Soon, Grandval announced a sweeping change in Protectorate personnel, closed Morocco's only internment camp, and promulgated clemency measures directly affecting 123 political

prisoners and exiles. Such conciliatory action during a wave of terrorist activity was a new technique; its major result, however, was
to make Grandval the focus of colon hatred.

On Bastille Day, July 14, a bomb explosion in a European café
in Casablanca inspired mass retaliation by French mobs, and the
battle of the streets was brought to a bloody climax. The Residency declared martial law in Casablanca (under the command
of General André Franchi), and the state-of-siege laws were now
applied in full force against both Europeans and Moroccans for
the first time. Foreign Legionnaires, Senegalese infantrymen, and
French paratroopers moved into the city to enforce order, while
armored vehicles patrolled the streets and men stationed on roof-
tops with bazookas and machine guns observed the city below.
By July 18, the tension had abated somewhat, but a strict curfew
was maintained.

As an aftermath to the tragic weekend, several Europeans, including the leader of the Présence Française, were deported. Si
Bekkai on the other hand, returned to his homeland on Grandval's
invitation. After a long conversation with the Resident General,
Si Bekkai proclaimed his belief that a formula could be worked
out that, with the consent of "His Majesty, Mohammed Ben
Youssef," would satisfy the "legitimate aspirations of the Moroccan people." Although Si Bekkai's later proposal for a popular referendum on the question of who rightfully belonged on the
throne caused some criticism, it still appeared possible for France
to reach a compromise, despite additional riots in Marrakesh and
Meknes, resulting in the death or wounding of more than 300
Moroccans.

Certain extremists, however, either felt that real compromise
could not be achieved or wished to avoid it at all costs in order
to further their own specific ends. This was true of several Moroccan terrorist organizations—such as the Black Hand, which
threatened to turn Casablanca into another Dien Bien Phu. It
was also true of colon diehards who asked Europeans to stand
by "to liberate, by force if necessary, our second fatherland."
Protectorate bureaucrats disobeyed Grandval's orders, and, through
influential French financiers, the colons persuaded certain members of the French National Assembly to threaten to bring down
the government if Grandval had his way. Bowing to this sort of
pressure, therefore, the plan for the Sultan's resignation and his
replacement by a regency council—which would have avoided
capitulation to the nationalists' demand for the immediate return
of Mohammed Ben Youssef—was rejected in favor of an ob-

viously unworkable scheme: Ben Arafa was authorized within a week to form a government composed of all shades of opinion except "avowed enemies" of France; if he failed, the most important representatives of Moroccan opinion would be invited to a conference in France where a final decision would be reached. When the nationalists, as expected, flatly rejected collaboration with the puppet Sultan, the French Government announced that a conference would begin at Aix-les-Bains on August 22.

The first three weeks of August witnessed growing demands from virtually all quarters for the return of Mohammed V, and Grandval's repeated plea for a settlement before August 20, the anniversary of Mohammed V's removal. (Among petitions to the Residency was one from four important Berber chiefs of the Middle Atlas, asking for a prompt settlement of the throne question. Rejecting el-Glaoui's claim to be chief of the Berbers, they asserted that in the mountains he was considered an agitator and an obstacle in the path of Franco-Moroccan friendship.) Delegations representing the major cities, tribes, caids, sherifs, brotherhoods, artisans, intellectual and youth organizations, businessmen, professionals, and even the unemployed and groups of mothers called for a return of Mohammed V. The ulema of Fez issued a communiqué decrying the current situation as "illegal, incompatible with our religion, with the history of our country, and with the claims of the Moroccan people." The honorary president of Casablanca's Moroccan Chamber of Commerce told Grandval that it would be dishonest to withhold from him the real feelings of the countryside, which was unanimous in its adherence to its exiled sovereign. Finally, a delegation from the Moroccan Communist Party demanded that the Moroccan people regain their sovereignty after the abdication of Moulay Ben Arafa and Mohammed Ben Youssef's return.

Even personages connected with the makhzen joined the growing chorus. The son of Moulay Ben Arafa's private secretary, a young Moroccan lawyer, declared that, like everyone conscious of his duty toward his country, he was ready to sacrifice his person and his family if need be, and he declared his attachment to the legitimate sovereign, symbol of Moroccan patriotism. Si Thami el-Mokri, the Grand Vizier, and Si Abbes Tazi, the Pasha of Rabat, also called for a prompt solution to the throne question. (Protectorate officials stated that these last two had told Moulay Ben Arafa they had been forced to make such a statement under threat of death, but both denied this claim and insisted no outside persuasion was involved.)

On the other side of the political fence, however, a telegram from fifty-eight caids of the Meknes and Tafilalt regions affirmed their support of el-Glaoui and demanded a solution that would not disappoint the friends of France. The Présence Française added a frantic warning that French *grandeur* would perish if the government bowed to the Moroccan pressures. With due regard for the welfare of the Moroccan people "whose lot it wished to better," it denounced the threat to the possessions and persons of French settlers as an attempt to influence France to renounce her rights in "our beautiful Moroccan country."

C. The Moroccan Liberation Army

The French prepared for August 20 only by putting the Army in the major Moroccan cities on alert and by announcing that insurance coverage against strikes, riots, and insurrection was available from practically all insurance agents. Nationalists of various persuasions, on the other hand, prepared for the fateful day in a variety of ways. In the medinas of most cities, on August 19, they distributed tracts calling for a one-day strike to mark the "day of mourning." Most of these tracts urged the population to protest peaceably, but inflammatory messages distributed in Casablanca by the Black Crescent, which had been infiltrated by Communists, made no such suggestion. Nevertheless, the demonstrations in Moroccan cities on August 20 did remain orderly. This was not the case, however, in the bled.

Many nationalist leaders had long been convinced that, while urban terrorism was useful as a means of consolidating popular support, wearing down French resistance, and attracting international attention, it would not suffice to expel the French, particularly after the humiliating concessions they had made in Indochina and Tunisia. A guerrilla army operating in the bled, however—and perhaps working in concert with the Algerians— could well administer the *coup de grâce*.

Abundant manpower was available among the tribesmen, particularly in the Rif. Training, indoctrination, and logistical work could be undertaken by experienced nationalists. Furthermore, a base for operations was available in the Spanish zone, as the Spanish authorities had long exhibited considerable sympathy for the French-zone nationalists and their activities, hoping thereby to win their friendship and retain a special place in Morocco once the French position had collapsed. Under the leadership of Dr. Abd el-Krim Khatib, the ex-French Army officer Mahjoub Ahardane, and the Communist Abd el-Krim bin Abdullah, therefore, preparations for and training of the fledgling Moroccan Liberation Army had begun in 1954 at Nador, in the Rif. Khatib was in charge of the top-level Committee of Resolution that maintained the crucial liaison with suppliers of the Moroccan Liberation Army outside Morocco. Ahardane, a Berber caid from Oulmes, in the Middle Atlas, who had fought with the Allies in World War II, recruited Moroccans from the French Army.

Whether the atrocities that occurred in the bled on August 20, 1955, were planned by leaders of the Moroccan Liberation Army, whether they were the result of harangues by Radio Damascus, as some Frenchmen unofficially suggested, or whether they were a spontaneous act is not clear. What is brutally clear is that on the morning of that day, Smala tribesmen attacked the town of Oued Zem with a savagery rare in any time or place. They massacred French men, women, and children in Oued Zem, and then repeated their actions in two other towns. Whether by design or default, the massacres played into the hands of extremists of all kinds by causing France to recall to active duty in Morocco 60,000 reservists. By the end of the week, France had doubled its force to more than 110,000 men in Morocco, including soldiers from three of the five divisions she had previously assigned to NATO—more than she had committed even to Indochina. Ruthless reprisals raised the death toll by the week's end to more than 1,000 and, by the end of the month, to 200 Europeans and several thousand Moroccans, the numbers varying according to the source of the reports.

Calls for a holy war resounded through the Arab world; Asian and African nations appealed for U.N. intervention in the Moroccan crisis. Meanwhile, Premier Faure conceded Moulay Ben Arafa's failure to form a government and convened at Aix-les-Bains the "Committee of Five," composed of the members of his coalition cabinet most concerned with Moroccan affairs. After a week of interviewing representatives of all political views in Morocco, including viziers, leaders of nationalist parties, the Pasha of Marrakesh, colons, traditionalists, ulema, and leaders of the Jewish community, the committee suggested a compromise solution to the Moroccans. It called for the removal of Grandval and Moulay Ben Arafa, the establishment of a throne council and of representative governmental institutions, the transfer of Mohammed Ben Youssef from Madagascar to a dignified residence in France, and negotiations between France and Morocco for a limited measure of home rule. The much-abused Grandval was

relieved by Lieutenant General Pierre Boyer de Latour, a former
aide of Marshal Juin, who arrived from Tunis on August 31; the
Sultan, encouraged by his colon supporters and not at all discour-
aged by the appointment of de Latour, refused to budge.

As September 12 approached, the deadline Faure had set for
carrying his Moroccan policy into effect, he further bolstered
French military forces in Morocco and sent General Georges
Catroux, a seventy-eight-year-old soldier-diplomat who had served
in Morocco with Lyautey, to Madagascar. Catroux was authorized to obtain an agreement with Mohammed Ben Youssef on the
Aix-les-Bains decision and to arrange for his return to France if
he approved the plan.

At the same time, a meeting in Rome between al-Fassi, Omar
Abdeljalil, Bouabid, and Ahmed Lyazidi revealed some sharp differences among Istiqlal leaders. Al-Fassi, in particular, opposed
any "solution" that did not provide for Mohammed V's immediate
return to Rabat. But a nationalist delegation headed by Si Bekkai
that had visited Mohammed Ben Youssef reported that he had
agreed to Faure's compromise proposals and had refrained from
raising the question of legitimacy. This quieted the controversy
momentarily and engendered new hope. It was decided in Paris
that Mohammed Ben Youssef would leave for France near the end
of September.

The composition of the throne council and the departure of
Moulay Ben Arafa remained the most serious issues to be solved.
The French and the nationalist leaders agreed that the throne
council would be a three-man body, including one nationalist,
one traditionalist (Protectorate supporter), and one neutral. There
was immediate accord on Si Bekkai as the nationalist representative; after the French retreated from the untenable position that
Si Thami el-Mokri was a neutral, he became the traditionalist
nominee. But the question of the third man was a stumbling block,
for there was no true "neutral" to be found.

Despite apprehensions, September 12 was observed with calm
in Morocco. Roadblocks, displays of strength by the French Army,
and stern warnings helped to maintain order, but quiet was also
assured by the nationalists' fear of alienating moderate French
and world opinion at a moment when a genuine reform in
Morocco's political status seemed now so close. In Paris, the
Cabinet issued a historic declaration that laid the groundwork
for a new Franco-Moroccan relationship, albeit with continuing
interdependence.* Although this declaration was not made public

* For the text of this declaration, see below, Appendix B.

until October 1, its content was indicated in July's communiqué
stating that the Government had decided to implement the decision of the Committee of Five immediately. Nationalist confidence was further bolstered by the realization that the French,
faced with unforeseen setbacks in Algeria, were rapidly concluding they could not hold all North Africa and should therefore
concentrate on keeping that "integral part of France" rather than
the two protectorates.

The days passed without action, however, and the colons and
their spokesmen in Paris again took heart. They were particularly
encouraged when the French Foreign Office indicated that, even
in an independent Morocco, it expected to retain exclusive control of Moroccan military and foreign affairs, in addition to its
authority to safeguard French rights in Morocco by means of
double citizenship and a temporary mixed council. In response
to such views and to France's failure to implement her many
promises, terrorism once again became rampant in Moroccan life,
as did various forms of colon intrigue.

Tribal leaders from various areas began visiting Rabat to encourage Moulay Ben Arafa to retain the throne. First, thirteen
caids representing (or, more likely, misrepresenting) 260,000 tribesmen, made the pilgrimage; an additional eighteen followed. In
all, about seventy-seven caids, or one-fourth of the country's total,
arrived; one of them went so far as to declare that Morocco would
"naturally" prefer to be a French protectorate than an independent state. The French noted for public consumption that these
men journeyed to Rabat on their own initiative, although it was
known that the caids had in most cases been appointed by the
puppet Sultan and wished to retain their positions.

The Présence Française also increased its activities. Its Meknes
chapter, 4,000 strong, demonstrated for "our strong-willed Sultan," and the Oudjda local, with 3,000 members, mailed soil
from the graves of terrorist victims to Premier Faure. In Rabat,
they kept a private detective at the palace at all times to inform
them of any developments. Acting on a false report that Moulay
Ben Arafa was about to be ousted and that Faure was coming
to Morocco to complete the coup, a group hurried to the palace.
Informed that the Sultan was still determined to stay, they cheered
and shouted, "If Faure comes, we shall meet him with guns!"
More than 120 veteran and patriotic associations even spoke of a
civil war.

In Paris, Marshal Juin led a die-hard group of military officers
in a campaign against the dissolution of the empire. Supported

by Generals Pierre Koenig and Duval, he was determined to sabotage the government's reform plans, and, to this end, he sought the cooperation of de Latour; General Pierre de Benouville, a right-wing deputy in the French National Assembly, was dispatched to Rabat to urge Moulay Ben Arafa to sit tight. De Benouville was followed by the Minister for Air, Pierre Montel, who came to Morocco ostensibly to see how the military reinforcements were being used and who ended by propagandizing in support of the puppet Sultan.

De Latour, supposedly still loyal to the official French Government position, flew to Paris and returned on September 21 with a virtual carte blanche to achieve government objectives. He thereupon resumed interviews with sundry personalities, allegedly to create a climate favorable to the government plan. On September 30, he met with the leader of the Présence Française, Raymond le Coroller, and a palace spokesman, Abd er-Rahman el-Hajoui. While 500 colons outside demanded action, the three men inside altered the Aix-les-Bains agreement until it was virtually a new one. Moulay Ben Arafa accepted it, after brief negotiation (which may have included a final financial settlement). The next afternoon, he announced his decision to leave Rabat for Tangier, and details of the de Latour plan, which dumbfounded both the French Government and Moroccan nationalists, were revealed: no formal abdication, no throne council, and certainly no return of Mohammed Ben Youssef; Moulay Ben Arafa was to delegate his seal to Prince Abdallah, the forty-five-year-old son of the former Sultan Moulay Hafid, a functionary in the imperial government.

D. The Battle for Independence

Controversy raged. The Istiqlal leaders in Rabat bitterly insisted that the Moroccan people would never accept institutions imposed by a minority rebelling against its own government, and nationalists elsewhere prepared to strike the final blows against colonialism and against what they feared would be a compromise settlement with France. From their headquarters in Cairo, al-Fassi and the seventy-four-year-old Abd el-Krim, who had organized and trained a special group of guerrilla agitators recruited from all over French North Africa, sent a "hard core" of fighters to Nador, where they contacted Khatib and the Moroccan Liberation Army. There, they passed on their techniques to an elite of several hundred tribal leaders from the Rif and from the

Marmouch tribe of the Middle Atlas. Two thousand tribesmen—
organized into 100-man commando groups, dressed in dark uniforms, and carrying English rifles, Herstal guns, Bren automatics,
Thompson submachine guns, Spanish Mausers with telescopic
sights, and Mills hand grenades—swore to free the entire Maghrib
and to force the return of Mohammed V. On October 1, al-Fassi
announced in Cairo that a Maghrib Army of Liberation had been
formed with headquarters "somewhere in North Africa," determined to wage war against the French colonialists to the death.
Before dawn of the following morning, this army had made its
initial attacks against French outposts, and an important new
military and political element had appeared on the scene.

The besieged area was a high plateau only sixty-five miles from
Fez. The guerrillas attacked and faded back into their craggy
lairs to snipe at search patrols and rescue columns, sometimes
disappearing among their fellow tribesmen and then emerging to
attack again. As in Kenya—and shortly thereafter in Algeria—
few natives ever betrayed the rebels. Communiqué No. 1 of the
new army, issued just after the initial attacks, made this appeal:

> O Muslim Soldier! The hour for the liberation of the Muslim Magh-
> rib has sounded; come join with us. The Maghrib Army of Libera-
> tion, which will not cease to rain pitiless blows on the forces of
> oppressive imperialism, sends you this appeal. Do not allow your soil
> to be used for the defense of the forces of colonialism. Be cannon
> fodder no longer. O Moor, ancient in glory, enlist in the array of your
> brothers to join in the liberation of your country and the elevation
> of the banner of your faith. Join your brothers, warriors for the faith,
> who fight to the death for the way of God, Country, and King. Long
> live the Liberation Army! Long live the Maghrib! Long live Mo-
> hammed V!

In response to the first attacks, the French sealed off the battle
zone, increased their available manpower in Morocco, and rushed
donkeys to the front. Planes dropped supplies to the French
forces but could not parachute in additional soldiers because of
the dangerous high peaks that encircled the area. Relieving forces
were compelled to wind their way through miles of high passes
to reach the scene. The forts were manned by *makhaznis* (palace
guards) commanded by French officers, while reinforcements were
principally goumiers and members of the Foreign Legion.

While the battle between the Army of Liberation and the
French Army continued in the Rif, Premier Faure obtained approval from the National Assembly to proceed with the original

throne-council plan and asked de Latour to act on it immediately. The Présence Française responded with strikes and riots and Istiqlal members demanded de Latour's resignation, but on October 15, the Resident General finally announced the creation of a throne council of four men. The council was formally installed two days later, and the PDI, seeking to maintain for itself a place in the Moroccan political spectrum in face of the predominant Istiqlal, accepted it on the ground that Mohammed V had given it his approval. The Istiqlal, UMT, and the Présence Française, however, voiced vehement disapproval. The Présence Française objected, labeling the throne council illegal under Koranic law and contrary to the agreement made with Moulay Ben Arafa. It warned Premier Faure of grave troubles that might ensue from his abuse of their confidence. Ahmed Lyazidi, now deputy secretary of the Istiqlal, on the other hand, protested against the plan's representation of the council as guardian of Moulay Ben Arafa's throne. Ben Barka, already known as one of the Istiqlal's most militant executive-committee members, angrily denounced the addition of a fourth man to the council and the ruling that its decisions must be unanimous; he demanded Moulay Ben Arafa's formal abdication and the immediate transfer of Mohammed Ben Youssef to France, as the Committee of Five had promised. Lastly, he made it clear that the Istiqlal would not join any government under the throne council, and the UMT concurred.

The throne council decided nevertheless to ask the moderate Pasha Fatmi Ben Slimane to form a government. Its plans were abruptly halted, however, on October 25, by the greatest political surprise of the entire Moroccan struggle. El-Glaoui, heeding the writing on the wall, suddenly announced his desire to see "His Majesty Sidi Mohammed Ben Youssef" restored to his rightful position and to see Morocco independent. With this astonishing development, Moroccans' enthusiasm for their exiled ruler grew virtually beyond control; even the Présence Française expressed its hope that Mohammed V would return.

Moulay Ben Arafa resigned at last on October 30. The last vestiges of opposition now eliminated, the French Government announced the next day that it "welcomes the possibilities that now appear of ensuring for Morocco a calm, orderly evolution of its destiny in permanent cooperation with France," and Pasha Sbihi, a member of the throne council, remarked that its sole mission was to re-install Mohammed Ben Youssef in Rabat.

E. *The Sultan's Return*

In the waning hours of October, Sidi Mohammed Ben Youssef arrived at Beauvillon, France, en route to Paris. It was the first step in his slow but triumphant return to his own capital in Morocco. On November 1, he met with Foreign Minister Antoine Pinay, and his arrival in Rabat was set for November 16; blueprints for future discussions were drawn up. Later in the day, in his Paris residence, Mohammed V received numerous French and Moroccan leaders: Ben Slimane, Si Bekkai, and el-Mokri, followed by Grandval, de Gaulle, and Pierre July. Delegations headed by Thami Ouazzani, Secretary General of PDI, Abderrahmin Bouabid of the Istiqlal; and Taieb Bouazza, Deputy Secretary General of the UMT, pledged him their support. An endless stream of callers and several thousand telegrams from the faithful at home arrived daily throughout the Sultan's stay in France. In Morocco, demonstrations for him were marred by only rare instances of violence and by the demand of the Présence Française for equal representation with Moroccans in all government agencies and for elections among the French residents to a special council to negotiate the future status of the colons, who now foresaw separation from France and integration into Morocco as an organized ethnic group, and hoped to ensure their rights to participate in the management of the country.

While members of the throne council continued, at the Sultan's request, to handle affairs of state, Mohammed Ben Youssef and Pinay hammered out a joint declaration: on November 6, at La Celle St Cloud, Mohammed V confirmed his intension to create a representative Moroccan government that would prepare reforms for Morocco's transformation into a constitutional monarchy, and to conduct negotiations "to permit Morocco to rise to the status of an independent state, united with France by permanent bonds of interdependence, freely consented to and freely defined." Both parties agreed that France and Morocco must build their future together without the intervention of "third parties," a phrase denoting France's serious attempt to relegate Spain to a secondary role in the new Morocco. Al-Fassi, in Cairo, criticized the compromising tone of this declaration, but an emergency meeting of the Istiqlal's executive committee in Madrid once again temporarily patched up party differences, and the Istiqlal officially supported the Sultan's position. After several days of ceremonies—including el-Glaoui's groveling apology to his sovereign, de Latour's replacement by André Dubois (former police commissioner of Paris), and Mohammed V's stirring address to his "dear and noble" people—the Sultan finally returned home.

On November 16, an Air France DC-6 deposited Mohammed V at the Salé airport, a mile from the Sultan's palace at Rabat. Wonders of the jet age and ancient Arabian Nights splendor combined in the tumultuous welcome that greeted the forty-six-year-old monarch; fighter planes saluted him from the sky, and a line of opulent native rugs was laid down before him. To the steady hum of the women's traditional wail, "you-you," an enormous crowd pressed forward to kiss the king's hand and to strew his path with flowers. Hundreds of white-robed tribal chieftains, the Resident General, the members of the throne council, and the Prime Minister-elect were on hand, and French troops stood at attention. Flags and ten-foot portraits of the monarch were displayed everywhere; cannon boomed a 101-gun salute from the ramparts of the capital. Great crowds from all over the country, which had camped along the roadside for days to await this moment, lined the streets to watch the Sultan's triumphal ride to the palace, chanting, "The Sultan is Truth! Long live Mohammed V! The Sultan means Independence! Our future will be ever more glorious! Mohammed Ben Youssef is the beating heart of the Moroccan people!" A double file of 15,000 French troops lined the road to do honor to the Sultan and to maintain order, but the crowd responded to Mohammed Ben Youssef's appeals and refrained from violence. (The French had contributed to the calm of the occasion by releasing 1,700 minor political prisoners and lifting the curfew.)

Passing under the flowered *arcs de triomphe* built especially for the occasion and pausing only to receive the traditional offering of dates and milk from the pashas of Salé and Rabat, the royal entourage at last arrived at the Mechouar, the Royal palace. Mohammed V appeared at the balcony to thank his people: "Here we are before you as you have always known us, at the service of our dear country. Praise Allah who in His mercy has put an end to our trials."

During the next delirious four days, business shut down completely, and Moroccans paraded, danced in the streets, and made merry day and night. Spontaneous joy extended from Rabat to the Sous, from the Rif to Casablanca. In Tangier, where the international administration had allotted $15,000 for the festivities, celebrants requested and received a donation of 1,000 cases of

Coca-Cola from the local distributor. The truck bearing the gift displayed a large picture of the Sultan on the side, and the crowd stopped it continually to kiss the likeness. The miniature Moroccan taxicabs carried flags so large they almost blocked the windshields. Water carriers hustled back and forth among the throngs, selling their wares (for five francs a cup) and pouring water from the traditional dark, dripping, goatskin bags.

The ex-Sultan Moulay Ben Arafa was almost the only Moroccan who took no active part in his country's celebrations. The French had provided a special police force to guard his Tangier residence, and he remained securely within the walls of his new home. Perhaps he noted with interest the report that an old man who resembled him and who had been taken for himself was beaten by the crowd. Several months later, he deemed it prudent to move to France, where he quickly faded into oblivion.

F. Preparation for Freedom

Once the initial celebrations were over, nationalist leaders urged the people to rally around the Sultan and reminded them that their work had only begun. Independence was yet to be achieved, since the Treaty of Fez was still in effect and would remain so until negotiations between France and Morocco had ended. The Istiqlal resumed publication of its long-suppressed Arabic-language daily, al-Alam, and in it called for the abrogation of the Protectorate treaty and creation of a constitutional monarchy. The Union of Moroccan Workers posed such demands as higher minimum wages, guaranteed civil liberties, collective-bargaining agreements, social security, the right to organize agricultural workers, the liberation of all political prisoners, the abrogation of the state-of-siege laws, the construction of low-cost housing, and a drastic change in the powers of the caids and pashas. The Sultan expressed general accord with all nationalist demands but also sought assurance from the nationalist leaders that no limitations would be placed on his power in order to assure order and avoid confusion in the ensuing reorganization.

Uncertainty already existed in many quarters. Moroccan soldiers previously loyal to the French Army had begun to defect even before the Sultan's return; they continued to desert, disappearing into the countryside, usually with their weapons. Stories spread through the European quarter of Casablanca that foreigners were about to be massacred; in the medina, it was rumored that the French had poisoned the local water supply. To offset such fears, the Sultan repeatedly took a positive stand concerning the French settlers. In an interview with Dubois, he expressed desire to see the colons cooperate fruitfully with the Moroccan people in an atmosphere of peace and concord, and in his Throne Speech on November 18, the twenty-eighth anniversary of his accession and his first major public address since returning to Morocco, he reminded his people of the settlers' contribution to the country's growth and economic prosperity. Most of the settlers, he said, showed a real spirit of understanding for the aspirations of the Moroccan people, and Morocco was disposed to guarantee their interests, rights, and personal status.*

Both the French Government and Dubois regarded these comments as renewed proof of the Sultan's good intentions, but Mohammed V left no doubt as to his sentiments concerning the settlers' future political role. He declared firmly that Moroccan nationals alone would exercise the right and prerogatives of sovereignty, and that guarantees to the French must not infringe on that sovereignty, on the institutions that expressed it, or on the national interest. Relations between Moroccans and Frenchmen, he asserted, must be founded on equality, mutual respect, and reciprocal esteem in economic, social, and administrative life. As long as Frenchmen respected Franco-Moroccan agreements, the "New Morocco" would welcome them sincerely.

Despite the straightforwardness of these remarks, many colons and their supporters in Paris clung to the unrealistic hope that further concessions could be forestalled indefinitely. At the very least, they envisioned special privileges for Frenchmen in an "independent" Morocco whose foreign affairs, army, police, and judicial system were controlled by France. Fortunately for both sides, however, there were also enlightened Frenchmen in Rabat and Paris with whom the nationalists could negotiate, while the much-feared Army of Liberation acted as watchdog for Moroccan interests.

Certain Moroccans also were jeopardizing the future with continued acts of violence, despite the Sultan's appeals for forgiveness and nationalist reminders that liberty did not mean license. The chief culprits were urban resistance groups such as the Black Crescent. To assist regular security forces in keeping order, an unarmed volunteer police force composed of members of the Istiqlal and PDI sprang into existence. Although they occasionally quarreled among themselves, the party stalwarts commanded

---

* For the text of this speech, see below, Appendix C.

considerable obedience and did a commendable job of maintaining order in the streets of the medinas. However, even their presence could not completely repress the desire for revenge against those who had collaborated with the French, especially the caids and other officials who had supported the deposition of the Sultan in 1953 or who had favored the retention of Moulay Ben Arafa in 1955. In this instance, violence was directed at Moroccans rather than at Europeans, but this did not fully comfort French bystanders, who feared that the terrorism might get out of control and perhaps even cause the downfall of their new-found friend, Mohammed V. The more pessimistic of them foresaw a return of anarchy and general insecurity; others hoped for such a deterioration, in order to reassert French military and political control over the country. These fears and hopes were not fulfilled and order was generally maintained, but many collaborators paid dearly for their earlier defection.

The most spectacular of the reprisals against "collaborators" occurred in the courtyard of the palace itself on November 19. The day started ominously with young Moroccans running through the area shouting, "This is the day of revenge!" A few hours later, the Khalifa of the Pasha of Fez, with his bodyguard, was walking across the courtyard when a large rock was thrown at him, crushing his skull. The Khalifa had come to seek forgiveness for having supported the Sultan's dethronement two years earlier, but the crowd had been less understanding than the Sultan might have been. The bodyguard and two companions were killed moments later, their bodies doused with gasoline and set afire.

Upset by these atrocities and wanting to begin the hard work of creating an independent state, the Sultan spoke to his people in a radio speech that night, asking the multitude that had come to Rabat to greet him to return to their homes. By the next morning, however, the word had not yet spread, and thousands of people demonstrated before the palace gates until they were opened. Once they were inside, native policemen ordered them to sit until the Sultan appeared, an order motivated by the Koranic injunction, "When you are angry, you should sit down, and if you are already seated, you should lie down." When the Sultan appeared to reiterate his appeal to return home, the crowd quickly dispersed.

On November 22, the Sultan accepted the resignations of the four members of the throne council and of Premier-designate Ben Slimane and then began consultations with nationalist and labor leaders, and with representatives of other shades of political opinion, to form a new, representative government. The country's three major organizations—the predominant Istiqlal, its political ally, the UMT, and its small rival, the PDI—submitted their respective choices for premier, their suggestions for a government program, and their recommendations as to the number and composition of the ministries to be created.

The Istiqlal asked for a government of twenty ministries, at least nine to go to its members, because of the majority of the population it claimed to represent. The PDI, greatly exaggerating its strength, demanded equal representation with the (far more popular) Istiqlal and with independent nonparty politicians. The UMT offered no candidates but generally supported the claims of the Istiqlal. The French, although not consulted, attempted to exert their limited influence on behalf of the PDI to provide a balance against the strong Istiqlal-UMT coalition. The three groups could agree only on the nomination of the widely respected, nonpartisan Si Bekkai as premier. To emphasize their other demands, each of the "Big Three" staged noisy public demonstrations.

At this decisive moment, it seemed essential that the two principal political parties be welded into an effective unit presenting a common front to France. The Sultan himself was loath to permit any single party a clear preponderance, not only because he disliked "one-party dictatorship" in principle, but also because he wished to retain as much power as possible in his own hands for the present. After many consultations and much soul-searching among the Istiqlal leaders, some of whom wished their party to enjoy a near-monopoly of government posts, a coalition government with a pivotal number of nonaffiliated members was approved. Of twenty-one ministerial posts, including the premiership, the Istiqlal was to have nine, the PDI six, and the independents six. The PDI criticized this distribution as artificial but agreed to cooperate for the good of the country. On November 27, the Sultan formally announced that Si Bekkai had been named Premier and given the responsibility of choosing a cabinet.

On December 7, Premier Bekkai presented his cabinet to the monarch. The ministers took the oath of office "to protect the sovereignty and territorial integrity of the country" (a sovereignty and integrity now threatened by Spain's reluctance to quit its zone). The government's first task was to implement the Sultan's program of abrogating the French Protectorate and replacing it with Faure's concept of "independence within interdependence." The Istiqlal ministers, however, regarded the implications of that concept with suspicion and remembered that at their first public congress, held in Rabat a few days before, 800 delegates had pointedly demanded the creation of a Moroccan army and Morocco's assumption of full diplomatic powers, as well as freedom to organize unions, religious tolerance, emancipation of women, and other political and economic reforms. The ministers also anticipated that al-Fassi, who had not even left Cairo to attend the congress because of his continued displeasure with the spirit of compromise favoring France and other political opponents, might well turn from passive to active opposition, thus weakening the ministers' own positions in the Istiqlal.

On December 9, the new Moroccan ministers were installed in the Residency offices previously occupied by French bureau chiefs, who now were called Secretaries General of their ministries and acted only in an advisory capacity. Four days later, Si Bekkai assumed the legal powers of the Prime Minister and issued the first ministerial declaration outlining the broad lines of governmental policy:

1. The protectorate is a thing of the past. A new agreement will be concluded by France and Morocco.

2. The exploitation of the country's assets requires the maintenance of order and stability, which are conditions essential to economic prosperity.

3. Without the economic and technical assistance of a friendly country—France—we would be incapable of solving all our problems.

4. The safeguarding of our freedom and independence implies a defense alliance with a friendly country. We shall be allies of the French people.

5. Our ambition is to make this country the meeting point of two civilizations that complement each other and have the same sense of values.

6. We propose these internal measures: reorganization and purification of the caid system; release of all political prisoners; a modern judicial organization; and the restoration of public freedom, particularly of the unions.

Although no mention of interdependence as such was made, the declaration showed a clear understanding of what France could still offer an independent Morocco.

The government's reference to order and stability was a realistic one, since daily murders of vengeance continued and clashes between adherents of the Istiqlal and PDI in their efforts to recruit new members had begun. The Sultan asked former administrative personnel to remain at their posts while power was shifted to new hands and bureaus, but many officials fled in fear of their lives, adding to the burdens of those who remained. Tax assessments by tribal caids were forgotten, litigants due to appear before the traditional native courts ignored their summons, boycotts and truancy were extensive. Internal security was clearly one of the most serious problems facing the government. The old specter of anarchy was a constant threat to Morocco in the following months, and only the prestige and power of Mohammed V served to stabilize the situation.

In a general effort to impress the authority of the new central government on the populace, the nationalists encouraged a second wave of pilgrimages to Rabat in early December. One day, 3,000 women from Fez appeared; on the next, 40,000 residents from the Oudjda area. On December 16, perhaps 150,000 people attended the Friday prayer. Some traveled by foot, bicycle, burro, or bus, but the majority entered the capital in tightly packed, flag-draped trucks, shouting pro-Sultan slogans and cheering continuously. (Before the visits were finally halted in January, 3 million persons had journeyed to Rabat.) Prince Moulay Hassan, the Sultan's popular eldest son, began to address the crowds, appealing for order and forgiveness, for justice administered by the courts rather than by individuals, and for payment of taxes. The traditional heyda was proscribed, but most of the faithful were satisfied with a single glimpse of their monarch, which many believed ensured eternal salvation.

In a more specific attempt to achieve internal security, the new cabinet divided the country into thirteen regions and three autonomous cities. An *amel* (governor) under the authority of the Minister of Interior was appointed to head each unit and was charged with police control. Finally, eighteen new caids and pashas were named to replace the most objectionable of these administrators, and it was announced that henceforth these local officials would be responsible directly to the Minister of the Interior and would eventually be deprived of their judicial powers.

While this painstaking reorganization continued in Rabat, dramatic events were unfolding in the Rif, a constant reminder to the French that the forthcoming negotiations for independence must not be too protracted. After a brief lull in the fighting, fires in the hills gave the traditional warning that warfare was about to resume. Groups of natives from hamlets on the edge of the Rif disappeared into the hills, their flocks guided by men in khaki carrying submachine guns. A guerrilla force organized with 2,000 men in October had tripled in size within two months, and rebels again ventured down from the hills to harass the countryside. Despite the presence of 16,000 French troops in the area, the Moroccan Army of Liberation, familiar with the terrain, soon held a line from Berkane to Ouazzane and continually launched successful attacks; its favorite targets were French soldiers and French farms. By the end of December even the 36,000 citizens of Taza (about 50 miles east of Fez) were within range of the guerrillas. Frenchmen feared to venture out on the city's streets alone; at nightfall, colons on isolated farms locked up and went into the city to sleep. In addition to their other problems, French Army commanders had to keep watch that their own Muslim troops (50 per cent of the total) did not desert or revolt.

As the attacks continued, the French settlers became increasingly critical of the Resident General's failure to give them adequate support. In January, 1956, seventy farm owners in the Taza area informed President Coty that, since their appeals for protection had remained unanswered, they had decided to abandon their property. Dubois urged the farmers to stand fast and dispatched troops to patrol at night. The farmers agreed to hold out a little longer, but several isolated forest-ranger stations were evacuated.

At this point, Allal al-Fassi suddenly appeared in Tetuán, proclaiming the Rif war as a struggle for independence. As it had been rumored that he had participated in directing the guerrilla activities from Cairo, his comments did not go unnoticed. France asked the nationalist leaders and the Sultan to appeal to the Rif rebels to cease fighting, but the request fell on deaf ears: Rabat authorities were in any case unable to control the irregulars, but they were also reluctant to antagonize them and their supporters, for the guerrillas were exerting useful pressure against France. The Liberation Army continued its harassment; when it became more daring, the French Army was forced to "readjust its line," withdrawing thirty miles. French officials estimated average casualties for each side at more than sixty a week by the end of January; the rebels painted a different picture in one of their communiqués:

In the name of Allah, the most merciful and compassionate; you do not kill them, but Allah has killed them. What I throw, if I throw, Allah has thrown. To the trials that oppress the faithful, Allah is all wise. The Army of Liberation has pursued its military operations, inflicting severe losses on the enemy. On the west front, our forces attacked the enemy at Tafraout, where enemy losses were 62; at Tizi Ouzar, enemy losses were 75, plus 5 military vehicles; at Khalala, we captured 112 arms and large stocks of food and ammunition. Our total losses for these ventures were 4 killed and 8 wounded. Long live the Maghrib! Long live Sidi Mohammed V!

In Rabat, meanwhile, the groundwork for Franco-Moroccan negotiations was being laid. Both sides had difficulty in selecting teams; Morocco lacked qualified officials at the top level, and few Frenchmen wanted the dubious distinction of presiding over the dissolution of part of their empire. A French cabinet crisis in December that overturned the Faure regime further delayed discussions. Finally, Mohammed V named the four new Ministers of State: Ahmed Reda Guedira, Mohammed Cherkaoui, Bouabid, and Driss M'Hammedi; and the outgoing Faure government selected Alain Savary, Secretary of State for Foreign Affairs; Jean Basdervant, his Staff Director; the Secretary of State for National Defense; and a member of the Conseil d'État. After Dubois and Bekkai had signed an agreement stipulating that the administration of Morocco's foreign affairs, defense, and finance would remain temporarily in the hands of the Resident General, it was agreed that negotiations would begin in Paris in February. In Rabat, Mohammed V, official head of the Moroccan delegation, expressed hope that they would fulfill the aspirations of the Moroccan people. Guedira observed further that, because the Moroccan people had considered themselves independent since Mohammed V's return, the monarch could not ask for less than formal recognition of this claim. The Istiqlal paper *al-Alam* warned that with or without France independence would be achieved.

Final indications that this time Paris intended to negotiate in good faith came on February 11, when a preliminary accord guaranteed that there would be no jurisdictional void between the recognition of independence and the final treaty, as France was to maintain control of government employees, public works, security, control of exchange, and administration of prisons in the interim. When the Sultan arrived in Paris later that day, he was greeted by the new French Premier, the Socialist Guy Mollet, who promised to carry on Faure's Moroccan policy.

The following day, at a sumptuous banquet luncheon, negotiations were formally opened. President Coty's speech was clear and to the point: he warned that numerous and complex problems awaited the negotiators, but expressed his hope that the final outcome would improve conditions of the masses, indeed the entire economic and intellectual life of Morocco. The Sultan, clad in a white silk djellaba, the usual tarbouche, and pointed Moroccan slippers, expounded Morocco's desire to achieve independence, define the basis of a close cooperation with France, abrogate the Treaty of Fez, and guarantee the interests of French settlers in Morocco. After noting his country's hopes for French technical, financial, and economic assistance, the Sultan concluded with a plea for territorial unity. Negotiations were then deferred for a week to allow both sides to examine the situation further.

The basic question was whether independence or interdependence would come first. To discourage any delay in obtaining the former, the Moroccan Army of Liberation stepped up its activities around Taza; the city was placed under a strict curfew. Tracts distributed throughout the country threatened total war if the Franco-Moroccan discussions failed, while a communiqué of the general committee of the Black Crescent (signed with a machine gun and a crescent) announced that urban terrorists would thenceforth operate as affiliates of the army. The communiqué was followed immediately by attacks on French soldiers in the larger cities, mostly in Casablanca, and French military authorities at once confined all personnel to their bases. The Army of Liberation denied any alliance with the Black Crescent, however, and emphasized its adherence to a previous decision to suspend all urban attacks. It warned against foreign "Communizing" influences and promised effective action to end that threat. Two days later, several members of the Black Crescent were shot in Rabat, initiating an underground struggle that was to last many months.

On the other hand, the Présence Française, 2,000 strong, met in Rabat and drafted proposals for equal representation in the local government of areas with heavy French populations, a representative in the National Assembly in Paris, and special status for the French community in matters such as education; since the French settlers were not a party to the Franco-Moroccan negotiations, they withheld approval of them. Lastly, they threatened to remove from Morocco entirely if their demands were not met.

As before, however, Moroccan demands prevailed in fundamental matters; a Franco-Moroccan declaration in which independence formally preceded interdependence was duly signed on March 2.* Pending its application, relations between France and Morocco were to be founded on the provisions of the following protocol:

* See above, Introduction, p. 3.

1. Legislative power shall be sovereignly exercised by His Majesty the Sultan. The representative of France shall be informed of all dahirs and decrees. He shall be consulted on all matters concerning the interests of France, of Frenchmen, or of foreigners, during the transitional period.

2. His Majesty Mohammed V shall have at his disposal a national army, for the formation of which France shall lend her assistance. The present status of the French Army in Morocco shall remain unchanged during the transitional period.

3. Administration of foreign affairs, defense, and finance, reserved to the Resident General until now, will be transferred by a joint agreement. The Moroccan Government shall be represented, with the right to speak and vote in the committee of the franc zone, the central directing organ of monetary policy for the whole of the franc zone. Moreover, those guarantees now enjoyed by French officials and agents serving in Morocco shall be maintained.

4. The representative of the French Republic in Morocco shall bear the title of High Commissioner of France.

A separate letter pledged French protection of Moroccan foreign interests pending the final agreement.

The Moroccan triumph was dimmed somewhat by the argument of some French spokesmen that the Treaty of Fez had been merely suspended, not abrogated, since only the French parliament could legally terminate the treaty, and that the Moroccan Government could not ask it to do so without first establishing new ties and new guarantees for French interests. Despite this view, a new era had begun, for, in negotiating with Morocco to protect French interests, France was now dealing with an independent and legally equal state.

G. *Spanish Morocco*

The status of Spanish interests in Morocco remained to be settled. Spain governed not only the 18,000 square miles of northern Morocco and a 10,000-square-mile extension of the Spanish Protectorate on the southwest, called Tarfaya, but also the five *presidios* (enclaves) of Ceuta, Melilla, Alhucemas, the Chafarinas Islands, and Peñon de Vélez de la Gomera. Their area comprised only 82 square miles, but it sheltered more than 100,000 Europeans (over 55 per cent of their total population). Spain also held title, by virtue of a disputed treaty, to the 741 square miles of Ifni which she had occupied in 1934, and the Spanish Sahara (composed of Río del Oro and Saguia el Hamra). Franco, who had played a long and complex carrot-and-stick game in Spanish

Morocco, was not to surrender easily the last vestiges of his empire —even the northern zone, which was Morocco's immediate concern.

Although the Spanish Republic had considered abandoning its Protectorate in 1936, Franco had relied heavily on Moroccan soldiers during the Spanish Civil War and was therefore inclined to retain the manpower, strategic position, and prestige of Spanish Morocco. However, Spanish Morocco was an arid, hilly territory with few natural resources; Spaniards had invested little development capital there; and the administration, in general, suffered from inefficiency and corruption. Yet, local conflict between Spaniards and Moroccans was minimized by the considerable assimilation of the Spanish settlers, most of whom were of the working class, into Moroccan life.

Although Franco had wooed the nationalists during World War II, giving them a freedom of expression unknown to Spaniards in Spain, economic and political reform lagged behind that of the French zone. After World War II, the nationalists grew tired of unfulfilled promises and covert obstruction, and the Islah became so critical of Spanish policies that the regime declared it illegal in 1948 and expelled its leaders from the country. Two years later, spurned by the Western democracies, Franco decided to seek the friendship of the Arab-Muslim peoples and to try to play the role of middleman between East and West. The Islah was legalized again in 1952, and Franco made Torres and another nationalist leader ministers in the Spanish Protectorate government. From 1951 through 1955, under the administration of the High Commissioner, General Francisco García-Valino, not only did Spain make unofficial promises of ultimate independence to Torres and his colleagues, but a haven was offered to nationalists from French Morocco as a base from which to carry out actions against the French. During this period, in effect, the Islah became part of the Istiqlal and never re-emerged as a separate entity.

The wave of nationalist terror that swept French Morocco following the deposition of Mohammed V thus had no true counterpart in Spanish Morocco until after France recognized Morocco's independence. On the contrary, the French charged that Spain not only tolerated the training of rebels in their zone but also did nothing to help the French stave off the initial onslaught of the Moroccan Liberation Army in October, 1955, or to curb subsequent guerrilla operations originating in Spanish Morocco. When Foreign Minister Pinay went so far as to submit a vigorous official protest to the Spanish Ambassador in Paris, the Spanish

Government denied any complicity and promised to reinforce its vigilance against the rebels. However, Spain threatened to denounce France in the United Nations for threatening the peace in Morocco, and she continued to attack France for having deposed the popular Sultan, for failing to initiate needed reforms, and for suppressing rather than properly channeling nationalist feelings.

Spain had no immediate intention, of course, of relinquishing her own protectorate and advocated instead a timetable for satisfying nationalist aspirations in the far distant future. And, when Mohammed V returned to his throne, Franco even deplored any attempt to introduce democracy into Morocco on the ground that this would only facilitate the entrance of Communism. He further warned that Spain would never accept agreements negotiated without her participation and would never allow herself to be replaced under the pretext of a "pseudo-interdependence" while another nation increased her influence in the northern zone.

When the Sultan demanded unification of all Moroccan territory, Torres and Abdellah Guenoun resigned their positions in the Spanish Protectorate. In a last attempt to offset the growing influence of the French, García-Valino then announced his intention of introducing political reforms that would facilitate Morocco's independence while respecting Spain's "legitimate interests." He declared that Morocco had the right to choose its own political institutions, with the protecting powers playing only the role of honest counsellors.

Spain then asked for a three-way negotiation on Morocco. García-Valino met with Dubois in a formal but cordial atmosphere, but France declined to second Spain's request. Although France kept Spain informed of the progress of her negotiations with the Sultan, Spain was relegated to the wings while France occupied the stage.

Immediately upon conclusion of the Franco-Moroccan accord on March 2, demonstrations and bitter clashes between Moroccans and Spanish troops erupted in the Spanish zone. Torres protested the troops' action and demanded that Spain begin negotiations without delay. A vague reply from the Spanish Government stated merely that the Spanish zone could be fully dissolved only with true independence and that Spain would never permit her sphere of influence to be "interdependent" with that of France.

García-Valino added that Spain would continue to aid Morocco to achieve total independence in peace and then ordered tight security and censorship throughout the Spanish zone. The zone's frontier was closely controlled, and French reporters were forbidden entry. Moroccans, south as well as north, reacted strongly to these measures; in Fez, students at the Karouine gathered before the Spanish Consulate to hurl invectives, while in Meknes and Casablanca less erudite Moroccans threw home-made bombs at Spain's consular offices.

These events during the first week of March inspired a prompt reappraisal of Spain's Moroccan policy. Moulay el-Mehdi, son and heir of the Khalifa of Tetuán, rushed to Rabat to see the Sultan on his return from Paris on March 5, and García-Valino was recalled to Madrid to discuss the rapidly deteriorating situation. When al-Fassi arrived in Madrid a few days later en route to a meeting of the Istiqlal's executive committee in Tangier, he was greeted by a government-inspired editorial in a Madrid newspaper which argued that the time had come to revise the Franco-Spanish agreement of 1912 and establish a relationship based on "free association."

By April 1, the stage had been set for Spanish-Moroccan negotiations. After ignoring two diplomatic invitations to Madrid that did not include the promise that talks would result in recognition of Morocco's independence, the Sultan accepted a personal invitation from Franco that embodied such a statement. Premier Bekkai and Spain's Minister Plenipotentiary in Rabat, José Felipe Alcover y Sureda, made the preliminary arrangements for the talks.

Mohammed V was the first Moroccan monarch to set foot on Spanish soil since 1492, and the Spaniards accordingly had prepared to receive him in state. Two days of feasting, sightseeing, and celebration preceded the business at hand, during which Franco bestowed on his guest the Imperial Order of the Yoke and Arrows, one of the highest decorations of the Spanish State. During this courtship, it did not go unnoticed that the French Ambassador to Spain, who was not invited to any of these functions, was received by the Sultan at his temporary residence.

At first, Spanish officials suggested to the Sultan that Spain should enjoy the same rights in Morocco as France and that full control in the Spanish zone should be turned over to the Moroccan Government only when "Morocco's independence from France was genuine." The suggestion reflected Spain's growing fear that the forthcoming negotiations in Paris on interdependence might extend French influence to the Spanish zone and place Spain in a subordinate position even in her own area. The Sultan and his party rejected this plan, however, and Premier Bekkai told the Spanish Foreign Minister, Martín-Artajo, that Morocco was, in fact, already independent and able to protect herself against attempts to undermine her sovereignty. Si Bekkai asserted that Spain must formally recognize the *fait accompli*, "in order to strengthen the friendship that unites the two states and to ensure a free and fruitful cooperation."

Given little choice, Spain signed the joint declaration and protocol recognizing Morocco's independence and unity on April 7.* Following the pattern of the Franco-Moroccan agreement, the declaration guaranteed the liberties and rights of Spaniards in Morocco and of Moroccans in Spain, and provided for negotiations "to lead to new agreements between the two sovereign and equal states, with the object of defining free cooperation in those spheres where their common interest is involved." The attached protocol was to govern their relations pending completion of the all-important agreements.

The documents were generally well received in both Morocco and Spain, although semiofficial opinion indicated that many problems remained to be resolved. For example, the Spanish enclaves were not mentioned in either the declaration or the protocol, an omission that the Spanish newspapers *Ya* and *A.B.C.* regarded as consistent with their status as *plazas de soberanía*, sovereign towns that were not part of the Protectorate. Some Moroccans, however, claimed that the *presidios* should ultimately revert to Moroccan sovereignty. Moroccan government spokesmen in Rabat said that the distinction between "interdependence" and "free collaboration" was based on the dominance of French interests in Morocco and the unavoidable need for French cooperation in all fields, but voiced a hope for continued close ties with Madrid.

Resolution of the Spanish Protectorate problem was also greeted with satisfaction by the representatives of the eight powers that controlled Tangier. † Their discussions on the status of the international city were not yet completed, but they had prepared for Tangier's continuance as a free port despite its integration into the Sherifian Empire, and had scheduled discussions with Moroccan Foreign Minister Balafrej on the future status of the International Zone.

Two events brought matters to a head more rapidly than either

---

* See below, Appendix D.

† The concentration of foreign diplomatic missions in Tangier in the nineteenth century and the extension of capitulatory rights evolved into history's only truly international (civil) administration early in the twentieth century. For details see Graham Stuart, *The International City of Tangier* (Stanford, Calif., 1955).

party had expected. On April 27, the Personnel Union of the international administration in Tangier, affiliated with the Union of Moroccan Workers, presented a long statement of grievances concerning discrimination against Moroccans in the international administration, claiming that Moroccans received only humble jobs, while responsible posts went to foreigners, and that, while Moroccans were required to know foreign languages for employment, foreigners were not required to know Arabic—a requirement which they considered made Arabic a secondary language. The report called for "Moroccanization" of the Zone's administration and the integration of Tangier into a unified, independent Morocco.

Three days later came another surprise. At a meeting of Tangier's Assembly, Sidi Benaan, a Muslim delegate, suggested that, since legislative power in the newly independent Morocco was exercised exclusively by the Sultan, the Assembly should confine its legislation to such matters as public order, public health, and fiscal affairs, normally handled by a muncipal council, until the status of Tangier was clarified. The United States delegate opposed this motion, and it was subsequently defeated. The Moroccan delegates then walked out and the Mendoub, who was presiding, said that there was no quorum and adjourned the meeting. This spontaneous action, which caught even the Moroccan Government unaware, could not be long ignored. Balafrej rushed to Tangier and presented the Sultan's plan to the Committee of Control.

The Sultan's proposal called for a transitional regime while formal negotiations were conducted between the interested powers to alter the basic statute on Tangier. The Committee of Control considered the plan during May and approved a preliminary draft on June 12. Finally, on July 6, the eight nations on the Committee of Control agreed to a protocol that, as an amendment to the 1945 statute, was temporarily to regulate the administration of Tangier as a city still under international jurisdiction. The Moroccan delegates returned to the Assembly, their objective achieved.

The July 6 protocol provided for: (1) the Sultan's exercise of legislative powers of a general or institutional nature to extend to Tangier when urgency so demanded, after the Committee of Control had been consulted on harmonizing his laws with those in force in the Zone; (2) the abolition of the post of Administrator, its functions to be assumed by the Mendoub, who would become Governor of the Zone and henceforth under the sole authority of the Moroccan Government; (3) the guarantee of the rights of the present administrative personnel, as determined by laws and usage; (4) the police forces to be integrated into the General Directorate of National Security in Morocco; (5) plenary meetings of the Assembly during the transition period; (6) application of the laws, ordinances, regulations, and decisions presently in force during the transition period, provided the Sultan agreed that they did not interfere with his sovereignty and Morocco's territorial integrity; (7) autonomy of Tangier's budget and fiscal system; and (8) the Committee of Control would not enact legislation by ordinance, but could exercise right of control over the decisions taken by the Assembly.

(Later in 1956, a conference of the interested nations was held at Fedala [now Mohammedia] to terminate the International Administration of Tangier. October 28 witnessed the signing of the agreement abolishing Tangier's international regime and recognizing that its future rested with the Sultan, as complete and exclusive sovereign. Morocco assumed the debts and other obligations of Tangier's international administration, repossessed the public and private domain that had been entrusted to it, promised to respect the status of professional persons, and agreed to decide within six months if administration employees would be retained. Tangier's existing statutes were to be effective until changed and concessions and leases were to be governed by Moroccan law. Non-Moroccan radio stations and communications networks were allowed to continue, pending a special agreement between Morocco and the interested parties.)

Three hours after he had signed the agreement with Spain on April 7, 1956, Sultan Mohammed V returned to his own country—via a quick circuit in southern Spain. Arriving in Tetuán, he was greeted by 250,000 of his faithful followers—tribesmen from the Rif who had come on donkeys and afoot, officials from all sections of the country who had traveled by train and plane. For the first time in more than forty years, Moroccans moved freely in their own country without passports or visas. Slowly, the Sultan returned to Rabat, making several stops en route. He headed a sovereign state that was unified and independent in name, but not yet in substance.

Part Two

New Nation

Introduction

SOME MOROCCANS had long appreciated and others quickly learned two basic truths of self-government: that independence on paper and in practice are two very different things, and that the latter is far more difficult to achieve or even to approach. Terminating the protectorates was hardly an end in itself, despite the belief of some nationalists. Even to consolidate their hard-won position, Morocco's leaders were obliged to maintain order, earn and retain the confidence and support of all the country's ethnic groups, develop political stability and an efficient centralized administration, promote economic and social reforms, and evolve a foreign policy and international relationships that would suit the varied material and psychological needs of the Moroccan people, while satisfying the other nations with which Morocco sought, or was compelled, to deal.

Theoretically, the Moroccan Government, a term now embracing the Sultan and the Council of Ministers, could handle these matters as it wished. Actually, its freedom for constructive action was sharply limited from the start by the lack of clearly defined political and administrative institutions; by the paucity of domestic Moroccan production, investment capital, and experienced or even trained personnel in most fields; and by the abundance of excited citizens of diverse backgrounds who little understood what they or their country should expect of each other. To these problems, which alone would have seemed insurmountable to many "new" countries, was added the need to integrate territories and an international city controlled for two generations by foreign powers; to find a *modus vivendi* with a sizable and economically dominant foreign population against which considerable popular antagonism had been aroused; and to respond to the opposing demands of the parties to a war raging just across the country's longest border.

To steer a smooth course under such conditions would have required a government of angels and not of men in Rabat, as well as in Paris, Madrid, and several other capitals. Morocco's leaders not only lacked harps and halos; they also lacked the basic unity of purpose that a longer period of nationalist gestation might have produced. Thus, the Moroccan political picture was unlike that of such countries as Tunisia, where independence was achieved gradually by a single group that held a monopoly of political power. In Morocco, actual authority was divided between various politicians and resistance groups, between the palace and the ministries, between the PDI and the Istiqlal, and among various factions of the latter. While this plethora of checks and balances prevented the establishment of that "one-party rule" so often deplored in the West, it also precluded a concerted national effort in handling internal and external problems.

The complexity of these problems was indicated as soon as the accords granting independence were signed, when differences arose concerning the meaning of "interdependence." To Morocco, the term connoted free cooperation and unqualified French assistance in economic and cultural activities and in the rapid resolution of unsettled matters such as boundary delineation and the withdrawal of French troops and bases from Moroccan soil. To France, however, interdependence signified the continuance of her special role in Morocco. Her troops would remain indefinitely to protect this position and the citizens who represented it, and she would give aid only after Morocco had signed an "establishment convention" determining the rights and privileges of French citizens.

Difficulties in bridging the gap between these official positions were immediately increased by the pressures of extremists on both sides. Most colons and their supporters in France felt that the "natives" were neither ready nor able to administer a modern state; they feared not only for their personal security, but also changes such as increases in taxes and labor costs. The colons also resented the apparent disregard of, and ingratitude for, their contributions to Morocco's physical development and were loath to admit any responsibility for their present plight. Many Moroccans, for their part, were unable to revise their ingrained feelings of suspicion or even hostility toward Frenchmen. Some, like al-Fassi, equated interdependence with neocolonialism, and a few even believed that

France would attempt to reconquer Morocco if the opportunity presented itself.

If the French Government had not been harassed by her struggle to retain Algeria, Morocco and France could probably have done much more to curb their respective troublemakers and reach a compromise. But France's condition for cooperation with Morocco—that she maintain a "neutral" attitude toward the National Liberation Front in Algeria (FLN)—gave her an additional reason to retain troops in Morocco, particularly along the eastern border. This, of course, only encouraged Moroccans outside the government to demand firmness in dealing with "colonialism" and to criticize or even defy the new regime if it appeared too ready to compromise. Furthermore, by undermining the authority of the Moroccan Government at home, these individuals simultaneously weakened its position abroad.

Chapter 4

Internal Security and National Unity

BEFORE UNDERTAKING any reforms, the young Moroccan Government was obliged to demonstrate to Moroccans and Europeans alike its ability to maintain internal order and security. To do so, it had to impose discipline on a people that had spent a lifetime systematically defying authority, and curb the antagonism and distrust of the various segments of a heterogeneous population. The difficulty was compounded by the fact that the Moroccan Government initially had few instruments of persuasion or coercion at its command, since under the reservation of powers of February 11, France had retained temporary control over security functions in that part of Morocco which had been a French Protectorate. Morocco thus had the responsibility but not the ability to maintain order, while France had trained personnel with a legal authority almost impossible to exercise under the political circumstances.

In view of these considerations, the success of the Moroccan Government in maintaining even a modicum of order, checking secessionist threats, and extending the scope of its authority in the early postindependence period was a significant achievement and one for which the leadership deserves considerable credit. However, since there had been so little time to formulate procedures for promoting public order, and few means at hand with which to implement such plans, measures adopted by the government tended to be impromptu rather than systematic and often only temporary in effect. Thus, many vestiges of the basic problems that existed nearly a decade ago remain today and will require many years to resolve.

The difficulties involved in maintaining security appeared the very day after France had recognized Moroccan independence, when Liberation Army fighters in the Rif attacked a convoy of Legionnaires, killing eight and wounding eleven. Although the army commanders were then unaware of the formal end of the French Protectorate, it was questionable whether such knowledge would have made any difference. Operating in areas historically beyond the pale of central authority and respecting Istiqlal suggestions only when it seemed expedient, the Liberation Army felt itself under no obligation to accept the terms recently agreed to in Paris.

On the other hand, most Liberation Army leaders, while lacking a sense of responsibility to the abstract Western concept of the state, felt a deep personal loyalty to the religious position of Mohammed V. Accordingly, in response to an appeal by the palace, on March 8 army headquarters announced:

> People of Morocco! Since 1800 hours on March 7, the soldiers of the Liberation Army have passed from the offensive to the defensive. They will no longer attack foreign forces stationed in our country, but they are ready to strike back if attacked. Likewise, they are ready to resume combat if the agreement signed is not respected or its promises unfulfilled.

The following day, 600 soldiers of the Beni Snassen tribe descended from Nador to a joyous reception at Taza and thence to a royal welcome in Rabat. This was the first of several contingents of the Liberation Army to leave the hills for the capital. The Sultan received each group in the Great Court of Honor of the Palace, where the chiefs presented him with a saber and a machine gun as a token of homage and obedience. Thanking them in the name of the country and promising that their memory would be cherished and their duty rewarded by God, the Sultan pointedly asked them to aid Morocco in its new struggle—for organization and order.

On March 26, however, Liberation Army headquarters stated that although it accepted the Sultan's authority, it would not disband until the country was free of the last vestiges of colonialism. As the Istiqlal leader still in closest contact with (and most respected by) the Liberation Army chiefs, al-Fassi explained that the army's position was to remain vigilant until all negotiations were ended and independence complete. The French negotiators were thus put on notice that the position of their countrymen in Morocco depended entirely on the decisions reached at the conference table. The Liberation Army statements were occasionally accompanied by kidnapings of French soldiers, who were usually returned unharmed in exchange for the release of Moroccan prisoners or the abandonment of a position by French forces. The Liberation Army thus served as an occasionally useful gadfly during Morocco's negotiations with France, but more often than not it was a cause of alarm or embarrassment.

A further, but temporary, source of concern to the authorities was the continued urban terrorism. During the first two months of independence, for example, violence in the cities resulted in the death of forty-four Moroccans and one European, and injury to twenty-three Moroccans and five Europeans. The government attributed this in part to displaced employees of the old regime who wished to embarrass their successors. But it was also obvious that many aggressive youths who had been active in the resistance found it difficult to adjust to peace and were turning to various illegal activities. Insufficient police control fostered this growth of common crimes which the French press, generally obsessed with "bad news," sometimes labeled as political. There were in addition several sordid attempts to settle old political scores, principally against former Protectorate Muslim administrators, who were eventually to pay dearly for their collaboration with the French by loss of their property and civil rights. Political organizations also jockeyed for position; the resistance groups of the Istiqlal (the Black Hand and Moundama Seria), the PDI (Seven Lions of the Liberation), and the Black Crescent waged an underground political struggle that nevertheless came to the surface in several dramatic, well-publicized manifestations.

In February, 1956, Touria Chaoui, Morocco's only aviatrix, was murdered for refusing to pay a tribute to the Black Crescent, and the President of the Istiqlal Youth Committee was killed in Taourirt; in April, Si Abdelouahad Laraki, a professor at the Karouine and General Secretary of the Fez section of the PDI, and Dr. Omar Drissi, one of the country's few physicians, were murdered. Retaliation against the Black Crescent, which the Istiqlal openly termed a "Communizing influence" despite its denial of Communist ties, was conducted on an eye-for-an-eye basis. Two members of the organization's hierarchy were killed (one, Abd el-Krim bin Abdullah, an Algerian-born Muslim citizen of France, was a geologist and an important figure in the Moroccan Communist Party), and an attempt was made on the lives of three ranking MCP members—Abdelslam Bourguia, Abdullah el-Ayach, and Edmond Malett—but all escaped alive from their bullet-ridden car.

At the end of July, an all-out crack-down on the Black Crescent began. Thirty members of the organization were arrested, and four of its leaders were killed when they attempted to escape. The Istiqlal and PDI were apparently prepared to kill every member of the Black Crescent, if necessary, to end its activities, but the group faded into anonymity when deprived of its leadership.

French criticism of the Moroccan Government's inability to secure and maintain order was generally severe, but Dubois showed more understanding when he remarked that the atmosphere in Morocco was comparable to that of France following the liberation in 1944. Many observers were surprised that vindictiveness was not more widespread, considering the bitterness of the fight for independence. In any case, the French appreciated the fact that the Sultan and his ministers, at a calculated political risk to themselves, repeatedly warned the Moroccan people that acts of violence against the foreign civilian populace would detract from Morocco's prestige and that the maintenance of order was evidence of patriotism. The Sultan further promised that the new government would protect the rights and interests of his country's European guests. For his part, French Minister of State Jacques Chaban-Delmas exhorted his countrymen to "play the game with independent Morocco openly and loyally" and urged his government to furnish Rabat with more effective means of keeping order.

The unworkable situation created by the February 11 reservation of powers was partially resolved at the end of April, when the Moroccan Government assumed full control of security services. Mohammed Laghzaoui, a confidant of the Sultan and formerly active in the Istiqlal in the Protectorate days, was appointed to the crucial post of Director General of National Security, retaining his predecessor under the Protectorate, Marcel Pettijean, as technical adviser. The Directorate was technically attached to the Ministry of the Interior but was responsible in fact only to the Sultan. Although three-quarters of the original 7,500-man security force was French, the dismissal of 272 Frenchmen a few months later initiated a gradual turnover; by 1964, only a handful of French experts, versed in such skills as fingerprinting, remained in a force estimated at perhaps 10,000. At Morocco's request, France maintained temporary control of the *gendarmerie*, but this likewise eventually passed to Moroccan control.

In the first major incident of violence after the change of security control, the Moroccan Government resorted to judicial rather than physical power. On May 2, 1956, in Marrakesh, mobs dragged from their homes, then burned and chopped to death, more than forty

supporters of the late Pasha, el-Glaoui. Security forces rushed to
the scene but, obviously instructed for political reasons to hold
their fire, were completely ineffective. Only personal appeals from
the governor, supplemented by an opportune hailstorm, quieted
the popular fury. However, forty-six persons were subsequently
arrested, and the guilty were promised severe punishment.

As a secondary result of the Marrakesh affair, the Minister of the
Interior, Lachen Lyoussi, an unschooled Berber leader who had
received his important portfolio (security affairs being under his
jurisdiction) because it was hoped that he could deal successfully
with the tribes during the transitional period, "resigned" and was
made a Minister of State. His replacement was the shrewder Driss
M'Hammedi, the Istiqlal stalwart who commanded the respect of
both the French High Commissioner and many Moroccan politicians. One of M'Hammedi's first actions was to confiscate whatever unregistered weapons could be uncovered in the hands of
French or Moroccan civilians. Following a few positive indications
of an intent to use the security forces effectively, violence in the
cities steadily diminished, with but one significant exception.

On the other hand, the problem of rural unrest, with its foreign
and domestic political ramifications, remained. Although the Sultan admonished his subjects to refrain from violence against
French settlers, he refused to take an unequivocal stand opposing
Moroccan attacks on French military patrols. This attitude reflected the government's continuing inability to control the Liberation Army, as well as growing popular resentment toward
French soldiers—and particularly those who temporarily entered
Morocco from Algeria after killing Algerian liberation fighters. Although the Moroccan Government asked the French commanders
to give advance information on troop movements so that it could
arrange for the "protection" of French soldiers, France was officially blamed whenever incidents occurred. Paris was perturbed by
this situation, but nonetheless proceeded with plans to give Morocco an army of its own on the theory that this would better
enable the Moroccan Government to control the Liberation Army
and thus protect the interests of both countries.

On May 9, at the N'Knehlia military center south of Rabat,
13,000 goumiers, the Berber warriors, presented their colors to
French officials for transfer to the Hôtel des Invalides in Paris to be
displayed with those of other disbanded units. In Rabat, four days
later, with 2,000 *mehallas* (Moroccans in the Spanish Army), they
took an oath administered by Prince Moulay Hassan, and a twenty-
nine-gun salute announced the birth of the Royal Moroccan Army,

which was shortly augmented by 7,000 additional mehallas and supported by donations of Spanish equipment and the services of officers and technicians. On May 14, the Sultan, his red-uniformed Senegalese Horse Guards, and 200,000 delighted citizens witnessed the first parade of the new army. The khaki-clad troops in their green berets comprised 13 infantry battalions of 900 to 1,000 men each, 35 cavalry squadrons, tank squadrons, an artillery group, a battalion of engineers, medical auxiliaries, and 6 reconnaissance planes piloted by Frenchmen. The Chief of Staff was Prince Moulay Hassan, an obvious symbol of central authority and a man his father could trust completely; the Field Commander was General Ben Hammou Kettani, formerly the only Moroccan general in the French Army.

France had given the Royal Army more than $3 million worth of equipment, including tanks, half-tracks, armored cars, cannon, jeeps, weapons carriers, trucks, and rifles, and the tricolor was still visible beneath the freshly painted Moroccan crescent. France also donated the services of 142 officers and 603 noncoms, since Morocco had only 200 ranking officers and 1,500 cadets in training at Dar el Beida, at St Cyr, in France, and at the Toledo Military Academy in Spain. These Frenchmen were transferred, despite their lack of enthusiasm, under individual one-year contracts to the Moroccan Government, wore Moroccan uniforms, and were responsible to the Moroccan command. The Sultan loudly praised French generosity, but his government also made it clear that Moroccans would replace these French officers as soon as possible. Talks looking to the creation of a Moroccan navy and air force were also initiated by the new Defense Minister, Ahmed Reda Guedira, chairman of the small Liberal Independent Party and confidant of the royal family.

Guedira's designation of the Royal Army as the "only recognized military force" in Morocco obviously made the Liberation Army's position more anomalous than ever. At first, the guerrillas indicated a willingness to retreat from the military limelight. They caused no disturbances at the military review on May 14, as had been feared, and, on May 18, their spokesmen announced that troops would thenceforth carry arms only in their immediate areas and that they would stop soliciting funds. A few days later, however, Liberation Army troops captured a seven-man French patrol in the mountains north of Oudjda. The government in Rabat feebly explained that such encounters were possible as long as the French Army insisted on performing reconnaissance missions in that area, while the Liberation Army accused the French forces of numerous provocative actions which implied that Moroccan independence was still an illusion.

Accusations flew back and forth with increasing intensity. The French commander in Morocco accused the Liberation Army of supplying the Algerian rebels with weapons and men, as well as with a rest center. The situation reached such a pitch that the French Chief of Staff of Ground Forces, Paul Ely, intervened: he suggested a demilitarized zone along the Algerian-Moroccan border, closer cooperation between French and Moroccan forces in safeguarding French lives and property, and permission for French troops to circulate freely in Morocco. In reply, however, he received a sharp warning from the Sultan that peace would return to North Africa only when the aspirations and rights of all its inhabitants were realized.

Foreign Minister Balafrej tried to minimize the disagreement with France, and he denied the French charges that Morocco was either conducting a second front for the FLN or trying to extend her boundaries by force. On the other hand, the Istiqlal organ, *al-Alam*, reflecting the growing impatience of al-Fassi and his followers, sharply warned France that she must not mount attacks against Algeria from Morocco. The frontier must be guarded by Moroccan troops, stated *al-Alam*, though a mixed commission might supervise the operation. Foreign Minister Pineau's insistence that France would continue to guard the frontier herself only encouraged the Liberation Army to extend its activities southward, resulting in further clashes and additional casualties. Franco-Moroccan tension was heightened in June, when the Moroccan Government refused to accept twenty-three former French civil controllers as consular officers on the ground that they were obvious symbols of colonialism.

A partial relaxation in the over-all tension occurred at the end of June, following the Royal Army's capture of a Liberation Army leader whose band had been preying on the countryside. After inducting the renegade's 400 apologetic followers into the Royal Army at their own request, Prince Moulay Hassan learned that this group had killed a top Liberation Army leader who had opposed them. The government thereupon decided to force the Liberation Army of the Rif to disband. This determination was implemented through negotiations combining flattery, threatened force, and a promise of such veterans' benefits as a monopoly of licenses to operate transport vehicles. As a result, 6,000 more irregulars were enlisted by the Crown Prince at Talamgnit on July 12. The remaining 3,000 Liberation fighters were excluded from service because of physical disqualifications or political unreliability, and were officially disbanded.

Further to strengthen central authority in the rebellious Rif, the Sultan and a large entourage toured the area—the first visit to that region by a Moroccan monarch since 1847. In speeches before hundreds of thousands of enthusiastic faithful, the Sultan repeatedly condemned all attempts to divide Arabs and Berbers "who were truly united by Islam" and announced his determination to abolish artificial barriers between them. This promise was fulfilled in August, when the Berber Dahir of 1930 was officially repealed.

Rural separatism continued to be encouraged, however, by the promulgation of a "Berber Tract" inciting tribesmen to revolt against Arab domination. The Minister of Information, Ibrahim, attributed the document to unnamed Frenchmen and the disgruntled Lyoussi; the latter was tried and found guilty (he was later pardoned). The subsequent seizure of various Présence Française members, their expulsion from the country, and the prohibition of their organization met with stiff protests from the French Embassy. But the rugged individualism of the tribesmen was unaffected by these developments.

Early the next year, internal dissension again marred the Moroccan scene. When the Sultan left for a Mediterranean cruise in January, 1957, the Governor of Tafilalt Province, the tribal leader Addi Ou Bihi, took the opportunity to announce that, although he recognized the Sultan's authority, he did not adhere to the Istiqlal-dominated government. He dismissed an official sent from Rabat to take over the police station in Midelt, refused an invitation from Prince Moulay Hassan to come to the capital, and alerted several thousand armed tribesmen. Royal Army troops and two Crown Counselors were unable to reason with Bihi, so the central Government sent Major Ben Larbi, Director of the Royal Military Cabinet, to replace him. Bihi surrendered without a fight to General Kettani and was taken to Rabat to await the Sultan's judgment. In the meantime, the Minister of Information charged that Bihi had acted under the inspiration of "foreign elements," but no elaboration or substantiation of this accusation was made public at the time. Two years later, in January, 1959, Bihi was tried by the Moroccan Supreme Court for conspiring with three French generals to incite tribal uprisings that would give France a pretext to re-occupy Morocco. Bihi and several codefendants were found guilty and sentenced to death, but Bihi died in jail.

Within two years after Bihi's rebellion, restlessness flared again in the Rif. Some of the outbursts were spontaneous, but others were instigated by former Liberation Army leaders, among them Khatib and Ahardane, who were in the process of organizing a new party, the Popular Movement. The arrest of Khatib and Ahardane on charges of sedition in October, 1958, and the removal of the latter from his administrative post, led to a campaign of warfare and passive resistance in the Rif and to the open revolt of their followers in the Oulmes region east of Rabat.

At this point, the leaders of the Rif rebellion expressed a marked nostalgia for pre-Protectorate days. They regarded themselves as Arab Moroccan nationalists, but they condemned the Istiqlal government's centralized control and, above all, the appointment of "outsiders" to political positions in the Rif. The Rif spokesmen also decried the antimonarchical tendencies of the modern party's "republican" elements. Reflecting in part the ideas voiced in Cairo by their still revered Abd el-Krim, they also demanded the immediate withdrawal of French troops from the Rif and increased Moroccan aid to the Algerian rebels. This concern with Algeria could be attributed to both political and economic causes: the Rif's local economy, upset during the guerrilla struggle before 1956, had failed to recover, largely because of the Algerian conflict next door, for in times of peace Rifians had traditionally sought work in Algeria during slack periods at home. There were also signs of Spanish intrigue, as well as evidence that Egyptian agents, opportunely fishing in troubled Arab waters, had encouraged the revolts in the hope of catapulting friendly Moroccans into power.

A sharp debate broke out within the Moroccan Government and between militant Istiqlal leaders and the Sultan concerning the degree of force to be used to meet this threat to internal unity. The Sultan agreed to send Royal Army units against the Popular Movement groups operating close to Rabat, and disturbances there quickly ended. He was reluctant, however, to feed the discontent in the north with "oppressive" measures. Although he dispatched troops to the Rif, he did not send them into action and merely reviewed them in Tetuán on November 16, 1956, at the start of the three-day national holiday in honor of the throne. After several scores of persons had been killed or wounded during that short holiday period, however, he declared martial law in the Rif and instituted an inquiry into the causes of the outbreak. And when the rebels attempted to seize the port of Alhucemas in January, 1959, Mohammed V dispatched Prince Moulay Hassan with 20,000 Royal Army troops to check the insurgents. In response to a final appeal and in the face of compelling force, the rebellion ceased, but military control of the region continued until October, 1962. If there was doubt before, it was by this time clear that Morocco's bled problem had not disappeared with the end of the Protectorate.

The problem of provincial separatism was closely paralleled throughout Morocco's first years of independence by the issue of supranationalism, raised and acted on in the name, but without the advice and consent, of the central government. The first instance of this occurred in July, 1956, shortly after the Liberation Army of the Rif had been disbanded, when a "Saharan Liberation Army" of about 3,000 men established headquarters at Goulimine. This force consisted mainly of castoff Liberation Army veterans who had not been absorbed into the Royal Army and disgruntled persons who shared al-Fassi's contempt for the moderate policies of the Bekkai government. Announcing irredentist claims to the south against both France and Spain, this new irregular force attacked the garrison at Foum el-Hassan that had shortly before been jointly occupied by French and Royal Army troops. The resulting tripartite quarrel, which set the pattern for many others, illustrates how unsolved domestic and foreign issues aggravated each other in independent Morocco.

The joint occupation of Foum el-Hassan had been the culmination of a drama that began when French troops moved into the Sous after an alleged theft of weapons, presumably by Moroccan irregulars, from five Royal Army posts south of Agadir and after the French had advised the Moroccan governor that they had orders to occupy three Moroccan posts. When an emergency meeting of French and Moroccan officials in Rabat achieved no solution to the critical situation, a French naval escort appeared in Agadir harbor, and a battalion of French troops parachuted into Foum el-Hassan. The UMT responded to these French moves with an appeal for a general strike in Agadir and instigated the local population to erect roadblocks to prevent movement by French troops. On July 4, the Sultan ordered the Crown Prince to Agadir with units of the Royal Army to retake the posts the French had occupied. At this juncture, General René Cogny, former military governor of Metz and France's youngest general, replaced Bourguny as commander of the French forces in Morocco and flew immediately to Agadir to confer with Prince Moulay Hassan. Although he denied that a capitulation was contemplated, Cogny acknowledged that French troops had been ordered to withdraw from the area immediately around Agadir. The impasse was resolved when the three posts in question were occupied jointly by French and Moroccan troops. A general outbreak had been avoided, but ill feeling persisted on both sides.

Throughout August, Moroccan leaders fostered further complaints against the presence of the French Army by continually characterizing it as an occupation force. Al-Fassi even declared that Morocco's struggle for liberation would continue until French forces were removed from their dominant position in four-fifths of the country. The government, however, while pressing its demands for a new agreement concerning French troops in Morocco, was anxious to avoid any further open clashes. Sensing that agreement was possible, the Sultan went so far as to ask the people to be friendly to the French troops and requested the latter to refrain from provocative action. Furthermore, the Moroccan Government succeeded in convincing the Saharan Liberation Army to cease its harassment of Foum el-Hassan. By the end of the year, the Istiqlal, which dominated the cabinet, appeared to have established considerable control over the Saharan Liberation fighters.

In September, the Sultan's moderate approach to the problem of the French Army in Morocco appeared vindicated when the French agreed to negotiate on the status of their forces. However, on October 22, the impending negotiations were seriously threatened by France: on that day, French officials forced down and "kidnapped" five Algerian nationalist leaders, including Ahmed Ben Bella, who were traveling from Rabat to Tunis in the Sultan's private plane. Popular support in Morocco for the Algerian revolution, added to the personal commitment of Mohammed V to the safety of the Algerian leaders, served powerfully to renew anti-French sentiment; protest riots in several Moroccan cities, notably Meknes,* were followed by the recall of the Moroccan Ambassador to Paris and the announcement that any further negotiation between Morocco and France must await the release of the five Algerians.

When France demanded punishment of the instigators of the Meknes riot, indemnities for losses, opening of credit for French farmers, and maintenance of the *status quo* for French troops, the Sultan was faced with a difficult decision. The future of French

* The fighting in Meknes began when the chief of the municipal police, a Moroccan, was killed while attempting to restrain a mob of angry demonstrators from stoning the French consulate. The French later alleged that he had shot himself accidentally while aiming at a demonstrator, but the people believed that he had been murdered by a Frenchman. Whatever the cause of his death, it infuriated the mob, which then proceeded to kill, pillage, and burn throughout the city. Fifty-three persons were murdered, including twenty-seven Europeans, before Royal Army troops restored order. When it was all over, 400 French farms in the Meknes region had been burned, with a total damage of 5 billion francs.

cooperation and the Sultan's personal prestige appeared to depend on a satisfactory balance of deeply felt antagonisms in the Meknes area, a stronghold of the colon mentality. The Sultan's response was, in any case, prompt and to the point: Morocco agreed to the first request, refused the second, explained that credits were possible only with French financial aid, and flatly stated that the Royal Army alone would maintain security in Morocco.

The Meknes area was declared a military region, and Major Driss Ben Omar of the Royal Army became its military and civil governor. A military court was established by dahir to administer all civil, criminal, and military justice, and Driss Ben Omar advised the populace that he would permit neither flouting of authority nor the slightest insurrection in his territory. Steps were taken immediately to bring the guilty to trial, and, within a fortnight, 600 persons were arrested.

In Rabat, Minister of Interior M'Hammedi warned that the government would hunt down criminals without mercy to assure security in both the city and the bled. A commission was appointed to examine the general situation with a view to assessing damages and restoring normalcy; the people were urged to return to work. Compliance was slow, however, and French merchants in Meknes continued a general strike for almost a week, while the police and other government employees remained idle until the end of October.

On December 2, the military tribunal finally convened in Meknes—a court composed of three Royal Army officers, a member of the Sherifian High Court, and one other civilian. Defense counsel were appointed by the court. The tribunal opened with routine criminal trials in order not to emphasize the cases of the rioters. Eventually, however, the rioters came to trial; ten death sentences were handed down, and eight men were given life imprisonment. On December 27, the first execution, by a Royal Army firing squad, took place. This example of Moroccan justice had the intended effect of impressing even the colons.

When the military tribunal acquitted several of the accused, however, in February, 1957, the colons of Meknes protested to the Sultan and the United Nations and threatened another general strike. In reply to their accusations that the trials were a show designed to conceal judicial impotence, the court's leading defense counsel, Jean-Charles Legrand, praised the conduct of all the trials. The recently appointed Defense Minister Mohammed Zeghari warned the colons that outside pressure on Moroccan courts would not be permitted, and Governor Driss Ben Omar forbade the proposed strike. The French consul in Meknes then convinced the colons to drop their protests, and Premier Mollet assured the French in Morocco of his government's solicitude, although he could promise them nothing that would increase their sense of physical security. This was gradually assured, however, as the Meknes incident faded and proved to be the last violent eruption of anticolonial sentiment.

Subsequent surveys of public opinion showed that, while many Frenchmen encouraged repatriation, there was also considerable sentiment for remaining in Morocco to assure France's position and safeguard her interests. Some Frenchmen were unable to adjust to the new conditions and left, but others remained to fill the need for professional and technical assistance. A newspaper survey revealed the Moroccans' desire to have well-disposed Frenchmen remain, despite their dismay at the tactlessness of so many French and the limited interest they showed in helping Morocco to assume her new responsibilities.

For more than two years after the Meknes affair, only limited progress was made on the problem of foreign troops in Morocco, and this by piecemeal action rather than formal, long-term agreement. By the spring of 1957, some 35,000 troops had returned to France. Moroccan demands in 1957 for the complete withdrawal of French troops resulted only in a counterproposal that France reduce her forces in Morocco to the pre-1955 level of 40,000 to 50,000, grouped primarily around the six French airbases (in Marrakesh, Meknes, Casablanca, Agadir, Port Lyautey, and Khouribga). In 1959, 25,000 additional French troops were withdrawn, but the French argued that total withdrawal involved major technical problems such as the disposal of equipment, the transfer of aviation and meteorological facilities, guarantees for the safety of Frenchmen, and clarification of Morocco's position vis-à-vis Algeria and NATO. In addition to further complicating Morocco's already serious security problems, this French attitude helped to foster an aggressive Moroccan foreign policy that visualized such anti-French, irredentist objectives as the annexation of Mauritania and also served to nullify the positive effects of France's substantial cooperation with Morocco in economic and cultural affairs.

While the problems involving the Saharan Liberation Army, the French Army, and the Rif tribes were the greatest source of domestic discord between 1956 and 1962, several other matters also created considerable official and popular concern. One was the status of the Jewish population, which had been the object of terrorist attacks in 1953 but which had shown slight interest in emigrating to Israel until the Petitjean outbreaks of 1954 (except for 1948–49, when 20,000 emigrated). Thereafter, many Jews considered the possibility of emigration, fearing that their position would be insecure under an independent Muslim government. Others, regarding Morocco as their home, were willing to accept the nationalist promises that Jews would be equal citizens both in law and in fact, and they were especially gratified by the Sultan's injunction to the Muslims to respect fellow "People of the Book."

The Sultan declared that Moroccan Jews, as an "elite" group (the term "elite" referred to the relatively large number of doctors, lawyers, teachers, and businessmen among them), had certain duties as well as rights. Skeptics, however, considered that the government wanted only to exploit these professionals and would tolerate them only briefly. Nevertheless, there was some satisfaction in the fact that a Jew, Dr. Leon Benzaghen, was appointed as a minister in the first Moroccan cabinet, a move described by the Istiqlal as an effort to include a "representative of a truly native element" rather than as "a concession to a racial minority." Subsequently, a Jew became Assistant to the Minister of National Economy, and another was appointed to the High Court of Appeals.

Despite such gestures, the counsel of some of their own leaders, and reports that non-European Jews were treated as second-class citizens in Israel, most Moroccan Jews were reluctant to commit themselves firmly to the new regime. For example, only one Moroccan Jew volunteered for officer training in the new Royal Army in 1956. In the first five months of 1956, about 17,000 Jews left Morocco; more would doubtless have departed if the necessary funds and ships had been available. While disapproving of the exodus, which it felt sullied its prestige, the Moroccan Government initially did nothing to prevent the flow, but a series of incidents and one provocative statement led to an abrupt change of this position.

In May, 1956, ten Jews in eastern Morocco were kidnapped for a forty-eight-hour period and held for ransom by persons identified in the French press as Liberation Army elements. Jewish shops in Oudjda immediately closed in protest, and telegrams were sent to the Sultan demanding his intercession in the matter. The Tunisian representative of the Joint Distribution Committee, an American organization aiding needy Jews, publicly declared that independence in Morocco was a disaster for its Jewish inhabitants. The weekly Istiqlal paper, *al-Istiqlal*, responded with an article by a Moroccan Jew entitled "The Hateful Campaign Against the Jewish-Muslim Entente," and characterized the emigrants as bad

Moroccans. In a more moderate vein, the Istiqlal referred to "colonial propaganda" based on the old divide-and-rule principle and pointed to the colons' anti-Semitic campaign against two French leaders of Jewish origin—Pierre Mendès-France and Gilbert Grandval—to indicate who were the "real hate-mongers" in Morocco. Balafrej asserted that in an independent Morocco, Jews would be equal citizens in law and fact, and al-Fassi asked Moroccan Jews not to swallow propaganda designed to incite them to leave their country for Israel. The government, irked by this barb, anxious to promote friendly relations with the Arab states, and still lacking in diplomatic finesse, went further.

On June 11, the Israeli Cadima Society, the Moroccan division of the Jewish Agency for Palestine, which sponsored and financed mass emigration, was ordered to cease its activities within twenty-four hours and to close its staging camp, where some 5,000 persons were awaiting transportation. The Cadima had issued single visas for an entire boatload of emigres, but now the Moroccan Government asserted that emigration would henceforth be permitted only on an individual basis. It justified this drastic move by referring to the economic dislocations caused by the mass departure of Jewish skill, energy, and capital, to the alleged return of many disillusioned Jews to Morocco in a destitute condition, and to the "threat" to fellow Muslims in the Near East. At the same time, it ordered twenty-three Israelis employed by the Cadima and the Joint Distribution Committee to leave the country, charging them with endangering public security by inciting Jews to emigrate.

Dr. Nahum Goldmann, President of the World Jewish Congress and of the Jewish Agency for Palestine, declared that these orders violated previous assurances, and he insisted that the Jewish people would never relinquish their right to emigrate to Israel or elsewhere. Alleging that Morocco had acted under pressure from the Arab League, he predicted that the move would cause great suffering. He disputed Morocco's charge that mass emigration disturbed the country's economy, and argued that it was usually the poor and untrained workers who wished to leave; such persons, he added, could finance a trip to Israel only through the Cadima. Goldmann intended, therefore, to appeal to various governments and possibly even to the United Nations to intervene.

On June 19, Morocco reversed its stand; Laghzaoui announced that the Jews in the staging camp would be permitted to depart. However, difficulties ensued when others outside the camp began to infiltrate it. It was not until mid-August that the Moroccan Government and the World Jewish Congress settled the problem by

Morocco's agreement to permit the 6,350 Jews then in the camp to emigrate at the rate of 600 weekly until October 10. The emigres were required to sign a statement that they departed of their own free will and relinquished the right to return. Although the latter provision was contrary to the agreement and to international law, for practical reasons it was not contested.

After the Cadima closed, an underground was set up via Tangier to a Gibraltar staging camp for Moroccan Jews who could not afford passage or obtain individual passports. Others left Morocco by traveling to Spain or France on a temporary visa and failing to return. By the end of 1956, the small Jewish communities in the Moroccan interior had almost entirely disappeared, and the total number of Moroccan Jews had dropped below 200,000, perhaps 50,000 less than the last Protectorate census had counted.

Since 1956, the Jewish exodus from Morocco has ebbed and flowed, depending in large part on the government's official policy on emigration. When curbs are imposed, interest in departure increases; when the restrictions are relaxed, tension and concern among the Jews diminish. These periodic changes in policy reflect the government's preoccupation with Pan-Arab influences.

Moroccan Jews have suffered from occasional hooliganism, which at times is abetted by their lack of police protection, and some newspapers have attacked Zionism. On the whole, however, both the government and the Muslim population have proved fairly tolerant. In September, 1957, for example, when it was rumored that a few Moroccan Jews might be tried as collaborators of the former Protectorate regime, Moulay Hassan ceremoniously denied the report while attending Yom Kippur services in a Casablanca synagogue. Economically, Moroccan Jews have fared well; politically, they have enjoyed official guarantees of their safety and liberty. Under the 1959 nationality law, Jews received the same legal status as their Muslim compatriots, and the 1962 Constitution guarantees them freedom of religion. Indicative of the virtual impossibility of separating Muslim-Jewish matters from Arab-Israeli politics, however, was the fact that, during President Nasser's visit to Morocco in 1962, numerous Jews were arrested on flimsy pretexts, and some were beaten.

The Jewish community in Morocco today numbers approximately 70,000. For the most part, the poor have departed and the middle class remain. They have their own newspaper, La Voix de la Communauté, and continue to have their own schools, now subsidized by the government, which two-thirds of the Jewish children attend. (One-third of the Alliance schools were nationalized in

1961, but this process has not since been repeated.) If official policy remains favorable, Moroccan Jewish leaders expect that at least a majority of the present Jewish residents will continue to live in Morocco.

Much greater obstacles to national unity have arisen in Morocco's northern zone, which posed such problems as those involving the transfer of powers still retained by Spain, guarantees for Spanish civil servants and settlers, the status of the Spanish Army, and the future of the peseta. Progress on these matters was delayed by Morocco's limited number of qualified negotiators and her desire to use them primarily to reach agreements with France, and also by the fact that Morocco's lack of European administrative personnel and capital was even greater in the northern than in the southern zone. In addition, the 30 per cent discrepancy in the level of wages and prices between zones would have caused a rush of population and goods to the south if the frontiers between the zones had been abolished immediately. The country remained divided in all but allegiance to the Sultan, therefore, for nearly two years after independence, much to the chagrin of nationalists on both sides of the border. Furthermore, Spanish political and military leaders were reluctant to implement their promises with deeds, and willingly waited for Franco-Moroccan negotiations to end before settling their own affairs with the new government. Nevertheless, both official and personal relations remained cordial, due largely to Franco's early pro-Arab policy and to the lesser antagonism and jealousy between Muslim and Spanish residents in the northern zone.

Formal negotiations pursuant to the April 7 declaration officially began in June, 1956, with the arrival of Prince Moulay Hassan and Balafrej in Madrid. A mixed commission was designated to meet in Tetuán to plan the transfer of administrative powers; pending its decisions, the northern zone was divided into five provinces headed by governors, four of whom were former leaders in the Liberation Army. The Istiqlal had hoped to name its own representatives to all five posts, but, recognizing its limited party strength among the rural citizenry and the popularity of the Liberation Army, it chose the candidates from the ranks of the latter. The Istiqlal stalwart Abd el-Khalek Torres, however, was given the ultimate authority to complete the transfer of powers from the Spanish administrators. Pending this action, the two zones remained under separate administrations. Each zone had its own budget; customs inspection was maintained at border stations; and, although Moroccans could travel freely between zones, foreigners were still required to show their passports.

In February, 1957, the mixed commission finally signed its first agreements: a judicial pact stipulating that Spain would continue to provide judges for the northern zone until Morocco's legal system was unified; and a diplomatic accord providing for consultations on matters of mutual concern. Four additional agreements were concluded in July, covering cultural affairs, administrative and technical assistance, commercial relations, and the replacement of the peseta as the official currency. The last measure, which was not executed until February, 1958, had political as well as economic significance, since for the first time it made the unity of the two zones more real than apparent.

The principal remaining point of negotiation was the status of the 30,000 Spanish troops. Emulating France, Spain at first refused Morocco's demands either for immediate evacuation or for an agreement on phased withdrawal, a decision based largely on the growing friction over the Spanish Sahara and the presidios. In June, 1958, however, following the French example, a slow exodus began with the departure of some 3,000 soldiers.

In recent years, the principal threat to internal security in Morocco has apparently shifted from rural unrest to urban-centered political conspiracies against the power of the monarchy or against its chief supporters. The government thus regards internal security as a major problem to this day, sapping much of the country's resources and energies. The Royal Army, now commanded by Prince Moulay Abdullah as Chief of Staff and led by officers carefully screened for loyalty to the King, is therefore better organized to combat internal than external threats. This well-equipped force by 1965 numbered 36,000 men, including 900 Moroccan officers, many of whom are graduates of the new military academy at Meknes, and 100 French officers responsible for training.

A Royal Navy, created in May, 1961, has only a few ships and little more than 400 men; the 2,000-man Air Force, created in 1961, is equipped with twelve U.S. transport planes, twenty American and French fighter planes, and twelve Soviet MIG-17 fighters. In addition to the help provided by the Sûreté, which is equipped with many modern devices for curbing subversion, there exists an auxiliary force of 10,000 men controlled by the ministries of Interior and Defense.

Since the nature of the tasks confronting Morocco's security forces today can be understood only against the background of Moroccan politics, we now turn to this subject.

Chapter 5

National Politics and
Morocco's Evolving Political Structure

A NY NEWLY independent state, however thoroughly groomed
for its debut, will have awkward moments as the leaders
attempt to evolve a new political system and the people
try to adjust to it. A fairly smooth transition is possible, but only
when the nationalist leadership has had sufficient time to develop
a consensus regarding basic national values and goals and to obtain
some practical experience in the responsibilities of self-government.
Single-party Tunisia, for example, with two generations of relatively
peaceful nationalist struggle capped by a brief period of internal
autonomy, or multi-party Nigeria, which the British endowed with
a functioning constitutional government well before their carefully
phased departure, had ample time to adjust to their responsibilities.
Morocco, emerging so quickly from colonial status, was less well
prepared. It was extremely difficult for her leaders to establish a
pattern of political relationships that would be understood, respected, and obeyed. Independence arrived without benefit of a
constitution, parliament or other elected bodies, experience with
national elections, or even a political party such as the Tunisian
Neo-Destour, which had, in effect, operated a government-within-
a-government before independence.

One generally respected authority, one universally understood institution did exist: "our beloved Sultan." As the symbol of the
Moroccan nation and as Imam, as a man known for his fairness
and firmness, his wisdom and integrity, Mohammed V could ex-

pect allegiance from politicians and *résistants*, from bourgeois and tribesmen. A shrewd politician, legally the unfettered depository of all sovereign powers, responsible for both the enactment and execution of laws, his power was unmatched by that of any individual or group in the country. The Council of Ministers was chosen by and responsible to him alone, as were the Imperial Cabinet and Secretariat General that comprised his personal administrative staff.*

A. King Mohammed and the Parties

Although there were no legal limitations on his power, Mohammed V could not have played the role of traditional Oriental despot, whatever his wishes. Even the least sophisticated among Morocco's nationalist groups would have revolted against a ruler who did not at least appear to be benevolent and progressive, particularly at a time when Arab nationalists in other countries were overturning monarchies. To Mohammed V, who felt a genuine sense of responsibility toward his subjects, a major consideration was the fact that the Istiqlal was strong enough to be of help in mobilizing the country behind progressive reforms, but also sufficiently powerful to block the implementation of royal decrees if he denied it an active role in charting Morocco's future. Recognizing both these positive and negative strengths of the major party, the Sultan had given it the leading place in his Council of Ministers and most of the choice local administrative posts. However, recognizing that its will was far from law throughout the country and realizing also that his own power depended inversely on that of the Istiqlal, he had insisted on diluting its strength by giving representation in the Council to all "nationalist viewpoints." The old alliance between the Sultan and the Istiqlal, born of mutual dependence, was thus gradually weakened as their differing interests became paramount. A struggle between the palace and the

* For several years after the end of the Protectorates, the subordinate administrative structure corresponded largely to the directorates and services that existed under the former regimes. In the bled, the traditional tribal structure continued to be the basis of local administration, while the French and Spanish regional administrations were transformed into provinces, headed by governors appointed by the Sultan. A new rural office, the supercaid, was created in 1957 to supervise local officials (500 caids and khalifas) in specified areas. The rural commune that ultimately developed under government sponsorship was patterned after the traditional djemaa, but was based on a division of the nation's 700 tribes into units that took into consideration economic viability, political manageability, and ethnic harmony.

more dynamic Istiqlal leaders ensued, with other political elements generally forced to side with one or the other major contestant in Morocco's special form of two-party politics.

Since independence had transformed the Istiqlal leaders from nationalists to politicians, personal differences and ambitions began to emerge beneath the cloak of patriotism. The "dosage" arrangement in the first Council of Ministers was tolerable to men such as Balafrej, who were familiar with multi-party rule and in any event were not personally committed to radical economic or social changes. Al-Fassi and his disciples, however, who had refused to participate in the original coalition cabinet, felt that a strong one-party government would combine the best of Moroccan-Muslim traditions with the most efficient means of building a modern state and removing the last vestiges of colonialism. These views, with republican and socialist ideas replacing al-Fassi's traditionalist concepts, were shared by younger Istiqlal members, led by Ben Barka, Bouabid, and the UMT leadership.

The lack of material accomplishment by the Bekkai government, which the Istiqlal could conveniently blame on the PDI economics ministers, encouraged more aggressive Istiqlal leaders outside the government to demand a change. Eventually, the Istiqlal members of the government, fearful of weakening their own positions within the party, were forced to concur in these demands. In early August, 1956, militant Istiqlal spokesmen openly attacked the government for its failure to launch a program that could "capture the enthusiasm of the masses." The Istiqlal's alleged membership of 2 million (compared with the PDI's 150,000) gave some support to the claim that only its leaders could effect a democratic revolution to replace colonialism. The UMT Council then demanded a "homogeneous" government and attacked the incumbent one for exorbitant administrative expenses, lack of progress toward social equality, a static level of employment, and the rising cost of living. It also asked for measures to assure protection against foreign commercial and financial interests.

At the end of August, an Istiqlal congress in Rabat moved to withdraw its members from the government, which "had lost sight of national goals," and to petition the Sultan to entrust to a "capable team" of Istiqlal ministers the powers needed to effect sweeping changes. Balafrej led the attack on Si Bekkai and the PDI ministers and also presented a program, which had been drawn up mainly by al-Fassi and Ben Barka. In the following days, al-Fassi toured the nation to rally diverse groups behind the Istiqlal's platform of an Arab-Muslim state and a "democratic constitutional monarchy." To Berbers, he stressed Moroccan unity under Islam; to Jews, he promised equality and individual liberties; to all, he declared that the Istiqlal desired power only to fulfill its program for the good of the country. At one point, his car was the target of bullets from an unknown source, but, uninjured and seemingly undisturbed, he continued his campaign. Si Bekkai answered the Istiqlal's attack by declaring that his government of "administration and negotiation" had not yet completed its work, and that, since its program embraced all national activities and forces, the government could not be entrusted to one faction of the population. Since there had been no popular election, he maintained that no political group could as yet claim hegemony.

The PDI supported the premier and called the Istiqlal's program dictatorial and unacceptable. The PDI Minister of Finance, Abdelkader Benjelloun, saying that his party would join the opposition only if forced to do so, charged that terror and repression had already swept the country and that the Istiqlal controlled the police and had used "fascist" methods in detaining several PDI leaders without charges. (These accusations were not without some basis in fact, since the lack of written guarantees for civil rights or liberties in effect left citizens at the mercy of security forces, and the latter, under Istiqlal influence, had singled out several PDI activists as public enemies.) He then called for free elections for a representative assembly. Although it seemed certain that the Istiqlal could win a majority and that the Sultan would not yet permit such elections, the PDI hoped to win support by posing as the champion of "democracy."

Additional opposition to the Istiqlal was voiced by ex-Minister of Interior Lyoussi, and by the French press. Lyoussi attempted to rally the Berber tribesmen, and also to court royal favor, by calling for unity in support of the Sultan and for "country above party." The opposition voiced by the French papers led Ben Barka, editor of the Istiqlal's French-language weekly *al-Istiqlal*, to demand legislation setting out the obligations of the foreign press in an independent state.

Two other political groups also asked for a united stand against the threat of Istiqlal dictatorship. One of these, the Democratic Front, was an insignificant PDI protégé. The Liberal Independents, however, led by Rashid Mouline; the Minister of Defense, Guedira; and Rabat's Governor Mahjoub Ahardane, enjoyed the support of the palace and of urban intellectuals, although it may not have had the membership of 50,000 that it claimed.

Unwilling to accept the Istiqlal's demands, the Sultan temporized, simultaneously and subtly spreading the notion that he alone stood above politics and should retain hegemony over all parties. Prince Moulay Hassan announced that the government crisis could be resolved only by the Sultan, who alone fully understood its cause and could end it at the appropriate time. The Sultan himself told Istiqlal ministers privately that he would not accept their resignations at that time, but he promised publicly to study their proposals. Unwilling to risk openly antagonizing him, the Istiqlal agreed to await his decision—thus enhancing the ruler's position. The Sultan added to his popularity in August by agreeing to form a Consultative Assembly, a promise that implied he had no desire to monopolize political power.

Many rumors, including one predicting a cabinet of technocrats headed by M'Hammedi, circulated during the following weeks. Impatient Istiqlal and UMT leaders could do little but foment demonstrations against French Army actions in order to dramatize their demands for a strong government. The PDI, on the other hand, sponsored a "National Front Congress" at the end of September to protest what it called a police regime, and in October it held its own first National Congress, after which it speciously claimed to have increased its membership by 80 per cent since the end of the Protectorate. Four PDI members of the Cabinet—Cherkaoui, Ahmed Ben Souda, Thami Ouazzani, and Abdelkader Benjelloun—then toured the Middle Atlas to campaign against one-party government. An automobile accident, an occupational hazard of Moroccan politicians since 1956, almost deprived the party of its leading representatives, but none was permanently injured.

Finally, following France's "air piracy" of the five rebel Algerian leaders in October, 1956, and the riots in Meknes, the Sultan permitted the first government to resign in order to give the Istiqlal a better opportunity to assist the monarchy in handling the crisis. While not precisely to the Istiqlal's specifications, the change met its major objective: although Bekkai remained premier, the PDI was eliminated from the cabinet,* which was thereafter composed of eight Istiqlal members and six independents; the post of Minister of Habous (religious groups) was temporarily vacant. (The PDI had been offered the ministries of Housing and Information

---

* For the first few years, the PDI increasingly resorted to a demagoguery that changed with every wind, accusing the Istiqlal of being fascists and leftists, Francophiles and Francophobes, pro-Cairo and anti-Arab. During this period, the PDI remained the principal political opposition in most urban areas but its national influence steadily decreased. In 1960, it reorganized as the Constitutional Democratic Party, but with no more success.

but declined them on the ground that the offer did not recognize the party's political strength.) At the same time, a three-member Private Council of the Throne, whose members were to consult with and advise the Sultan in his executive capacity, was established.

Only two new faces appeared among the ministers in the reorganization, but several officeholders changed posts. The most sweeping change was in the consolidation of several offices, particularly those that were combined in the Ministry of National Economy. To aid him in the heavily burdened and extremely important post of minister of this enlarged department, Abderrahmin Bouabid appointed two undersecretaries.

While the Sultan personally assumed the delicate task of mending fences with France, the ministers of the second government focused their attention on the pressing problems of re-establishing the confidence of European settlers after the Meknes riots, of trying to improve the deteriorating fiscal and economic situations, and of staffing the growing administration with qualified personnel. At the same time, a number of Istiqlal leaders continued to put pressure on the Sultan for further democratization of the government.

A short step in the direction of constitutional monarchy was taken in November, with the debut of the Consultative Assembly, an embryo parliament created mainly to give a small number of Moroccans some experience in public affairs. Its seventy-six members were drawn from all walks of life, on the theory that this would encourage the voicing of many opinions. However, the democratic aspect of the Assembly was limited by the fact that its members were selected by the Sultan, and its powers were limited to advising the monarch on national policy, propounding questions to government officials, and scrutinizing the national budget. These factors, moreover, limited the influence and interest of political parties in the new body.

Scheduled to meet twice yearly, with extraordinary sessions as needed, the Consultative Assembly first convened on November 12. Ben Barka's subsequent election as President of the Assembly, with Mahjoub Ben Seddik as Vice President, transformed the Assembly into a forum for more progressive Istiqlal-UMT ideas but otherwise accomplished little, since the Sultan was not compelled to heed its suggestions. In 1959, when twenty-two members of the progressive factions resigned in protest of the body's shallow role, the ailing assembly died.

The basic question of how to channel and express popular opinion in the political system thus remained open, despite the fact

that, in his Throne Speech of 1956, the Sultan had promised that
"we will follow the natural process by ordering first of all municipal and rural elections, then the creation of regional assemblies,
and finally the establishment of a Constitutional Assembly to draw
up a constitution in the framework of a constitutional, Arab,
Muslim, democratic monarchy." At first, there was general agreement in principle that municipal and rural elections should precede elections on the national level, in order to teach inexperienced voters the fundamentals of the democratic process. The first
Bekkai government had been asked by the Sultan to prepare for
such elections, but it had been diverted by more pressing matters.
Subsequent delays were due to Istiqlal insistence on election procedures that would assure sweeping electoral victories for their
party; to minority parties' reluctance to accept procedures that might
permit an Istiqlal triumph and their repeated demands for guarantees of civil liberties that would permit fair elections; and to
difficulties in deciding on such technical matters as size and numbers of electoral districts, requirements for voters, and methods of
election. That any progress was made at all was due largely to
Mohammed V, despite his attitude of furthering democracy at
levels that could not directly diminish his own powers.

Politically sophisticated persons agreed that Morocco should become a constitutional monarchy, with the true separation of powers
that the Sultan himself had proposed in his Throne Speech of 1955,
and with an elected national parliament. Political leaders differed
sharply, however, on when, how, and by whom this constitutional
monarchy was to be achieved. The Sultan's repeated promises of
local elections, announced early in 1957 for that year, did not result in rapid action, and he felt no compulsion to commit himself
to any timetable at all for national elections. He feared, evidently,
any steps that would entrust too much responsibility too soon to
inexperienced persons, whether potential voters or the delegates
they would elect. In this general view, he was supported by Balafrej, who considered a strong monarchy an indispensable guarantee
of stability and unity, and to a lesser extent by al-Fassi, an autocrat
in his own way. The progressive wing of the Istiqlal, headed by
Ben Barka, Bouabid, and Ibrahim, was less patient. It was unsym-
pathetic to monarchy in principle, although it dared not attack the
Sultan, and wished to move as rapidly as possible toward a government in which major decisions would not rest or even be shared
with the crown. The PDI, fearing to antagonize the palace with
too much talk of "democracy" but also fearing that it might lose
what support it retained if it did not advocate reforms, said little.

Even had there been agreement as to the time for initiating particular changes, opinions still varied as to who should institute them. Should the task of writing a constitution be left to the Sultan, the only repository of legal power, or to a popularly elected constituent assembly, as the progressives advocated? Whatever the duties assigned to this national body, how would its membership be chosen? By universal, male, or limited male suffrage? By direct or indirect election? Mohammed V and Balafrej, both fathers of unveiled and educated daughters, were theoretically as willing as Istiqlal progressives eventually to accept universal suffrage. Al-Fassi, by contrast, while radical on other issues, recommended literacy requirements for voting and restriction of the franchise to men. These questions were widely debated, but neither the government nor the Istiqlal was able to formulate definite plans; as a result, events moved along the path the palace preferred.

In July, 1957, the Sultan formally invested Moulay Hassan as Crown Prince, a "progressive" or "Westernizing" step that broke with Muslim tradition (the Sultan was supposed to be appointed by the ulema) while significantly bolstering the Prince's position.

The eldest son of Mohammed, Moulay Hassan had studied law at the University of Bordeaux and had earned a doctorate in France. A young man (twenty-nine years old) of abundant charm, wit, and energy, he was thoroughly modern in outlook. During the struggle for independence, he was extremely popular with the young people of his country, although republican nationalist elements regarded him with strong reservations. In the following month, Mohammed V also changed his own title from Sultan to King (without otherwise altering his dominant position) and the official name of the country from Sherifian Empire to Kingdom of Morocco. This was recognized as merely a token change by most Istiqlal leaders, however, and by the fall of 1957 they decided to force the creation of a homogeneous regime.

The popular mandates given single parties in other Arab and African countries incited in dynamic ministers such as Bouabid a resentment of their own incapacity even to seek such a mandate. The fact that Tunisia's Constituent Assembly had been able to overthrow the Bey of Tunis in July only aggravated their grievance. Furthermore, they were by this time irked by the King's plan to subordinate national to local elections, a procedure they regarded more as a means of forestalling a devolution of power than as an expedient to give voters some electoral experience. Finally, the party as a whole had been disturbed by the development during the year of the rural-based Popular Movement.

The Popular Movement—whose official spokesman was Professor Haddou Riffi of Alhucemas, but whose prime movers actually were Lachen Lyoussi, Mahjoub Ahardane, and the former Liberation Army leader Abd el-Krim Khatib—augured organized political opposition in the bled, where the Istiqlal had been trying on its part to enroll young people. Since the Popular Movement was strongest in the Middle Atlas, the home of many members of the Saharan Liberation Army, it also threatened to withdraw the loyalty of the guerrilla army from al-Fassi, who was at that time stepping up his irredentist program to extend Morocco's southern borders down to St. Louis, in Senegal. Al-Fassi's campaign, which aroused popular resentment against the Spanish and the French, was extremely useful to all factions of the Istiqlal and to the King: it diverted dissatisfaction with domestic conditions from the ministers responsible for them, as well as from the palace, and at the same time encouraged militants to demand stronger and more radical measures against the internal and external opponents of progress. What might have remained exclusively a foreign-policy issue in the Sahara thus became, with the conflict between al-Fassi and the Popular Movement, a domestic issue as well.

During November, 1957, in this atmosphere of popular unrest and sharpening political ambitions, the Istiqlal ministers began their power play by causing the government to declare the Popular Movement illegal on the ground that it had been organized without official permission in violation of an unrepealed dahir of 1917. Interior Minister M'Hammedi explained that the move was designed to maintain order and respect for law. The fact that the law in question was "colonial" in origin made little difference on this or other occasions when repressive measures seemed opportune. The Istiqlal paper *al-Alam* even added that this dahir preserved the principles of a healthy democracy, since a multiplicity of parties constituted an obstacle to national stability!

The next major round in the Istiqlal's fight for one-party government occurred in February, 1958, when the government banned public speeches, meetings, and demonstrations and suspended all PDI daily and weekly newspapers. Ostensibly, the action was taken to prevent anti-French demonstrations protesting the bombardment by French airplanes of Sakiet Sidi Youssef, a Tunisian village. However, the government was planning to draft an election law and to designate local election committees; the ban was imposed when the PDI assailed these moves as steps designed to "rig" an election and to circumvent its demand for the creation of a committee of all parties to formulate this legislation. Furthermore, the government's arbitrary act was questioned by the very Frenchmen it allegedly sought to protect.

These complaints did not disturb the Istiqlal, however, since it seemed to be gaining political ground through its anticolonial and irredentist policies. In a speech in February at M'Hammedi-les-Gazelles ("the gateway to the Sahara"), the King had for the first time officially demanded the "return" of Mauritania, seconding the irredentist Istiqlal position. On the other hand, the PDI and Popular Movement spokesmen who protested government "totalitarianism" enjoyed little support. Many were arrested, and some who attended now forbidden meetings were fired upon by security forces. When Premier Bekkai, in a final attempt to prevent one-party rule, approved a PDI complaint to the King, the Istiqlal ministers seized the opportunity to resign. On April 15, after eighteen months in office, the second government was officially dissolved by the crown.

The Istiqlal now renewed its demand for, and apparently expected to receive, a one-party mandate. However, the King, using the tactics of delay and diversion which had worked so well in the past, unhurriedly consulted all factions of opinion and made it clear that he intended to retain his freedom of action and choice. Several days later, he suddenly announced plans for a program of civil rights, political liberties, and constitutional procedures. The Istiqlal took up the cry for this "Bill of Rights," but the initiative had been seized by the King, an important victory. On May 8, 1958, the King proclaimed a Royal Charter that promised (a) the creation of communes to replace tribal structures as units of local administration and representation; (b) a Deliberative Assembly, to share legislative power with the King, whose members would be selected by communal and municipal councils, in turn to be elected by popular vote; (c) written clarification of the individual and collective responsibilities of the ministers, which implied a certain limited delegation of the King's executive authority; (d) a Bill of Rights allowing freedom of assembly, association, and speech; and (e) the eventual election by universal suffrage of a National Assembly. The charter was to be implemented by royal decree at an appropriate time. Finally, the King again called for early local elections.

On the next day, the King asked Balafrej to form a new government. It was to be composed predominantly of Istiqlal members, with one important exception: M'Hammedi, whose vigorous action against political opposition had aroused such strong protests, was to be replaced. As compensation to the Istiqlal, Mohammed V

ruled that the Defense Minister would replace Crown Prince Hassan as head of the Royal Army. This compromise enabled the King
to appear progressive and statesmanlike and gave to the Istiqlal
what was in many ways only an empty victory.

The decision of Prime Minister Balafrej and the Istiqlal "conservatives" to accept the King's program, thus tacitly approving a
policy of gradual political and economic change, brought them
into sharp conflict with the "progressives," who sought to erect
new mass-based political institutions and to inaugurate centralized
and somewhat socialized economic planning. The progressives, led
by Ben Barka, went openly to the attack. The conservatives forced
Ben Barka to resign his post as editor of *al-Istiqlal*. With the intra-
party split absorbing much of its energies, with goals and programs
no more clearly defined than those of previous regimes, and with
no desire to espouse radical measures, the Balafrej government
was as unsuccessful as its predecessors in strengthening the popularity of the party. Even increased Royal support for the irredentist
issue did little to help its sponsors. On the contrary, the fact that
the Istiqlal now controlled the Council of Ministers and the administration, the scope of whose functions was steadily increasing,
sorely aggravated existing popular dissatisfaction with the party in
particular and overcentralized authority in general.

The Balafrej government revealed its inability to come to grips
with the major problems facing the country by diverting attention
to minor concerns. For example, it bore down on the Moroccan
Communist Party, arresting a dozen members for questioning and
raiding party headquarters in Casablanca. The MCP, which had
been banned in 1952, had been unofficially tolerated after the
Protectorate until it was formally declared legal early in 1958, a
move based in part on the recognition that its influence was very
limited and in part on the MCP's decision not to espouse aggressive policies. Most Moroccan political leaders recognized the
MCP's dual loyalties, but international considerations and its confidence that it could keep Communist aims in check persuaded the
government to allow the MCP to pursue certain limited activities.
The action of the Balafrej regime therefore reflected its own
weakness more than the strength of the MCP.

The failure of Balafrej and his new Minister of the Interior
Chiguer to end the revolt in the Rif precipitated the most serious
crises in both the government and in the Istiqlal. Protesting the lack
of firmness in the government's handling of the situation and in dealing with the country's economic problems, Bouabid resigned as
Minister of National Economy. He and Ben Barka, Abdullah

Ibrahim, and Thami Ammar then launched another bitter attack against the conservative wing of the Istiqlal—Balafrej and his son-in-law Mohammed Douiri, Omar Abdeljalil, the Lyazidi brothers, and their followers—and demanded a new regime that would give greater representation to labor and to former resistance leaders. With superior strength among the intellectuals, labor unions, resistance veterans, and student organizations, the progressives were able to swing the balance of power. Al-Fassi's efforts to prevent a deep split between the wings were futile, for he had little rapport with the younger activists, and the latter had no intention of compromising. After achieving no more than the promulgation of a Bill of Rights, Balafrej resigned as Premier and the King spent the next few weeks in seeking a leading independent or Istiqlal conservative, of which faction al-Fassi now became the leading representative, to head a new government. On December 16, after repeated failures to find someone who would risk survival in such muddied political waters, he finally asked Ibrahim, in his "personal" capacity and not as a leader of the Istiqlal progressives, to form a cabinet of "technicians" rather than politicians. Ibrahim himself assumed the posts of Premier and Foreign Minister, with the understanding that his main task was to prepare for municipal and communal elections and that his term would be a limited one. He designated Bouabid as Vice Premier and Minister of National Economy, M'Hammedi once again as Minister of Interior, and Thami Ammar as Minister of Agriculture.

The political victory of the progressives soon proved a hollow one, since it led, not to their control over the Istiqlal, but to a final schism in the party's ranks. After five months of discussion, a committee representing both factions failed to agree on terms for holding the party congress proposed for January 11, 1959. Ben Barka resigned from the executive committee and called a special meeting of twelve Istiqlal sections in Casablanca for January 25. There, he attacked the old guard for "three years of weakness, negligence, and neglect" and proposed that the Istiqlal be reorganized as a "party of the masses" without the highly centralized control that had alienated younger members and contributed to the split in its ranks. Although Ibrahim and Bouabid preferred not to jeopardize their work in planning for the elections by taking a definite stand on this proposal, Ammar, Ben Seddik, and the Istiqlal's leading ex-resistance chief, Faik Mohammed Basri, immediately announced their support of Ben Barka. The following day, al-Fassi read the dissidents out of the party. The next several months witnessed vitriolic charges from both sides in their attempt to win over the rank and file, but neither achieved a definite success. The regime was able to accomplish little during this period; the only notable improvement in Morocco's internal situation, the abrupt ending of the Rif revolt, was due mainly to the King's efforts.

The following months of party strife were highlighted by al-Fassi's attempts to form "free" unions as a possible competitor to the UMT and by several violent incidents, the most notable of which occurred on April 24, when al-Fassi's friend, Abdel Ben Driss, a member of the Istiqlal's executive committee, was assassinated. The same day, al-Fassi officially ousted Ibrahim from the party, charging that his government's negligence was responsible for Ben Driss's death, and the UMT opened its second congress at Casablanca. Ibrahim and Bouabid were present; rioters from the free unions gathered outside.

In September, the dissidents formally baptized themselves the National Union of the People's Forces (UNFP), added a few strays from the PDI to their following, and assumed open opposition to the Istiqlal. Rejecting capitalism and favoring socialization of the means of production, industrialization, and agrarian reform, the UNFP clearly stated its objective as the transformation of Moroccan society through a "struggle for democracy and the conquest of power." Istiqlal stalwarts, personally vindictive against their former comrades and, in many cases, somewhat fearful of their radical ideas, tried to arrange an understanding with the palace. The King replied only that he welcomed their opposition to "socialism" and "radicalism." He also observed that the bickering caused public dissatisfaction with the politicians and provided him with reasons for placing himself still further above the political struggle. At the same time, like many others who were genuinely concerned about Morocco's future, he deplored the general confusion and unrest consequent on party dissension.

Further indications of basic instability were, in fact, not long in coming. In December, another small uprising occurred in the Rif; for his part in instigating the trouble, Basri was arrested and held for nearly six months. In February, 1960, eleven other UNFP leaders were arrested on charges of plotting to kill Prince Hassan. The following month, amid rumors that they would be arrested, several UNFP officials from the Marrakesh region fled to the Atlas after the police moved against "leftists." Those whom the authorities apprehended were detained; their less fortunate comrades were killed. Drawing obvious conclusions from these events, Ben Barka left the country in order to avoid arrest.

These sordid developments, which added rancor to the preparations for the forthcoming elections, also embittered relations between Ibrahim and the King. In addition to his long-standing objection to the Premier's demand for a national parliament and a constitution, the King blamed Ibrahim for negligence in apprehending the plotters against his son's life. Ibrahim in turn resented the King's apparent collaboration with M'Hammedi, which bypassed him, and suggested that the accusation of complicity in the plot and other charges leveled at UNFP members were fabrications. He had little opportunity to push his case, however, for on May 20 he was retired from office on the ground that the mission for which he had been appointed was accomplished.

Four days later, after publicly claiming that the selfishness and ineptitude of the politicians were responsible for Morocco's chronic unrest, Mohammed V took the extraordinary step of assuming the premiership himself and naming his son Prince Hassan as Vice Premier and Minister of Defense. Portfolios in this "Royal Government" (or "Presidential Monarchy") were distributed among a few trusted Istiqlal, Liberal Independent, Popular Movement, and unaffiliated persons. Si Bekkai became Minister of the Interior while his predecessor, M'Hammedi, was shifted to Foreign Affairs. By simultaneously satisfying many of his urban supporters and neutralizing the key spokesmen of the rural opposition, the King evidently hoped to check the growth of the UNFP. His reliance on men whose political fortunes depended mainly on him rather than on popular support implies that he also expected firm allegiance from his cabinet. There was certainly nothing to unite this polyglot group other than a general respect for the establishment and a vague desire for orderly changes first in the economic and social, then in the political, spheres. Personalities had always been far more important in Morocco than programs or ideologies; no party had ever filled all the seats in a cabinet; and the last premier had officially headed a regime of technocrats, *à titre personnel*. An apolitical patchwork regime was therefore not without precedent, and it was now explained as a significant and necessary step to serve the people rather than satisfy ambitious politicians. Lest the UNFP capitalize on doubts concerning his democratic intentions, however, Mohammed V promised a Constituent Assembly in the near future and a constitution by the end of 1962.

The aim of keeping parties out of politics and politics out of elections was pursued in the nationwide elections on May 29, 1960. Assisted by noted French legal and technical advisers, the election committee had decided to enfranchise all citizens over twenty-one years of age and divide the country into 800 communes and municipalities, for which more than 300 local assemblies were to be established. From among 47,000 candidates (including ten women), 10,000 delegates were to be elected in 11,000 polling places by a total of 4.2 million registered voters (including 1.6 million women, many of whose husbands forced them to forgo what they regarded as a male prerogative); members of the civil service and armed forces were excluded. Democratic procedures yielded to certain peculiarities at the ballot box, as candidates were not permitted to list party affiliations. For voters unable to read the campaign literature or the ballots, candidates were identified by special colors.

The absence of party labels hardly concealed the candidates' politics from the 70 per cent of the electorate that turned out to vote, but it did serve in several ways to stunt the growth of party organizations, as the King had intended. For one thing, many simple people voting for the first time received the impression that candidates *should* be nonpartisan, that elections *can* be held without parties, and that parties serve no useful purpose other than perhaps to help their supporters through slush funds and influence. In the bled, for instance, voters took individualism seriously, and often voted for the candidate who, whatever his politics, was known not to drink or steal. Even where there was open discussion of his political affiliation, the candidate would try to identify himself with a party notable who was highly respected in the area, rather than with the party or its platform.

The lack of certainty regarding party affiliations of the winners also seemed to encourage exaggerated claims of victory and bitter charges of fraud and corruption on all sides, all of which reinforced the existing public distrust of politicians. Unofficial figures (whose compilers, when uncertain, apparently gave the Istiqlal the benefit of the doubt) gave the Istiqlal 44 per cent of the seats, the UNFP 23 per cent, and other groups and individuals the remaining 33 per cent. The UNFP carried far fewer communes than did the Istiqlal, as the King had hoped, but it did win in Casablanca, Rabat, and Tangier. The Istiqlal, as expected, carried Fez, al-Fassi's home town, and several Saharan Liberation Army strongholds.

In addition to its setback at the polls, the UNFP was significantly weakened during 1960 by a basic disagreement with the UMT. Several UMT leaders, fearful of becoming mere political tools of the UNFP and in certain cases nurturing high political ambition, proscribed pro-UNFP activity in the union locals and forbade political strikes. The latter decision deprived the UNFP of its principal means of wringing political and economic concessions from the government. However, the UNFP maintained its verbal offensive, publicly and behind the scene, against the forces of conservatism.

The King reacted to UNFP pressures in his usual way. First, he continued to advocate a more radical foreign policy than the UNFP, in order to be free by contrast to pursue a conservative domestic policy without being attacked as a reactionary. He repeated demands for the "return" of Mauritania, despite the fact that the French were then on the point of giving that territory its independence. Second, in November, he inaugurated the promised 78-man Constitutional Council, another "representative" advisory body with perhaps more prestige but certainly no more power than its predecessor.

Whether the new Council would have evolved into an effective consultative organ under King Mohammed's direction was a question never to be answered. On February 6, 1961, at 1:00 P.M., during minor nasal surgery, the monarch's heart stopped. While the tragedy stunned the nation, the individual most affected obviously was the thirty-two-year-old Crown Prince; he was promptly designated King Hassan II by a decree signed by the Government Council and the ulema.

B. *The Accession of King Hassan*

Hassan's eventual assumption of power had long been anticipated as creating a crisis for Morocco. Mohammed V had held the respect of the seasoned politicians and the adoration of the ordinary people, but Moulay Hassan possessed neither asset. He had ably pursued legal studies in France, but his reputed lack of discretion in affairs of both heart and pocketbook and his alleged lack of "spiritual" qualities had led Moroccans and foreigners alike to doubt that he could rule for very long, if indeed he succeeded in occupying the throne. But these prophecies overlooked the exceptional political acumen the Crown Prince had acquired since his student days, the disunity of his opponents, and the twist of fate that brought him to power at a time when France, preparing to shed her Algerian albatross, was ready to make marked concessions to Moroccan nationalism and pave the way for other countries to follow suit.

Hassan demonstrated his *savoir faire* immediately upon learning of his father's death. Before making the news public, he and Ahardane, soon to be named Minister of Defense, alerted the army and police to be on guard against any possible disturbances, which could even have included assassination attempts against the new ruler. Not until 6:oo P.M. did Hassan announce Mohammed V's death and his own accession to the throne. His caution was justified during and after the week of mourning that followed: Although the late King's funeral was attended by spokesmen for all progressive elements except Ben Barka, the UNFP formally boycotted the investiture of Hassan II to demonstrate their disapproval of the new sovereign. The snub, perhaps a bit too broad for the party's own good, was duly noted at the palace. To counter a possible outburst of republican sentiment, Hassan proceeded to polish his somewhat tarnished image through an intensive public-relations campaign. A highly successful visit to Casablanca, the center of the strongest existing and potential opposition, was followed by personal appearances elsewhere. While addressing the Casablanca Municipal Council, composed mainly of UNFP adherents, he declared that the government was giving priority to a vast public-works program designed to "promote real social democracy." Political democracy, he noted, while of "extreme importance," must follow later.

Hassan also lost no time in taking the initiative with those foreign countries which most influenced Morocco's domestic affairs. Following Mohammed V's funeral, he met with Ferhat Abbas, Premier of Algeria's Provisional Government, and the President of Tunisia, Habib Bourguiba. Shortly thereafter, he concluded an agreement with France whereby the latter promised to begin immediately to withdraw all regular troops from Morocco and to vacate her six remaining aviation training schools and stations by October. Paris also assured Morocco of renewed economic aid. Hassan, whose own promises to his subjects concerning reforms were rendered more convincing by these prospects, continued to emphasize that his "people's monarchy" could be trusted to provide the best in modern benefits while maintaining the proper respect for traditional Islamic values. In this heady climate, UNFP demands for political change via a new "transitional" government and an elected constituent assembly and its attack on French aid as neocolonialism had little popular appeal. Nevertheless, the party's continuing support among labor, students, and intellectuals made its unremitting attacks on "personal" rule a source of some concern to the new King.

On May 3, 1961, as a gesture toward devolving some of his power upon other officials, Hassan shifted many of his functions to Guedira by officially naming him Executive Director of the cabinet. Guedira, who had earned the new King's trust while working in the palace for several years prior to Mohammed V's deposition, thus capitalized on his realism, efficiency, and devotion to the crown to become the number-two man in the government. On June 2, the King announced further cabinet changes, obviously designed to cement the loyalty of the conservative parties and to isolate the UNFP in opposition: the King continued as Premier; Guedira held the key Interior and Agriculture ministries as well as being Executive Director of the cabinet; Douiri became Minister of National Economy; Mahjoub Ahardane was named Minister of Defense; Mouline and Khatib were Ministers of State; and al-Fassi finally entered the lists as a Minister of State. The Ministry of Foreign Affairs was temporarily left vacant while Balafrej, who would settle for nothing less, refused the Justice portfolio. Hassan Ouazzani was given the less significant title of Minister of State in charge of foreign affairs. The principal responsibility for conducting external relations, however, was left in the hands of the King.

A noteworthy indication of Hassan's *realpolitik* was his naming of Mohammed Fall Ould Omeir, former Mauritanian Emir of Trarza, as Minister of State for Mauritanian and Saharan Affairs. Mauritania had become a *cause célèbre* in Morocco ever since al-Fassi had made it the major target of his irredentist campaign. Ould's presence in the cabinet thus mollified supporters of the Istiqlal's expansionist program, while posing no genuine threat to Morocco's growing *rapprochement* with France. The move did little to satisfy the UNFP, however, which had been lukewarm to irredentism both because of its primary concern with modernizing Morocco and because the Mauritania issue was the child of the Istiqlal. The anticolonial overtones of the Ould appointment, on the other hand, vitiated some of UNFP's criticism of the government as being too pro-French.

Hassan also responded more directly to the plea for more democracy by issuing a "Fundamental Law" setting out the basic principles of government for Morocco.* The Fundamental Law stated that Morocco was "an Arab and Muslim kingdom . . . on its way to becoming a constitutional monarchy" and characterized the current political system as "a phase preceding the promulgation of a constitution." It also proclaimed the rights of individuals and the equality of all Moroccans and for the first time officially described the country's foreign policy as one of "nondependence."

The UNFP leaders loudly protested that this latest document, like its predecessors, created no new national political institutions,

* For the text of the Fundamental Law, see Appendix E.

set no date for elections for a representative assembly, and provided no real guarantee of civil liberties. They were also distressed about the provisions in Article VI for "the elimination of any obstacle" that might "thwart" the achievement of national goals. Lacking patronage and other favors to dispense to potential adherents, and fearing that general obstructionism, its primary means of exerting influence, might be further suppressed by determined advocates of Article VI, the UNFP resorted increasingly to raucous and often unconstructive criticism of the establishment.

The UMT also found little comfort from its anti-government position at that time. On May 13, 1961, the UMT newspaper *Avant Garde* accused Douiri of participating in, or at least tolerating, attempted corruption in handling the bids for a contract to construct a phosphate plant near Safi. Douiri filed a libel suit against the paper, but outside the courtroom the most notable result of the Safi scandal was the apparent strengthening of Hassan's determination to show that he would tolerate no stabs at the regime's weak spots or anything smacking of treason. This was demonstrated in August when the government brought to trial thirty-one men implicated in the February, 1960, plot against the regime and sentenced to death six Liberation Army veterans, along with several other *accusés*. In October, judgment rendered in Douiri's case found for the plaintiff, and *L'Avant Garde* was ordered to pay a substantial fine and to print retractions in all major newspapers.

By contrast, the Istiqlal's support of the new King appeared to be paying some dividends, although it involved a parody of the postwar *entente* that had obtained with Mohammed V. After the great schism in 1959, party leaders had abandoned all hope of one-party rule, and, at the fourth meeting of the National Council of the party, al-Fassi formally wrote into the platform a statement that the Istiqlal never had and never would seek more than a majority voice in a democratic multi-party system. This represented a realistic recognition that the UNFP was undermining the Istiqlal's urban strength and that the Popular Movement, after regaining its legal status, was acquiring considerable strength in the bled. (The UNFP was also gaining ascendancy over various student groups, including the National Union of Moroccan Students, which remained faithful to the exiled Ben Barka, but which did not formally adhere to the new party for fear of losing such favors as government scholarships.) Under the circumstances, the Istiqlal would have been satisfied to retain a few responsible posts in a coalition cabinet. Accordingly, despite dissatisfaction with

Guedira's growing influence, the Istiqlal hoped that a spirit of compromise toward the King might gain it further favors. Balafrej, who had been irked by the King's independence of him, was mollified in December, 1961, when he was again named Foreign Minister. However, the still-proud al-Fassi continued to resent his secondary role in the government, although he generally voiced his complaints only in terms of the loyal opposition.

Partly to placate al-Fassi and his supporters, partly to obtain greater administrative efficiency, but mainly to create new dependents by a wider distribution of favors, Hassan changed the cabinet again in 1962. In March, he named Driss Slaoui Executive Director of the cabinet, thus relieving Guedira of some minor chores. On July 18, he created new portfolios, the most notable innovation being his creation of a Secretariat of State for the Interior, an office under Guedira's control. The new post relieved Guedira of the responsibility for certain administrative details, but did not detract from his power, particularly since it was filled by his close confidant, M'fadel Cherkaoui, the former Governor of Rabat. The expected complaints from the UNFP and protests from the Istiqlal were forgotten by the end of the summer, when the attention of Moroccans was riveted on developments in Algeria, which were becoming increasingly entwined with Moroccan internal politics.

Algeria had achieved independence in July, 1962. By the end of September, general elections for a Constituent Assembly had been held and rough blueprints for new democratic and socialist institutions adopted. Algeria thus accomplished more in terms of political evolution in two months than Morocco had achieved in six years. Inspired by these developments next door, the UNFP and UMT renewed their demands for sweeping reforms on the Algerian pattern and forthrightly criticized the slow pace at which their King and his selected French and Moroccan advisers were framing a Moroccan constitution. *Avant Garde* went so far as to print sinister references to the Yemeni rebels who had recently assassinated their Imam.

Such attacks by opposition papers resulted, in September, in the "mysterious" bombing of the left wing's printing plants. The UNFP charged the government with responsibility for the incident, which it called a callous mockery of earlier promises of freedom of expression. Statements of sympathy came even from the rival *al-Istiqlal*, an indication that the Istiqlal was concerned with the Interior Minister's apparent condoning of the bombings. Soon, however, fearing the specter of revolution, Istiqlal spokesmen resumed their praise of the monarch; later, *al-Istiqlal* also protested the coercive, "nondemocratic" Algerian elections and predicted turmoil among the "misguided" Algerian people.

King Hassan, fully cognizant of the threat to his throne posed by Algerian republicanism, proffered his friendship to the victorious Ahmed Ben Bella. He even minimized a potentially serious border incident in order to demonstrate to reformers both in and beyond Morocco that he wished the Algerian revolution well—provided, of course, that it remained outside his borders. At the same time, however, he also accelerated the preparation of the constitution, and on November 3, while the Istiqlal National Council was holding its fifth session, he informed al-Fassi that the promised document was ready. After two weeks of discussion with trusted politicians, and after several planned leaks to the public, the King chose the traditional holiday of November 18 to present to his people the constitution "that I have made with my own two hands." Simultaneously, his government made preparations for a referendum by which the people could accept or reject their ruler's "handmade" gift.

C. The Moroccan Constitution of 1962

The Moroccan Constitution is based in large part on the Gaullist French Constitution of 1958, which Hassan greatly admires, and on the Tunisian Constitution of 1959. It first sets forth the political, economic, and social rights of Moroccan citizens, including equal political rights for women; freedom of movement, speech, assembly, and association; inviolability of domicile; secrecy of communication; the right to work and strike; the right to an education; and the right to own property. These rights are not in all cases absolute, but subject to regulation by law.*

Clearly reflecting the interests of its maker, however, the constitution characterizes the King as the symbol of national unity and guarantor of the state and requires him to safeguard respect for Islam and the laws. Deviating from Islamic tradition, the crown and its rights are declared hereditary and transmitted through primogeniture, with provision for a regency in the case of a minor. The King's person is inviolable and sacred, in apparent contradiction to the Islamic tradition that condones the overthrow of a ruler under certain circumstances. The King's power includes the right to appoint and dismiss ministers at his pleasure; preside over the Council of Ministers, as well as the Supreme Council of Justice and the Supreme Council for National Reconstruction and Plan-

* For text of the Constitution, see below, Appendix F.

ning; submit legislation that has been approved or rejected by parliament to popular referendum; dissolve the Chamber of Representatives under specified conditions; address to the nation messages not subject to parliamentary debate; exercise regulatory authority in specified domains; command the armed forces; accredit foreign diplomats and ratify treaties; exercise the right of pardon; and declare a state of emergency and take "necessary" measures when such "events occur as may interfere with the functioning of constitutional institutions."

The realities of Moroccan politics are recognized by a clause prohibiting a single-party state and by a provision that cabinet ministers need not reflect the strength of the parties in parliament. Local administration is the responsibility of assemblies elected by the prefectoral, provincial, and communal units and of governors of prefects and provinces.

The parliament consists of a Chamber of Representatives and a Chamber of Councilors. Members of the former are elected for four years by direct universal suffrage. Members of the latter are chosen for six-year terms by and from colleges composed of members of prefectoral and provincial assemblies, municipal councilors, and chambers of agriculture, commerce and industry, artisans, and trade-union representatives. Matters subject to legislation include individual rights; fundamental principles of civil and penal law; judicial organization; and basic guarantees to state officers. Other matters are subject to regulation. However, parliament may authorize the government, for a limited period and for a definite purpose, to decree measures normally in the legislative domain. Between sessions of parliament, the government may issue decrees with the approval of appropriate commissions, subject to ratification by the next session of parliament. Texts existing in legislative form prior to the constitution may be modified by decree only when they concern matters within regulatory authority. The government may declare unconstitutional any bill it regards as in conflict with the basic law, and its decision can be upset only by the Constitutional Board of the Supreme Court.

The Prime Minister and members of parliament may initiate legislation, which becomes law when approved by a simple majority vote of both houses. If the two houses cannot agree on an identical text or if the government declares a matter urgent after only one reading of a bill, the general question is submitted to the Chamber of Representatives, which may adopt it by a two-thirds majority, leaving the exact language to be determined by the King. Parliament also has the authority to declare war or impose martial law. The Chamber of Representatives can, with an absolute-majority vote, force the government to resign by a motion of censure or by a refusal of confidence when requested. Censure may be called for only once a year.

The relative positions of the King and parliament are established by the right of the King to refer legislation to referendum or to return it to parliament for another reading; by his authority to let a bill die by not affixing his seal; and by his power to dissolve the Chamber of Representatives after consultation with the President of the Constitutional Board and after informing the nation. If, in a referendum, the people approve a measure rejected by parliament, the Chamber of Representatives is dissolved; the succeeding Chamber may not be dissolved for a year after its election.

The Council of Ministers, or Cabinet, supervises the execution of the laws and may exercise such regulatory power as the constitution does not expressly reserve to the King. It must also adopt the national economic plan, which the Supreme Council for National Reconstruction and Planning formulates, and submit it to Parliament for approval.

The judicial authority, officially independent of legislative and executive power, is exercised by native magistrates trained in the National Institute of Judicial Studies and appointed for life from a list drawn up by the Supreme Council of Justice. This Council, presided over by the King, includes the Minister of Justice, the Chief Justice, the Attorney General, the President of the First Chamber of the Supreme Court, and six representatives elected from their own ranks by magistrates of the ordinary tribunals. The Constitutional Board of the Supreme Court, over which the Chief Justice presides, includes a magistrate of the Administrative Board of the Supreme Court and a professor from the School of Law, both appointed by royal decree for six years, as well as two members appointed respectively by the President of the Chamber of Representatives and the President of the Chamber of Councilors at the beginning of each legislative term. This board exercises certain prerogatives under the constitution, rules on the right of members of parliament to hold their seats, and conduct all referendums.

The constitution may be amended on the initiative of the Prime Minister and parliament. A projected amendment is formulated in the Council of Ministers and debated in both houses, where it must be adopted by an absolute majority of the members before submission to referendum. The monarchy and provisions relating to the Muslim religion are not subject to constitutional amendment.

In sum, Morocco's first constitution formally established the state as a "social, democratic, and constitutional monarchy" with the emphasis on the monarchy. Recognizing the existing power structure and the post-1955 tendency to deliberation, the constitution established the relatively new principle of separation of powers without creating any balance among them. This tended to emphasize the King's political power and his already significant spiritual authority. As in the past, Morocco thus remains in large part legally dependent on the personal capacity of the ruling monarch.

In keeping with the palace-to-people theme, a popular referendum on the proposed constitution was scheduled for December 7, 1962. In order to simplify their tasks, voters were to answer **Yes** or No to only one question: "Do you approve of the draft constitution?" To assure a respectable turnout and the proper response, the regime first sought to register as many as possible of the 5.5 million Moroccan citizens over the age of twenty-one. A disgruntled former UNFP leader, Abdelhai Boutaleb, was named Minister of Information and put in charge of a propaganda barrage that included the distribution of radios and television sets to public places and virulent anti-opposition attacks spearheaded by *Les Phares,* Guedira's paper. In addition, new governors loyal to the King were appointed to administer such potential centers of opposition as Casablanca, where they were to entice UNFP adherents with promises of a better future.

The Istiqlal, in what was to be its last show of support for Hassan, did most of the active campaigning for the constitution, which was supported also by the Popular Movement, the Liberal Independents, and the Constitutional Democratic Party (the erstwhile PDI). The UNFP, the last of the five parties authorized by royal decree to campaign, advocated a boycott on the ground that the proposed constitution did little to enhance the concept of government by the people. The UMT, although noting that the document suffered from basic deficiencies, refused to support the UNFP boycott and remained uncommitted. This decision was part of the union's effort to strengthen its own position. Guedira had encouraged this attitude by picturing the important role a strong and independent union could play; other officials, such as the Minister of Labor, were more forceful in suggesting that power could be brought to bear against a belligerent union.

The Communist Party was the only group that vetoed the new constitution, marking the first time the MCP had directly opposed the monarchy. The reaction of the government and the Istiqlal to the Communist campaign of speeches, pamphleteering, and slogan-

writing against the Constitution was quick and pointed. The
Istiqlal denounced the MCP for opposing the constitution because it proclaimed Islam as a state religion, and this led to a wave
of anti-Communist sentiment, highlighted by tactics reminiscent
of those of the late United States Senator Joseph McCarthy. For
example, when Sheik Mohammed Ben Larbi, a traditionalist and
former member of the King's Court Council, condemned the constitution because it would give the executive legislative powers, *Les
Phares* stated that the Moroccan patriarch had evidently been in-
fected by the virus of Communism.

Assisted by loyal new governors in provinces where the UNFP's
ideological strength could be offset by popular reliance on government representatives for bread and butter; by a massive communications campaign on government and private facilities; by the proclamation of election day as a paid national holiday; by the alerting of
the troops in Rabat; and, finally, by beautiful weather, the King's
efforts paid off handsomely at the polls. Of 4.6 million registered
voters, 3.8 million turned out, 3.7 million of whom cast the white
ballots indicating Yes. In other words, about 80 per cent of all
registered voters and perhaps 95 per cent of those voting heeded
their sovereign's wishes. Even Casablanca met government expectations, thanks partly to the large numbers of women who were
encouraged to use their new prerogative. While the disgruntled
UNFP charged corruption and coercion at the polls, the triumphant Hassan began making plans for local elections and promised
that the newly accepted "democratic institutions" would materialize the following November.

D.   *The Front for the Defense of Constitutional Institutions*

The prospects for putting Morocco's political house on some
firmer democratic foundations were never better, but the old
rivalry between the palace and the politicians again emerged as an
obstruction. While the King had benefited by the Istiqlal's campaign on behalf of the constitution, the Istiqlal itself had profited
equally, for in praising the King's achievements since independence, Istiqlal politicians likewise lauded their own accomplishments. Simultaneously, they had had the opportunity to examine
promising party recruits and test the effectiveness of their campaign techniques. The immediate result of their success was to
arouse apprehension in the highest ruling circle and to lead King
Hassan to contemplate steps to prevent a renaissance of the party
before future elections were held.

Suspecting that the King was considering a reorganization of the cabinet which would be unfavorable to the Istiqlal, al-Fassi decided to rally popular strength behind the party by dramatizing its claim to be the stanch defender of faith and country. An opportunity presented itself in the activities of an "alien" religious sect, the Bahai, which was beginning to attract attention and some converts among younger intellectuals and professional people, particularly in Nador. The attractiveness of the movement stemmed from its belief in world brotherhood (a factor in its recent appeal in certain parts of Africa), the dedication of its organizers, and the vitality of its discussions, which contrasted sharply with the small concern in Morocco with the possibility of modernizing Islam. It is also probably true, as some Moroccan spokesmen have claimed, that many of the new converts to Bahaism were unfortunate youths who had grown up during a troubled period in which they had no opportunity really to study Islam. An incident was created with the discovery of a "plot," announced in a provocative article in *al-Istiqlal*, allegedly to overthrow the government, subvert religion, and disrupt public order. On December 16, 1962, the regional tribunal at Nador, under the jurisdiction of the Istiqlal Minister of Justice, M'Hammed Boucetta, sentenced three of the accused Bahaists to death, five to life imprisonment, and one to ten years' imprisonment.

Unwilling to let the Istiqlal make political capital of this supposed threat to Morocco's security and faith, Interior Minister Guedira used the pages of *Les Phares* to denounce the tribunal's judgment, declaring that its action contravened Morocco's guarantees of religious liberty and could set a precedent for discrimination against Christians or Jews. The Istiqlal and its papers contended that Bahaism was not a religion, since it advocated secular, international substitutes, not only for the Koran and for Mecca, but also for loyalty to the Islamic country of Morocco.

The widely publicized affair was now considered in a cabinet meeting, and the King appointed a commission consisting of the ministers of Interior, Justice, and Islamic Affairs, to investigate. The two Istiqlal ministers saw to it that the commission's report confirmed the action of the Nador tribunal, whereupon Guedira used *Les Phares* to attack the report. At this point, the extraordinary volume of criticism abroad prompted King Hassan to broadcast reminders that the constitution conferred on him the power to reprieve the condemned. The controversy gradually lessened; nothing was done in the next few months, and popular attention was soon diverted elsewhere. However, in December, 1963, the Supreme Court reversed the convictions of the Bahaists on the ground that there existed no law under which persons could be tried for attempting to convert Muslims to another faith.

With the cabinet split over the Bahai affair, the King announced that he was indeed considering some changes at the Istiqlal's expense. Al-Fassi, Douiri, and Boucetta conferred with the Istiqlal's executive committee and decided they should resign rather than accept a humiliating loss of authority. When, on December 28, 1962, the King informed al-Fassi of his intention to discontinue the Ministry of National Economy, to make the Liberal Independent Driss Slaoui responsible for finances, and to move Douiri back to the Ministry of Public Works, the three Istiqlal ministers proffered their resignations, effective at the end of the year.

A few days later, another meeting of the National Council of the Istiqlal was called to explain the leaders' decision to the rank and file, which gave its approval and support. The party also proclaimed a new doctrine of egalitarianism, which contrasted sharply with its traditional policy to revive, rather than change, Moroccan society. This deviation reflected the party's growing responsiveness to the expectations of the masses in Morocco, as elsewhere in the "Third World." Al-Fassi explained the doctrine as Istiqlal socialism: it involved agrarian reform, nationalization of resources and means of production, social justice, and organization of the country into four sectors: nationalized, mixed, private, and cooperative. The Istiqlal leaders hoped that announcing this program in advance of the forthcoming elections would enhance the party's chances for popular vindication.

In the midst of preparations for what was to be an extremely bitter election, Prince Fall Ould Omeir, still Minister of Mauritanian and Saharan Affairs, quarreled with the King and Guedira over their now frequent hints of willingness to compromise on Mauritania's future now that Morocco's position had become a source of difficulty in diplomatic affairs. Apparently concluding that he would receive no support from them in his effort to "liberate" his country, Fall Ould Omeir resigned his cabinet post at the beginning of March and returned to Mauritania, where he apparently hoped to engage in more direct activities. His ambitions, whatever their precise nature, were, however, doomed, for he was arrested shortly after crossing the border into his native land. Al-Fassi thereupon charged that the Moroccan Government had deserted the cause, urged a plebiscite for Mauritania, and thus created an additional issue against Hassan's regime.

The odds against both the Istiqlal and the UNFP, however, were growing stronger, due mainly to Guedira's plan to organize a political "third force." This plan, which had King Hassan's tacit support, called for mobilizing many dissatisfied conservative elements and the largely uncommitted rural populace behind the King. This had been in the back of Guedira's mind ever since he launched the public-works program Promotion Nationale in the fall of 1961.* By the spring of 1963, his aides in the Agricultural and Interior ministries had built up considerable support among persons they had assisted in the bled, while the backing of most of the army officers, the police, and many civil servants was assured. Other aid was promised by the smaller parties, notably the Popular Movement, that heretofore had enjoyed little political influence, by businessmen, and by politicians disappointed in their former party affiliations. Guedira even expected to obtain some help from the UMT and implied that it would be given preferential treatment vis-à-vis the pro-Istiqlal UGMT † in exchange for continued non-alignment with the UNFP. On March 30, 1963, therefore, he confidently announced the creation of the Front pour la Défense des Institutions Constitutionelles (FDIC), or Front for the Defense of Constitutional Institutions.

A "front" rather than a genuine "party," this inchoate mass was firmly united only in its general support of the palace, which its various members considered the most certain source of support for their respective group or individual interests. Nevertheless, the FDIC announced a program advocating constitutional monarchy, freedom, economic liberalism, Maghrib unity, reform of the agrarian, fiscal, and commercial structure, equitable distribution of national revenue, and recovery of colon lands.

In a further attempt to destroy the two most powerful political parties, the government announced on April 18 that the forthcoming elections, to be held on May 17, would be for representatives to the House of Representatives, rather than for the expected municipal posts and consultative bodies such as chambers of commerce. The switch was obviously motivated by Guedira's desire to compete with neither the UNFP nor the Istiqlal for seats in local councils, where they were already entrenched, but to hold an election whereby candidates could choose the districts in which they wished to run. With the scenario and the staging so firmly controlled by the FDIC and the latter openly, though not officially, backed by the palace, Guedira's Front expected to carry two-thirds of the 144 contested seats on the claim that the King had replaced a "fumbling" party government with a program of expansion. Once

* See below, chap. 6, pp. 187–88.
† See below, chap. 7, p. 208.

again, however, Morocco gave the pundits some surprises. For one thing, news of a reported *entente* between Ben Seddik and Guedira leaked out to an angry UMT rank and file, upon whose insistence the union leadership took a last-minute stand in favor of the "progressive" candidates of the UNFP. During the campaign, which officially opened on May 2, the UMT denounced the elections as "a masquerade of democracy" that sought to divert attention from genuine problems by fostering interest in a parliament without real powers. Rural support for the FDIC cracked when adherents of the Popular Movement balked at domination by city politicians and at the last minute supported independent local candidates. Furthermore, the King was unwilling to endorse FDIC candidates either collectively or individually or to give the Front unlimited use of propaganda media and other resources. The King's insistence on remaining above politics had the virtue of obviating too great a dependence on Guedira and the Front, but it also weakened pro-Throne FDIC candidates in several areas. Finally, the government cause was hurt by the miscarriage of the Marrakesh conference of the Casablanca group of African nations planned for May 8.* Largely as a result of these unforeseen developments, a vitriolic campaign fought on nebulous issues and uncertain affiliations left the country's political future even more clouded than before.

A total of 3.5 million votes was cast for the 500 candidates, who included three Communists, two Jews, and one woman. The Front was expected to carry the 117 posts allotted to the rural areas, but it won only 69 seats. Probably most humiliating were the losses sustained by seven of the nine cabinet members backed by the Front, including Ahardane and Abdelhai Boutaleb. Guedira alone triumphed, but not in his home town of Rabat; a shanty town outside Casablanca was the scene of his victory. The Istiqlal won 41 seats, showing its greatest strength in Marrakesh and Fez, but al-Fassi won by only 735 votes. The UNFP carried 28 seats, again finding its greatest support in Casablanca, Rabat, and Agadir; the winners included Bouabid in Rabat and Ben Barka in Kenitra. Among the losers was the lone woman, an Istiqlal candidate named Halima Ouarzzazi, who lost in Casablanca to the UNFP candidate; and the three Communists, one of whom, Chairman Ali Yata, lost to Meyer Obadia, president of the Jewish community in Casablanca, who was backed by the Front. Six independents gained the remaining "swing" seats.

The Front's failure was due in part to its inability to harmonize

---

* See below, chap. 8, pp. 241–44.

and smooth over the conflict between Ahardane and the Popular Movement on the one hand, and Guedira, the regional governors, and urban factions on the other. More important, however, was the superior organization of the Istiqlal and UNFP. Only the fact that these two major parties were unable to coordinate their efforts in the voting saved the Front from complete disaster.

The Front's poor showing in the parliamentary elections encouraged both parties to intensify their political attacks upon the FDIC and its leaders. In response, the government increased its efforts to weaken its opponents, even though this created doubts involving its intentions to establish constitutional rule. On May 17, four Istiqlal deputies and a mayor addressed a letter to the United States Embassy in which they accused the FDIC of buying votes with wheat donated by the Food for Peace Program and used in Promotion Nationale. The United States thereupon protested the incident, and the government's response was to arrest these five, despite the parliamentary immunity that the new constitution guaranteed four of them. It also brought libel suits against *La Nation* and *al-Alam* for printing the letter. On July 16, two weeks before the scheduled communal elections, police stormed a meeting of the UNFP National Council and arrested 130 of its party leaders, including Basri and Abderrahim Youssefi, a lawyer, who was a member of the UNFP Secretariat and the editor of the UNFP journal *Al Tahrir*; twenty-one elected members of the House of Representatives were also detained. Bouabid was arrested but later released. Ben Barka, who was in Cairo at the time, was charged with supplying funds to aid the plotters, and vague charges also implicated the United States and the United Arab Republic. One month later, it was announced that the arrests were connected with a plot to overthrow the King and that the accused would be tried in a civil court. To offset charges that the government was detaining the suspects illegally and the police were treating them brutally, the Ministry of Justice declared that French and Algerian lawyers would be allowed to defend the accused and that they would be accorded "all the guarantees afforded by Moroccan law." The UNFP and Istiqlal responded with further charges, the former alleging that 5,000, and the latter 4,000, party members had been arrested. The National Union of Moroccan Students (UNEM) announced that thirty of its members, including its president, Hamid Merada, had been incarcerated.

The communal elections, held under this cloud on July 29, were ultimately to determine the composition of the upper house of parliament. Boycotted by both opposition parties and the UMT, which closed ranks once again with the UNFP over the issue of royal suppression, the elections resulted in an easy victory for the FDIC, which won 9,479 posts, compared with 1,091 for all other parties and independents combined. The Front announced that 71 per cent of the eligible voters had participated in the elections, but the Istiqlal ridiculed this claim. The Istiqlal daily newspaper *La Nation Africaine* deemed the Front's success a hollow victory, alleging that in some districts abstentions ran as high as 97 per cent.

E. New Developments

The dependency of Moroccan democracy upon the will or whim of the ruler, rather than of the ruled, was further revealed during a trial in 1963–64 of 100 Moroccans charged with plotting against the state and against the person of the King. These proceedings demonstrated even more clearly than the Bahai affair the weakness of the Moroccan judicial system and the shallowness of the concept of separation of powers when the King is involved. The proceedings began on November 23, 1963, before a regional criminal court in Rabat; seventeen of the defendants, including Mehdi Ben Barka, were to be tried *in absentia*. The government immediately moved to bar the French and Algerian defense attorneys, chosen by their clients because of their foreign nationality as well as their expertise, on the pretext of "extenuating" circumstances. William Thorp, one of the banned counsel, who was also President of the French Bar, declared that this violated the provisions of the Franco-Moroccan Judiciary Convention that gave French lawyers the right to practice before Moroccan courts. Disturbed by this obviously true accusation, the court adjourned five days after the trial began, apparently awaiting the enactment of new laws to meet objections raised by the defense counsel on points of procedure.

On December 26, the trial resumed. The following day, Mamoun Diouri, one of the accused, charged with acting as the contact between two clandestine revolutionary organizations headed by former resistance leaders Basri and Sheik el-Arab, startled the court by testifying that he had been tortured by the police—in an effort to obtain a confession that would destroy the UNFP. This threatened the prosecution's carefully built case, but the attorneys alleged that there was sufficient evidence to establish the defendant's guilt without the confession.

On January 28, 1964, however, Maoti Bouabid, one of the defense lawyers and President of the Casablanca Bar, apprehended a court magistrate and several policemen as they were handling the weapons that the plotters had supposedly stolen from the U.S. naval base at Kenitra and that had been presented in court as one of the main pieces of evidence against the accused. This tampering with the evidence, following previous legal acrobatics on the part of the prosecution, convinced the defense counsel of the impossibility of obtaining justice for their clients, and they announced their decision to withdraw en masse from the case, "at the demand and with the consent" of their clients. Declaring that the trial had revealed numerous irregularities, their statement on the matter revealed that the court had rejected requests submitted by counsel for a medical examination of the accused to determine whether they had been tortured, as almost all of them had charged; and that the court had also refused to consider objections raised by the defense lawyers to the many contradictions and ambiguities in the inquiry. The integrity of the examining magistrate was questioned, they said, by the majority of the defendants, and they protested the removal of evidence from the courtroom without the knowledge or consent of counsel.

The climax of this judicial nightmare occurred on February 12, 1964, when the prosecuting attorney asked permission to play a tape-recording of statements Basri had allegedly made to the police. The defendants, who had thus far remained silent, objected, on the ground that a damning recording could easily be fabricated. When the court allowed the prosecutor's motion anyway, the accused men attempted to drown out the tape by making an uproar, and the presiding judge ordered them removed from the court and the trial continued without them.

On March 14, after deliberating 160 hours, the court finally sentenced eleven of the defendants, including eight who were not present, to death. Notable among them was Ben Barka, who had already been sentenced to death *in absentia* in November by a military tribunal for inciting Moroccans to revolt during the conflict with Algeria. The three present were Basri, Diouri, and Omar Benjelloun. Three others received life imprisonment, forty-four received lesser prison sentences, and forty-two were freed.

Although the sentences were milder than anticipated—apparently a government effort to thwart the rising tide of criticism—the trial had further repercussions. In Morocco, the UNEM (National Union of Moroccan Students) called a strike in protest; its Secretary General was subsequently arrested, although soon released. In France, the student organizations of France, Algeria, and Tunisia appealed to King Hassan; in Damascus, students demonstrated against the death sentences and occupied the Moroccan Embassy, refusing to leave until they were allowed to give the chargé d'affaires a petition asking King Hassan to annul the verdicts. In Moscow, the Moroccan Embassy headquarters was invaded by about fifty irate Moroccan students.

Further criticism came from the Committee for the Study of and Information on the Situation in Morocco, which UNFP exiles and French liberals had formed in France immediately after the discovery of the "July Plot." Condemning the verdicts and the failure of the French Government to protest more vehemently against the circumstances surrounding the trial, it also repeated the charge that the Rabat government had violated the Franco-Moroccan judiciary agreement in denying French lawyers the right to plead in Moroccan courts. The committee declared its resolve "to make contact in France and elsewhere with all organizations and high officials, being determined not to allow such a denial of justice."

By the end of March, twenty of the condemned men had appealed for a retrial, among them the three sentenced to death. The condemned were regarded as martyrs, and the affair had become a *cause célèbre* that would not soon be forgotten. From plot discovery to verdict, it served as a major factor shaping Moroccan domestic and foreign developments during the country's first attempts at parliamentary democracy. The King's desire to rally the people behind him and the FDIC, shortly before the trial began, contributed to his decision at the end of September, 1963, to try to enforce Morocco's territorial claims on Algeria.* (The move succeeded, and political leaders of all factions, with the exception of Ben Barka, supported the government in its campaign. They also agreed to attend parliamentary meetings despite their continued protest against election irregularities.) And, in an effort to consolidate his personal support in the Council of Ministers prior to the opening of parliament and the start of the trial, King Hassan asked Guedira to replace Balafrej as Foreign Minister, and he promoted M'Hammed Bahnini of the FDIC from Minister of Justice to the premiership. The Istiqlal was thereby eliminated completely from the government. This of course increased the risk that the party might form a parliamentary *entente* with the UNFP, but the threat of such an occurrence was balanced by the fact that the man who now headed the cabinet could rally support from non-FDIC members better than Guedira.

On Throne Day, November 18, 1963, the King formally opened

* See below, chap. 8, pp. 232–34.

the two houses of parliament. The two opposition parties were present, but their leaders declared that their presence did not condone the "illegal" character of the "fraudulently" elected body. Their participation, they explained, was only a reprieve designed to enable the government to deal with immediate problems and avoid discrediting Morocco in international circles.

The opposition's acquiescence did not continue long, however. When the FDIC in the House of Representatives, having moved the nomination of a provisional board of officers and the appointment of a rules committee, called for a vote before the motion had been debated, both the UNFP and the Istiqlal balked, and the Istiqlal members actually left the hall. A provisional board was then nominated and presented to the House, together with a set of rules on procedure. These, however, were rejected at the next meeting on the ground that they represented a clumsy reproduction of the rules of the French National Assembly and were unsuitable to the Moroccan legislature. A new committee including al-Fassi and Torres was then formed to redraft the rules.

On January 2, partial elections were held in seven districts where the previous vote for the lower house had been annulled by the Constitutional Chamber of the Supreme Court. The UNFP, again declaring that the voting was "rigged," did not enter candidates. The Istiqlal also charged that there was government intimidation, but it entered candidates and won two seats; the FDIC won the balance. The Front thus controlled 79 of the 144 seats and forced the selection of Abd el-Krim Khatib as Speaker. However, after several skirmishes, the Istiqlal-UNFP opposition momentarily united and won a point by forcing the adoption of the much-debated Article 37 of the House rules, which provided for proportional party representation on the House committees. Twelve committees were appointed in accordance with the principle of proportional representation; this was perhaps a small victory for democracy, but hardly one for effective government. After debating the budget, the first Moroccan parliament adjourned.

The tense political atmosphere within and without parliament, aggravated by increasing economic distress, was causing dissension within the conglomerate ranks of the majority, but hardly dominant, FDIC. In the hope of strengthening it, as well as of showing renewed concern for his subjects, King Hassan decided it might be wise to heed the growing demands for "socialism." As this had become a catchword throughout Africa, with different loosely defined meanings in each country, no great doctrinal surrender was involved. Since Guedira had maintained contact with labor leaders

—in his attempts either to reach an agreement with the UMT or perhaps to create a third labor force—it was not too difficult for King Hassan and his supporters to sponsor a Moroccan version of the New African Look. Accordingly, the formation of the Democratic Socialist Party (PSD), a name that connoted it had something for everybody, was proclaimed on April 12, 1964. At the party's initial congress, attended by 1,500 delegates, Guedira and Bahnini announced that the PSD was designed to establish wide support for the King and government through its advocacy of a "liberal" brand of socialism under which "state guidance" and private enterprise would work together. Neither the composition of the new party, nor its platform, nor its relationship to the FDIC was clearly explained. Subsequently, it became known that the erstwhile Liberal Independents and Constitutional Democrats would form its nucleus, but that it would continue as part of the FDIC, in which the Popular Movement still played a major role. However, personal and philosophic differences appeared increasingly to be splitting the FDIC apart.

At a PSD party congress on May 10, 1964, Prime Minister Bahnini was named President, Foreign Minister Guedira Secretary General, and Mohammed Laghzaoui Treasurer of the new organization. Some of the party's objectives were indicated to be long-range economic planning; direct state control of the basic sectors of the economy; industrialization; redistribution of revenues; reform of the commercial structure, including Moroccanization of internal trade; and agrarian reform, including appropriation of land held by foreigners, subject to equitable indemnification.

The second session of the Moroccan parliament, which had commenced on April 24, ended abruptly on June 29 while opposition members were preparing to debate precisely this last point: the question of *colon* lands. The closing came four days after a vote had been called on a UNFP motion of censure against the government's economic and financial policies, the increase in sugar prices, the high cost of living, and the poor conditions of the working classes—an occasion on which the UNFP had failed by only eleven votes to bring down the government but had succeeded in arousing public interest in the questions involved. The Popular Movement, which for a while had appeared to support the censure, voted against it amid rumors of government promises of greater cabinet representation for the party.

The premature cloture of parliament brought a swift reaction. On July 3, the Istiqlal and UNFP demanded that a special session be called to take up the unfinished business. At this point, Hassan made conciliatory gestures to the more responsible leaders of the opposition by accepting the "resignation" of Guedira, Abdelkader Benjelloun, and Driss Slaoui from the Council of Ministers. On August 20, he announced that a reorganized Council had been formed, headed again by M'Hammed Bahnini but including seven newcomers, among them Taibi Benhima, former chief of the Moroccan Mission to the U.N., as Foreign Minister; General Mohammed Oufkir, former head of the Sûreté Générale, as Minister of Interior; and General Mezzian of the Royal Army as Minister of Defense. (For the first time, two career soldiers assumed top civil posts.) In another significant move, Ahardane was shifted to the Agriculture Ministry in an effort to enlist Popular Movement support in the forthcoming debates on colon lands and agrarian reform. Next, King Hassan announced that the special session would be held; finally, as a concession to the UNFP he commuted to life imprisonment the death sentences of three of the men—Basri, Diouri, and Omar Benjelloun—who had been convicted of attempting his assassination.

On September 14, an extraordinary session of parliament was convened upon the request of the opposition, under the terms of Article 40 of the constitution, which permits such a session to be called on request of one-third of the members. However, its time was largely consumed by a dispute as to the legality of the session and the validity of the agenda. Hassan decided the conflict in favor of the opposition, but the session adjourned on November 12 with no tangible results. The regular session which commenced shortly thereafter was equally fruitless. Debate on the colon lands and the foreign press consumed much of the time in the first weeks. Then, when the President of the House of Representatives ruled against debate on the creation of a special court with jurisdiction over offenses involving bribery, corruption, and abuse of public authority, the fifty-one representatives of the Istiqlal and UNFP withdrew from the session. The opposition parties subsequently returned to the parliamentary session, but positive results remained unattainable.

While the nation's responsible adults were mired in the quicksand of polemics, high-school students sparked an abrupt change in the country's political life. On March 22, 1965, the youths staged demonstrations in Casablanca that snowballed into violent riots and burning of public buildings, and spread to Rabat, Fez, and Marrakesh. The demonstrations began as a protest against a Ministry of Education decree preventing students over the age of 17 from enrolling in the second stage of high school and relegating them instead to technical schools. A general sympathy strike called by the Moroccan Federation of Labor (UMT) paralyzed railroads, ports, airports and most industries.

The government reacted promptly and sharply to the actions, which some feared might even destroy the monarchy. A curfew was imposed in Casablanca and army units were called in to restore order. (Official government figures put the casualty toll at seven dead, forty-three wounded, and 168 arrested, but the Istiqlal claimed that fifty were killed, hundreds injured, and thousands arrested.) Hassan responded to the critical situation by inaugurating a series of consultations with representatives of the country's major political groups, with the aim of establishing a coalition government of "national unity."

The UNFP's conditions for agreement were the release of their members previously arrested on political charges, and the conclusion of a Palace-UNFP agreement to define precise limits on palace involvement in party affairs, and to draw the lines of responsibility for UNFP leaders. The first condition was met in the release of political prisoners (including Mohammed Basri) under a general amnesty granted by Hassan, but the King was not inclined to comply with the second demand.

The Istiqlal's response was predictable: it affirmed its support for national unity but emphasized that it conceived of such unity only within the institutional framework outlined by the Constitution. Party spokesmen said new elections would have to be held as a prerequisite to the Istiqlal's participation in any coalition government.

Al-Alam commented that the political consultations have revealed that there are three groups proposing different solutions to the present crisis: 1) those who believe that the present institutional structure is satisfactory, although an addition of a minister from this or that group is needed to satisfy the dissidents; 2) those who say that the present government structure is imperfect, but that the weaknesses could be rectified by an arbitrary action by the King alone, without resort to democratic means; and 3) those who believe that the country is in the process of political, economic, and social reconstruction, and that the people—being the essential builders and beneficiaries of the process—should be consulted on any changes made in the government.

Endorsing the third viewpoint, *al-Alam* said any change would be initiated through democratic institutions and should follow the people's will as to the selection of the government, its manner of functioning, the programs to be adopted, and the political and economic doctrines to be followed.

When it was finally apparent to the King that conciliation with the opposition was impossible, his response was quick and severe. On June 8, he announced on a nation-wide broadcast that a state of emergency had been proclaimed, Parliament was suspended, revisions of the Constitution were projected, and a new government would be formed under his own premiership. As authority for his actions, he cited Article 35 of the Constitution, which gives the King the right to assume full powers in both the executive and legislative branches of the government.

The major surprise was Hassan's decision to "revise" the Constitution. The King said that certain constitutional provisions did not presently guarantee conditions for a normal function of parliamentary institutions, but he did not specify exactly how or to what extent the Constitution was to be revised. He merely indicated that the new Constitution would be submitted to referendum and new elections held.

Immediately after King Hassan's address, Bahnini's cabinet resigned, and a new cabinet was formed under the King's chairmanship. Many old cabinet members were retained, but Bahnini and several other ministers were dropped.

The nation's reaction to Hassan's speech was varied. The left was reportedly optimistic, since prospects for a possible truce with the authorities had not been disrupted, and the delay engendered by Hassan's reforms would enable them to organize for the future. The Communists, however, were more cautious and demanded that a constituent assembly be elected. Other political groups expressed their dissatisfaction with the new measures in no uncertain terms. The Istiqlal reaffirmed its stand that the "return to democratic principles and procedures" was the only way to solve Morocco's political and economic problems. The General Federation of Moroccan Workers issued a communiqué charging that the King's projected actions would result in the "same failures" as all previous attempts that did not take the people into active consideration. The only equitable solution, said the UGTM, would necessitate new elections. The National Union of Moroccan Students called the present situation a "return to the autocratic system of the past."

A week later, Hassan signed a decree establishing a Council of Regents, composed of eight members and led by Prince Moulay Abdullah. The new government, composed of ministers loyal to the King, has committed itself to a determined effort to remedy unemployment and the other economic ills besetting Morocco. Its first action in this regard was announced by the King on July 1:

Morocco had decided to nationalize a substantial segment (35 per cent) of the country's export industry. Since the phosphate industry is already in the public sector, 60 per cent of Morocco's exports are now effectively nationalized. Immediate opposition to the move was indicated by the resignation of Mohammed Laghzaoui from his post as Minister of Industry, Mines, and Tourism (he was also Director General of the Royal Department of Phosphates). But the influential Paris daily *Le Monde* sympathetically observed that the measure would stop foreign companies and individuals from depriving Morocco of all but a meager part of the exports value while investing little.

In view of the augmenting concern with economics, it is to that subject we next turn.

Chapter 6

Economic Development in
Modern Morocco

U NDER THE French Protectorate,* the traditional economy
of Morocco was not modernized; rather, a separate economic structure was superimposed upon it. To accomplish
this, considerable capital and Western methods of technology
were introduced, physical barriers to communications were overcome, a feeble financial structure was reorganized, and the basic
facilities for economic development were constructed. While these
economic endeavors of the French administration were highly
significant in the over-all picture of Moroccan development, the
benefits devolving on the Moroccans themselves were small, particularly before 1949, in comparison to those bestowed on European
settlers and investors. This was due in part to official policy, which
geared development primarily to French interests, and in part to
the Moroccans' slowness to adjust to the new conditions. After
forty-four years of Protectorate rule, the standard of living of 90
per cent of the Moroccan population remained far below that
of the average European; the gross national product was only
$179 per capita in 1956.

* Statistics concerning the Protectorates used in this chapter refer to French
Morocco unless otherwise noted. Information for Spanish Morocco is inadequate
and in any case relatively unimportant in the national picture. Unfortunately,
politics often influenced statistics in French Morocco, making necessary a careful analysis of figures given by both Protectorate and nationalist sources. In
independent Morocco, there is a remarkable variance in the "official" statistics
in the government publications released by different, sometimes even the same,
departments.

Defenders of the Protectorate's economic policy cited the adage, "As ye sow, so shall ye reap," to explain the continued poverty of most native Moroccans, but this reasoning could not obliterate the fact that Europeans regarded the basic purpose of the French and Spanish administrations to be the resolution of indigenous problems to the advantage of the "protecting" people. It was therefore natural that Moroccan nationalists attacked Protectorate policy on economic as well as political and social grounds. They accused France and Spain of integrating Morocco's economy with their own and of using Morocco as a reservoir of raw materials for their industries and a dumping ground for their manufactured goods. They criticized the Protectorates' failure to alleviate the continuing poverty of the Moroccan masses and to provide technical education; finally, they blamed the Protectorates for the rising cost of living.

Contrary to the claims of some Frenchmen that France's economic prosperity depended on continued political control of her overseas territories, Morocco, viewed as an investment in the narrow economic sense, was a net expense to France. French government loans were repaid only in part, and then with inflated francs; French military expenditures in Morocco exceeded $70 million a year before 1955 and more than twice as much in that year; France's commerce with Morocco amounted to only 5 per cent of her foreign trade. Nevertheless, France's special economic position in Morocco was of great concern to her, principally because of the human and financial investments Frenchmen had made in Morocco in expectation of a profitable return.

Although many Moroccans believed that the end of the Protectorate would soon be followed by increased prosperity, the leaders of the country lost no time in emphasizing the real state of affairs. Shortly after Morocco became independent, Premier Bekkai cautioned the people that they could neither live by slogans nor could they allow themselves to be misled into believing in a paternalistic state; only hard work would strengthen the economy.

The efforts made by the government and the early enthusiasm of a large segment of the population bore some fruit after 1956. Morocco unified her currency, broke her ties with the French franc, revised her tariff structure, promulgated an investment code intended to attract foreign capital, reduced her trade imbalance, and attempted to formulate comprehensive economic plans. Still, ten years of political independence have failed to achieve anything approaching a commensurate economic independence.

Morocco continues today to rely on French investment capital (estimated at $3 billion in 1963), agricultural subsidies, and technical know-how. Furthermore, a wide technical and cultural gap still exists between the modern sector of the economy (involving approximately one-fourth of the labor force, which produces two-thirds of the total national output) and the traditional pastoral sector, which continues mainly at subsistence level. The cost of living continues to increase and the population to grow, but agricultural production has not expanded proportionally. Domestic capital remains scarce, and the reserves of managerial-technical talent are even weaker, while bureaucratic *immobilisme* and corruption have become a major problem. Foreign capital has been cautious in making new investments, and unemployment and underemployment are at critical levels. The French and Spanish governments, furthermore, have been slow to negotiate economic *rapprochements*. These shortcomings may be explained largely by the immensity of the problem, but Morocco's lack of clear purpose in her economic planning, which in turn has been largely the by-product of political squabbling, cannot be overlooked.

In sum, Morocco has barely maintained the low standard of living of the mass of her population. Although the gross national product rose to $2 billion in 1962, the population increase forced a drop in annual per-capita income to $165. The prospects for the future are dimmed by the fact that the gross national product must grow annually by $43 million simply to keep pace with population growth. On the other hand, considerable natural resources, a large young labor force, and a sound infrastructure left by the Protectorate—in fact, developed beyond the capacity necessary for self-maintenance—continue to mark Morocco as a country of tremendous opportunity. Given substantial and continuing foreign economic assistance, the development of a substantial cadre of technicians, and the political stability needed to create a favorable climate for foreign capital, the promises of the future could still be realized.

A. *The National Budget and Morocco's Plans*

The first financial reforms in Morocco under the French Protectorate had significant success in ending the economic crisis that had led to the Treaty of Fez. The Sultan's private finances were separated from the public treasury; improperly appropriated state property was recovered; a properly organized service for the assessment, collection, and guardianship of taxes was instituted; and new taxes were imposed. For the European settlers, these taxes were less than those paid by their countrymen at home, but to Moroccans they seemed considerable. Direct taxes were levied sparingly; according to later nationalist economists, this placed the bulk of the tax burden on the Moroccan population, which in turn received only a small part of the benefits. There was no single graduated tax on income, and the collection of a "professional" tax on income was never strictly enforced. The most efficiently collected tax was the tertib, an agricultural levy which affected Moroccans much more than Europeans, who received a rebate for modernization of their farms.

Each Protectorate zone had its own budgets: an ordinary budget financed for the most part by local sources, and a development or equipment budget financed principally by the protecting powers. By 1955, the annual ordinary budget of the French zone had reached 69.5 billion francs ($240 million); in the Spanish zone, the ordinary budget was 519 million pesetas ($11.8 million).

Modern economic planning, in the broad sense of the term, was instituted by Marshal Lyautey in 1912, but it was not until 1949 that the first long-term program was adopted for Morocco as a whole. Actually, the 1949–53 plan was a combination of sector programs prepared by the French Protectorate's departments. Only rudimentary efforts were made during this period to coordinate either departmental programming or private and public investment. As was the first, a second plan (1954–57) was implemented through annual capital budgets.

In July, 1957, King Mohammed authorized a Superior Planning Council, headed by Prime Minister Bekkai and including other ministers and representatives of various sectors of the economy, to prepare a transition plan for 1958–59 and a five-year plan for 1960–64. The objectives of the two-year plan that the Council drew up were basically realistic: to increase agricultural production, stimulate industrial output, and increase the number of educated and technically trained Moroccans. Although it included projections for each sector, the plan was unfortunately no more than a public-investment budget, like its two predecessors, and included few concrete methods to realize its goals.

The transitional period was intended to provide time to gain general acceptance of the need for broader planning and to prepare the comprehensive five-year plan. But Morocco's disappointing economic progress during the interim period demonstrated the need for more thorough, immediate planning and augmented the demand for a "socialist" government. Yet many leaders of the government, while desirous of seeing Morocco on a sounder economic footing, were consciously or unconsciously opposed to governmental controls that might limit the activities of their supporters in the business community. This feeling, coupled with the administrative chaos in the government departments responsible for planning, made the subsequent plan no more effective than its predecessor.

The Five-Year-Plan published in November, 1960, was described by its authors as "the first Moroccan experience with true economic planning, going beyond the stage of simple annual investment programs." Critics labeled it "a catalog of desires." In reply, the authors conceded that current facilities for planning permitted no more than a general definition of needs and methods. In truth, the lack of adequate statistical data and trained economists was a serious impediment to effective long-term planning.

The two main objectives of the Plan were to lessen Morocco's dependence on foreign technicians, capital, and markets, and to integrate the traditional sectors into the national economy. To achieve these objectives, it was proposed (1) to increase the number of technicians and qualified personnel by intensive educational and training programs; (2) to stimulate agriculture through reform of traditional practices and the application of modern technology; (3) to encourage private investment to establish basic steel and chemical industries; and (4) to train Moroccans for the civil service and to reform administration practices. The state planned to finance a public-investment program from import taxes, profits from the export of phosphates, and special funds, but it in fact relied on domestic and foreign loans for the greater part of the budget.

The expenditures of these new programs were justified by the assumption that gross domestic production would increase at an average annual rate of 7 per cent during the years 1960–64. (The anticipated percentage increases ranged from a low of 5.5 for mining to a high of 10.5 for industry and handicrafts, and were expected to bring about increases of 30 per cent in private consumption, 30 per cent in exports, and 50 per cent in imports over the five year period.) In fact, however, local production showed an annual progress of only 1.6 per cent during this period. In view of its undeniable failure, the government quietly scrapped the Plan and replaced it with a three-year plan (1965–67) that envisaged an average outlay of more than 800 million DH * per year and a

* The dirham (DH) is Morocco's gold-backed currency introduced in 1959 and valued at 5 to 1 U.S. dollars.

3.5 per cent annual growth in investment. It designated three priority areas: agriculture, tourism, and training.

While planning in Morocco since 1956 can hardly be called successful, it is not anticipated that economic plans will be discontinued. Indeed, the UNFP is committed to more and better planning. But if it is to avoid haphazard and hasty action, the government must take very careful stock of the nation's political, economic, and social situation. Although the latest plan is less ambitious than previous ones, it still poses basic financial and economic problems so that once more its over-all success must depend on the cooperation and initiative of the private sector.

Throughout the periods covered by these plans, independent Morocco's budgets were generally balanced, on paper, that is, but the estimates of domestic income on which they were based have not been realistic. Therefore, Morocco has had to rely on foreign aid to underwrite her economic development. The success of this aid is indicated by the fact that the national debt has remained relatively moderate, usually below one-third of the yearly gross national product. By 1963, the national debt was $543 million, 75 per cent of which was owed to France and the United States. (The burden of direct foreign aid shifted from France to the United States between 1957 and 1962, but France resumed her predominant role in 1963.) But the cost of government can be expected to increase in the future; if foreign aid does not increase correspondingly, the debt is likely to mount critically.

The first budget of independent Morocco was not a national budget but was divided by the former protectorate zones. The government insisted that the operational budgets of the two zones be balanced by internal taxes, since to do otherwise would be inconsistent with the principle of independence. To meet this need, indirect taxes—on items such as gasoline, tobacco, electricity, and commodity transactions—were raised, nullifying the hope that the cost of living would not increase. Following the French example, the new government continued to limit direct taxation in order to encourage investors (it also recognized the difficulties in collecting direct taxes), but when it became apparent that indirect taxation alone was not enough, the tax on professional profits was raised from 18 to 20 per cent (although the personal exemption for individuals was at the same time increased from $700 to $860); the charge on urban residents of 6 per cent of rentals to defray the cost of street cleaning, garbage disposal, etc., was converted into a tax; and finally, treasury bonds were issued to raise an additional 5 billion francs ($14 million).

In contrast to the pride that insisted on balancing the operational budgets, Morocco had no qualms about eagerly seeking foreign aid to finance her development. In 1956, immediately after gaining her independence, Morocco asked France for 35 billion francs ($100 million) and hoped to receive the equivalent of an additional 7 billion francs ($20 million) from the United States. Negotiations between France and Morocco broke down after the French "air piracy" of the five Algerian leaders and the subsequent riots in Meknes. By the year's end, Morocco had received only 9 billion francs ($25 million) from France and a $700,000 technical-aid grant from United Nations agencies, but nothing at all from either the United States or Spain. The year 1957 opened with the government in a precarious economic condition.

In 1957, expenditures remained unchanged while French aid dropped to 5 billion francs ($14 million). Some assistance was forthcoming, however, in a 4-billion-franc ($11-billion) loan from the Banque de Paris et des Pays-Bas and an equivalent of 10 billion francs ($28 million) from the United States.

In 1958, the first actual national budget provided 134.5 billion francs for ordinary expenditures and 36.7 billion for development. The latter amount was to be raised by 14.5 billion francs in local receipts (including 6.5 billion from exports of phosphates); 10 billion in United States aid; 4 billion in foreign bank loans; 4 billion in Moroccan treasury bonds; and 4 billion from a reserve fund. Local sources were relied on to balance the ordinary budget, but a sizable deficit eventually resulted.

In 1959, French aid to Morocco was terminated, but the United States increased its assistance to 16.8 billion francs ($48 million) —more than 40 per cent of the nation's entire development budget. During the next two years, while estimates for ordinary expenditures rose by about 7 per cent annually and for development expenses by 9 percent, foreign assistance remained unchanged except for a $23 million loan from the Development Loan Fund in 1960, extended to complete an irrigation project near Berkane. Meanwhile, local revenue continued to fall short of expectations.

In December, 1961, King Hassan and his new government announced an important fiscal reform designed to increase domestic investments and decrease the tax burden on the peasants. It called for the creation of a national investment fund into which all companies must invest from 3 to 15 per cent of their annual profits. This contribution to the fund could be regained under certain conditions. In addition, individuals were to pay a tax on net professional profits at rates of from 5 to 30 per cent. Salary taxes, collected by payroll deduction, were also progressive. The traditional tertib on agricultural production was replaced by a tax on agricultural capacity, and, under the new farm law, peasants with an income of under $280 were exempt from taxes altogether. Municipal property taxes were increased, and a single 30-per-cent tax was placed on all company profits. By special statute, oil companies pay a tax of 50 per cent on distributed profits.

Morocco had been led to expect a reduction of American assistance in 1962 to the original 10-billion-franc level ($30 million), as well as a significant loss of revenue from the cutting back in the French and United States military establishments, and a serious loss stemming from the 1961 drought. But an unexpected increase in American aid balanced the development budget, and a 5 per cent treasury loan balanced the operating budget.

By July, 1962, Morocco's balance of payments with France showed a 30-billion-franc ($90 million) deficit, but in that month, a new financial accord with Paris was finally reached. The agreement provided 400 million dirhams ($80 million) in treasury advances, including 150 million DH ($30 million) for financing public investment, 40 million DH ($8 million) for financing imports from France, and 190 million DH ($38 million) to guarantee export credits. Morocco's outstanding debt to France was consolidated into a 25-year loan at 1.25 per cent interest. The first amortization payment of 25 million DH fell due at the end of 1963.

France, however, reacting to Morocco's threat to nationalize French-owned farmlands, failed to meet its promises in the early part of 1963. The principal aid received during the first part of the year was therefore American; additional support was forthcoming in West German assistance for a chemical complex and a Development Loan Fund grant for development of the valley of the lower Moulouya River. This was a long-term 80-million-DH loan at 3 to 3.5 per cent interest. But French aid increased as the year advanced and by the end of 1963 totaled perhaps 210 million DH.

The Constitution of 1962 had set forth certain requirements regarding the national budget, linking it with the National Plan. Parliament had to pass on the budget; expenses for investments resulting from application of the Plan were to be voted on only once during the period of the Plan; after the Plan was approved, the government alone could introduce bills to modify it. If the budget was not approved by December 31 of a given year, the government could allocate by decree the funds necessary to maintain public services.

The first budget submitted to the Moroccan parliament was offered in January, 1964. Expenditures in this 1964 operational budget were estimated at 2.1 billion DH ($400 million). Of this amount, only 8.8 per cent was to be balanced by income; and the resulting deficit was emphasized by the fact that phosphate profits, which had previously been allocated to the capital equipment budget, were shifted to the operational budget, as were tax revenues normally allocated to the National Investment Fund. The capital equipment budget allocated 860 million DH ($172 million) but showed only 27 million DH of income and 250 million DH in grants from France. Although 150 million DH was subsequently promised to Morocco by Kuwait, a deficit of 43 million DH still existed.

By the fall of 1964, the total deficit for the two budgets was estimated at 788 million DH ($157 million). To meet this crisis and to correct a rapidly deteriorating balance of payments, the government announced a number of austerity measures on October 9, to be effective immediately. The new policy curtailed the use of government-owned cars by public officials; discontinued costly special missions abroad, except to countries where Morocco does not have diplomatic envoys; eliminated 20 per cent of the posts formerly held by foreign technical assistants; and reduced by half government administration posts not held by Moroccan citizens. It was announced that no new expenditures would be made unless they could be offset by corresponding income, that nonpriority public works would be suspended, and that importation of automobiles and other luxury products would be strictly limited. Finally, prices of basic commodities were strictly controlled.

The effect of the austerity policy on the worsening financial situation is not yet clear. The future therefore remains clouded, although foreign aid may delay the eventual day of reckoning. In the long run, however, improvement must come from within if political independence is to remain meaningful.

B. Money, Banking, and Investments

In 1920, the Protectorate powers discontinued the hassani, Morocco's national currency, and substituted the Moroccan franc in the French zone and the peseta in the Spanish zone. The Moroccan franc was placed on the same gold basis as the French franc and was correspondingly devalued several times after its initial appearance. Despite the official exchange rates, the currencies varied slightly on the Tangier black market. In 1955, the legal exchange rate was 350 francs to the dollar for both the French and Moroccan francs, but the Moroccan franc sold in Tangier at 370 to 440. The peseta of Spanish Morocco was the same as that used in Spain itself (8 francs=1 peseta). In the international zone, it was the primary currency, although Moroccan francs, dollars, and pounds sterling circulated freely.

The first major financial accomplishment of independent Morocco was to unify the country's currency. In February, 1958, the peseta was withdrawn from circulation in the former Spanish zone; by agreement, 1 billion pesetas ($23 million) were redeemed at the rate of ten Moroccan francs to the peseta and were then paid to Spain as partial satisfaction of Morocco's debt, which amounted to 2.3 billion pesetas ($52 million). But the Moroccan franc passed from the scene less easily. Morocco's final decision was to cut her ties with the French franc zone, a decision that was forced by a series of unilateral measures taken by France which had adversely affected Morocco's economy. When France indirectly devalued her franc in August, 1958, Morocco, fearful of a sharp price rise, refused to follow suit, creating a rate of exchange of 100 Moroccan francs for 117.5 French francs. Six months later, Morocco imposed a 10 per cent tax on financial transfers from Morocco to the rest of the franc zone, but by July, 1959, $80 million of capital had nevertheless fled. The devaluation of the peseta that summer only exacerbated the situation.

In October, 1959, therefore, Morocco took a number of important steps. First, she devalued her currency by 20.44 per cent, enabling Moroccan exports to compete favorably on the world market. At the same time, the new, gold-backed dirham was announced, and the French-controlled bank of issue was replaced by the new Banque du Maroc. Exchange controls with the French franc zone were tightened (although foreigners were permitted to transfer part of their wages, and corporations their dividends, abroad), and Moroccans were obliged to declare their foreign holdings. The groundwork for a tighter and more independent economy was thus laid.

Private banking in French Morocco had been regulated for forty years by the State Bank of Morocco, an institution created at the Algeciras Conference whose charter had been extended in 1946 for another twenty years. The Banque d'État also served as repository for government funds; it controlled credit and issued currency. It also operated in Spanish Morocco, but government services there were handled by the Bank of Spain and a General Credit Bank. Controlling shares in the Banque d'État were owned by the Banque de Paris et des Pays-Bas and by the French and Spanish governments. In the later years of the Protectorates, there were about twenty-five banks in French Morocco, more than half of them affiliated with banks in France, and eight in Spanish Morocco.

When the Banque du Maroc was organized in 1959, its capital of 2 billion francs was held entirely by the state. The National Bank for Economic Development, the country's only financial institution making long-term loans to industry, had been organized two years before (its stockholders include the International Finance Corporation and the Morgan Guaranty Trust Company of New York); in 1962, it received a $15 million loan from the World Bank. Morocco's banking system today comprises approximately fifty banks. In 1958, Morocco became the sixty-seventh member of the International Monetary Fund and the International Bank for Reconstruction and Development. Her quota in the former was $52.5 million in 1964 and her capital in the latter was $70 million.

Foreign currency brought into Morocco must be exchanged for dirhams at licensed banks at the official rate. Except in limited amounts for travelers, dirhams (including earnings from the sale of imported merchandise) may not be transferred outside the French franc zone without authorization from the Moroccan Exchange Office. (On January 22, 1958, a Royal decree modified Protectorate legislation of 1939, which had instituted in French Morocco the exchange regulations of the franc zone, by charging the Moroccan Exchange Office with the responsibility for exchange operations, capital exports, and trade in gold.)

In theory, foreigners need not obtain authorization to make a capital investment in Morocco. In practice, however, their investments must be made pursuant to the exchange-control regulations. Thus, a foreigner cannot open an internal bank account until he qualifies as a Moroccan resident after six months of continuous residence or establishes a main office in Morocco. Branch offices and agencies of foreign companies must obtain from the Exchange Office authorization for investments in Morocco except for day-to-day expenditures incurred in the normal operation of their business.

Investments exempt from the exchange regulations include the purchase of government bonds, and bonds and shares issued by a Moroccan corporation through the proper channels, and the application for new shares involving an increase of capital of a Moroccan company. However, even where prior authorization is not required, investment must be financed, according to the general exchange regulations, by transfer of convertible currencies negotiated by the Bank of Morocco, or, alternatively, by (1) debit in convertible dirhams of foreign accounts opened on the books of authorized intermediaries in Morocco; (2) transfers of convertible currencies not negotiated by the Banque du Maroc or nonconvertible currencies from countries with which Morocco has bilateral payment agreements; (3) debit of capital accounts, suspended accounts, or internal accounts of nonresidents; or (4) assets in kind and settlements of debts.

Once investments are authorized by the Exchange Office, they may be repatriated only by consent of that office. When such permission is refused, the proceeds from the liquidation of a foreign investment are deposited in a capital account in a licensed intermediary bank and may be used only in Morocco according to the conditions prescribed for such funds.

Between 1912 and 1955, French capital invested a total of 300 billion francs in Moroccan real estate, 285 million francs in agriculture, and 800 billion in industry—a total outlay of almost $4 billion. During the struggle for independence, there was some initial hesitancy to invest new capital, followed by the departure of capital, and private investment between 1951 and 1954 amounted to only $2.2 million a year.

In the first year of Morocco's independence, investment totaled 79 billion francs ($225 million), but fear of the future caused the withdrawal of about half that amount. In 1957, 69 billion francs ($200 million) were invested, while 31 billion ($90 million) fled. Alarmed, the government took steps to give assurance to foreign capital in September, 1958, with a program for duty rebates on imports of capital equipment; guaranteed convertibility of profit; repatriation of invested capital within limits set by individual contracts; tax exemptions on patents; and concessions in the professional profits tax and the commercial license fees. It also organized a special government bureau to be concerned with foreign investments and the National Bank for Economic Development (BNDE). Due largely to these measures, investment for 1958–59 rose to 158 billion francs ($450 million), starting an upward trend.

The National Bank for Economic Development is Morocco's only institutional source of long-term industrial capital. It also makes medium-term loans, discounts medium-term credits made by commercial banks, establishes enterprises on its own initiative, subscribes to shares in new or expanding enterprises, and guarantees investments by others. Its capital stock, 30 million DH, is owned by the Moroccan Government, private Moroccan investors, leading financial institutions in Europe, the Morgan Guaranty Bank, and the International Finance Corporation, an affiliate of the World Bank, which has itself loaned $15 million to the BNDE. By 1963, the BNDE had loaned 63 million DH, assisting both public and private enterprises in establishing new plants, or expanding existing ones, in the fields of electric power, transportation, agriculture, textiles, food and beverages, chemicals, leather, paper, petroleum, refractory materials, car and truck assembly, and metallurgy.

In conjunction with its first Five-Year-Plan (1960–64), Morocco adopted a new investment code in 1960 that was intended to encourage the investment of 850 billion francs (more than $2 billion) during that period. The new law has been administered by an Investments Commission in the Ministry of National Economy.

The code was designed to encourage investment capital through various concessions. It exempted equipment and capital goods not available locally from customs duties, reduced registration fees for new companies, and allowed greater freedom in the amortization of new capital expenditures. Within reasonable limitations, it permitted tax-free reserves for new equipment and guaranteed the right, also subject to reasonable restrictions, to transfer between nonresidents the proceeds of partial or total liquidation, without time limit. (These provisions apply without exception to both "basic" and "priority" industries. The so-called basic industries embrace mining; iron and steel and related industries; chemical industries and their supporting plants; fuel and petroleum-processing facilities; and shipyards. Priority industries were defined as those which fill a definite need and demand; those which added significant value to imported semifinished products; and those that utilized native raw materials or semifinished products, or Moroccan-manufactured machinery or machine parts.) All industries established in Tangier prior to December 31, 1961, benefit by these advantages; furthermore, vacant land intended for industrial plants was to be exempt from transfer fees until April 18, 1962.

American investments are further protected by a special agreement concluded between the United States and Morocco on March 31, 1961, whereby the former promises that, in accordance with the provisions of the Mutual Security Act of 1954, it will guarantee no project undertaken in Morocco by United States nationals until the project is approved by the Moroccan Government. When an investment project is approved and guaranteed under the Mutual Security Act, Morocco accords in the subrogation to the United States Government of all rights and privileges granted to the American investor.

The fiscal reforms introduced in late 1961 by King Hassan included a forced-savings scheme to make self-financing more attractive to businessmen—a law requiring all firms to contribute to a national investment fund, amounts ranging from 3 to 15 per cent of their taxable profits. Such a measure appeared necessary because Moroccan merchants, like most Arabs, were accustomed to making quick profits from sales and had never learned to make long-term investments that would return gradually increasing dividends as the scope of the enterprise increased. (A company could avoid the levy by independently investing within the year a sum twice as great as the contribution would have been.) It is still too early to judge the long-range effect of the measure, but the immediate effects were a sharp rise in prices, followed by wage increases.

The 1962 constitution contains an important provision on the delicate subject of nationalization. Article 15 guarantees the right of property, although the law may limit its extent and use, should the planned economic and social development of the nation require it. Expropriation cannot, however, be carried out except in cases (and subject to forms) stipulated by law.

C. Industry

One of the most notable achievements of the French and Spanish Protectorates in Morocco was the construction and modernization of a transportation and communication network, so essential to the development of Moroccan industry. Although Spanish success in these fields was considerable, the French constructed a more extensive road network in the southern zone. By 1955, there were more than 6,000 miles of paved two- and three-lane highways and another 22,500 miles of secondary roads (of which only 15 per cent are passable all year round). The highway network is most extensive near the coast, but paved roads cross the Atlas at several points, and even the secondary roads in the southern desert region are satisfactory in dry weather.

The roads were constructed largely by hand labor and provided an excellent source of employment throughout the Protectorate.

Dramatic testimonials to the determination with which the work was pursued are to be seen at points where roads were cut through rock and twist about the mountainsides. At the entrance to one tunnel, a plaque reads: "The order was given, the Legion went through."

Moroccan nationalists claimed that road construction was merely part of the French program to pacify and exploit the country. Indeed, it was indispensable to the former and useful for the latter, but the independent Moroccan Government received an indisputably valuable legacy.

Since independence, Morocco has added several important bridges, 2,500 miles of roads of all classes, and the spectacular, if short, "Unity Road," built in 1957 to link the former northern and southern zones through the Rif Mountains. Although the roads are heavily utilized, they have been well maintained. Road signs, following the style of the International Geneva Protocol of 1949, were all in French until 1956 but are generally bilingual today. There are approximately 220,000 registered vehicles, including 1,500 for public transport. The volume of merchandise transported by road exceeds 2.5 million tons on controlled public trucks and perhaps another 4 million tons on private vehicles. Gasoline is very expensive, the premium grade selling for 59 cents a gallon in Casablanca in 1964, but modern service stations are numerous in the larger cities and gasoline is available throughout the country.

Good roads and numerous vehicles have made the staggering accident rate—due primarily to nonenforcement of traffic laws, animals and other road obstructions, and a casual attitude toward the hazards of driving—even higher. In 1955, for example, there were 25,000 highway accidents, resulting in 784 fatalities and 12,500 injuries.

The first commercial railroad in Morocco began operating in 1915 along rail lines laid from Casablanca to Khouribga and from Rabat to Fez. By 1955, there were more than 1,100 miles of standard-gauge lines, more than 40 per cent of which was electrified; 200 more miles have been added since. The principal lines in operation connect Casablanca and Marrakesh; Petitjean and Oued Zem; Oudjda and Bou Arfa; Tangier and Fez; Fez and Oudjda; and Benguerir and Safi. In addition, the first section of the Mediterranean-Niger line runs south from Bou Arfa. Rolling stock totals about 6,000 cars and 120 locomotives. Revenue covers only half of the annual cost of operation, despite the fact that more than 5 million passengers and more than 10 million metric tons of freight travel by rail each year. Until 1963, the railroads were operated under private concession, although heavily financed and controlled by the government. In February, 1963, negotiations were concluded for the cancellation of the concession in return for a heavy indemnity, and the process of nationalization, promised by King Hassan, was begun.

Traffic by inland waterway in Morocco is limited to the Sebou and Moubouya rivers, which are navigable inland only by small boat for 50 and 30 miles, respectively. Sea traffic is handled principally for foreign shipping, since Morocco's merchant fleet in 1959 consisted of only 30 ships totaling 33,000 tons. The most important foreign passenger line is the Compagnie de Navigation Paquet.

Casablanca, Morocco's first modern port, built by the French at the beginning of the Protectorate, was chosen by Lyautey because of its geographic position. By 1955, it was the third largest port in the French franc zone and the largest in Africa. Today, it handles more than 9 million tons of traffic a year, 67 per cent of Morocco's total; 2 million tons are handled by Melilla and Ceuta. With roadsteads 26 to 33 feet deep, it can accommodate the largest ships, but the inner harbor is already too small for increasing traffic. Congestion is aggravated by slowness in unloading, a normal six-hour task often requiring three days. A new outer harbor has been under construction for several years, but it is likely that a larger role will be played by the nation's other ports in the future. Safi is the second largest port in the former southern zone, followed by Mohammedia, Kenitra, Agadir, Mogador, and Mazagan. In the north, main ports exist at Larache, Tangier, and Alhucemas.

Air transportation was inaugurated by the Toulouse-Casablanca Airline in 1919, but it was not until World War II that Morocco acquired sufficient airports and was served by international companies. In 1946, the Air-Atlas line was organized as a semiprivate company; later, it absorbed Paquet's Air Maroc line to become the primary domestic airline in the southern zone. In the northern zone, Iberian Airlines provided local service. In 1957, Morocco incorporated the new national air service under the name of Royal Air Maroc; 55 per cent was owned by the Moroccan Government, 30 per cent by Air France, 5 per cent by Iberian Airlines, and 10 per cent by private interests. Royal Air Maroc serves all of the country's internal routes and flies to France, Spain, Switzerland, Germany, and Algeria. In 1964, its fleet comprised four Constellations, two Douglas DC-3's, and two Caravelle jets to serve the

Casablanca-Paris route. In 1963, the line carried 180,000 passengers and 6 million tons of freight. Service to the Soviet Union was inaugurated in 1962, and direct flights to New York in 1963 (both by non-Moroccan airlines).

Apart from the beginnings of these basic transportation networks, industrialization in Morocco proceeded very slowly before World War II. Some capital was attracted by Morocco's natural resources, low wages, and favorable tax structure. Progress was limited, however, by the Protectorate's policy of exporting Morocco's raw materials while using the country as a market for European manufactured goods, by the shortage of skilled workers, by the inadequate replacement of industrial equipment, and by the lack of power. Traditional handicraft industries continued to account for most local production, and the Protectorate encouraged them by establishing foreign markets for the products. Carpets from Rabat and the Atlas Mountains, pottery from Safi, filigree silver, basketware, ceramics, leather, and copper goods became known the world over. In 1953, 200,000 persons worked as artisans, and handicraft exports were valued at $3 million annually.

With the installation of modern harbor facilities and the growth of a fishing fleet, fishing has acquired real importance in Morocco and now supports perhaps 80,000 persons. In 1925, the fishing fleet numbered only 230 boats, but by 1955 there were 1,800 trawlers and other craft. The average annual catch was less than 20,000 tons between 1925 and 1935, but about 100,000 tons between 1951 and 1955. The number of fishermen likewise increased from 1,400 in 1927 to 9,000 in 1955, and the proportion of Moroccans thus engaged increased significantly. Of the 89,000 tons of fish caught in 1956, 2,500 were exported fresh; 14,500 were consumed locally; 61,000 were canned for export; and 11,000 were utilized for their by-products.

The principal fish caught today are herring (141,000 tons in 1964), constituting 70 per cent of the total catch, anchovy (2,000 tons), mackerel (7,500 tons), and tuna (2,000 tons). The peak year for the export of canned sardine was 1950, when 2 million cans were sold; by 1957, this figure had fallen to 1.1 million as the world demand decreased, canning costs and competition increased, and the fish became relatively scarce off the Moroccan coasts. But the situation has improved markedly, and Morocco is now canning 2.5 million cans of herring and other fish annually. There is still little local demand, despite the government's advocacy of the consumption of fish for nutritional reasons. In a further step to aid its fishermen, Morocco extended its territorial waters for fishing purposes from 6 to 12 nautical miles in July, 1962.

In 1955, heavy industry was still nonexistent, and light industry concentrated on processing raw materials. About 100,000 persons were employed in these light industries (as compared to 7,000 in 1924) and another 100,000 in construction work. Most of the industry in the French zone was French-owned. Seventy per cent was concentrated near Casablanca; Meknes and Port Lyautey were secondary areas; Safi and Agadir were important fish-canning centers.

This concentration of industrial activity around Casablanca continued after 1956. In 1961, in order to relieve the urban congestion created by this centralization, the government began to offer inducements to factory owners to locate their plants in other areas. Supporters of the move argued that this would also decrease corruption in the larger plants, but some critics charged that the dispersion of plants would increase graft by placing administrators beyond the reach of central authority, a fear that proved to be not without foundation.

Prior to independence, the food-processing and chemical industries were the leading modern industrial activities in Morocco. Morocco was, in fact, one of the top ten nations in fish-canning; other processed foods included cereals, sugar, chocolate, candy, fats and oils, fruit juices, beer, yeast, and carbonated beverages. Morocco was also the world's fifth largest producer of superphosphates; other industries and producers included textiles (which satisfied only one-third of the domestic need), leather and hides, tin cans, metal-stamping, and fish by-products. (In addition to these, between 1950 and 1954, a boom occurred in the construction business, and it became a focal point for foreign speculative capital. But it was adversely affected by the nationalist rebellion and has not even now recovered.) Except for its canned goods, the bulk of Moroccan manufactured goods was consumed in the domestic market; except for sugar and some tobacco, the raw materials used were primarily of Moroccan origin.

After 1956, the atmosphere of general insecurity made both local and foreign businessmen loath to expand their activities in Morocco, and no immediate effort was made to broaden the now independent country's industrial scope. In fact, in May, 1956, a leading Moroccan economist advised his countrymen that the nation must inevitably suffer French protection a little longer. During 1957, however, a new tariff structure gave increased protection to Moroccan industry, and the government began a campaign to entice foreign private and public investment to the country, with a view to encouraging the local processing of raw materials and reducing imports of consumer goods. Processing industries were of particular interest to the government as they would provide numerous jobs for unskilled workers and would also create products for internal and foreign consumption.

Slowly, in 1958, capital ventured into Morocco. The Berliet Company opened a heavy-vehicle assembly plant; Labouri started production of tractors and agricultural equipment. Simca (French) and Fiat (Italian), together with the Moroccan Government and private Moroccan investors, inaugurated the Moroccan Company for Automobile Construction (Somaca). Somaca has begun assembly operations and hopes eventually to manufacture more than 7,000 cars per year. Renault also announced tentative plans in 1964 to build an automobile factory in Morocco in conjunction with a similar plant in Tunisia.

In other fields, $50 million of Italian capital has been invested in the Samir oil refinery; a spinning mill is now under construction by Cofitex; Unilever is preparing to manufacture detergents in Morocco; and a $55-million chemical complex at Safi will annually produce 200,000 tons of superphosphate, 150,000 tons of phosphoric acid, and 50,000 tons of sulfuric acid—a project financed in considerable part by foreign interests.

In February, 1960, Spain granted oil exploration and development rights in the Spanish Sahara to six United States companies; other than that, American investment has been limited to Procter & Gamble's detergent plant; a General Tire factory that will supply 85 per cent of Morocco's needs; and a very successful business established by Jerry Nusbaum, an enterprising individualist who has lived in Morocco since World War II. In 1957, Mr. Nusbaum, one of the few American entrepreneurs who remained in Morocco after the end of the Protectorate, opened Morocco's first chewing gum factory, which captured the local market and now exports to three continents.

In 1960, industry in Morocco was valued at $280 million; the index of industrial production rose between 1958 and 1962 by 19 per cent. During those four years, the Moroccan Government also showed considerable interest in offers from the Soviet Union and Poland, respectively, to establish a shipyard and a sugar-beet factory. But time showed these and other offers to be ephemeral, since the Communist nations have far less capital and capital equipment to spare than do the Western nations. Morocco had

no alternative but to turn back to the West for her capital investment needs.

Morocco is now anxious to develop further her textiles, food-
processing, ore-conversion, sugar-refining, and a national iron and
steel works. Although coke must be imported, the excellent iron
in the Rif makes this worth while, provided the necessary financing
can be arranged. The government is presently planning a mill to
process 250,000 tons of scrap iron and imported semi-finished
steel a year. Nine groups, both United States and European, have
submitted bids on this mill.

It is hoped that auxiliary plants will develop around the planned
basic complexes, but the need for capital and technical know-how
remains great, and confidence in government protection must be
increased. Given these ingredients, Morocco's industrial potential,
particularly in consumer goods, is unlimited.

Perhaps the most important of Morocco's industries is, however,
mining. During the early years of the Protectorate, inadequate
transportation facilities and sources of power were obstacles to a
full exploitation of Morocco's abundant mineral wealth. And,
although considerable progress has been made since World War
II, hopes for mineral development remain unfulfilled. Nevertheless, mining is second only to agriculture in Morocco in the value
of production, and it accounts for 40 per cent of exports.

Since 1914, over-all control of mining has rested in the hands
of the state. All ore deposits except at the phosphate mines,
however, are operated by private concessions. Phosphates are a
state monopoly and are administered by the Office Cherifien des
Phosphates (OCP), created in 1920. The state also plays an important role through a bureau organized in 1928 to assist pros-
pectors.

Under the Protectorate, the country's mineral production was
almost entirely exported, generally in a raw state. Moroccan
nationalists accused their protectors of draining the country's resources for the benefit of foreigners, but it was true that the mining
industry, supported almost entirely by French and Spanish capital,
employed 40,000 workmen who received a minimum wage that was
15 per cent higher than the average agricultural wage. The independent Moroccan government has concentrated on research
and on efforts to establish domestic ore-processing facilities, but
84 per cent of the total tonnage is still exported.

When Morocco became independent, the total annual value
of mineral production in the southern zone was $128 million.
Although this was only one-tenth that of France and one-one

hundredth that of the United States, Morocco was second in the world production of phosphates (17 per cent—only the U.S. exceeds her); third in cobalt; fifth in manganese (5 per cent); seventh in lead (7 per cent), and fourteenth in zinc (2 per cent). In the Spanish zone, iron ore was the only important mineral; in 1957, more than a million tons were produced (less than 0.5 per cent of the world total) from mines 15 miles south of Melilla. It has been estimated that iron reserves will last at current production rates from 25 to 30 years. Production of copper and coal is negligible.

Phosphates, first mined in 1920 and still of very high quality, account for half the total value of Morocco's mineral production. Morocco retains little of its output for domestic use and has become a principal supplier to virtually every West European nation. When the Khouribga phosphate mines were heavily damaged during the insurrection in 1955, it was feared that production would decline considerably, but the mines were quickly repaired, and production figures for the year exceeded those for 1954. The rate of expansion has fallen off, employment dropped to 30,000 in 1962, and world prices have declined since Morocco became independent; but her total mineral production expanded steadily through 1962 due to an increase of 13 per cent in phosphate production after 1958. In 1962, over-all production was valued at $125 million.

The future holds promise of further increase, both in production at present mines and by the discovery of new lodes. In 1956, potassium was discovered near Khemisset and also near Zian, where a mine established in 1957 now produces 530 tons a month, with a potential two to three times that figure. An intensive search is under way for coal, oil, phosphate, lead, cobalt, iron, potash, silver, and copper lodes; attention is also fixed on the disputed areas of the Sahara, where iron ore, copper, manganese, tin, oil, and natural gas are believed abundant.

In the early years of the French and Spanish Protectorates, coal was the major source of energy, but hydroelectric power now greatly exceeds that of coal and petroleum combined. In 1963, consumption of energy, expressed in coal equivalents in thousands of tons, was: coal, 250; electricity, 1,000; and oil, 900. Nevertheless, Morocco today produces only half of the energy resources she requires.

The fact that no bituminous coal has ever been found in Morocco has severely limited the development of her heavy industry. Although anthracite reserves are considerable, the mines have been developed at high cost, since the coal runs in thin seams, which are expensive and difficult to mine. In 1961, about 430,000 tons of anthracite were nevertheless extracted, of which 205,000 tons were exported. Morocco had to import an additional 100,000 tons of hard and soft coal.

Local oil production was stabilized at about 90,000 tons annually during the 1950's, satisfying only 10 per cent of domestic needs. Exploration for new oil wells has been intensified in recent years, both in the Sahara and in Morocco itself. The Société Cherifien de Petrole, owned by French and Moroccan public and private interests, spent 1.5 billion francs prospecting in 1956, and Italian and American companies have joined the search for "black gold." In 1963, oil production rose to 150,000 tons; reserves are estimated at 2 million tons.

Paralleling efforts to extract oil is the government's interest in increased refining capacities. The existing refinery at Sidi Kacem has an annual capacity of only 180,000 tons, but the new Samir installation at Mohammedia will have a capacity of 1.2 million tons. The Moroccan government hopes that future discoveries will permit full use of that facility.

The most recently developed and now most important source of energy is electricity, produced primarily for waterpower. In 1925, consumption of electric power was only 25 million kilowatt hours, but by 1956 it had reached 830 million and in 1963, more than 1 billion. Half of Morocco's fifteen hydroelectric plants are located in the Oumer-Rebia basin, where the Bin el-Ouodane Dam, the largest hydroelectric plant in Africa and the tenth largest in the world, with a capacity of 1 billion kwh, was opened in 1955. More recently, important dams have been completed at Mechri Homadi and Mechri Klila on the Moulouya River.

These electric power plants had been developed by Électrique Énergie du Maroc, a private company operating under government supervision. To reduce charges to the consumer, the government canceled the private concession in February, 1963, and began operating the utility itself.

Extensive natural-gas deposits exist in Morocco, but to serve the urban centers, the gas must be piped across the Atlas Mountains. There is not yet sufficient demand to make such a costly project worth while.

D. Trade

Under the French Protectorate, Morocco's trade was in theory regulated by the Act of Algeciras, which continued the provisions of earlier conventions with Great Britain (1856) and Spain (1861) that provided for economic equality for all states, and that established a maximum duty of 12.5 per cent on all goods entering the country. In practice, however, both Spain and France imposed trade controls and currency restrictions by which they secured a major percentage of Moroccan trade. French Morocco's imports from the franc zone reached a high of 68 per cent in 1950, and her exports to that area totaled 77 per cent of her total in 1948. After 1950, these percentages gradually declined. By 1955, imports from the franc zone were 54 per cent and exports to the franc zone 57 per cent of Morocco's total. The principal causes of this change were an improvement in world prices, the politically motivated boycott of certain products advocated by Moroccan nationalists, and the growing non-franc competition, especially from Germany and Italy. (Morocco's chief customers in that year were, after France and Spain, West Germany, Italy, French West Africa, Great Britain, Algeria, and the United States, in that order. Principal suppliers were the United States, West Germany, Cuba, China, Great Britain, the Netherlands, Italy, Belgium, Luxembourg, and Algeria.)

During the Protectorate period, the total volume of Morocco's trade increased steadily. In 1921, imports were 510,000 metric tons and exports 480,000 tons; by 1955, these figures were, respectively, 2.278 million tons (valued at $500 million), and 8.3 million tons (valued at $320 million). The increase in imports was principally in consumer goods, which Morocco did not produce in sufficient quantity to meet the demands of her growing population and her improved standard of living: sugar, tea, fabrics, and automobiles; industrial and capital goods; raw materials and semimanufactured goods; and fuel. The increase in exports was primarily in mineral and agricultural products. Minerals, especially phosphates, account for a large part of Morocco's exports, but agricultural exports led the field: cereals (particularly barley), citrus fruits, wine, tomatoes, and cork.

Although the rapid increase in volume of trade was a stimulant to the country's economy, Morocco suffered from a steadily worsening *balance* of trade under the Protectorate. This was due to several factors: the influx of European settlers whose wants were not satisfied by native goods; French and Spanish policies of limiting Morocco's manufacturing industries; the high tariffs set by the Act of Algeciras; and an increase in the cost of imports over exports. The nationalists charged that Protectorate economic policies were deliberately designed to perpetuate Morocco's dependence on France and Spain and to benefit and enrich European interests. While this was partially true, there was also a genuine conflict between the immediate need to meet the population's growing demands for consumer goods and the more idealistic, long-term goal expressed by the nationalists and some Frenchmen of augmenting the national income by bringing in capital goods.

Independent Morocco established a program designed to permit better government control over the balance of trade, and to broaden the base of the country's foreign trade, thus reducing French and Spanish dominance. The first steps to this end were taken by the successful 1957 negotiations to abrogate Morocco's early tariff-limiting treaties with the United Kingdom and Spain. (There was no need to abrogate the Act of Algeciras in order to enact a higher tariff, but since the Act compels Morocco to extend equal treatment in trade matters to all countries, it has been attacked by Moroccans as an affront to their country's freedom of action. At the same time, it has been advanced as a reason to deny French demands for special economic privilege.) Thereafter, a new customs schedule, based on government evaluations, was established, with imports divided into five categories: primary products needed by agriculture or industry, a maximum *ad valorem* duty of 10 per cent; semifinished products, 5–20 per cent; finished products, 15–30 per cent; luxury goods, 35 per cent; and a special group of commodities, up to 50 per cent. In addition to these duties, all imports are subject to a special 2.5 per cent tax, a 5 per cent transactions tax, and a 1 per cent stamp tax. Subsequent bilateral trade agreements were negotiated; by mid-1965, Morocco had such agreements with most of the nations of the world.

Another stimulant has been broader participation in international trade fairs. Morocco participates in twelve to eighteen foreign fairs each year; and the Casablanca Fair is continued annually. More than 30 nations were represented at the twenty-first fair, in 1965; China and the Soviet Union, customary exhibitors since independence, were not represented.

In addition to tariffs, other restrictions have been placed on imports and exports. Foreign products may be imported only within the provisions of the foreign-trade and exchange regulations. Tariff-free goods may be imported from the French franc area, except in the case of a few prohibitions and certain quotas fixed to protect domestic production. (In 1961, in order to offset the unfavorable franc zone balance of payments created by the reaction of investors to exchange controls, the end of military expenditures, and the drought affecting grain exports, Morocco temporarily suspended *all* imports from the franc zone; at the same time, she required a deposit of 25–50 per cent of certain imports.) The currencies needed to pay for imports are delivered to the importer without restriction, by means of deposit and registration at an authorized intermediary bank.

Importation of goods from countries outside the franc area is subject to prior authorization or import license. These authorizations have been granted liberally for goods within the "general import program"—raw materials, equipment, and some manufactured goods necessary to local industries and ordered from countries in the convertibility area. Authorization has also been given bilateral exchanges of goods under a trade agreement, when their economic utility is proved and they are competitive in price. There are no nationality discriminations against import authorizations.

Importers dealing with all countries outside the franc zone with which Morocco has entered a special payments agreement must place in a blocked account a prior deposit based on the undelivered value of the incoming merchandise. An exception is made, however, in the case of equipment approved by the Moroccan Investment Commission when the goods are imported directly by users. This deposit is refunded after the purchase is completed or, in the case of barter-type agreements, after goods have been shipped to the foreign supplier.

In general, export licenses are required, and an *engagement de change* (by which exporters agree to repatriate the proceeds of the sale) must be filed with a bank. To uphold the reputation of exports and provide market research in a given area, Morocco has an Office of Export Control, where products are inspected for conformity to government standards. Subsidies are provided for exports such as grain, the domestic price of which is usually higher than the world price, and sardines.

The new program has achieved some success in increasing Morocco's total volume of trade and reducing her adverse balance of trade, but a slackening of imports has occurred in capital goods rather than consumer goods, and Morocco still exports too great a volume of unprocessed raw materials. There has been a slight increase in the number of her trading partners and in the types of goods exchanged, but a considerable rise in the cost of living, resulting largely from the new tariff regulations, has affected the psychological gains resulting from decreased dependence on France.

There has been a significant rise in exports—textiles, vehicles, phosphates, and other natural resources—to the Communist countries, but the bulk of Morocco's trade remains with Western Europe. In fact, Morocco's continued dependence on trade with the European Common Market (EEC) poses a serious problem. France, which still takes 40 per cent of Moroccan exports, continues to admit many items on special preferences; sardines, citrus, cork, and wine enter France duty-free; and France also supplies price supports for grain. This policy has been sharply criticized by the other members of the EEC, and, as an EEC agricultural policy takes shape, rival citrus producers in Italy and Greece are particularly likely to protest Moroccan privileges.

A protocol to the basic charter of the Common Market (the Treaty of Rome), indicated a willingness to discuss the possible association with the EEC of former African territories of EEC members. Until recently, domestic and foreign political considerations compelled the Moroccan Government to indicate that it did not desire this associated status with the EEC because of the neocolonialist overtones of the organization.* It did, however, ask EEC members for the present to maintain their quotas at reduced tariffs on farm products from Morocco. In 1962, the French Government agreed to maintain the quotas and subsidies and promised to ask the other member states to do the same. The following year, there were hints that Morocco's attitude toward affiliation with the EEC was changing, and the government followed with keen interest the discussions conducted by the Tunisian Ambassador in Brussels concerning ways in which Tunisia might affiliate with the Common Market. In 1964, Morocco commenced informal discussions with the EEC, but with de Gaulle's rupture of France's EEC relations and the outspoken criticism of the Istiqlal, Morocco's future policy toward the EEC remains unclear.

E. Agriculture

Morocco is today, as she always has been, principally a rural country. Seventy per cent of the population depends directly on

---

* As an alternative to association with the EEC, African nations of the Casablanca bloc envisioned their own common market. It planned to reduce tariffs by one-half initially, to eliminate them completely within five years, and to lift quotas on all except competing products and luxury goods. Similar aims were expressed by Morocco, Tunisia, and Algeria, but this also holds little promise, even if political differences are resolved, because the economies of the three members do not complement each other sufficiently.

the land for its livelihood, and 10 per cent rely on it indirectly. Since agriculture represents 35–40 per cent of the gross national product, the general prosperity of the entire country continues to a very high degree to reflect the success or failure of the harvest, which in turn is largely determined by the varied and irregular rainfall.

Approximately half of Morocco's total land area of more than 40 million hectares is arable. (One hectare equals 2.47 acres.) The region most favorable for agriculture, known as the Gharb, embraces the plains and uplands of western Morocco lying between the mountains and the Atlantic, where the soil is moderately fertile and the weather generally mild. Only 8 million hectares are currently under cultivation. A breakdown of land utilization shows that, in millions of hectares, 7.2 are devoted to grazing, 6.5 remain in forests, 4.6 are devoted to field crops, 2.8 are steppe lands, and considerably less than 1 is occupied by orchards, vineyards, and market gardens. Perhaps 90 per cent of the field-crop acreage is devoted to the production of cereals, with the remainder scattered among vegetables and truck crops, forage crops, and cotton. In 1962, the principal crops yielded some 32 million quintals (one quintal equals 220 pounds)— 14.6 million of barley, 8.9 million of hard wheat, 3.9 million of corn, and 3 million of soft wheat, with the remainder composed of oats, sorghum, peas, beans, and lentils.

The large acreage devoted to forest land does not represent either an agricultural or economic loss, as more than 90 per cent of the area is productive. Productive crops include thuja and cedar woods, used by cabinetmakers and builders, as well as juniper, eucalyptus, and evergreen oak. Morocco has 300,000 hectares of cork oak, and two-thirds of its cork is exported; indeed, cork is the only agricultural commodity that constitutes a significant proportion (6 per cent) of world production.

In 1962–63, the steppe lands produced 125,000 tons of alfa grass, most of which was exported to produce paper. Vineyards covering nearly 75,000 hectares produced 2.6 million hectoliters of wine in 1963. Other economically productive crops include tomatoes (mostly exported), and the produce of 9 million almond trees, 13 million olive trees, 9 million fig trees, and 5 million citrus-fruit trees.

Of the 8 million hectares of land presently under cultivation, 7 million are farmed using traditional techniques. Of this 7, 1 million belongs to collective societies and 6 million to individuals. Due to the antiquated methods of cultivation, total annual crop production averages only about 30 million quintals and varies

widely, depending on the weather. Since this is roughly the amount
needed to feed the present population, even in the better years,
crops are neither sufficiently large nor diversified enough for
commercial marketing abroad. The alternation of good and bad
crop years runs in cycles of three or four years. In the droughts
of 1937 and 1945, an estimated 1 million persons and 60 per
cent of the country's livestock died; a 50-day drought in 1961
cut grain production in half and caused a significant recession
in every sector of the economy. On the other hand, some of
Morocco's arable land is threatened regularly with too much water,
either because the water is too close to the surface, due to lack
of storage facilities, or because of faulty drainage. Other perennial
natural problems are locusts and hot desert winds.

Natural problems are not, however, the only ones facing Moroccan farmers. The overwhelming majority of farmers earn extremely low incomes in even the best years because their land
holdings are too small to be farmed economically with mechanized
equipment. The average holding is less than ten acres. Only 33
per cent of Moroccans working on farms own their land, and 90
per cent of these own less than two acres.

Many rural Moroccans of nomadic heritage prefer stock-raising
to farming. Animal production yields an annual income of $220
million. The more than 25 million animals (and 50 million fowl)
include 15 million sheep (in 1963, Morocco produced 16,000 tons
of wool); 2.8 million cows; 7.2 million goats; 1.8 million horses,
mules, donkeys, and camels; and 50,000 pigs.

Under the Protectorate, Morocco became for the first time an
importer of agricultural products, a fact that nationalists were
quick to point out in criticizing the French administration. But
to cite this simple fact of national economic history is hardly to
tell the full story: in the same period, the country's population rose
spectacularly, while the percentage of Moroccans living on farms
steadily declined, and methods of cultivation usually remained
primitive. Today, the country is almost self-sufficient in food-
stuffs, a fact due to the presence of European farmers and the
Protectorate administration's introduction to a small number of
Moroccan farmers of modern equipment and methods: fertilizers,
plant protection, modern storage and processing techniques, rotation of crops, irrigation methods, water conservation, and an important long-term contribution in agronomic research and agricultural education. The French also introduced a vast reforestation
program to replace the Moroccans' previous indiscriminate cutting,
and the Protectorate's development of communications and trans-

portation facilitated access to new domestic markets. The raising of livestock was improved by modern methods of animal husbandry and veterinary facilities. Arable land increased by more than half a million acres by the construction of dams, aqueducts, and irrigation projects; vast stretches of land were also reclaimed by the installation of water filtration systems.

The Protectorate also instituted a system of land registration to replace the inadequate and infrequently used traditional method of establishing legal title in the bled el-makhzen. (In the bled essiba, there had been no system of written title, and personal knowledge was relied on to settle claims.) The new procedure was patterned after the well-known Torrens System; today, title is recorded at registries in Rabat and Tetuán.

In addition to these accomplishments, the Protectorate administration attempted to improve rural life by making a start toward creating an adequate supply of potable water, rural electrification, and storehouses to replace some of the *nouallas* (mud-and-reed huts). These limited efforts were not always appreciated, for the village women lamented the end of social gatherings at the communal well, and peasants often quartered their animals in the new stone houses while they remained in the huts.

Despite these efforts, the standard of living of the vast majority of the 850,000 Moroccan families living on farms did not progress proportionally with that of their 6,000 European counterparts during more than four decades of Protectorate rule. Nationalists considered that this disproportion of Moroccan holdings to European ones (there were more than 55 times as many Moroccan farmers as European ones, but they owned only nine times as much land) and the differing quality of their lands were indicative of official injustice.

One of the Protectorate's first steps concerned land tenure. Lest Moroccan control of public-domain and habous lands hamper the expansion of urban areas, mining enterprises, or public utilities, the domain lands were placed under the guardianship of the Customs Department and could be acquired only for purposes approved by the Protectorate administration. Some of the habous lands could be exchanged, on approval of the makhzen, for other properties producing equal revenue. Land under collective, or tribal, title was also opened to private purchase. The French claimed that they took only land that was uncultivated or barely arable; the nationalists alleged that they took only the best. The French colons obtained about one-third of their land through the processes outlined above and acquired the remainder either by reclaiming wasteland or by purchasing acreage for legal, if inadequate, consideration from private landowners. Europeans settled principally in the Gharb, and rarely in the less-watered areas. Settlement was most rapid between 1923 and 1930, when 10,000 hectares were made available annually by the administration for colonization. After the beginning of the depression, land grants almost completely ceased.

By Moroccan standards, the Europeans were large landowners. In 1955, their average farm was approximately 70 hectares, as against 4 hectares for a Moroccan farmer. The European farmer earned, on the average, $7,000 a year; in 1955, the average Moroccan agricultural wage laborer earned $230, the average fellah, $850. Europeans cultivated more than 400,000 hectares and grew 10 per cent of the total field crops, yet their advanced methods and the better quality of their land returned them 30 per cent of the national yield. While Moroccans farmed mainly for subsistence, the European preferred "cash crops," some of which could be sold abroad. In addition to growing most of the country's soft wheat, they owned most of the vineyards, citrus orchards, and market gardens. Livestock farming, except for pigs, was generally left to Moroccans.

Protectorate fiscal policy also enhanced the European farmer's net profit. A 30 per-cent rebate on the tertib (land tax), designed to encourage the extension of modern farming methods, applied to all land owned by European farmers but benefited only 200,000 hectares of land owned by Moroccans, less than 5 per cent of their total. The government also subsidized the production of soft wheat; its incentive bonuses and easy credit loans were not available to Moroccans.

The Spanish zone accounted for 10 per cent of the country's total agricultural products, despite the fact that 1.3 of its 2 million hectares were useless for agricultural purposes, due to topography and climate. Only in the western part of the Spanish zone, where there was sufficient water, was land cultivated productively; even there, the steepness of much of the land limited the planting of field crops to 280,000 hectares. The principal field crop was barley. In 1951, vineyards and orchards covered 40,000 hectares (the latter consisting principally of citrus, olive, and fig trees). Livestock totaled almost 2 million in that year, half of which were goats. There were few European farmers in Spanish Morocco. In the Tangier zone, soil was too poor for crops and the climate unfavorable for cattle.

The Moroccan insurrection against the Protectorate affected

European farms and farmers adversely, and forest land also suffered. Between 1953 and 1956, Moroccan terrorists destroyed more forest acreage than the Protectorate was able to replant. In addition, forest stations were so often attacked that 320 of 400 were closed. Terrorists destroyed equipment and crops, and farmers were threatened and even murdered. In many cases, when their work became both unprofitable and unsafe, they simply abandoned their land but the majority stayed, determined to salvage what they could in independent Morocco. When independence was achieved, the Moroccan Government attempted to reassure the colons and urged them to pursue their efforts. In July, 1956, the French Embassy made 250 million francs ($700,000) available for loans to small farmers, but on August 1, Mohammed V signed a dahir rescinding the rebates Europeans had previously received on the tertib. The move was calculated to bring the government an additional 500 million francs ($1.5 million) a year, as well as considerable native political popularity. A few days later, al-Alam called for the expropriation of "feudally owned lands" and their return to their original owners.

Then, in October, disaster struck the colons in the Gharb. Six hundred farms, 75 per cent of the total in the region, were damaged to the extent of 5 billion francs ($15 million) when irate Moroccans burned agricultural machinery, farm buildings, vehicles, haystacks, and field rubble. Fifteen thousand agricultural workers were deprived of work, and banking institutions and retail firms that had sold equipment to the colons on credit were seriously hurt, all on the eve of the planting season. The immediate provocation for this attack had been France's arrest of the five Algerian rebel leaders, which to the colons failed to justify such violence. Since that time, the Moroccan Government has been able to maintain physical security of the European farmers, and most of those who survived the first difficult years have remained. Moroccan farmers entertained great hopes for the future during the first years of independence, but they have since learned that their government can give them little more than token assistance.

Immediately after independence, the government supported a farm labor agreement in the Moulay Idris region that it hoped would be a model for the nation. It provided for a 6-day, 54-hour week at a minimum daily wage of 300 francs (85¢) for men and 225 francs (64¢) for women. After two years, all laborers were to receive a 5 per cent increase, and another 5 per cent three years later. This scheme placed the minimum wage at a level 17 per cent higher than the previous national average for agricultural workers. Today, the minimum daily wage has been raised to about one dollar; the average annual income of agricultural workers is only one-fourth that of nonagricultural workers.

As a second step, a small quantity of state and reclaimed land was turned over to the fellahs; this included land that had been held by the state for centuries, farms confiscated from Moroccans who had collaborated with the French, and land abandoned or sold by Europeans. In some cases, title was retained by the government; in others, ownership passed to the fellahs, subject to payment over a 20-year period of 600,000 francs in wheat.

Third, the government has tried to alter Moroccan eating habits, both to make the country more self-sufficient and to improve the balance of trade. It has urged the consumption of fish, long neglected by Moroccans; the use of granulated instead of the more expensive loaf sugar; and the local production of tea and cane or beet sugar—to reduce the annual importation of $17 million of green tea from Communist China and $45 million of sugar from Cuba. (Morocco had never produced a significant quantity of tea, but, in the sixteenth and seventeenth centuries, she grew a considerable amount of sugar cane.) Other cash crops, such as rubber, cotton, and tobacco, have been encouraged. Morocco now cultivates 2,500 tons of tobacco annually, which produced a revenue of $22 million in 1962.

These efforts were supplemented by an increase in irrigation, which had been practiced for centuries by a simple diversion of water from streams or pumping from wells. In 1915, only 125,000 hectares were irrigated, but a large-scale program of dam construction, begun in 1926, placed more than 750,000 hectares under irrigation by 1957. The year 1960 witnessed the creation of a National Office for Irrigation, which established a 20-year program of watering perhaps one-third of about 900,000 hectares suited to irrigation.

Perhaps the most ambitious program that Mohammed V attempted was an effort to increase agricultural production under "Operation Plow." Inaugurated in 1957, this program formed 100 cooperatives, managed by locally selected committees, which were given tractors, small equipment, high-grade seed, and fertilizers at cost; farmers were then instructed in modern farm techniques such as crop rotation. In its first three years, Operation Plow concentrated on small, individual, uneconomic plots and increased the yield on 1 million acres. Unfortunately, enthusiasm waned after the 1961 drought as the peasants realized that they must pay for the equipment whether the harvest was good or bad. Furthermore, the instruction and machinery that the work centers provided too often proved inadequate. Probably more successful, although far less sweeping, was a corresponding reforestation project under which volunteer workers planted an estimated 10 million trees.

King Hassan's first agrarian reform was the revocation of the tertib in June, 1961. This was followed by the inauguration of the Promotion Nationale, an interministerial agency created to ease rural unemployment and further rural development through public-works projects: drilling wells, digging irrigation canals, and reforestation. The management of the projects was left to the provincial governments, while technical advice and general supervision were provided by a central office. In 1961, perhaps 80,000 persons were engaged on Promotion Nationale projects; long-range planning calls for the employment of 1 million Moroccans. Its ambitious goals notwithstanding, Promotion Nationale has been handicapped by its occasional use to increase the political support of former Defense and Agricultural Minister Guedira. Much of the work has been done, in fact, not by unemployed farmers, but by Royal Army troops. Exaggerated charges by opposition parties concerning the political morality involved have further undermined the program.

In January, 1962, the problems of agricultural development were taken over by the National Office for Rural Modernization. This was supplemented in August by the creation of a centralized agricultural credit system, under the direction of a new Agricultural Credit Bank, to establish local credit committees in rural areas. Finally, in answer to the growing demands for land reform, the government announced in February, 1963, a plan prepared by the National Office for Irrigation to overcome this long-time obstacle to agricultural development. The plan called for limitation of land ownership to 50 hectares of irrigated land or 300 hectares of dry land and the distribution of expropriated land according to a system of priorities favoring small landowners and landless peasants: indemnities for expropriated land would be paid over 30 years; recipients would pay for land over a 10-year period.

The plan was soon modified by the government's determination to maintain existing production levels while advancing toward the announced goal. By the fall of 1963, it became clear that only one-quarter of the land owned by Europeans would be included in the first phase of nationalization, which was planned to take three years and affected land colonized by former French Protectorate officials. Furthermore, while the land would be distributed among Moroccan peasants, it would be retained in manageable production units supervised by government technicians. Wherever possible, cooperatives were to be created. In other cases, the new occupants would become owners of the land only after a probationary period of ten years.

Opposition to the amendments was sharp and loud. Leaders of the Moroccan Agricultural Union, representing landowners, declared that too much stress was placed on state control. On the other hand, the Istiqlal and the UNFP demanded immediate recovery of *all* colonized lands and future limitation of ownership to Moroccans. Tunisia's expropriation of French-owned farmland in May, 1964, increased the pressure on King Hassan to follow suit. Although the pace of nationalization was accordingly intensified in 1965, the government still stood by the principle of negotiations with the French concerning compensation. This continued to arouse the opposition which questioned the propriety of the compensation principle. The outcome will depend on the future course of Moroccan politics.

F. Tourism

At the end of the Protectorate, tourism in Morocco was still an underdeveloped but potentially great industry. The country offers an ideal climate on the coast for most of the year and inland during the spring and fall; good roads; some fine hotels; excellent sea and mountain resorts, two with skiing facilities; and a fascinating contrast between two eras and two cultures. Morocco is, in a sense, a travel agent's dream, a delightful taste of the Orient only a few hours from Europe.

The government's early recognition of this potential resulted in the construction of casinos in Mohammedia and Tangier to supplement Marrakesh's existing one; folklore festivals; tax exemptions on gasoline; and abolition of visas for some countries, including the United States. On the other hand, additional facilities and the uses of publicity and salesmanship developed slowly. Nevertheless, by 1964 tourism had become a primary exchange earner, second only to phosphate exports, as 375,000 visitors enjoyed the many attractions. The 1965–67 plan indicates the government's determination to attract even more tourists and currencies to Morocco in the future.

Chapter 7

Social Problems and Cultural Affairs

A. Basic Problems of a Growing Population

ONE OF the most impressive and laudable achievements of the Protectorate administrations in Morocco was their remarkable legacy to the new nation in the field of public health. The initial French (and, to a lesser degree, Spanish) efforts had been directed primarily at overcoming native fear and superstition, but, in 1926, a Directorate of Public Health was founded in French Morocco to supplement the work previously carried on by military medical missions, and, as private doctors were beyond the means of most Moroccans, free services were steadily, though slowly, increased. By 1953, French Morocco had almost 400 private doctors and 300 in the public service. There were 12,000 hospital beds in 15 general hospitals, 35 city and rural hospitals, 73 infirmaries, 287 consulting rooms, 23 mobile public-health units, and 38 special clinics. In addition, auxiliary services provided blood-transfusion units, drugstores, and a training school for nurses and medical assistants. As a result, there was no plague after 1945, few cases of typhus, and considerably less epidemic disease than before 1912. Malaria, tuberculosis, dysentery, trachoma, conjunctivitis, and venereal diseases, however, remained prevalent.

The Protectorate powers also actively sought solutions for medico-social problems such as sanitation and care of the aged, infirm, and orphans. Used to capacity, water and sewage facilities functioned well in the larger cities, but were lacking elsewhere. Public institutions aided the indigent, corrected the abysmal ignorance of even elementary rules of hygiene, and provided care and advice for expectant mothers. Finally, the Protectorate administra-tions attempted to coordinate and guide, as well as to subsidize, the private agencies that fought disease and poverty.

Moroccan nationalists, at least in their public utterances, were unimpressed by these official facts and figures, but they did not dis-pute them. Instead, they pointed out that the well-intentioned French efforts were still hopelessly inadequate. Three hundred doc-tors in the public-health service, for example, meant only one for every 30,000 Moroccans. (The average was somewhat better in urban areas but considerably lower in the bled.) Moreover, only 14 of the total of 700 doctors were Moroccans, and no medical school existed prior to 1956. Finally, one-quarter of the country's hos-pital beds were reserved for Europeans, leaving one bed for every 1,000 Moroccans.

Despite the widespread poverty, rapid urbanization, and confu-sion of values resulting from the clash of French and Islamic cul-tures, crime and juvenile delinquency rates during the protectorates were no higher than those in many Western countries. In 1951, for example, 20,385 Moroccans (including 30 women) and 615 Euro-peans were convicted of offenses other than petty crimes, larcency being the most common offense. There were fifteen penal institu-tions in the French zone.

Moroccan (and Anglo-Saxon) observers often complained that prostitution remained unregulated under the protectorates, facili-tating the spread of venereal diseases, and that efforts to curb the use of narcotics were inadequate. In 1954, French Morocco offi-cially prohibited the use of *kif*, the local variety of hashish, but, in the Spanish zone, the growing of Indian hemp, the source of kif, was legal, and the drug was easily transported across the frontier. It was a not uncommon sight to see Moroccans smoking kif in their long-stemmed pipes, undisturbed and comatose.

The improved standard of health under the French Protectorate was confirmed by the rapid increase in population. Official esti-mates showed a native population of 4.2 million in French Mo-rocco in 1921 and of 5.1 million 10 years later. The first "exact" census in 1936 counted 6 million, and by 1956 this figure had reached 8.4 million. In addition, there was a population of 1.1 mil-lion in the Spanish zone and 183,000 in Tangier—a total of 9.7 million Moroccans (including 200,000 Jews), plus approximately 567,000 Europeans. The general death rate unquestionably de-clined, but the infant mortality rate was disputed between Pro-tectorate officials and nationalist spokesmen, the former claiming 129 per thousand, the latter 283, in 1948.

At the end of the Protectorate, Morocco possessed an excellent base for improvement in public health, but there were far more people, many of them still superstitious and ignorant of modern medicine, than the existing programs could hope to serve effectively. The government continued to rely on European doctors, although a medical school in Rabat will eventually increase the number of Moroccan physicians. Medical facilities expanded until, by 1964, more than 16,000 hospital beds were available and there was a physician for each 20,000 persons. A Red Crescent Organization, affiliated with the International Red Cross, has also been formed. Other measures undertaken since 1956 include attempts to suppress prostitution and the use of kif; aid to the needy in the Rif, who were dislocated during the struggle against France; a requirement that all doctors work for two years in public service before entering private practice; the inauguration of professional social-work training schools; and plans for a "city of the blind" in Casablanca.

New facilities, however, have barely kept pace with the population explosion. The average annual birth rate of more than 40 per 1,000, one of the highest in the world, means that Morocco's population has been growing at the rate of 3.5 per cent, or about 420,000 persons, a year, although the European population has had a birth rate of only 1 per cent. In 1960, a national census showed a population of 13 million, of which almost half are women. Fifty-one per cent of the population are under 20 years of age; 29 per cent are aged 20–39; 13 per cent, 40–59; and only 7 per cent over 60. These figures reflect both the high birth rate and the low life expectancy of about 43 years. A steady emigration of Europeans after 1955 continued until 1960, when the census showed approximately 300,000 remaining. The exodus abated from 1960 to 1964, but its resumption in 1964 brought the number of European residents in Morocco to less than 200,000 by mid-1965.

The government has not yet taken any serious steps to curb the troublesome population increase, not only because of its preoccupation with other matters, but primarily because of the widespread belief that children, like other natural phenomena, represent the will of Allah, which must not be thwarted. Assuming that the poorer classes, which stand most in need of birth-control information and devices, could be educated in birth control, a heavy investment of money and time would be required to produce any noticeable results.

The increased population has created problems in several areas other than that of public health. For example, it has caused a migration from the country to the cities. Whereas only 10 per cent of the population was urban in 1936, 22 per cent lived in the cities in 1952; today, the urban population constitutes 30 per cent of the national total and is increasing almost twice as rapidly as the national growth rate. Droughts in the bled and hope of work in the cities have motivated this trend, sometimes regarded as a stampede, which the government is now futilely attempting to curb by improving the standards of rural life and by decentralizing industry.

In the meantime, the cities continue to grow. In 1917, Fez alone had a population of more than 100,000; in 1926, Marrakesh exceeded this total, joined within ten years by Casablanca, which developed from a mere fishing village in 1900 to Africa's fourth largest city with a population of 965,000. Other major cities have grown proportionately: Marrakesh, 243,000; Rabat, 225,000; Fez, 216,000; Oudjda, 129,000; Meknes, 176,000; Tangier, 147,000; Tetuán, 101,000; Kenitra, 86,000; Safi, 81,000; and· Salé, 75,000. Population density in the cities varies greatly, from 153 per square mile in Casablanca to only 22 in Oudjda, and from 60 in the southern zone to 140 in the northern. In Tangier, it is 1,250 and in some medinas may exceed 2,000.

This rapidly expanding urban population has created a critical housing problem. Whereas the European residents and the small number of Moroccans in the villes nouvelles enjoy a high standard of living, the residents of the medinas continue generally to live as their ancestors had in crowded, poorly ventilated, and ill-lighted rooms, lacking even elementary sanitary facilities or any modern conveniences. Even worse than the medinas are the post-World War II *bidonvilles*; these shantytowns, sheltering the lowest-income groups and the unemployed, were built from discarded gasoline cans, cardboard, and old rags. They are unbelievably congested —one near Casablanca had 60,000 persons living on 130 acres—and the lack of sanitary facilities is appalling. At least 500,000 Moroccans lived under these conditions in 1953, when the Protectorate inaugurated a program to sanitize these villages by deconcentrating the huts, building streets, constructing public toilets, drinking fountains, and washhouses, and installing sewers. The French also built several low-cost housing projects, including three large centers in the Casablanca area. Ain Chock, which houses 15,000 persons in 26-foot-square single-story dwellings of two to three rooms, was the showplace of the Protectorate propagandists and was, indeed, a notable achievement, but the rental of 3,000 francs per month was still too high for the average Moroccan worker. In addition, the Service de l'Habitat also completed an average of 1,750 lodgings a year between 1944 and 1955.

The independent Moroccan Government has intensified the efforts to decongest the medinas and abolish the *bidonvilles*. In addition to advancing credit for private home construction, the state built 22,000 low-cost dwellings between 1956 and 1962, but this effort failed to meet the demands of the population expansion. Even had the intention expressed in the 1960–64 plan to build new housing for 1.4 million persons been fulfilled, there would still be a slum population of 400,000 and another 500,000 living in congested housing conditions.

B. Arabization and Education

The high proportion of children in the Moroccan population has created a formidable education problem. Although the Moroccan Government has raised the literacy rate substantially over that existing under the Protectorate, largely by building on the French heritage, illiteracy and the lack of adequate vocational and professional training remain major obstacles to progress. The national literacy rate in 1963 was 11 per cent; only 18 per cent of the men were literate and only 4 per cent of the women; about 7 per cent of the rural population was literate, by contrast with 23 per cent of the urban population.

Immediately after signing the Treaty of Fez, the French planned a new educational system for Morocco. A Department of Public Instruction, including a Youth and Sports Service, was founded, and a program was instituted to construct schools, recruit teachers, and install equipment. The traditional Koranic and Jewish schools were allowed to continue concurrently with the new structure, which consisted of two separate systems. First, Franco-Moroccan schools, designed for all French children living in Morocco and a small, select group of Moroccans, offered instruction similar to that given in France, but with such curricular additions as Moroccan history and geography and elementary dialect Arabic. By 1953, primary instruction was being given to 60,000 students, of whom 6,000 were Moroccans who received an additional 6–8 hours of instruction in Arabic each week. In the same year, 13,300 French children and 2,700 Moroccans attended Franco-Moroccan secondary schools, courses in which led to a French *baccalauréat* (the equivalent of a high-school plus junior-college diploma).

The student body of the second system of Protectorate schools was entirely Moroccan; unlike the Franco-Moroccan schools, these were not coeducational. In the elementary classes, 10 hours per week were devoted to Arabic, Moroccan history, and the Koran, and 20 hours to French, science, mathematics, and geography. The five secondary schools, where classes were taught entirely in French, led to the French, or a special Moroccan, *baccalauréat*. In 1953, about 5,000 pupils (including 200 girls) attended the secondary schools and 187,000 (including 40,000 girls) the primary schools. Although these figures increased steadily until 1956, only 12 per cent of Moroccan children of school age were then enrolled in schools.

Under the Protectorate, advanced and technical instruction was available but limited. In 1953, for example, 15,000 students, two-thirds of whom were Moroccans, attended agricultural, industrial, and other special secondary schools, distinct from either of the two school systems mentioned above. Advanced instruction included courses in law and literature at the Institute of Higher Learning in Rabat, a Moroccan Studies and Administration College, an agricultural college, a scientific-research institute, and a center for advanced scientific studies. There were preparatory courses in other subjects toward degrees obtainable only at universities in France; by 1956, several hundred Moroccans were pursuing studies at French universities.

In justifying the separation of education under the Protectorate, the French maintained that it was necessitated by differences in language, the location of students' homes, and the administration's desire to provide Muslims with some religious training. Many Muslim families were in principle opposed to completely secular schools and would have forbidden their children to attend them. Whatever the reasons, the attendance at Franco-Moroccan schools was limited primarily to Europeans. Theoretically, a Muslim child might attend, but the nationalists charged that this was possible only when the parents had unblemished political records. The Protectorate authorities reiterated their obligation to look after the children of European settlers first, so that they would stay in Morocco, and explained the low enrollment of Muslims in both school systems as due to a limited budget and the reluctance of Muslim children to attend school. The nationalists scoffed at French excuses and charged that both the separation and the low number of Muslims were motivated by the French desire to maintain political and economic supremacy. They also attacked the Protectorate's educational policy as one designed to replace Moroccan with French culture. While it is an exaggeration to say that the French followed a deliberate policy of keeping the Moroccan masses ignorant, the figures show that, under the Protectorate, French children in Morocco were obtaining an education similar to that of their cousins in France (94 per cent were enrolled in schools), but by and large Muslim children were no better educated than were their grandfathers before the Protectorate began. (By contrast, 67 per cent of the Jewish children were enrolled in their own schools, which educated 29,000 Moroccan Jews in 1956.)

In response to these "outrages," the nationalists opened a number of "free" schools (so named because they were free of French control, not of tuition fees) beginning in 1938, with money provided by well-to-do urban Moroccan families. The education at these schools was conventional, supplemented by extensive nationalist political indoctrination; as a result, they were abolished by the Protectorate in 1944. Two years later, they were permitted to reopen but only under individual permits granted in cases where no political activities were involved. In 1948, there were approximately fifty such schools with a total enrollment of 20,000.

Other nationalist complaints related to the personnel employed by the Department of Public Instruction both as teachers and in administrative capacities and to the budgetary allocations to the two school systems. Of 9,000 employees in the Department, only one-third were Moroccans; in the Franco-Moroccan schools, the teachers were almost all Europeans; even in the Moroccan schools, three-fifths of the teaching staff were French. While it is true that there were few qualified Moroccan teachers, the lack of schools to train them explains, though it may not justify, this situation.

The nationalist complaints about educational inadequacies, voiced by persons of both traditional Islamic and French educational backgrounds, had the positive result of creating an awareness of the importance of education in Moroccan national life. This was shown almost immediately after the country gained her independence. Even before taking concrete steps to expand the educational system, the Moroccan Government initiated a "crash" literacy program to help adults who could not benefit by the anticipated expansion of primary educational facilities. In the spring of 1956, under the direction of Minister of Education Mohammed El Fassi, it inaugurated an anti-illiteracy campaign for the older generation and established a League designed to teach children not yet in, or destined never to attend, school the Three R's, domestic sciences, farm-implement repair, and other practical skills. In its first three years, the adult program enrolled 800,000 persons. These efforts were furthered by the publication of the first newspaper, *Moroccan Lighthouse*, printed in a simplified form of Arabic (with all vowels indicated) and in the simplified Arabic typography invented in 1957 by Ahmed Lakhdari, head of the Adult Education Service, consisting of 67 characters instead of the 475 found in classical written Arabic.

The importance attached to education was further emphasized by the added funds that the far from prosperous country was willing to allot to it. With the government committed to the principle of ultimately providing free public instruction to all Moroccans and thus expanding it beyond a monopoly of the prosperous, 16 per cent of the first national budget, totaling 19 billion francs, was allotted to the Ministry of Education. By 1960, this allocation rose to 27 billion francs, or 25 per cent of the total. More than 900 primary classrooms were built between 1959 and 1960, while the Five-Year Plan for 1960–64 called for the construction of 1,200 new classrooms each year.

In addition, an agreement with the French Government allows a few Moroccan children to attend French *lycées* under French subsidy. The problem of affording French children the same quality in education they would receive in France without violating Moroccan sovereignty was settled by a convention of June, 1957, under which a French Cultural and University Mission was to administer these foreign schools. (The agreement also included French promises to provide Morocco with qualified schoolteachers, to help found a university, and to make annual contributions to Morocco's cultural program.) In 1957, these French Mission schools enrolled 38,500 pupils, including 6,000 Muslims and 2,000 Jews; the secondary schools were attended by 9,000, including 1,100 Muslims and 1,100 Jews.

The efforts of the Moroccan Government, seconded by French help, have produced impressive quantitative results. By the fall of 1963, 1.3 million children, including 200,000 girls, were enrolled in primary schools. Since this enrollment embraced only 50 per cent of all school-age children, it is obvious that still greater expenditures will be required, especially to keep pace with population expansion.

Progress in secondary and higher education since 1956 has also been impressive. By 1961, the number of secondary schools had increased from seven to twenty-two, to serve the needs of approximately 30,000 pupils. An additional 27,000 students attended traditional Muslim secondary schools; 10,000 were enrolled in French or Moroccan schools; and 30,000 Jews continued their education at

Alliance centers. The total came to approximately 130,000 by 1963. Since 1956, five new institutions of higher learning have been opened. In 1957, the University of Rabat, also called Mohammed V University, became Morocco's first modern top-level educational institution, absorbing the Institute of Higher Moroccan Studies and the Center of Advanced Scientific Studies and offering courses in law and liberal arts. An engineering college was added in 1961 to supplement the pitifully small number of trained native engineers. The following year, a medical school opened with more than 180 students. As of 1964, the university had an enrollment of more than 6,600 students, two-thirds of whom were Moroccans. These included 2,500 studying law, 1,000 in liberal arts, 1,000 in the sciences, and nearly 200 in medicine. In addition, more than 1,000 Moroccans were studying in universities abroad (including approximately 650 in France, 100 in Spain, and 150 in the Middle East); between 1953 and 1963, 1,270 Moroccans pursued their studies in other countries under scholarships provided by the United States. The ancient Karouine in Fez and the traditional Islamic colleges in Marrakesh and Tetuán added modern science courses to supplement their curriculums in Islamic law and literature and Arabic grammar. Their total enrollment in 1964 was approximately 26,000.

The urgent need for skilled workers has also intensified technical education and training in Morocco; several ministries have sponsored training programs for government employees and other interested persons. One of the most important has been the Centres d'Instruction Professionelle of the Ministry of Labor, which have ten-month accelerated programs designed to train mechanics, plumbers, electricians, and skilled workers in other trades. Notwithstanding this noteworthy effort, these programs still fail to meet the demands of Morocco's economy.

Despite the millions of still uneducated persons, Morocco's problems in this sphere could be gradually resolved if this involved no more than teaching a population to read a simplified newspaper or perform semiskilled work, with a small elite trained in the professions. Or if the problem were confined merely to expanding classroom space until every qualified child could begin and pursue formal studies through the secondary level, technicians in the Education Ministry could at least define the parameters of the task in terms of facilities, funds, and persons needed, and decide upon a systematic approach. But the program has extended beyond such physical matters to an attempt by the Ministry to unify the diverse school systems. This was to be accomplished by appointing only Moroccan teachers at the elementary level, by making Arabic the universal language of instruction, and by offering courses on Islamic history and culture—all the while maintaining the general standard of instruction and preparing young Moroccans for constructive roles in modernizing the nation. The impossibility of reconciling and realizing these diverse aims within a foreseeable period was apparent from the beginning to professional educators and many political leaders, but few would admit this in the emotion-charged atmosphere of the early post-Protectorate years, when independence was popularly regarded as a solution for all problems.

The basic difficulty was the lack of Moroccan teachers and especially of Moroccan teachers trained to instruct in Arabic. Early in 1956, according to the Ministry of Education, the number of Moroccan teachers available for primary and secondary teaching, including those qualified to teach only in the French language, totaled only 4,500, as compared with 7,800 French colleagues. Unless school enrollment were to drop drastically or the quality of teaching to be diluted by employing inadequately trained Moroccan instructors, it was obviously necessary not only to retain the French teachers already in Morocco, but to increase their number to cope with the growing population of school age. This necessitated the deferment of "Moroccanization" and, to some extent, the unification of the school system, but such a course of action was preferable to the potentially disastrous alternative of asking them to leave. Unfortunately, many French teachers were reluctant to work in an atmosphere of political instability and job insecurity, and their numbers steadily decreased until there were barely 5,000 in 1958–59. A slow upward trend began the following year, however, when the total reached 6,400. As part of the Franco-Moroccan *rapprochement* begun in July, 1962, Paris promised at least 1,000 additional teachers, and, by the end of 1963, there were well over 8,000 in Morocco, a number still insufficient for the country's needs.

To fill the gaps, the Moroccan Government has tried rapidly to expand its very limited facilities for training teachers. The principal normal school, which admitted only 280 prospective pedagogues in 1956, graduated approximately 2,000 teachers in 1962, while hastily improvised regional training centers, which raised the total number of normal schools from 6 in 1956 to 29 in 1964, rapidly increased the total Moroccan teaching corps to 19,000 in 1963. Since few of the graduates of these regional schools had more than a primary education, their effectiveness has been limited. On the secondary level, a newly formed Pedagogical Institute of Secondary Education initiated one-year teacher-training programs for high-school graduates in the fall of 1957, and subsequently provided a two-year curriculum for its few hundred students, most of whom were taught to teach in French.

While there have been some administrative changes within the Ministry of Education, designed to unify the primary and secondary school systems, both complete unification and Moroccanization have necessarily been deferred. It was understood that the French Mission primary schools would eventually be turned over to Moroccan administration. Lacking native teachers to replace the French instructors, however, the government has postponed the matter, contenting itself with nationalizing certain schools operated by the Universal Jewish Alliance. By the fall of 1960, 40 per cent of these schools had been incorporated into the national system.

The shortage of qualified, or even quasi-qualified, Arabic-speaking teachers has been the most obvious cause of the delay in Arabization, a step that such men as Allal al-Fassi and Mohammed El Fassi still regard as necessary if Morocco is to develop along Islamic lines and consummate her renaissance as a nation. Widespread enthusiasm for Arabization led Education Minister El Fassi, a former rector of the Karouine, to initiate a plan for 1956–57 whereby children would be taught exclusively in Arabic in the first two grades and half in Arabic and half in French in the next four grades. After this, the ratio was to be two hours of Arabic to one of French instruction. With teachers fluent only in French unable to comply, with many of the hastily trained normal-school graduates unable to teach properly in classical Arabic (dialect Arabic is not written) and with unsatisfactory new Arabic textbooks, the program failed to give many children a proper foundation in their mother tongue. It thus discredited the whole concept of Arabization in the eyes of many parents.

A cultural agreement with the United Arab Republic signed in August, 1957, brought 300 Egyptian teachers to Morocco, but their use of their own dialects, preoccupation with their own national accomplishments, and their tendency to propagandize quickly led to the termination of the program.

In 1958, when only 50 per cent of primary-school graduates passed the examination for their certificates, Education Minister Omar Abdeljalil reorganized the Arabization program along gradualist lines, following a pattern adopted in Tunisia. Since then, primary-school children have been taught in Arabic exclusively in the first grade, and thereafter half in Arabic and half in French. In secondary schools, where overemphasis on Arabization had produced negative results, French has been used for 20 or more of the 30 hours of instruction.

In 1964, King Hassan established a National Arabization Center to train Arabic instructors and education administrators. It began its assignment by reviewing the Arabic texts used in the primary grades and by examining all the technical terms used in French texts with a view to establishing a common vocabulary for use in Arabic-speaking countries. Workers in this field recognize the problems involved in preparing textbooks in Arabic, and more serious, the dubious possibility of developing a modern Arabic vocabulary. This is a particular problem in science, and many authorities, including educated Arabs, doubt that the flowery Arabic language can be transformed into a suitable vehicle for teaching subjects requiring precision. An Institute of Studies and Research for Arabization was established in Rabat in 1960 under Lakhdari, but its work in compiling Arabic lexicons and textbooks suitable for teaching modern subjects progresses slowly. It has been under little pressure to hasten its work, which would benefit primarily the secondary and advanced levels of teaching, because most students prefer to pursue advanced studies in French (or even English, which is also taught in secondary schools), and because French is still the preferred tongue in intellectual, government, and some business circles. While the Moroccan Government has Arabized street names, added Arabic translations to commercial signs, and created a national Arabic theater, her future leaders, sometimes enriched and often confused by this duality, will continue to follow two cultural lines in their thoughts and acts.

Remembering the intimate relationship between the Arabic language and the Islamic religion, of which Arabic is still the most significant medium of expression, many traditionalists fear for the future of their faith because of the growing interest in secular subjects and the Western languages that usually expound them. Some of these apprehensions, notably those voiced by leaders of the Istiqlal and the Istiqlal paper *al-Alam*, are mainly a means of attacking their opponents in the government; those of the ulema and recent Karouine alumni are more sincere and apolitical. On the other hand, modernists in the FDIC or, in far larger numbers, in the UNFP, usually worry little about the future of Arabic and less about Islam. (This is true even of the antimonarchist Faïk Mohammed Basri, the only Moroccan politician of note who speaks no French.) Many of the younger element would even like to see Islam modernized *à la tunisienne*, but popular resistance to such change and a general inability to comprehend the issues involved will defer such changes indefinitely.

As most Moroccans are still illiterate or semiliterate, communication throughout the country is oral, and the most powerful instrument of information, education, and, of course, propaganda is the radio. In 1963, there were 625,000 radio sets in Morocco, many of them in public places. In 1959, the Moroccan Government created a state monopoly of radio transmission by closing the two commercial stations in Tangier. (The Voice of America was permitted to continue by special agreement until the end of 1963 but was obliged to allow the government 80 hours of broadcast time per week.) A year later, Moroccan radio transmitters totaled 700 kilowatts, twice their strength in 1955. Broadcasts are generally in Arabic, but some programs are offered in French, Spanish, English, and occasionally—as before elections—in Berber. Technicians are chosen from among Moroccans, even at the expense of ability, in order to avoid such situations as the 1956 strike of French technicians that was called in response to anti-French broadcasts. In addition to regular broadcasts, there are about 300 hours a week of short-wave programming to the Middle East and to Africa south of the Sahara. A recently established television network employs the European 625-line system, with 25 pictures per second.

For the literate, the most popular reading material is the newspaper. Under the Protectorates, the press, save for semiclandestine nationalist newspapers, was foreign-owned and printed principally in French or Spanish. American and British interests respectively operated weeklies in Casablanca and Tangier. Local reporting and news dispatches sent abroad were generally very procolonial. Just prior to independence, the first Arabic nationalist paper appeared, and, by 1958, there were two important Arabic dailies and five weeklies; five French dailies and more than a dozen weeklies; two Spanish dailies and six weeklies; and three weeklies in English. Total daily circulation is approximately 150,000, although dissemination is wider due to the common practices of reading newspapers aloud for the benefit of illiterate relatives and friends and of passing the papers onto others. In 1963, the first North African press agency, Maghreb Arabe Presse, was organized.

The Arabic press, generally composed of partisan journals, is vulnerable to political fluctuations. The UNFP papers, *al-Tahrir* and *L'Avant-Garde,* have been hard pressed by the government since independence and have often been suspended or experienced suppression of individual editions. Since the end of 1963, the Istiqlal papers have also been subject to attack.

The European press has fared even worse. It has been continually harassed and at times also banned. For example, the *Tangier
Gazette* was suspended when it denounced the economic integration of Tangier into Morocco; *L'Echo* was seized for criticizing the
FLN; and an economic weekly, *Stocks et Marché*, and even the
United Press were barred at one point. Then, early in 1963, the
Istiqlal initiated a vitriolic campaign designed to close all foreign
papers. The attack was leveled principally at the two papers owned
by a French banker and businessman named Yves Mas: *La Vigie*
and *Le Petit Marocain*. These two Casablanca dailies, published
by the Mas family for more than fifty years, have a combined circulation of 80,000. Since independence, neither paper had commented on Moroccan political affairs but had contented itself with
publishing all government press releases. When Istiqlal members
were in the government, they accepted this free publicity. When
in opposition and without benefit of government subsidy for their
own journals, they resented these facilities provided to the official
view and would gladly destroy the Mas press and obtain its circulation and advertising for its own financially strapped papers.

King Hassan upholds freedom of the press in theory but qualifies
this support by the statement that "no sanction, however severe,
can be too great in meeting abuses of this freedom." Nevertheless,
Moroccan papers continue to discuss fully and criticize all aspects
of public policy. In sum, freedom of the press in Morocco is hardly
absolute but is notable compared to the strict censorship prevailing
in many other newly independent states.

C. The Status of Women in Morocco

Whatever the gaps and flaws in pedagogy, the large increase in
the number of schools is fostering a high level of social mobility in
Morocco. Formerly, only the children, usually the males, of well-
to-do families could attend schools; this upper-class near-monopoly
of education created a climate that confined the social contacts of
educated persons to those of their own (generally urban) class.
Within the last few years, however, the children of fellahs and
laborers have often attended schools with the children of the
bourgeoisie, presaging a decline both in snobbery and rural-urban
separateness. Since most of the schools are coeducational, many of
the social barriers separating men and women will probably fall
within a generation. For the population at large, however, the
status of women is changing very slowly as compared with that of
women in some other Muslim countries.

The first leaders of the feminist movement in Morocco were to be found in the royal family. Mohammed V initiated this emancipation by encouraging his daughters (although not his wives or concubines) to adopt Western ways. The eldest princess, Lalla Aisha (born in 1930) at her father's request delivered a speech in Tangier in 1947 urging that traditional restrictions on women be removed. Nationalists with a Western orientation also encouraged a change in the status of women; in the struggle for independence, women sometimes fought beside men in the streets in hope of liberating their sex as well as their country. Lest they break too sharply with Moroccan traditions and alienate people from the nationalist cause, however, women's branches of nationalist political parties met separately. In some conservative areas, such as Tetuán, girls and women involved in political activities continued to wear their cumbersome haiks over modern French dresses. A few younger women discarded or never adopted the veil; they were usually from well-known and respected families and thus could appear unveiled in public without being mistaken for prostitutes. Other girls, including many with good education and progressive ideas, found it less complicated and less embarrassing to themselves and their families to continue wearing the veil in public.

Within the last few years, the royal family's interest in female emancipation has cooled somewhat. Although Lalla Aisha was appointed Ambassador to England in 1964, her sisters Lalla Malika and Lalla Muzna are not active in public life. Their brother King Hassan, by following tradition in not making his wife queen and by keeping his marriage secret until the press fortuitously learned of the birth of a daughter in Rome in 1962, has not advanced the feminist cause. The government has issued decrees, however, establishing fifteen as the minimum age for marriage and abolishing the traditional marriage contract between parents. Although polygamy has not been prohibited, since it is sanctioned by the Koran, plural marriage is now a ground for divorce. Men still can obtain a divorce with little difficulty but must now pay compensation to the wife.

On the other hand, employment of women in the modern economic sector still encounters resistance. The reasons usually given by men—and sometimes women—are fear of promiscuity, a reluctance to break with tradition, and an unwillingness to allow wives to become financially independent, although in some areas the wife has greater opportunity for employment in unskilled tasks or as an artisan than her husband and is often the breadwinner. Even the younger men who are attracted to emancipated European girls sometimes find it difficult to accept a Moroccan woman in the professions, because she presents so striking a contrast to the familiar pattern. A similar attitude prevails with regard to chastity: whereas many Moroccan men will grant European women the right to sexual freedom, they cannot break with Islamic custom to adopt the same attitude toward Moroccan girls. Many Moroccan women endorse this viewpoint because they fear that to challenge the traditional attitude toward chastity may jeopardize their chances of finding a husband. It will probably be some time, then, before more than a very small number of Moroccan women achieve a sense of freedom of action and opportunity equal to that accorded to men. If the process is accelerated, it will probably be due to the efforts of, and examples set by, the *avant garde* who are active in political and educational affairs. Their efforts to awaken in their juniors a sense of responsibility toward the nation and their sponsorship of serious discussion and evaluation of problems facing Moroccan women have done much to make both sexes realize the importance of developing the potential of this half of the population.

D. *Labor*

While the question of women's rights aroused considerable controversy, it has never posed a critical problem for the government. Feminists never organized the mass demonstrations that occurred in Egypt a generation ago when women sought to drop the veil, and no one has seriously suggested any sweeping reforms that might conflict with the Koran's concept of women and their proper place in society. Such inactivity has not characterized another traditionally underdeveloped group, the Moroccan workers, whose demands for social, economic, and political equality have continually plagued independent Morocco, as they disturbed the French and Spanish protectorate administrations.

Most of the inadequacies in the status of Moroccan labor under the protectorates were inherited from the period before 1912. The French failure to improve conditions, however, created a fertile field for nationalist propaganda. There continued to be large numbers of unemployed and underemployed persons, whose problems were intensified by the heavy migration to the cities and the overall increase in population. Although public employment agencies existed in the larger cities, labor was normally recruited by word-of-mouth. Apart from the artisans, most of the Moroccan labor force was unskilled by Western standards, due to a combination of impoverished background and lack of training, for which European employers and the Protectorate educational system were largely to blame. Employers did not generally permit Moroccans to develop skills that would raise them to an equal status with European workers, and off-job training facilities such as vocational schools were generally inadequate.

The French had enacted considerable labor legislation, however, providing compensation for occupational accidents and disease, a 48-hour work week for industrial workers, paid yearly 12-day vacations, safety regulations, unemployment insurance, child labor laws, and a code for industrial relations including inspections and conciliation boards to settle individual disputes. Unemployment insurance, however, was available only to European workers, and the other provisions were inadequately enforced. Employer-employee relations were controlled entirely by management. This was due to a law prohibiting strikes; poor labor organization; a high labor supply; the workers' reluctance to submit disputes to the conciliation boards for fear of reprisals; doubt concerning the boards' impartiality; or actual ignorance of the board's existence.

Equal pay for equal work did not exist under the protectorates; Moroccans received less than Europeans, and women less than men. Additional differences in fringe benefits increased the discrepancies. Between 1950 and 1955, a semiskilled European worker averaged 20,000–50,000 francs a month; skilled European workers, 100,000 francs; and administrative personnel 120,000 francs. Moroccan industrial workers received 39–100 francs an hour; agricultural workers were allowed 240 francs plus meager rations for a 12- to 15-hour day. As fringe benefits consisted principally of family allowances allotted only to industrial and business employees, the mass of Moroccans working on the land shared none of these advantages.

By 1955, the fully employed Moroccan labor force consisted of 2.25–2.5 million persons; a seasonal force totaled another 1 million. Except in agriculture and domestic service, women played a minor role. The permanent work force included approximately 1.7 million Moroccans, 136,000 Frenchmen, and 53,000 Jews. The majority of Moroccans (800,000), plus an almost equal number of wives, were engaged in agriculture; 400,000 were in industry or were artisans; 120,000 were in commerce; and lesser numbers in fishing, mining, domestic employment, and transportation. As might be expected, the smaller French labor force dominated the public services; their positions elsewhere were generally supervisory.

Prior to 1946, Moroccans had been permitted neither to join existing French unions nor to form their own, and thereafter they

could join only French unions. In order to facilitate a gradual shift
from tribal organization to the industrial pattern, however, some
firms had sponsored quasi-tribal labor councils composed of elected
representatives who brought complaints to the employer's attention. As many as 200,000 workers had been thus represented. The
largest French union was the General Union of Confederated Moroccan Syndicates, to which 18,000 Europeans and 20,000 Moroccans belonged in 1952. Technically affiliated with the Communist-
dominated General Confederation of Labor in France, the nationalists took it over in that year just before it was banned. Two
smaller unions were the Moroccan Federation of Christian Unions,
affiliated with the Confédération Française des Travailleurs Chré-
tiens in France, and the Workers Force. None of these organizations, however, afforded any significant benefits to their Moroccan
members.

The Union of Moroccan Laborers (UMT), formed in March,
1955, and claiming half a million members in industry and agriculture by the spring of 1956, was Moroccan labor's first effective bargaining agent. Although the UMT could not enforce its original
demands for general pay increases in the French zone, in January,
1956, it gained a 13 per-cent raise in the legal minimum wage for
workers in industry and commerce, making the minimum 56–66
francs per hour; it also enforced a similar 10–15 per-cent increase
for agricultural workers, raising their minimum hourly wage to 23–
35 francs. In the Spanish zone, although the Spanish authorities
opposed the UMT as long as their control there lasted, the minimum wage for unskilled laborers was increased from 19 to 23
pesetas a day. Finally, in 1958, a minimum-wage scale for industry
and commerce, based on a division of Morocco into four zones of
productivity, was introduced. In 1964, the minimum wage varied
from .73 DH to .85 DH per hour, with a minimum for agriculture
of 3.89 DH per day.

Moroccan independence brought more jobs but no decrease in
unemployment, which indeed was expanded by the general economic retrenchment and the rapidly increasing potential labor
force. While the permanent labor force was approximately 3.5 million in 1962, unemployment estimates ranged as high as 500,000; in
addition, 50 per cent of 3.2 million rural laborers were underemployed, working less than four months a year. Although unemployment benefits are not paid, a social-security program, supported
by employers' contributions, was instituted in 1961 and within two
years covered more than 300,000 workers. Relatively few Moroc-

cans have sought employment abroad, but the government has encouraged them to do so. It has also tried to combat unemployment by extensive rural development and public-works projects and by establishing *bourses du travail* (labor exchanges). However, large-scale industrialization and better training facilities are indispensable to solve this critical economic and political problem. As of 1963, the majority of all workers, 57.8 per cent, were still employed in farming, fishing, and hunting; no other category absorbed as much as even 10 per cent of the working population. It is obvious that only an industrial revolution can basically alter this situation.

In the first few years after Morocco gained her independence, strikes were not infrequent and, at least on one occasion, were violent. Since trade unionism has been strongest among transport, mining, and administrative workers and longshoremen, effective obstructionist activities were easily organized. These strikes were usually due less to wage or similar issues than to political ones, notably French Army movements and the existence of American bases on Moroccan soil. For several years, the UMT restrained its demands for wage increases in the national interest, but this has become increasingly difficult to do with the rising cost of living. Labor courts have been functioning since 1950 to settle disputes and labor inspectors are available to pass on complaints, but neither commands much respect. When labor and management cannot solve a dispute, government officials seek to bring about a solution, which all too often results in misunderstanding and resentment.

Although it is one of the most powerful political organizations in the country, both because of the votes it controls and the economic activities it can disrupt, the UMT is neither tightly knit, nor centralized, nor well disciplined; it suffers from too rapid growth, the limited experience of its 1 aders, and a tendency to dissipate its energies in political agitation and demonstration. A fortunate byproduct of this concern with, and commitment to, the national picture, however, has been the exclusion of Communist influence.

Until 1960, the UMT had a virtual monopoly over organized labor in Morocco. Its allies in the Istiqlal-controlled government, such as Labor Minister Abdullah Ibrahim, effectively crippled the French unions in 1957 with legislation requiring that all union officials be Moroccan nationals and by refusing contracts to unskilled European workers. French employees thus had no alternative but to seek redress of grievances through their former unions in France or the French Government itself.

A dahir of July 16, 1957, guaranteed the right of Moroccans to organize unions, although a "temporary" decree enacted the same day permitted the Secretary General of the government to forbid the creation of new unions. This decree has not been enforced, but, for several years, the government let it be known that it accurately reflected its views. In November, 1957, an electrician named Mohammed Jorrio, who had been ousted from the UMT for failure to obey a strike order, attempted to set up a rival labor union. This effort was frustrated by King Mohammed's call for "labor unity" that "encouraged" all workers to discuss their differences with the UMT, which, he said, had shown itself capable of defending the rights and interests of all the working class. As long as the UMT remained loosely affiliated with the Istiqlal, which was itself straining at the seams, the King apparently preferred labor unity to further politically oriented divisions that might strengthen the hand of malcontents in the bled.

In 1960, however, after the UMT had announced its support of Ben Barka and the socialist-minded UNFP, the King supported an attempt to form a conservative counterpart to the UMT. The Union Générale des Travailleurs Marocains, sponsored by the Istiqlal, has found it difficult to gain popular support to offset the economically and politically stronger UMT, yet this split in the labor movement has led to an increasing number of jurisdictional strikes and contributed to the general growth of labor unrest since 1960. Guedira has hinted that the FDIC might sponsor a third "nonpolitical" union; this might succeed, because of the jobs and other favors the FDIC could dispense to disgruntled workers. By mid-1965, however, no such body had materialized, and the UMT retained its strong position.

In sum, ten years of independence have seen limited evolutionary, but certainly not revolutionary, social changes in Morocco. There has been no attempt by those in power to erase completely the privileges conferred by high birth, no thought of redistributing wealth to end sharp class distinctions, no efforts, in other words, to attain "social equality" or realize the other goals demanded by many labor and student leaders and by persons in the UNFP. Most of the King's pronouncements regarding "socialism," first made in early 1964, have referred to a continuation of the pump-priming practice whereby the government helps the rich to provide jobs and other benefits for the poor or whereby excess wealth can be drained from the prosperous—preferably rich colons—and given to the poor, not as a right, but as a boon.

If developments were shaped by internal matters alone, these prevailing attitudes might continue for several generations. However, Morocco no longer lives in a vacuum, as she did a century ago, and it is increasingly difficult for the establishment to counter the siren calls for revolutionary change that are sweeping Africa.

Chapter 8

Foreign Affairs

I N ANALYZING the policies of any country, whatever its size, strength, or form of government, it is impossible to distinguish completely between domestic and foreign considerations. In the case of a newly independent state, preoccupied with shedding the vestiges of colonial control while still heavily dependent on external assistance for the economic and technical means necessary to run its internal affairs, the distinction becomes even more blurred. Foreign policies of new states must thus be viewed, in large part, as a dependent variable of domestic policies. (This applies even to such nations as Ghana or Egypt, whose leaders consider such aggressive foreign policies as Pan-Africanism or Pan-Arabism as the best means of serving their purely national or personal interests.)

One of the major reasons for nationalist demands for independence is a people's desire to let others know that they exist and must be reckoned with, to be accepted by other nations and independently to establish relationships with them. This impulse toward self-assertion usually involves several contrapuntal themes. An eagerness to be met on equal terms by the stronger, older powers, combined with the fear, and then the experience, that they will not be accepted, usually fosters a converse desire to work with other peoples who will treat them as peers, or possibly as superiors in certain respects.

At the same time, there is usually a desire to give the new nation a legitimate place in history; this manifests itself in an eagerness to affiliate even nominally with an international movement such as socialism or Pan-Arabism. National pride and a sense of uniqueness counter this wish to belong to something larger, and are shown clearly in the eagerness with which new nations proclaim their own special concepts of socialism or neutralism.

Frustration in trying to satisfy these conflicting desires, coupled with the need to unify a heterogeneous populace around a national ideal, or to divert them from pressing domestic problems, accounts for much of the sound and fury that often characterizes the foreign-policy pronouncements of new countries. On the other hand, the wish to lessen some of the mounting pressure can also serve to make foreign-policy actions actually more temperate than the language in which they are couched. This is particularly true when a matter that could minimize foreign or domestic criticism of the regime, such as substantial foreign aid or a decolonization measure, is at stake. It is within the context of these complex considerations, as well as the peculiarities of her internal politics, that Morocco's foreign relations must be viewed.

While internal matters almost entirely monopolized the attention of the Moroccan Government during its first months of independence, the new state was also endeavoring to gain recognition in the community of nations. The first step in this direction was the creation of a Foreign Ministry in April, 1956. Morocco's sovereign assumption of legal control of her foreign relations depended, however, on the conclusion of a diplomatic agreement with France, and France was not eager completely to cut the umbilical cord. Nevertheless, Morocco proceeded with plans to exchange diplomatic representatives with certain countries and notified their consular agents of the Foreign Minister's assumption of his duties and the Sultan's desire to establish diplomatic relations with them.

In the first week of May, 1956, the governments of Pakistan, Albania, Portugal, Switzerland, and Belgium recognized Morocco's independence. Spurred by this action, the newly appointed Foreign Minister, Ahmed Balafrej, and Premier Si Bekkai went to Paris and then Madrid in an attempt to reach diplomatic agreements with the former protecting powers. In Paris, they met with icy resistance, but in Madrid, the Franco government expressed its willingness to accredit an ambassador to Rabat. The British, American, and Italian representatives informed the new government of their countries' intentions to raise the status of their Moroccan consulates to embassies in the near future.

The prospect that four major Western powers would precede

France in diplomatic exchange with Morocco finally roused the French Government to action. Alain Savary, Secretary of State for Moroccan Affairs, hastened to Rabat in an effort to break the impasse that blocked the conclusion of a diplomatic accord. During these talks, a member of his party made the unfortunate statement that, if the International Court at The Hague were to consider an issue involving Morocco's presentation of diplomatic credentials before the French National Assembly abrogated the Treaty of Fez, it would certainly find such procedure illegal. Moroccan statesmen retorted that, since the French parliament had not ratified the treaty in 1912, it need take no legal steps to effect its termination; the March 2 Franco-Moroccan declaration of Moroccan independence, they argued, brought this about. To end the squabble, the Sultan advised M. Savary that both governments should act quickly, lest further disagreements terminate the negotiations. Moroccan opinion was as "sensitive as the skin of a flower," the Sultan observed, and could not be denied the full fruits of independence.

For a week, both sides argued over the draft of a diplomatic treaty. Procedural matters became as important as substantive issues when France demanded that her future representative in Rabat be given a special title and be recognized as dean of the diplomatic corps. While the haggling continued, the Sultan used the occasion of Aid es-Seghir, the holiday that marks the end of Ramadan, to receive the consular corps for the first time without the presence of a French representative. On the following day, Spain named José Felipe Alcover, Spanish Consul General in Rabat, as Ambassador Designate to Morocco, a selection the Sultan promptly approved. Alcover did not present his credentials immediately, however, giving France a few more days to reach an agreement. Savary, scheduled to leave Rabat on May 18, postponed his departure one day; toward midnight on May 19, the agreement was at last reached. The terms were not made public until May 28, however, when French Foreign Minister Pineau and Balafrej formally signed the treaty and exchanged supplementary letters.

The agreement immediately provoked controversy on every side, most of it involving the question whether the various provisions concerning consultations required Franco-Moroccan unity of action. The most controversial item was Article 4, in which both parties promised not to adhere to a policy that, after joint examination, was recognized as incompatible with the interests of either. Some French journalists interpreted this to limit Morocco's freedom of action, precluding her, for example, from becoming a member of the Arab League. Istiqlal spokesmen flatly rejected this interpretation and contended that none of the provisions was to be interpreted as limiting either party in concluding treaties, conventions, or other international acts. *Al-Alam* noted that Morocco was not obligated to adopt any policy but retained the right to negotiate and reach understandings in her own interest with all nations. Balafrej further asserted that both countries must agree that questions raised under Article 4 were of common interest. The issue of Algeria, for example, was in his view not subject to Article 4, since Morocco could not find it a "common interest" to support a colonialist policy. It thus appeared to Morocco that the two states would merely discuss matters of common interest and then act independently. Nevertheless, the opposition PDI criticized the treaty as incompatible with real independence, in that it included provisions that bound Morocco to the will of France. Although not hostile to voluntary collaboration with France, Ouazzani said he could not accept interdependence, which imposed restrictions under the guise of technical assistance, a common interest, and traditional Franco-Moroccan friendship. Other, though lesser, difficulties were posed by Spain's vain protest over the treaty's grant of precedence to the French ambassador after her envoy had been accepted by the Sultan.

Following the signing of the Franco-Moroccan diplomatic accord, the nations that had not already done so extended their recognition to the new state. In July, in response to France's formal request, the United Nations Security Council unanimously voted to admit Morocco to the world organization. Subsequently, Morocco became an active member of all the principal organs of the international body.*

Although the rupture of formal Franco-Moroccan diplomatic relations following the Meknes riot in 1956 continued until September, 1956, a *détente* was reached in January, 1957, and negotions on agreements governing their post-Protectorate relations were resumed. The first result was a convention on technical and administrative assistance that permitted Morocco to retain temporarily as many of the 41,000 remaining French civil servants as

---

* Morocco's first act in the United Nations involved a resolution condemning Soviet intervention in Hungary. In abstaining, the Moroccan representative explained that, while he agreed with the principles of the resolution, he believed it inconsistent to condemn the U.S.S.R. and not the British-French-Israeli "aggression" in Egypt. Primary Moroccan interests at the General Assembly have revolved about the question of Algeria, the need for technical assistance in the Maghrib, African freedom, and Mauritania.

she chose and included a French promise to train prospective
Moroccan civil servants, who would gradually replace the French
cadre until only approximately 10,000 (including 8,500 teachers)
remained in 1965.

Thereafter, until 1962, Franco-Moroccan relations were determined principally by the statements and actions of the two
nations in regard to Algeria. However, the similar attitudes of
King Hassan and de Gaulle on the principles of interdependence
and cooperation foretold an early and substantial *rapprochement*
of the two countries after Algeria became independent. This came
about to a considerable extent, although Morocco's internal politics
required King Hassan to minimize the change.

For Morocco, the significance of her revitalized relationship
with France is principally economic and cultural. For France,
Morocco continues to represent a foot in the door to Africa and
the Arab world. The future, however, is clouded by such Moroccan
economic problems as nationalization of the colon lands. It is
therefore necessary, as a matter of economics as well as of politics,
that Morocco continue to seek additional friends abroad. In this
perspective, the importance of Morocco's relations to other countries becomes clearer.

While Morocco's leaders, after 1956, contended that their major
aims were to bridge the East-West gap and eliminate colonial
exploitation, they also expressed more specific goals: the removal
of foreign troops from Moroccan soil; the final definition of Morocco's frontiers; the termination of the Algerian conflict; a broad-
ening of Morocco's political economic ties with other countries
to lessen her dependence on France; and consolidation of her
contacts with other Arab and African states.

In trying to implement the first objective, they soon found that
diplomatic issues with France and Spain were inseparable from
domestic politics. All too often, these problems were handled with
more emotion than reason and more with a view to increasing
individual political popularity or diverting the masses from mun-
dane problems than from a considered appraisal of Morocco's best
interests. The immediate agitation over French troops, for example,
embellished the political reputations of men such as al-Fassi. While
it undoubtedly convinced France that Morocco intended to force
withdrawal of the troops, it also wasted energy, destroyed hope
for French and Spanish aid, and made foreign investors wary. The
treatment of the Mauritania issue likewise antagonized not only
France but also several African governments.

French intransigence on the troop question was motivated by

her desire to protect French settlers in Morocco, but it was also influenced by the view that the pacification of Algeria must precede friendship with Morocco. King Mohammed V and Balafrej understood this and might initially have postponed their demands for the early removal of the troops, had it not been for the pressure exerted by al-Fassi and his adherents, the Liberation Army, and other active supporters of the FLN. The vicious circle of threats and counterthreats, which was not broken until France was ready to make peace with the Algerians, resulted in other troublesome diplomatic repercussions.

With French financial and technical help both diminishing and increasingly unpopular, it became not only desirable but imperative to solicit new support. In 1956, it appeared logical to appeal to the West, especially to the United States. Washington and other Western capitals, however, were reluctant to replace French influence. Against a background involving the issues of foreign troops, frontiers, Algeria, and the nuclear threat, this denial strengthened popular demand for a policy of nonalignment. In addition, the Sultan regarded a "third-force" foreign policy as a good method to balance out a conservative policy at home. Consequently, Morocco began to look toward the East, but with disappointing results, since the Communist countries offered few benefits and those not entirely without strings.

With the major powers treating Morocco as the weak and inexperienced parvenu that she in fact was, it might appear that the one group of countries with which Morocco might reach satisfactory understanding would be her fellow Arab states. Unfortunately, however, they entertained ambitions that often conflicted with those of Morocco and were unable to offer much material help. There were even serious difficulties with the other peoples of the Maghrib, with whom Morocco shared such obvious bonds as a common history, geography, a Franco-Islamic culture, personal friendships formed as students in Paris or as exiles in Cairo, and a common colonial opponent.

During the first few years of Moroccan independence, the Franco-Algerian-Maghrib tangle consistently elicited the greatest concern. Once Algeria became independent, it was Morocco's border disputes with Algeria that aroused intense interest. However, other frontier problems have also commanded attention. The Protectorate had hardly passed into history when al-Fassi announced that Morocco must liberate all her territory remaining under colonial jurisdiction. (He established the newspaper *Sahara al-Maghrib* to voice this demand.) This call was based on the contention that foreign officials had arbitrarily defined the Protectorate's boundaries in secret agreements, ignoring areas historically, ethnically, and popularly regarded as parts of the Sherifian Empire. This claimed Moroccan territory included Tarfaya, the Spanish presidios, and a vague area referred to as the Moroccan Sahara. The latter—which extends from the Senegal River, 1,000 miles south of the Dra River, to Figuig, Algeria, 600 miles inland—included Ifni, the Spanish Sahara, Mauritania, and part of southern Algeria. The addition of this land would have increased Morocco's total area by 400 per cent and its population by 20 per cent.

The Spanish-French Treaty of 1912 defined Morocco's southern boundary as the Dra River. Morocco never ratified this demarcation, however, and Tarfaya, whose administration Spain turned over to Morocco in 1958, actually is south of that line. Furthermore, until France actively began to administer the Sahara as part of Algeria in 1928, she called it often as not the "Moroccan Sahara." Still, although the area south of the Dra was within Morocco's historic sphere of influence, the river had generally represented the limit of effective Sherifian jurisdiction.

The first objective of independent Morocco's irredentist fervor was Ifni, a 676-square-mile Spanish enclave north of the Dra with a population of 38,000, where the inhabitants and Spanish soldiers clashed in April, 1957.* The Istiqlal paper al-Alam noted that the peoples of both Ifni and the Spanish Sahara were drawing closer to Morocco and would inevitably seek incorporation, and a delegation of Ifni tribesmen journeyed to Rabat to demand the integration of their territory into the "fatherland." The Spanish authorities suppressed Istiqlal activities in Ifni, but in July the party was still able to organize a general strike there. An Istiqlal governor was then sent south to Agadir, near Ifni, thus permitting al-Fassi not only to continue his political harangues in the south, but also to staff the Saharan Liberation Army with local pro-Istiqlal sympathizers and dismiss most of the Middle Atlas veterans. Following an intensive propaganda effort by al-Fassi, 1,200 troops from Ifni, together with the Moroccan irregulars, attacked Spanish

* Prior to the fifteenth century, Ifni was controlled by the Ait Ba Amran confederation of Berber tribes. In 1476, Spain built a fort at Sidi Ifni, which was recaptured by Morocco fifty years later. In 1860, the Moroccan Sultan and Spain agreed on a Treaty of Uad-Ras, in which, Morocco claims, it granted Spain fishing rights and land at the site of the old fort to facilitate its development; Spain, however, maintains that the entire enclave was permanently ceded to her. The enclave's present boundaries were defined in the Franco-Spanish accord of 1912. Ifni's chief administrator is a military governor appointed by the Spanish Council of Ministers.

garrisons throughout the enclave on November 23, while the King of Morocco was out of the country visiting the United States. Despite Crown Prince Moulay Hassan's denunciation of "adventuresome people who act contrary to the intent of the government," the King and the Council of Ministers perforce accepted the popularly supported rebellion, and, when Spain warned against providing aid to the rebels, the Moroccan Government declared that the Royal Army stood ready to defend Moroccan soil. However, the palace's official protests, even against Spain's alleged bombing of Moroccan territory and the dispatch of eight Spanish warships to Agadir harbor, remained courteous and mild. Morocco had no desire to embitter relations with Spain while important issues were under negotiation. King Mohammed called for a peaceful settlement of the conflict, and Prince Moulay Hassan offered to use his influence to effect a cease-fire if Spain would cede Tarfaya.

Meanwhile, the insurgents managed to penetrate the town of Sidi Ifni before a Spanish contingent of 4,000 troops from the Canary Islands (tripling the Spanish forces in Ifni to 6,000) succeeded in repulsing them beyond a 5-mile perimeter of the town. Then, in early 1958, Spanish forces and French units from Mauritania joined to crush the Moroccan irregulars still operating in the Sahara, and the Liberation Army of the Sahara faded into oblivion.

Although Ifni, per se, meant little to Spain, she could not relinquish it in the face of force. Indeed, she had wished to trade Ifni for a general border delineation in the Sahara and continuation of Spanish control of the northern enclaves of Ceuta and Melilla, which have predominantly Spanish populations. Morocco was not anxious to bring to a head the issue of her Saharan irregulars, however, and she remains unwilling to limit her territorial interests in the Sahara to Ifni. Consequently, talks with Spain produced concrete results only in the case of Tarfaya. In April, 1958, Morocco finally obtained an agreement for the transfer of authority in Tarfaya without offering any significant concession in return. Spain asked only that the transfer be effected without ceremony. However, when 1,000 Moroccan troops attempted to occupy Tarfaya's capital, Cape Juby, Spanish forces barred the way; but by May all Spanish troops had departed from Tarfaya, and Moroccan control was established.

Meanwhile, the Spanish Sahara, an area of about 100,000 square miles, was itself not free of tension during this period. Sporadic fighting, initiated in December, 1957, became fierce early in 1958. The Saharan Liberation Army and the Spanish Army each claimed to have inflicted heavy casualties on their opponents; al-Fassi claimed that Spain had effective control over only the cities of El Ayona and Villa Cisneros. As the year wore on, fighting was limited to military and political sniping, with no immediate conclusion in sight.

Between 1958 and 1963, Spanish-Moroccan relations remained unsettled and strained. For internal political and economic reasons, the Moroccan Government continued to voice its demands for the Spanish Sahara, while Spain continued to oppose Moroccan claims and to express concern for her citizens in Morocco and adjacent territories. The pride of the Spanish African Army influenced this position, although the most important factor was probably the domestic prestige of Franco's regime. Gradually, however, these points of contention were minimized as other matters assumed greater importance. A mutual desire for better relations developed; in July, 1963, Franco and King Hassan met in Madrid to negotiate a settlement of outstanding issues. Late in the year, Spain assumed a more flexible attitude toward the Sahara question, probably because extensive oil prospecting there had been unsuccessful, but expressed concern over Mauritanian claims to the territory sought by Morocco. A concentrated Spanish radio and press campaign sought to create an image of Spanish friendship for Morocco. There were also indications that General de Gaulle was urging Spain to resolve the issue quickly, probably because he hoped to expedite his own plans for *rapprochement* with Rabat or perhaps create a "vertical axis" of Paris, Madrid, and Rabat.

Relations were further improved by Spain's agreement in January, 1964, to evacuate her troops from Ifni. Implementation of this accord has been slow, but by mid-1965 only a small number of Spanish troops remained and Spain had indicated to the Moroccan Government that she was prepared to relinquish her claims to sovereignty over Ifni. The future of Saguia el Hamra, however, remains clouded: significant phosphate desposits have been discovered there.

The activities of the Saharan Liberation Army were not restricted to attacking French Army outposts * and Spanish enclaves within Moroccan territory. One year after Morocco gained her independence, al-Fassi announced that Liberation Army forces were moving against French West African territory (Mauritania), but his clearly irredentist proclamations have ultimately proved to be not much more than words. Moroccan interests and claims

* See above, chap. 4, pp. 107–8.

to this desert area of some 400,000 square miles, with its population of perhaps 650,000 Muslims of Arab-Berber origin, was founded on the fact that Sultan Maulay Ismail had been the first Emir of Trarza, one of three Mauritanian emirates. Moroccans who knew that their country's suzerainty was only nominal until the French occupied Mauritania early in the twentieth century were nevertheless interested in that area's rich iron (100 million tons), copper (27 million tons), coal, manganese, oil, lead, and uranium deposits. They were thus moved to support al-Fassi's emotional claim and to bolster it with the allegation that the Franco-German agreement of 1911, with its vague reference to Morocco's southern regions, recognized Mauritania as part of Morocco.

Initial French efforts to exploit the Sahara's resources had been made through the Office Commun des Régions Sahariennes, established in January, 1957. The OCRS planned to develop untapped resources in an area more than eight times the size of France, covering parts of Algeria, the Sudan, Niger, Chad, and Mauritania. Paris had claimed that the plan would not affect the political status of these territories and that Morocco would be invited to participate within the framework of interdependence. Balafrej had nevertheless insisted that the plan implied nationalization of Moroccan territory; and al-Fassi had said that Morocco would participate in it only if France recognized that some areas of the Sahara were integral parts of Morocco. Undisturbed, in March, 1957, France had asked the World Bank for a loan to exploit Saharan mines.

Although most Mauritanians had indicated satisfaction with French rule in elections held under the Loi Cadre of 1956, small groups of Mauritanian nationalists had visited Rabat since early 1956 to seek support in obtaining independence from France and association with Morocco. Some stayed as refugees in southern Morocco; others went on to Cairo; and some lived as guests in Rabat. The propaganda of these allegedly oppressed fellow Muslims and would-be Moroccans, coupled with limited fighting by Mauritanian "nationalists," provided an extremely popular issue for men like al-Fassi. The fact that attacks on French troops coincided with an Algerian offensive in the Sahara made it all the more difficult for either the government or the King to disavow the Mauritanian cause, despite the additional problems it posed in dealing with France. The government, in fact, created a separate office of Saharan affairs in the Foreign Ministry in November, 1957, for the purpose of supervising developments concerning Mauritania. In September, 1958, Morocco even sponsored a Mauritanian and Saharan conference in Rabat, where 200 delegates claiming to speak for more than a million persons met to deny the legality of de Gaulle's constitutional referendum and reaffirm their desire to integrate their territories into Morocco.

The objections of Morocco notwithstanding, Mauritania proceeded with other territories of French West Africa to achieve independence in 1960 (i.e., from France and from Morocco). Rabat then waged a vain struggle to preclude diplomatic recognition of the new country and its acceptance into the United Nations. Failing in these aims, Moroccans nevertheless continued firmly to support King Mohammed in this general policy.

King Hassan did not share his father's views on Mauritania. To appease the Istiqlal and generally to curry internal political support, however, he at first maintained Morocco's formal position on the Mauritania question. But by 1962, when it became apparent that this stand rendered Morocco's relations with other independent African states more difficult, Hassan launched a trial balloon suggesting a negotiated settlement. The UNFP accepted the plan quietly, but the Istiqlal reacted violently. The Istiqlal, however, was steadily losing both popular as well as official support on this position. Accordingly, in August, Fall Ould Omeir, then Moroccan Minister of State for Mauritanian Affairs; El Moktar Ould Bah, former Mauritanian Minister of Education; and Ahmedou Ould Sidi, ex-president of the Mauritanian Youth Association, went to the Mauritanian capital, Nouakchott, to further their aims from within.

Mauritania's existence as a sovereign entity was further confirmed when she was invited to become a charter member of the Organization of African Unity (OAU) in May, 1963. Morocco boycotted the conference at Addis Ababa that had conferred this status on her, but soon realized that the only consequence of her adamant stand was to alienate potentially friendly states. Accordingly, she adhered to the OAU in October, while King Hassan continued to press for special concessions from the Mauritanian Government in return for Morocco's formal recognition of it. President Daddah of Mauritania, however, refused to make this a subject for negotiation. He cited an old Moorish proverb: "So much the worse for him who cannot see the sun; we shall not wear ourselves out showing it to him."

By mid-1964, Morocco appeared to have seen the sun. Hassan admitted the obligation to respect an established regime and agreed that meddling in the domestic affairs of another state courted grave dangers. Daddah responded by advising the Mauritanian

Assembly that the way to cooperation with Morocco was now open. This *détente*, while not representing a diplomatic triumph for Morocco, was at least a victory for common sense over irrational emotion.

A. Morocco and the Maghrib

When the founding fathers of the FLN, despite the opposition of many fellow Algerian nationalists, fired their first anti-French broadsides on November 1, 1954, they had aroused mixed reactions among Moroccan nationalists. To al-Fassi and his supporters, who had been working closely with them, the move had been the long-expected signal for an all-Maghrib liberation campaign. Suspicious of France and of attempts to compromise with her, and sharing the FLN view that force was the one language France understood, they had wished Morocco to fight alongside Algeria and, hopefully, Tunisia, in order to remove France once and for all from the Maghrib. Tunisian nationalists, however, led by Habib Bourguiba, had indicated their disagreement when they agreed to accept internal autonomy from France in the spring of 1955, thereby incurring the wrath of both the FLN and al-Fassi.

Not all Moroccans were out of sympathy with the Tunisian position. Balefrej, for example, who was more a Moroccan nationalist than a Pan-Arab or Pan-Maghribian, could understand Bourguiba's wish to serve his own country first. Himself disliking violence, he could see little reason for Morocco to fight on if she received independence, and he realistically appreciated the constructive role France could continue to play in Morocco. Furthermore, he had been unimpressed with several of the Algerian leaders whom he had met and was reported to have shown this disapproval openly. In addition, there was an egalitarian air about the ragged Algerian fellaga and their political leaders, and strong ties bound the FLN and republican Egypt. In these circumstances, Balafrej and the Sultan contemplated the possibility of cooperation between the Moroccan monarchy and Algerian rebels with concern.

Mohammed V had had no personal disagreements with the FLN, but Prince Hassan was to many Algerians, and to Tunisians as well, an object of scorn. Feeling some sympathy for the Algerians, some fear of an attempted French reconquest of Morocco if the Algerian war continued, and great apprehension regarding the popularity of the Algerian cause within Morocco, on the eve of Moroccan independence Mohammed V had casually offered to act as a mediator in the conflict. When his offer was rejected, he and his advisers decided to pursue a careful policy of watchful waiting, hoping desperately that France could somehow be made to regard Algeria as an entity independent of France or that the FLN could be persuaded to accept a compromise short of full independence. Noninvolvement, or even benevolent neutrality toward the FLN, soon proved impossible.

Evidence of Moroccan sympathy for the cause of the Algerian rebels appeared immediately at the end of the Protectorate. In March, 1956, the French High Commissioner's Office in Rabat discovered that Radio Maroc's Arabic program was carrying messages of encouragement to the rebels. When it protested, the Moroccan Government denied responsibility on the ground that it lacked any legal means to prevent the broadcasts, since the station was still under French control. Less than a month later, the French were further embarrassed when, as the local populace gathered at Salé to greet the Sultan on his return from a triumphal Spanish trip, two youths suddenly appeared atop a baggage shed displaying the Algerian rebel flag and a banner proclaiming "Algeria needs its Moroccan brothers!" French policemen hastened to the roof to arrest the defiant standard bearers, but the rumbling of the 50,000 onlookers quickly turned into a chant of "Algérie! Algérie!" Powerless, the French could do nothing but ignore the incident.

While the Moroccan Government remained officially silent on the Algerian question after the Sultan's abortive offer of mediation, individuals in and out of the government were less reticent. Al-Fassi declared that Morocco was ready to assist in preventing a permanent rupture between France and Algeria but contended that an effective solution of the conflict must assure the Algerian people of their liberation and end the illogical state of affairs whereby Algeria remained a colonial regime while Morocco and Tunisia were independent. Adopting this line, al-Alam warned that, if Algeria was not liberated, Morocco would be isolated from the Arab world. It contended that Morocco could not stand idly by while French forces butchered fellow Arabs on the country's eastern border, and solicited aid for the Moujahadin (holy warriors) to deliver the Moroccans' brother Muslims from slavery. Torres predicted that Morocco would join the struggle for Algerian independence and envisioned a United States of North Africa.

At the end of May, Robert Lacoste, now Governor General in Algeria, warned Morocco to stay out of the Algerian struggle. The suggestion was summarily ignored, and French troops were attacked by Muslims from both sides of the border. The attackers from the Moroccan side of the vaguely defined frontier were generally Algerians who used Morocco as a base of operations. France retaliated, bolstering her twelve garrisons along the 600-mile stretch of oasis outposts from Figuig to Tindouf and increasing the number of armed patrols between these points. Electrified barbed wire was eventually installed on the Moroccan border to supplement the fence already erected on the Tunisian side. Planes patrolled the extended line and a no man's land in which intruders would be shot was demarcated. However, arms and men still filtered through where the barbed wire was cut and in areas that roving patrols could not adequately cover at night, and moral encouragement continued.

In August, while representatives of the Mollet cabinet and the FLN were conferring secretly on a "phased" independence for Algeria, the Sultan visited Oudjda. There, near the frontier, before a huge throng, he called for an end of the Algerian war and a solution that would satisfy the national aspirations of the Algerians, simultaneously respect the interest of France, and guarantee the rights of the French who chose to stay in Algeria. Immediately, representatives of the FLN and French spokesmen suggested the Sultan as a mediator. As a first step, plans were made for him to visit Tunisia in mid-October to discuss the basis for an honorable peace with another vitally interested party, the Bey of Tunis; but the trip was clearly the occasion for a meeting with Tunisia's real ruler, Premier Habib Bourguiba. Both Mohammed V and Bourguiba expressed hope for a solution that would give Algeria independence within the framework of a North African Confederation composed of Algeria, Morocco, and Tunisia, loosely allied to France by economic and cultural links.

The Sultan then received the Mollet government's unofficial blessing to discuss peace talks with France with the leaders of the FLN. The French asked that the meeting not be dramatized, but the five Algerian leaders—Ahmed Ben Bella, Mohammed Khider, Hussein Ait Ahmed, Mohammed Boudiaf, and Mustafa Lachraf—were acclaimed on their arrival on October 20 in Rabat, and Mollet was displeased with the Sultan's open cordiality. Nevertheless, when Secretary of State Max Lejeune suggested that the five Algerians be arrested, Mollet rejected the proposal categorically, for he had promised the Algerian negotiators safe passage. Lejeune was not easily dissuaded, however, and joined with Lacoste, other officials, and French officers in Morocco to set his plan in motion. A plot to arrest the Algerians was implemented when French advisers subtly suggested to the five Algerians that they leave Morocco in a separate plane so as not to antagonize France.

On October 21, the Sultan and his official entourage left for Tunis on an Air-Atlas-Maroc plane; the rebel leaders left on a separate craft manned, as were all such flights at the time, by a French crew. (Two French women journalists and Thomas Brady, North African correspondent for *The New York Times*, were with them.) Their first scheduled stop was at Palma, in the Balearic Islands, a site chosen to avoid passing over Algerian territory. But at Palma, the schedule of the second plane was altered, unbeknownst to the plane's passengers, on orders from French military forces in Morocco. The Moroccan Government learned of the plot shortly after the plane had landed in Palma and sent an urgent message ordering it to stay grounded, but the message was never delivered. After it left, the Moroccans sent another message ordering it to return, but this likewise was never received. The plane's pilot flew in wide circles after leaving Palma until it became dark, and then landed at the scheduled time—but at Algiers' Maison Blanche military airfield, ringed with waiting *gendarmes*, instead of at Tunis. The rebel chiefs were completely surprised, but not at a loss for words. "This is how you can trust the French," cried Ben Bella; another commented, "They don't want peace!" When the Sultan heard the news, he lamented, "I would rather it had been me or my son. This is a worse blow to my honor than my exile. These men were my guests. They trusted me, and now they are in a French prison!" Publicly, he referred to the French action as a violation of international law and of elementary morality.

With the Tunis talks necessarily suspended, Mohammed V decided to cut short his stay and return to Rabat. Before leaving, however, he announced that a treaty of cooperation and alliance between Morocco and Tunisia had been discussed and would be signed at a later date. Ben Barka said that Algeria's struggle with France would continue, and the Conscience Française deplored the action of its countrymen. A spokesman for the FLN, now deprived of its top leadership, speaking of the abduction as an "unprecedented betrayal," called for a renewal of the struggle against France. In Paris, the Mollet government, although it had not endorsed them, justified the arrests. (Later, an international commission of representatives of France, Morocco, Belgium, Italy, and Lebanon, was created to inquire into the affair. But, when France refused to allow the five Algerians to testify in person, the Moroccan delegate walked out, and the hearings were indefinitely adjourned.)

The response in Morocco to the French "piracy" was instantaneous. All stores were shut down, a general strike was called, and demonstrators cried for "Free Algeria" and "Lacoste to the Gallows!" The green-and-white flag of the Algerian rebels, heretofore seen only rarely, appeared everywhere, and the Meknes riots were indicative of the prevailing tension.

With a protracted war in prospect and local sentiment running high, the Moroccan Government resolutely faced the problem of forcing France to accept the prospect of Algeria's eventual independence. The strategy involved two tactics: to demonstrate to the world that Algeria was not a "part of France in rebellion," as the French contended, but a "part of North Africa fighting for freedom," as the FLN claimed, and to strengthen inter-Maghrib ties to foster this belief; and, second, to have the Sultan make repeated offers of mediation.

Morocco's initial efforts to build North African unity were made in the areas of labor and education. Leaders of the UMT and its counterparts in Algeria and Tunisia met yearly to consider the Algerian problem and discuss plans for a North African Labor Confederation; representatives of national student organizations in the three countries likewise considered amalgamation. Somewhat more concrete was the Moroccan-Tunisian friendship pact, forecast during the Sultan's visit to Tunis and finally initialled in Rabat on March 30, 1957, which provided that the two countries would hold frequent consultations on a common foreign policy, have joint diplomatic representation in some countries, take steps to abolish visas, maintain a permanent commission to coordinate their economies and standardize their economic systems. A joint commission to implement the treaty then proposed measures for the common protection of products common to both countries; increased trade in noncompetitive products and more flexible customs regulations; exchange of judges and a joint study of judicial codes; consultations to draft legislation to improve the living conditions of workers; and exchange of postal and communications specialists. Both countries agreed to these proposals in January, 1959.

Morocco and Tunisia were even more eager to reach a common solution on the matter of Algeria. They were thus willing to act as official spokesmen for the FLN at the 1957 session of the United Nations General Assembly and to propose there a joint mediation effort. Both countries were also eager to remain on speaking terms with France, a fact which the FLN appreciated, since each country would thus offer the entree to official French circles it wanted to keep open. As of early 1958, the FLN was therefore willing to heed Tunisian and Moroccan pleas that it postpone formation of a government-in-exile, a move that would force both countries to choose between recognition of it and breaking off with France. The FLN was satisfied by the assistance and commitment it then received from these neighbors. Furthermore, Algerians were eager to loosen their connection with Egypt, and strengthened inter-Maghrib ties appeared to afford an excellent means to that end. This was compatible with the interests of Bourguiba, who long had been the object of Egyptian intrigues, and of many Moroccans, who were suspicious of Pan-Arab activities in their country.

With closer cooperation appearing to offer advantages to each participant, a significant step toward Maghrib unity occurred in April, 1958, when delegates of the Istiqlal, Neo-Destour, and FLN met at the Marshan Palace in Tangier to pave the way for eventual political federation. Libyan observers were also present, because of the prospect that Libya might join a North African Confederation.* The resolutions adopted by the conference recognized Algeria's right to independence and promised total support for the rebels there; recommended establishment of an Algerian government-in-exile after consultation with the Tunisian and Moroccan governments; denounced aid afforded France by certain Western powers to prosecute the Algerian war and demanded withdrawal of foreign forces from North African territory; expressed solidarity with Mauritania's struggle for liberation from France and advocated Mauritanian integration with the union; proposed a Maghribian Consultative Assembly to examine questions of mutual interest and make recommendations to national executive organs; urged periodic meetings to discuss common problems and evolve means of executing recommendations of the Consultative Assembly; asked individual governments not

* Tunisia was especially eager to include Libya in order to strengthen that country as a bulwark between herself and Egypt. A "Treaty of Fraternity and Good Neighborliness" signed on January 7, 1957, between Libya and Tunisia was hailed as a significant step to greater Maghrib unity; subsequent general agreements provided for closer cooperation between Libya and Morocco. Leaders of the Libyan labor movement participated in the second North African Labor Conference; indeed, the third conference was held in Tripoli.

Linking Libya to the prospective North African Confederation was geographically plausible; and it had ethnic, historic, and economic ties with the Maghrib. Its propinquity to Egypt, however, can be expected to influence Libya to remain a buffer between Cairo and the Maghrib rather than become a partner of either.

to act wholly separately in the fields of foreign affairs and defense until colonialism was abolished; and created a permanent secretariat of six members.

Of primary interest to France and the West were the references to total support of the Algerian rebels and the prospective formation of an Algerian government. There was no indication how far this support would extend, beyond the fact that the Moroccan and Tunisian borders would remain open to provide sanctuary to the *fellaga*. France and such countries as the United States, which would be confronted with the delicate question of recognition, accordingly continued to hope that Morocco and Tunisia would restrain the FLN from forming an exile government.

Little clarification of these two points emerged from further talks held by the three countries in Tunis in June. The participants rejected integration into France as a solution for Algeria but did not otherwise elaborate on the Algerian question, despite vague French suggestions for the creation of a western Mediterranean pact to guarantee common defense and cooperation in the Sahara and an equally vague proposal for union of the Maghrib and France, with Paris as a common capital.

The Tangier Conference and its aftermath were the apogee of Maghribian cooperation. Notwithstanding their warm words, Morocco and Tunisia were in the last analysis reluctant to alienate France, pending clarification of de Gaulle's intentions. The inscrutable French leader, upon taking over the French Government in May, 1958, had expressed his desire for friendship with Morocco and Tunisia, and there was considerable hope that he would end the Algerian war and settle France's future relations with the Maghrib.

Initial signs of discord between the FLN and its neighbors, particularly Tunisia, appeared during the summer of 1958, when the Algerians objected bitterly to a Tunisian agreement to permit France to build an oil pipeline from southern Algeria to the Tunisian coast, believing that such arrangements should await FLN control of an independent Algeria, including the Sahara. Bourguiba replied that in the four years required to complete the pipeline, Algeria would achieve independence. Then, in August, Tunisian police seized the printing plates of the FLN's official organ *El Moujahid*, whose radical editors had been critical of Bourguiba's pro-Western and anti-Nasser policy. Despite these strains, Morocco and Tunisia immediately accorded recognition to the FLN government-in-exile when it was formed in September, 1958. Bourguiba, with only a poorly equipped 6,000-man army, was reluctant to oppose the FLN, which itself had more men under arms in Tunisia than he. The Moroccan Government did not want to thwart popular sentiment in favor of the FLN and thus give an opening to the waiting political opposition, but Balafrej contended that Morocco did not intend any hostility to France.

Within two years of the Tangier Conference, the brief *rapprochement* between Morocco and Tunisia ended in a formal separation. Several points of conflict had never been resolved: the personal and political clash between al-Fassi and Bourguiba; the sharp criticism in the makhzen of the deposition of the Bey of Tunis in 1957; Tunisia's dissatisfaction with Morocco's policy toward Jewish emigration; and Morocco's closer participation in the Arab League.* Furthermore, Morocco's deeper religious orthodoxy, which had led to widespread condemnation of Tunisia's outlawing of polygamy in 1956, produced an even more violent reaction in January, 1960, when Bourguiba announced that fasting might be ignored during Ramadan: such actions were sacrilegious in the eyes of Moroccans, since they directly contravened practices either specifically permitted or prescribed by the Koran. And the Moroccan Government had aggravated the tension by answering Tunisian criticisms with repeated personal attacks upon the "unmanly," "pro-French" Bourguiba. Differing policies during the Congo crisis further widened the split. The *coup de grâce* to Moroccan-Tunisian relations, however, was Tunisia's recognition of Mauritania's independence in November, 1960, and her sponsorship of Mauritania for membership in the United Nations. (This was done not merely to placate France, but also to increase Tunisian influence among the less radical, newly independent states of Africa that appeared to be potential allies of Tunisia in any clash with Algeria.) The Tunisians justified their action on the grounds that the Mauritanian people had voted for independence in a plebiscite and that there was little evidence of any popular Mauritanian desire for union with Morocco. Morocco, however, considering Tunisia's action a direct affront, recalled her ambassador from Tunis and thereupon concentrated on closer ties with Algeria and other African states that entertained irredentist or expansionist claims.

Rabat's growing closeness to the FLN, however, was due to more than the disagreement with Tunisia. The Algerians, increasing the scope of their diplomatic activities after forming their

* See below, pp. 235–38.

provisional government, sought increased support from the Communist bloc and closer direct cooperation with their North African neighbors. The two objectives merged when shipments of arms were promised by the East and the FLN ordered them delivered to ports in Morocco and Tunisia. The Tunisian Government voiced strong objections to such entanglements; the Moroccans were equally disturbed when in May, 1960, the FLN announced that an arms shipment from Communist China was scheduled to arrive in their country. But Morocco's closer involvement with Algeria continued, producing the expected frictions with France, and the French stopped a Morocco-bound Czech freighter carrying arms in November. Occurring two months after Rabat and Paris had accused each other of fomenting border incidents, the event further encouraged Morocco to strengthen her ties with the FLN.

Near the end of 1960, de Gaulle finally indicated his willingness to grant independence to Algeria and to open negotiations with FLN representatives. Attempts to reach a settlement foundered, however, on France's desire to retain control over the entire Algerian Sahara and the FLN's insistence that it was an integral part of Algeria—an issue of intense importance to Morocco. France based her stand mainly on the fact that the desert had always been administered separately from Algeria's northern provinces; the Algerians retorted that France had never administered the Sahara at all until 1930 and that Algeria's northern and southern provinces were not effectively separated until after oil had been discovered in the south during the war. Morocco's interest in this controversy was more than academic: with Tunisia and other states bordering the Sahara, she shared a claim to portions of the desert that France had thus far refused to concede. Morocco thus faced the alternatives of trying to force France to settle these claims while this was still possible or of agreeing with the FLN's contention that it had the exclusive right to settle claims to the Sahara and would do so immediately upon receiving independence.

Particularly significant to Morocco was her border with Algeria. This border had never been formally defined beyond a point about 50 miles from the Mediterranean. France had gradually extended her administration of the disputed area as part of Algeria, but Morocco never acknowledged her right to do so. After 1956, France had not directly refuted the merit of some of Morocco's border claims but was anxious that Morocco should not gain control of certain areas lest they serve to provide sanctuary or supplies to the FLN, and she demilitarized and neutralized the border zone. For practical reasons, Morocco had accepted this decision.

In view of her Saharan interests, Morocco compromised—by confining her pressure on Paris to behind-the-scenes suggestions while publicly espousing Algeria's claim to the entire desert. Simultaneously, in conversations during 1960 between Ferhat Abbas and al-Fassi, the former promised a fair settlement as soon as Algeria was independent. The Algerians reinforced these promises by asking Mohammed V to mediate with de Gaulle and by giving assurances that a monarchy next door was acceptable to them.

Throughout 1961, Moroccan-Algerian relations were centered on establishing the Casablanca Bloc,* smoothing relations between the new King and the many Algerians who had openly criticized him, and paving the way for Franco-Algerian peace talks. Morocco criticized Bourguiba's attempt in July, 1961, simultaneous with the Tunisian blockade of French naval bases at Bizerte, to occupy Saharan territory that the FLN had refused to promise Tunisia formally, although backing Tunisia on the Bizerte issue. By January, 1962, with plans for final negotiations of Algeria's independence well under way, Algerian and Moroccan leaders met in Fez to discuss anew the concept of a North African confederation. But even as the Evian accords ending the Algerian war were being completed in March, eliminating the greatest obstacle to North African unity, tension flared again among the prospective partners. That month, a little-known Tunisian named Mohammed Abdelkefi arrived in Morocco and was permitted, if not encouraged, by the government to hold a press conference in which he denounced Bourguiba's government and announced the creation of a mythical Tunisian National Democratic Front to combat Bourguiba's alleged dictatorship. Tunisia replied in kind in April by asking Bouabid to participate in a program in which Ahmed Ben Salah, Tunisian Minister of Planning and Economic Affairs, attacked Morocco's "feudalism" and lack of "social justice." Government spokesmen in Rabat reacted by suggesting that Ben Salah "must have been thinking of Tunisia"; such things "simply could not occur in Morocco."

Another Maghrib conference at Tangier convened in this uncertain climate. Economic and technical unity were discussed in detail, and al-Fassi urged common political institutions in the form of an advisory assembly and agreement on a common foreign policy. (The articulate Istiqlal leader subtly skirted the Moroccan-Algerian border dispute and suggested the use of all Maghribian

* See below, pp. 242–44.

natural resources for the common good.) Only very general resolutions resulted from the meeting, however, and by July, when Algeria became independent, Rabat and Algiers were again tiffing. With the FLN wracked by internal feuds and increasingly reluctant to discuss cession of territory, King Hassan received the chiefs of the Tindouf region, part of the undemarcated border area, who came to swear allegiance to him at Rabat. Then, impetuously, his government rushed troops to that key border town. After several armed clashes with Algerian fighters, however, Morocco chose not to escalate the affair into a larger conflict, and the territory remained under *de facto* Algerian control. But in September, tension flared anew when the Algerian leader Ben Bella asked the people in the disputed border areas to participate in the Algerian elections. Morocco denied the legality of the procedure, but King Hassan, faced with more serious domestic problems and fearing the growth of revolutionary republican sentiment, had to face the possibility that Abd el-Krim, who was in touch with Ben Barka *and* Ben Bella, would try to instigate another revolt in the Rif (an apprehension terminated only by Abd el-Krim's death a few months later), and he therefore chose to underplay the border issue for the moment.

At that point, Morocco decided to mend its fences with Tunisia. The first big step in this direction was a meeting in December between Balafrej and Tunisian Foreign Minister Mongi Slim —two men who shared a personal preference for moderation and apprehension over the course of events in Algeria. When Slim defended Tunisia's recognition of Mauritania and expressed the hope that Morocco would not interpret it amiss, Balafrej indicated his government's willingness to see this point of view. Thereafter, Morocco made efforts to pacify Ben Bella (including an announcement in December of a forthcoming [but never realized] alliance between King Hassan's younger sister and the Algerian leader), and, in February, 1963, a Maghrib foreign ministers' conference attempted to settle differences between Algeria and Tunisia.

During the next six months, Morocco and Algeria concentrated on internal affairs, and a policy of watchful and somewhat suspicious waiting prevailed on both sides of the unsettled border. At the end of September, however, internal dissensions in Algeria precipitated further deterioration. Following demonstrations and outbreaks in the Kabylia Mountains against the Algerian regime, Ben Bella charged that Morocco had troops poised ten yards from the Algerian border and supporting the Berber uprising against his government. Without substantiation, Ben Bella charged that Belkacem Krim, a former Algerian Provisional Vice Premier whom he had ousted from the national leadership group, had visited Tangier to seek Moroccans' help against the Algerian regime. Algerian newspapers and radio even alleged that King Hassan himself was supporting the rebels.

A momentary respite occurred at a meeting in Oudjda on October 5, at which Guedira and Abdelaziz Bouteflika agreed to implement bilateral agreements between Morocco and Algeria signed in March for economic, cultural, administrative, and technical cooperation; they also reaffirmed the principle of nonintervention. This reaffirmation, however, was soon to be dishonored. The Moroccan Government, badgered by internal political woes, seeking to divert attention from its recent *de facto* acceptance of Mauritania's independence, and also anxious to warn Ben Bella against taking aggressive action, took the initiative. On October 14, 250 miles southwest of Colomb Bechar, Moroccan forces— with an eye on Tindouf, gateway to Mauritania and reputedly rich in iron ore—captured Hassi Beida and Tinjoub, two palm-fringed oases in the desert. The Algerian Government immediately charged that 4,000 Moroccan soldiers received air and tank support in this attack against an area now 25 miles within Algerian territory. (French maps, drawn before independence, had included it in Morocco's borders.) Morocco replied that only one small battalion was engaged in this battle to recover Moroccan territory; despite the difference in details, it was clear that Morocco had determined to bring the border question to the point of negotiation. Ben Bella, however, demanded not negotiation but a general mobilization of the Algerian Army to meet "Moroccan aggression"; the Algerian National Assembly was suspended to enable the deputies to join their military units. Still, the sequel involved no more than an all-out war of words. Ben Bella charged that Moroccan troops were in the pay of international capitalists and that King Hassan was encouraging chauvinist forays in order to protect his throne against the Arab socialist revolution. There were even false and emotionally charged reports from Radio Algiers that American pilots, members of a training detachment with the Royal Air Force, were airlifting Moroccan troops to the fray. Morocco retaliated with more credible charges of Cuban, Syrian, and Egyptian aid to Algiers. (Cuba had, indeed, sent a shipment of weapons to Algeria, and the United Arab Republic had 1,000 troops there. Five Egyptian officers captured in Moroccan territory were paraded before journalists to prove the charge. Although Ben Bella claimed the Egyptians were merely a military training mission, Cairo admitted taking Algeria's side in the dispute. After bitter denunciation of Nasser's interference in Maghribian affairs, King Hassan recalled his ambassadors from Cairo and Syria and severed diplomatic relations with Cuba.

Four days later, on October 18, the Algerians attacked Ich, a town clearly within Moroccan borders to the northwest of the original area of conflict. In the following days, however, Moroccan troops began soundly to defeat the ill-equipped Algerians. Inconclusive dispatches furnished no clear picture of the scale or intensity of the clash, but light casualties were reported, and it appeared that the troops on the ground, if not in actual combat, numbered several thousand on each side and were supported by armored vehicles.

Calls for a truce by Tunisia and by Emperor Haile Selassie of Ethiopia, who arrived in Casablanca from a visit in the United States, went unheeded when Ben Bella rejected King Hassan's insistence on an Algerian commitment to negotiate the borders. Fortunately, steady pressure from Africa and the West prevailed. At the invitation of Modibo Keita, Hassan and Ben Bella met at Bamako, Mali, with Keita and Selassie acting as mediators. In addition to accepting a cease-fire, they agreed to establish a commission to set up a demilitarized zone supervised by Mali and Ethiopian officers; to form a committee under the Council of Foreign Ministers of the Organization of African Unity to resolve the dispute; to discontinue propaganda attacks; and to reaffirm a noninterference policy. A new outbreak at Figuig occurred after the cease-fire accord, and Algerians occupied the town in a last effort to achieve a bargaining position. But by November 5, the fighting had ceased at all points and the cooling-off began.

Ten days later, the foreign ministers of OAU member states met in Addis Ababa, in the first special session of the thirty-two-nation organization, to name a commission to ascertain the facts of the Algeria-Morocco quarrel and recommended a solution. The importance of this effort went beyond the Maghrib, since its success could serve as a significant precedent for other border disputes in Africa. Although many African states support the principle, espoused by Algeria, that borders inherited from colonial powers should not be questioned in the interest of law and order, it is agreed that attempts to solve disputes by force will not be limited to the Maghrib. If such problems can be solved by negotiation and in the absence of outside interference, African nations may take an important stride toward meaningful independence.

The commission, composed of representatives from the Ivory Coast, Mali, Nigeria, Senegal, Sudan, and Tanganyika, met twice early in 1964, and direct talks between Morocco and Algeria began simultaneously. Finally, on February 20, 1964, an accord was announced; it was understood to provide for a no man's land of seven kilometers on either side of the positions held on October 1, 1963, and a resumption of diplomatic relations. In particular, Algeria agreed to withdraw from Figuig and Ich; the status of Tindouf remained undecided. Several weeks later, 379 Algerian and 57 Moroccan prisoners were exchanged. The principal remaining task of the commission was to define the border.

Morocco's *détente* with Algeria was followed by her resumption of formal diplomatic relations with Tunisia. In October, 1964, economic ministers from Morocco, Algeria, Tunisia, and Libya attempted again to reestablish Maghribian economic coordination. A protocol called for formation of a permanent consultative committee, freer trade, harmonization of customs policies, coordination of export and industrialization policies, and adaptation of Maghrib policies to those of the European Common Market.

The coup d'état in Algiers which led to the replacement of Ben Bella by Colonel Hourari Boumedienne on June 19, 1965, set the stage for further amelioration of Moroccan-Algerian affairs. While the new Algerian Premier had been generally regarded as an austere revolutionary, the initial months of his rule have indicated that he is principally an intense nationalist who favors Islamic to Marxist ideology. Boumedienne has made clear his desire to strengthen Maghrib ties and has even blamed his ambitious predecessor for the military conflict with Morocco.

Thus, by mid-1965, the Maghrib faced the future in an atmosphere of growing understanding. Nevertheless, the scars of past schisms cannot be expected to disappear for some time. Moreover, the disparate political systems of the three North African states make close cooperation difficult. A Maghrib political union therefore appears visionary; increased economic coordination and cooperation, on the other hand, are not only possible but likely, in view of their practical importance.

In the past, plans for economic development in North Africa were completely nationalistic and resulted in such duplication of facilities as construction of separate steel complexes and in the cancellation of cooperative phosphate marketing agreements. These failures have now been replaced by joint marketing arrangements for esparto grass and some Saharan oil, the agreement to construct a complementary rather than competing automobile

factories in Tunisia and Morocco, and plans to construct communication lines across the Maghrib.

B. Morocco and the Pan-Arab Movement

Despite Morocco's initial enthusiasm for ties with fellow Arabs
and her attraction to the Pan-Arabism espoused by Nasser, her
relations with the Arab states of the Middle East have, with
occasional exceptions, been generally cool, covered by an occasional verbal gloss of brotherhood. For some time, Morocco's
embroilment with France and Spain and other issues peculiar to
Morocco and the Maghrib reinforced the government's philosophic reluctance to involve itself in Arab affairs. Also, Morocco's
geographical distance from the Middle East operated initially to
minimize her concern with Israel, although her recent policy in
this respect has more closely followed that of Israel's neighbors.*
(This change did not stem so much from strengthened foreign
ties as from a desire to curry domestic favor by refuting the
charges that the monarchy was pro-Zionist—and therefore pro-
imperialist. In addition, inevitable suspicions of local Zionist
agents were exaggerated into charges that attributed internal disturbances to Zionist action, and the government fostered this as
a safety valve for domestic dissatisfaction.) Morocco's tentative
approaches to closer cooperation with the Arab Middle East were
also limited by Eastern suspicions of any tendency to Maghrib
unity, and by violent attacks of hereditary "bourgeois" systems.
The precarious conditions of Moroccan-Arab relations is best
illustrated by reference to Egypt, the pivotal country of the Arab
Middle East and the most influential member of the Arab League.

Shortly after Sultan Mohammed had returned to his throne,
several Egyptian dignitaries, including the director of the Voice
of the Arabs radio and Hassan El Bakkouri, Minister of Religious
Endowments, paid him an official courtesy call. But, following
Morocco's independence, her official relations with Egypt were
limited to cultural exchanges. Egypt sent teachers to Morocco
and allocated funds to donate books to Moroccan libraries, while

* In a joint statement in September, 1963, Morocco and Libya guaranteed
that their Jewish nationals would not be allowed to supply men or money to
Israel and promised to block Israeli cultural or economic infiltration into their
countries. At the Arab conference called in January, 1964, to consider Israeli
diversion of the Jordan River waters, Morocco offered military support if the
Arab League requested it and supported a National Liberation Front, organized by Palestinian Arabs with the help of the other Arab states, for guerrilla
warfare.

Morocco appointed a cultural representative to the Arab countries, with an office in Cairo. In October, 1956, the two countries exchanged ambassadors.

Morocco initially reacted to the Arab League by announcing her adherence, as a Muslim country with an Arab culture, to nations of a similar heritage. But the government remained politically aloof from both Cairo and the Arab League on the grounds that involvement in inter-Arab disputes could only increase her own difficulties. This did not, of course, prevent her establishing ties with her brothers to the East when the time seemed opportune.

While the sentiments toward President Nasser publicly expressed that Morocco's leaders reflected those of the masses, their true feelings were often markedly different. Moroccans generally respected Egypt as technologically the most advanced Arab state and recalled with gratitude her past diplomatic and material assistance. And they admired Nasser's uncompromising attitude toward the colonial powers and his vocal demands for Arab self-determination, feeling that he had the welfare of all Arabs, not merely that of the Egyptians, at heart. Nasser's picture was often displayed next to Mohammed V's in private homes and public establishments. By contrast, government praise for the Egyptian leader was proclaimed only during political crises and went no further than oratory: for instance, in the Suez crisis of November, 1956, when the Sultan supported Egypt and praised Nasser's leadership. (*Al-Alam* decried the "imperialist" action of the Western powers and later credited the Soviet ultimatum to Britain and France with a major role in achieving the cease-fires; the Istiqlal, like other parties throughout the Arab world, called a one-day general strike in sympathy with Egypt's position.) The Lebanon crisis in July, 1958, provided a similar occasion for friendly Pan-Arab words.

While willing to bow to an inescapable tide of sentiment, the King and many moderate leaders of the Istiqlal privately thought that Nasser's Pan-Arab policy was designed to promote the personal ambitions of an imperialistic demagogue. Nasser was scorned in these circles as an apprentice dictator whose policy of playing one side against the other could result only in his being rejected by the West and swallowed by the East. This opinion was made public in March, 1958, when *al-Alam* denounced Cairo's "insane" policy toward Morocco after President Nasser had warmly received a former Moroccan collaborator with France, and attacked

Cairo's charge that the proposed Maghrib Union was an American maneuver.

The ideological disapproval of Cairo, the need to maintain a climate favorable to negotiations with France, and the desire to enjoy American aid were not enough, however, to sustain indefinitely Morocco's official coolness to Egypt and the Arab League. As time failed to bring complete satisfaction with her Western allies, Morocco drifted slowly closer to the Middle East. In April, 1958, despite the Tangier Conference, Morocco was host to the Arab states at a meeting intended to strengthen cultural ties through UNESCO; it was later announced that she planned to provide an inter-Arab coordinating center for cultural affairs. Then, late in 1958, Morocco joined the Arab League.

The decision to do so, and King Mohammed's trip to the Middle East in January, 1960, were motivated not only by popular pressures and frustrations but also by the abrupt failure of Morocco's own feeble attempts at inter-Arab intrigue. Fearful of Nasser's ambitions, the government had sought to curb them by enhancing the prestige of Iraq, a fellow monarchy and possibly a counterpoise to Egypt. In May, 1956, King Faysal of Iraq had been the first foreign chief of state to visit Rabat since independence. (The ostensible purpose of the trip was ceremoniously to initiate Iraqi-Moroccan relations at the top level; it was known, however, that the young king hoped to obtain the hand of the Sultan's oldest daughter in marriage. Lalla Aisha, who, at twenty-seven, was six years Faysal's senior and too Westernized to accept a prearranged match, declined his offer, and her father could not well reverse her decision after he had encouraged her to support women's rights.) Faysal had been enthusiastically received by the populace, however, and he left Morocco with good wishes and promises of future cooperation. He had been followed by Iraq's Premier Nuri al-Said and ex-Premier Fadhil Jamali, who came to lay the groundwork for the cooperation agreement between the two nations that was formally signed in February, 1957. These Iraqi-Moroccan relations had been of considerable interest to Tunisia and to the free world, because of distrust of Nasser. There were even suggestions in some French and American circles that, with Iraqi support, King Mohammed could become a rival to Nasser in the Arab world.

But the Iraqi republican revolution of July, 1958, abruptly terminated all Moroccan hope of alliance with another monarchy and served to illustrate the fate in store for those who attempted directly to thwart Nasser. Impressed with the wisdom of consolidating her position in the Arab League, Morocco joined other Arab members of the United Nations in August to sponsor a resolution calling on the Arab states to solve their problems independently.

The index to Morocco's new spirit of compliance could be found in her attitude toward the quarrel that erupted between Tunisia and Egypt in the Arab League; it was made clear by the loud support given Egypt by Torres, Morocco's chief delegate in the League, in a speech that did much to worsen Moroccan-Tunisian relations. Morocco's subsequent cooperation with Egypt in the Casablanca Bloc strengthened the (still rather superficial) ties between them and staved off antimonarchist attacks in a period when they might well have hurt the new King. This friendship with Egypt was put to the test, however, in Morocco's attempt to increase her influence with Algeria and by the intense propaganda of Egyptian schoolteachers in Morocco. Indeed, by the time those teachers left Morocco at the end of 1961, the Egyptian press had in fact become highly critical of Morocco's constitution and general political orientation. Another divisive issue was provided by the Yemeni revolt, Nasser's role in it being highly criticized in Morocco. But the low point of Morocco's relationship with Egypt occurred when Cairo supported Algeria in her border dispute with Morocco. Diplomatic relations were suspended, and King Hassan even refused Bourguiba's invitation to attend ceremonies in Tunis celebrating the French evacuation of Bizerte in order to avoid facing Nasser. It was not until early 1964 that Morocco resumed relations with the U.A.R.—an official reconciliation effected principally in recognition of Nasser's announced abandonment of a policy of "union of purpose" in favor of a policy of "union of ranks," a change that frustrates Arab socialist attacks on "bourgeois monarchies."

C. Morocco and Africa

At present, the Moroccan Government is not too concerned about the vicissitudes of its relationship to Egypt or the other Arab states, however, since it has formed more satisfying friendships with other neighbors. Before 1955, some contacts between Moroccan and other French African intellectuals had already been established in student circles in Paris; other friendships blossomed among Moroccan exiles in Cairo; and many of these contacts were renewed at the Bandung Conference in 1955. But, despite the anticolonial grievances they generally shared with African leaders and despite their government's claims to territory deep into the Sahara, few Moroccans considered their newly independent nation to be part of the Dark Continent. The only historical relationship Morocco had had with Negro Africa that most of them could recall, furthermore, was as conqueror or slave trader.

One of the factors that altered Morocco's outlook on Africa south of the Sahara was the Algerian war. The FLN leaders, in trying to convince the world of Algeria's right to independence, had concluded that the emerging states of Africa could help them considerably. Not only did these countries presently or potentially hold many votes in the United Nations, but the African countries, which in most cases had never themselves been nations before the advent of the Europeans, furnished a convincing precedent for Algeria, which had not been a sovereign nation-state in the Western sense prior to the French occupation. Mutual anticolonialism became far more important than ethnic ties; the Sahara, traditionally regarded as an ocean separating the people north and south, now became a link to join them; Islam, to which more than a quarter of all "Black Africans" adhere, acquired a new significance (particularly since President Nasser had begun to employ it to extend his own influence in Africa). Since Algeria was involved with Tunisia and Morocco in schemes for Maghrib unity, the two countries were therefore under some pressure to support the Algerians in the Pan-African political world. Then too, the Moroccans desired friends other than the Tunisians, whom they considered unreliable. Africa also provided an excellent forum for airing the anticolonial views the Moroccan Government itself was expressing with growing force. Furthermore, after years of petitioning superior powers for independence, for aid, and for acceptance as equals, Moroccans were happy to deal with peoples who treated them with genuine respect.

Morocco's active participation in African affairs began in 1958 with attendance at three conferences. At the Cairo People's Conference in January, 400 nongovernment delegates from thirty-nine African and Asian states including Morocco, violently criticized "Western imperialism," but they voted down resolutions opposing the United States in Korea and its treatment of the American Negro. The Istiqlal was not represented in Cairo, ostensibly because it had been invited too late to participate, but really because it disapproved of the leftist orientation of most of the conferees and the fact that such opposition groups as the Moroccan PDI had been invited.

At Accra, in April, representatives from Morocco attended the first conference of independent African states. Although they urged the liberation of colonial Africa, condemned racism, and announced a policy of noninvolvement in the cold war, the resolutions adopted were relatively moderate. The point of the meeting, as Balafrej explained, was to make it possible to exchange views on common problems arising out of independence and to coordinate the refutation of European plans to exploit African riches exclusively for Europe's benefit.

In the first All African People's Conference, held in Accra at the end of the year, attended by 500 delegates from political, economic, and social groups throughout the continent, the delegates mapped an independence strategy for Africa's remaining colonial territories and committed the participating parties to a policy of nonviolence, except when attacked.

In January, 1959, the Balafrej government sent delegates to the thirty-nine-nation economic conference meeting at Cairo. In February, an Afro-Asian Youth Conference in the same city, attended by Moroccan students, returned to political discussion: this time, however, the participants condemned Western and Eastern imperialism equally and staged an anti-Communist demonstration.

While the Cairo conferences of 1958 and 1959 produced considerable talk and heat, the two meetings at Accra were of greater long-range significance to Africa. Their effect on Morocco was shown in 1959 when Mohammed V delivered a speech calling for independence for all African territories.

At the end of January, 1960, the Second All-African People's Conference opened in Tunis and passed resolutions resembling those of its predecessor. From the Moroccan viewpoint, however, the most important development was Belgium's announcement that she would grant full independence to the Congo on June 30, 1960. (Noteworthy, also, as an indication of Morocco's troubled domestic situation, was the fact that Mohammed Douiri used the conference platform to inform the delegates that there was no freedom to organize unions in his country, a reference to the Istiqlal's failure to create a union to compete with the UMT.)

In February, the U.N. Commission for Africa met at Tangier, where participants engaged in hopeful discussions of the possibility of diminishing competition among African states and of making the continent viable. Another Afro-Asian meeting at Conakry in April presented further opportunity for delegates to denounce colonialism, while a twelve-nation conference at Addis Ababa in June concentrated on economic matters.

Opportunities for more than talk materialized that summer when the Congo became independent and shortly thereafter was thrown into chaos. This situation spurred King Mohammed to take direct charge of the cabinet and embark on a more aggressive foreign policy. The subsequent events in the Congo were to transfer Morocco from the sphere of negative nonalignment to the realm of active involvement with such other "radical nationalist" states as Ghana, Guinea, the U.A.R., and Mali.

When the U.N. intervened in the Congo in July, 1960, Morocco accepted its policy and dispatched to the U.N. operation in the Congo 3,100 troops under General Kittani, who was named commander of the U.N. force. However, when President Nasser and President Sékou Touré of Guinea announced their preference for an all-African force, King Mohammed agreed with their position. The King's decision was based in part on his government's genuine apprehension that the presence of Europeans might foster fragmentation of the Congo, a problem that France's divide-and-rule policy in Morocco had clearly dramatized; in part on the belief that only Patrice Lumumba could build national unity; and in part on popular support for Lumumba. As the quarrel between Lumumba and Joseph Kasavubu deepened during the next month, Kittani, who had been reorganizing the Congo Army at Lumumba's request, transferred his allegiance to Congolese General Joseph Mobutu. It is unclear whether this was because he liked having a protégé or whether he genuinely thought that Mobutu had a better chance of restoring order. Whatever his motives, Kittani's actions were sharply criticized by both major parties at home—contributing momentarily to Moroccan, if perhaps not Congolese, unity.

Chagrined at Lumumba's subsequent fall and the U.N.'s failure to prevent bloodshed in the Congo, Morocco, Ghana, Guinea, the U.A.R., and Mali announced in December that they would withdraw their forces, which totaled nearly one third of the 19,400 U.N. troops. To consider the consequences of this decision and to discuss such possible alternatives for the Congo as the formation of an all-African administrative and security force, King Mohammed invited the four heads of state to a conference in Casablanca on January 4, 1961. Ferhat Abbas, King Idris of Libya, and Lumumba were also invited. The notable omission on the guest list was Habib Bourguiba, whose ambassador to the Security Council, Mongi Slim, had been a major draftsman of the U.N. Congo plan.

The first meeting of this short-lived and never robust Casablanca

Bloc produced a charter that, among other traditional anticolonialist points, pledged its members to nonalignment and invited
other Africans to join the signatories in building African unity. At
King Mohammed's suggestion, the members also agreed to consider
the formation of a consultative assembly and an African defense
system comparable to NATO, and to withdraw their Congo contingents when each government deemed it necessary. Another
resolution approved any action Morocco might take on Mauritania
to restore her legitimate rights. (The impact of this resolution was
somewhat weakened, however, by the fact that Ghana had recognized Mauritania's independence the previous week.) A temporary
rift was created by Nasser's insistence on a resolution condemning
Israel as an imperialist agent, a stricture that Ghana and Mali,
which had profited from Israeli economic aid, were reluctant to
endorse. However, a show of unity was produced after Morocco
acted behind the scenes to dilute the attack on Israel, and the
conference closed with promises of future meetings to implement
action in several spheres.

In May, 1961, Africa was split into rival camps by the meeting
of twenty-one African nations in Monrovia. In January, 1962, the
same group met in Lagos to hear Nigeria declare that the time for
anticolonial harangues was past. Between these meetings, King
Hassan played host to a gathering of trade-union delegations for
several African countries that met ostensibly to coordinate labor
activities throughout the continent. It was scarcely a surprise when
the delegations soon split on the question of whether affiliation
with an all-African brotherhood should be followed by resignation
from other bodies; this referred primarily to the International
Confederation of Free Trade Unions (ICFTU), to which many of
the strongest African unions belonged. Tunisia's Ahmed Tlili and
Kenya's Tom Mboya refused to sever a relationship that had
brought them many benefits; joined by the Senegalese delegation,
they rejected adherence to the newly formed All-African Trade
Union Federation. The latter thus became a "Casablanca Bloc"
union, its members promising to leave the ICFTU, which soon
faced further competition from the rival African Trade Union Confederation founded by the unions in the "Monrovia bloc" and in
countries not yet independent. In a meeting in August, the
Casablanca countries established a General Secretariat (subsequently headed by a Moroccan, Thami Ouazzani) and later sent
delegates to the Belgrade Conference in September, which was,
in the words of King Hassan, a step to "collective nonalignment."
Two months later, as a further step in this direction, Morocco

and her Casablanca partners, alone among the African nations, voted unsuccessfully with the U.S.S.R. in the United Nations to proclaim 1962 "the year of elimination of colonialism"; all other African states either abstained from voting or opposed the motion. The high point in Casablanca Bloc cooperation was achieved in April, 1962, when a meeting in Cairo created the long-awaited joint defense command and also decided to establish a postal and telecommunications union, a payments union, and a development bank with a capitalization of $30 million; to organize and co-ordinate development projects; and to sign a maritime accord.

On the negative side, Morocco and the Casablanca powers did little to achieve their original purpose of unifying the Congo behind Lumumba and in fact contributed to African disunity by encouraging the division of the continent into blocs. Furthermore, Morocco received little help from her partners in regard to matters of particular interest to her. For example, Mali began a *rapprochement* in 1962 with Mauritania that was climaxed by formal recognition. Morocco also encountered some new difficulties in mid-1962 when Senegal's President Léopold Senghor implicated some Moroccans in subversive activities allegedly launched against his regime. Mali, which was by then patching her own tattered relations with Senegal, declined to defend her presumed ally. And the fact that Mali and Libya as well as Morocco presented Algeria with claims to the Sahara served only to weaken the unity of the Casablanca Bloc. Furthermore, with the specter of colonialism rapidly fading, the Casablanca Bloc slowly lost its reason for being and also much of what distinguished it from the more moderate, but decreasingly Western-aligned countries of the Monrovia group.

At the end of 1962, the Moroccan Government attempted to revive the faltering Casablanca Bloc by calling another conclave of heads of state. However, Nkrumah, Nasser, and Touré found it "impossible to attend at that time," and the conference was rescheduled for Marrakesh the following May. By then, many of the Monrovia Group countries had indicated their desire to put an end to African blocs, and Morocco entertained grave doubts concerning her role at the meeting in general and the disposition of the Mauritanian issue in particular. Although, after his visit to President de Gaulle in 1962, King Hassan had dropped hints that he would consider a compromise solution, he could not meet officially with Mauritania and thus tacitly admit her independence. When Nasser and Ben Bella indicated they would not attend, plans for the Marrakesh meeting collapsed. Morocco, alone of the independent African states, failed to attend the historic Addis Ababa Conference, but subsequently indicated her willingness to extend her cooperation to the new Organization of African Unity.

Recent indications of a new determination by Morocco to play an active role in African life include the signing of trade agreements with Senegal on February 14, 1963, and overtures in this direction to Nigeria in September, 1963. The *détente* with Senegal was followed by discussion between President Senghor and King Hassan on the possibility of cooperation between regional unions of North and West Africa. By 1964 there was even talk, although no more than that, of a stronger "vertical" alliance between the two moderate "socialist" regimes.

Recently, the Moroccan Government has expressed its intention to help the nationalists of Portuguese-controlled Africa and has occasionally played host to gatherings of representatives from Angola, Mozambique, and the Cape Verde Islands. In August, 1963, Rabat recognized the revolutionary Angolan government-in-exile led by Holden Roberto and announced that it would break diplomatic relations with Portugal in conformity with an Addis Ababa resolution. However, such action had not been taken by mid-1965. On the other hand, in 1965 Morocco opposed the anti-Tshombe activities of Algeria and Egypt as reprehensible efforts to meddle in the internal affairs of an independent African nation.

D. *Morocco's Relations with the Communist World*

Her avowed policy of friendship to all nations notwithstanding, Morocco avoided diplomatic ties with the Communist states for a number of years. The government's hesitancy stemmed partly from its members' personal and cultural ties to Western Europe, partly from a reluctance to become too quickly involved with strong regimes with which it had no personal dealings, partly from a pragmatic neutralism that implied that the Communists must indicate the potential benefits to be gained by diplomatic exchange. From the beginning, however, contacts with Communist nations did exist.

One of the earliest occurred at a high level, when Prince Hassan met Russian Foreign Minister Dmitri Shepilov in Cairo in June, 1956. Shepilov urged Prince Hassan to establish formal relations with the U.S.S.R. and invited him to visit Moscow. Although this invitation was not accepted, other Moroccans, principally students and labor officials, enjoyed Communist hospitality in several countries. In April, 1957, for example, three UMT representatives went to Peking to study Chinese factories, social organizations, and medical establishments. (Upon their return to Rabat, *Le Petit Marocain* quoted one of them as saying that the standard of living of most Chinese workers was inferior to that of some Moroccans and that individual liberty was unknown among them. Several days later, the quoted labor official denied this report, saying that he and his colleagues had been impressed with China's "reconstruction" efforts and that the workers there had enormous social advantages. It remained uncertain which of these reports represented the true views of the delegation.) Another Moroccan labor delegation visited East Germany later in 1957. Moroccan visitors to the Soviet Union in subsequent years included al-Fassi, who praised its accomplishments and advocated coexistence between Communism and Islam.

The Communists did not, however, stay at home waiting for Moroccans to call. Cultural groups and trade delegations seeking to develop reciprocal relations soon became frequent visitors to Morocco. One early delegation from Communist China subtly included four Muslims. In August, 1956, exhibits by Yugoslavia, Poland, Romania, China, and Czechoslovakia at the Casablanca International Trade Fair were the focus of attention. Their featured heavy machinery was considerably more impressive to the unworldly Moroccan than the scanty Western exhibits. Although trade with the Communist states constitutes a minute fraction of Morocco's commercial activity, direct negotiations soon replaced the earlier procedure of having arrangements handled through Paris, and several bilateral agreements have been effected.

These manifestations of Communist friendship with Morocco were contradicted by such statements as the thinly veiled threat contained in a letter from Marshal Bulganin to the Moroccan Government concerning "imperialist" bases in Morocco. Officially, the letter was rejected, but among Moroccans, as among other peoples, Communist propaganda has always won at least a few listeners. In April, 1958, the Soviet publication *International Affairs* argued that the Moroccan economy was controlled by French and United States (Morgan) interests, and inveighed against the presence of foreign troops, the repression and exploitation in the Sahara, and the imperialists' efforts to abolish Morocco's national independence and turn the country into a NATO bridgehead.

The Moroccans' increasing demand for true nonalignment in the Cold War and the government's wish to prove that it was not tied to colonial apron strings finally led Morocco to effect diplomatic exchanges with Communist China and the Soviet Union in the fall of 1958. Accords with other Communist nations followed. But Morocco continued to deal with the Communist countries cautiously, confining her formal actions to the extension of trade with Russia and China. (The total value of trade with the Soviet Union rose in 1959 from $8 million to $12 million, while a commercial agreement with China provided for $11 million worth of trade.) The psychological advantages of this trade apparently outweighed the material benefits, since they not only promised Morocco some refreshingly balanced trade figures, but also seemed to open the way for positive neutralist bargaining with Western countries.

Limited politico-military cooperation with Communist states entered Morocco via the Algerian back door. The provisional Algerian government had concluded an arms deal with Peking in April, 1960; since these arms could not be shipped directly to Algeria and since Bourguiba did not want them in Tunisia, Morocco was the obvious landing site. Unwilling to face UNFP accusations that it was obstructing the Algerian cause and bowing to French pressure, the Moroccan Government soon agreed to this. The popular furor caused by French seizure of arms on a captured Czech freighter, coupled with other clashes with France, furthered its determination to pursue this aspect of an activist anti-colonial foreign policy.

Morocco could not appear actively nonaligned, however, without some additional dealings with Moscow. Russia apparently appreciated the King's political dilemma—and also the issue that it might employ as an opening wedge to gain his good graces: Mauritania. Cordial Soviet-Moroccan talks preceded the Soviet Union's veto of Mauritania's application for membership in the United Nations in December, 1960. At the same time, Soviet arms destined for Algeria began to arrive in Moroccan ports.

The year 1961 witnessed the apogee of Morocco's relationship with the U.S.S.R. At the beginning of the year, it was announced that Crown Prince Hassan would attend May Day festivities in Moscow. On February 10, 1961, twelve MIG-17 fighter interceptors and two MIG-15 training jets, accompanied by twenty technicians to assemble them, arrived in Casablanca. The following day, Leonid Brezhnev visited Rabat en route to Guinea and offered Morocco "all the aid needed" for her economic development. Information Minister Moulay Ahmed al-Alaoui announced the same day that negotiations were under way for an exchange of newsreels between the two countries and that cultural ties with Czechoslovakia had been arranged. In that same month, Moroccan delegates traveled to Czechoslovakia and Yugoslavia to examine prospects for further aid.

In March, a two-man Soviet mission arrived to study the possibility of constructing a shipyard at Tangier, while Casablanca was host city to a meeting of the Prague-based International Students Union. This Communist-oriented conclave, to the surprise of many native and foreign observers, provided an opportunity for Ben Seddik to denounce the recent Soviet gift of MIG's as "a useless drain on the economy" and to suggest that the Soviet Union provide aid for development if it really wished Morocco well. The labor leader's speech was partially intended to criticize the government, but it also reflected a growing awareness that, while military equipment conferred prestige on the régime and perhaps excited the populace, it consumed funds that could better be spent elsewhere. The speech was also the first clear indication to the West that Morocco's pursuit of an activist nonalignment and willingness to accept Communist aid did not preclude criticism of Moscow and Peking.

Military aid continued, nevertheless, to overshadow other forms of Soviet assistance. In early 1962, a six-man military training group arrived, and, on April 6, a Soviet cargo ship unloaded weapons, vehicles, and tanks for the Royal Army. The beginning of September brought a shipment of seventy tanks, and, on January 25, 1963, a freighter delivered more equipment.

In the nonmilitary realm, there have been continuing cultural exchanges and the ratification of an agreement providing for Moscow-Rabat air service. However, the U.S.S.R. itself has invested little in Morocco; most of the expenditure has been borne by the Russian satellites. In April, 1962, for example, an agreement for the delivery of mining equipment and the construction of a copper-processing plant was signed in Rabat with Technoexport, the Czech foreign-trade corporation, and Poland undertook to design a sugar-beet processing factory at Sidi Slimane. Two additional accords with Poland were signed in 1962: the first provided for economic and technical cooperation; under the second contract, Poland was to loan industrial equipment worth $12 million to Morocco. (Eighty per cent of this advance was to be repaid over an eight-year period at 3 per cent interest, the remaining 20 per cent to be refunded in whatever commodities Morocco wished to export.) Lastly, a Moroccan-Cuban trade pact signed in Rabat on December 13, 1962, provided for the import of 105,000 tons of unrefined Cuban sugar beyond the 250,000 tons already delivered by annual contract.

Morocco's dealings with China have in general been limited to cultural exchanges, trade, and the arms shipments to the FLN. Chou En-lai's visit to Morocco in December, 1963, was clearly designed to serve China's interests, and in fact, Chou received a somewhat cool welcome in Rabat, due principally to the anti-Moroccan position Peking had adopted on the Algerian-Moroccan border conflict, but also in part to China's very obvious efforts to gain African support against the U.S.S.R. in particular and against the West in general.

The Moroccan Government, if perhaps not all of the Moroccan people, viewed benefits from the East with some skepticism and did not expect miracles from this new relationship. Doubt quickly turned into disillusion, and Morocco's "turn to the East" proved to be a very transient phase. For one thing, the Kremlin had major interests more vital than building Moroccan friendship, and its veto of Mauritania's bid for U.N. membership was resented by many countries it otherwise wished to impress. This factor, combined with considerations closer to home, led the Soviet Union in November, 1961, to play off the West's interest in Mauritania against her own concern for Outer Mongolia, and in a diplomatic horse trade with the West to vote for the simultaneous admission of both countries to the world body.

Except for some smaller agreements, Communist trade and aid also failed to live up to promises and expectations. Soviet plans for the shipyard, for example, failed to materialize, and, by 1963, the government was discussing the matter seriously with a Greek shipbuilder. Plans for the sugar-beet factory progressed slowly, and China, despite Morocco's vote for her admission to the U.N. in 1961, was delivering only half the products she had promised. Much of the manufactured goods from the East, furthermore, were of shoddy quality. Perhaps the most striking instance of this were six of the MIG's, which became mechanically useless within several months after delivery. In addition, military aid became a sharp political issue when the UNFP charged it would enable King Hassan to institute a virtual military dictatorship if he so desired. Finally, by 1962 France was willing to supply more of the goods and services that Morocco required.

Repeated disappointments with the Communist bloc and diminishing grounds for controversy with the Western democracies have recently persuaded Morocco to strengthen her ties with the West. Relations with the East remain formally cordial, but trade with the entire Communist bloc remains at only 6 to 7 per cent of Morocco's total.

Moroccan foreign policy, in sum, has progressed from preoccupation with her own decolonization to an active interest in the decolonization of others, and from absorption with France and North Africa to an interest in relationships with whatever countries seem to have something useful to offer. The change has been marked by a decrease in emotion and impetuosity, as evidenced by the declining interest in irredentism, and by a corresponding growth of pragmatism and diplomatic skill—as shown in her profitable *rapprochements* with Paris and Madrid, her willingness to accept, if not embrace, the governments of Tunisia and Algeria, and her cordial yet somewhat distant relations with Communist states. Perhaps most interesting and most indicative of a future trend, however, is the change in Morocco's self-image, her progress from considering herself primarily a part of the Arab world to identifying herself with Africa. This was sharply implied in a speech that King Hassan delivered in April, 1964:

> We must organize our culture and our instruction . . . in order to turn it into an instrument capable of shaping our children, who hope thereby to become citizens of the country—and of a continent that does not speak Arabic. We live on a continent that speaks English and French. . . . We [should] make our teaching homogeneous, preparing us to be citizens of our country, of the African continent, and of the world.

The psychological benefits conferred by growing ties with Africa, if combined with the material income supplied by numerous countries, East and West, should enable Morocco to remain genuinely and profitably nonaligned.

Chapter 9

The United States and Morocco

PRIOR TO World War II, United States contacts with Morocco
were few and far between, if somewhat dramatic.* This
situation changed on November 8, 1942, when American
soldiers launched Operation Torch, the long-awaited second-front
invasion of Europe. General Noguès, Resident General and commanding officer of the Vichy forces in Morocco, met the "invaders"
with bullets, but fortunately the fighting, later described by the
French as a "gesture," was short. The bad impression created by
this "gesture," contrasted with the welcome offered by the Sultan
and his entourage, doubtless influenced President Roosevelt's
famous words at Casablanca.†

With the end of the war, American interest in Morocco waned.
Excepting the several hundred Americans who settled in Tangier
and Casablanca for business reasons, the only American community, and the only official stake in the country, was Port Lyautey
(now called Kenitra) where a United States naval base, built in
1942, was retained to provide logistic support for the Mediter-
ranean-based Sixth Fleet. This 3,500-acre base, then the U.S.
Navy's largest in Europe or North Africa, was leased from the
French Protectorate government, which retained title to the land
and shared the use of its facilities.‡ Construction on the base,

---

* See above, chap. 1, pp. 17–20.   † See above, chap. 2, p. 46.

‡ France presumably acted under the authority of Articles 2 and 6 of the
Treaty of Fez, which provided that the French Government was entitled to
"proceed to such military occupation of Moroccan territory as it might deem
necessary for the maintenance of good order" and "represent and protect
Moroccan subjects and interest abroad."

which cost $40 million, originally consisted of temporary quonset huts and tents, and facilities were initially meager. Large ships could not berth, although the base was located on the Atlantic; but planes from the base carried supplies to the fleet.

Morocco's long struggle against the French for independence at first attracted little attention in Washington. Out of strategic considerations and a continuing recognition of spheres of influence, the American Government uncritically accepted French and Spanish policies. Nor were the dangers inherent in the Moroccan situation—or in the State Department's detached position in regard to it—realized. There was one notable exception: Demaree Bess, of the *Saturday Evening Post*, observed that, after years of carefully differentiating between the French Protectorate government and the Sultan's sovereign one, the United States had treated them as one in the Marshall Plan, thus immeasurably aiding France to strengthen its control over Morocco.

After the outbreak of the Korean War, however, the United States recognized the need for a series of foreign air bases from which long-range bombers armed with atomic weapons could retaliate against enemy attacks. Although Morocco was 2,400 miles from Moscow, its natural defenses of water, mountains, and desert made it ideal as a base not only for offensive operations but also for defense of the Mediterranean seaways, Europe's southern flank, and the Middle East's western flank. In thus choosing Morocco, as one military man put it, "Ten per cent less hitting power was sacrificed for 90 per cent more staying power." Furthermore, Morocco's high average of perfect flying days per year made it ideal for training purposes. To acquire these advantages, the United States negotiated a hurried agreement with France on December 22, 1950, permitting construction of five air bases. In addition, the headquarters of the Seventeenth Air Force was set up in Rabat, and several communications and radar facilities were established.

Like the one at Kenitra, the air bases were leased by the United States, but France was to share their use, provide local protection, and station customs officials at each. The American Government asked France to give prompt formal notification of the arrangement to the makhzen, as required by the Treaty of Fez, but the Sultan heard about the decision only through the French press and naturally concluded that the agreement had hardly been negotiated on Morocco's behalf. This slight to Moroccan sovereignty and pride was later to cost the American Government more than mere embarrassment.

Unfortunately, time was of critical importance, and the air bases were built on a "crash" schedule. Waste, faulty construction, and even corruption were the result. Work was begun in July, 1951; by October, 14,000-foot runways were in operation at Nouasseur and Sidi Slimane. Benguerir was ready the following summer and Boulhaut shortly thereafter; the fifth site, El Djemma Sahim, was soon abandoned. The cost of construction, carried out by the Atlas Company, a combine of five American concerns, and supervised by the Army Corps of Engineers, approached $500 million, an extravagant sum which a House of Representatives investigating subcommittee found to be due to a failure to demand competitive bids and to overcharges involving collusion that together wasted more than $50 million.

Rubbing salt into these financial wounds, the French insisted that American personnel on the air bases be limited to 7,500. (This total was later raised to 10,000.) The result was that Boulhaut, a base 35 miles southeast of Casablanca, was manned only by a handful of men. France also insisted on other restrictions—permitting only a specified number of planes on a base at one time—motivated principally by her fear that her political and economic position would be threatened by unrestricted American activity. The effect was seriously to curtail the military investment that was designed to protect France as well as the United States from a common enemy. By constantly rotating its units, however, the U.S. Air Force was able to familiarize a large number of pilots and crews with the bases, circumventing the limitations.

Sidi Slimane, 60 miles northeast of Rabat, became the Air Force's main center for operational training. The Strategic Air Command operated under simulated combat conditions at Sidi Slimane, and a jet-fighter school and a fighter defense squadron was based there. Benguerir, 25 miles north of Marrakesh, was used principally for heavy bombers.

In the years preceding Morocco's independence, the bases and their personnel worried France, irritated the nationalists, and posed many problems for the United States. The official American policy remained one of neutrality in Morocco's struggle against the Protectorate. Hoping for a peaceful evolutionary settlement, the United States left matters in the hands of France and refused to recognize the nationalists. This, of course, bolstered the French position; the nationalists, recalling America's espousal of the principle of self-determination, sarcastically referred to the United States position in Morocco as "anticolonialism on Sundays." Balafrej even asked whether a people who stood ready to fight for everything Americans held dear did not deserve freedom and self-government. He declared that Morocco could be of far greater assistance to the West as a free people and appealed to the United States to bring its influence to bear on France. Such appeals brought favorable response by a few groups, such as the American Federation of Labor, but the State Department remained unmoved and even refused to support Morocco in the United Nations on the ground that its problems could be solved only by the parties concerned.

Similarly, the United States acquiesced in the deposition of Mohammed V in August, 1953. American inaction was attacked by Moroccan nationalists, and Adrian Fisher, former legal advisor of the Department of State, charged that the U.S. had violated its own treaty obligations in failing to protest the French action. The American inaction was also questioned by *The New York Times*, which declared that it would be a great day when the methods of French colonialism were changed to conform to the high ideals of the French people.

During the next two years, American prestige in Morocco continued to drop among both colons and nationalists. Although the French Government appreciated United States diplomatic support and military equipment, designed for NATO use but often diverted to North Africa by France, the colons chastised the American population in Morocco and several vocal Americans across the sea for their sympathy with the nationalists. On the other hand, the nationalists criticized a noninterference policy that enabled France to use American guns against Moroccans and permitted Americans to forget their "moral obligations." There was some truth in the charges by both sides, but the State Department continued to hope that the problem would be settled without American involvement. Eventually, it was resolved, but only after America's vital interests in North Africa had been seriously endangered. The fact that American lives and interests weathered the resistance struggle with little damage can be attributed only to the appreciation by nationalist leaders that they were, in fact, supported by many Americans and that Moroccan interests required the friendship of the United States.

Although French Resident General Guillaume continually minimized American interests in Morocco, his successor, Lacoste, repeatedly sought support from the Americans resident in the country. On July 4, 1954, he appealed to Americans in these terms:

Remember, you are serving here in close cooperation with France, who, from the beginning of your national independence and even before that, has been a comrade in arms, a friend in good times and bad. The peaceful struggle we are waging here together is a battle for freedom and peace, a struggle that is perhaps more arduous if less glorious than war because it demands constant vigilance and unflagging effort on the part of every one of us to be ready and stay ready.

The main French propaganda campaign, however, was aimed at the United States itself, where a flow of press releases, television movies, and lecturers attempted to keep American public opinion in line. While the Residency had little success with Americans in Morocco, French propagandists did arouse opinion in the United States with reminders of historic Franco-American amity, appeals for Western solidarity, and dire warnings that France's loss in Morocco would be Communism's gain. "The United States thought Ho Chi Minh was a nationalist," they said. At a time when Senator McCarthy was active, the threat of the "Red menace" was effective.

The French Government's conciliatory words to Americans were in contrast to the attitude of the French press in Morocco, even during Lacoste's residency. The French journals lost few opportunities to cast the United States in a poor light. American segregation problems continually received the most unflattering attention, and rumors abounded that Americans were attempting to replace French economic interests in Morocco. At times, it was also charged that the United States was supplying arms to the nationalists. In March, 1954, a French paper in Morocco reported that the United States was trying to gain control of the Banque d'État.

The grant of independence for Morocco did not end such charges. When Max Lejeune announced that an American economic mission was in Rabat, L'Écho elaborated fancifully: "Contributions to the methodic deterioration of Morocco are coming from without as well as within. The American economic mission currently in Rabat is endeavoring under the direction of a State Department official to supplant Franch financing of the Moroccan Government." After 1955, French attacks were also leveled at American "cultural imperialism" in United States-sponsored programs for teaching English and technical subjects.

On the other side of the fence, the nationalists admonished and pleaded Abdel-Khalek Torres set the example for the former approach in a speech entitled, "You're too late, Mr. Dulles." Torres reproached the Department of State for "breaching the principles of the American Revolution and the teachings of the United States Constitution, as well as for breaking its promises to the Moroccan people." Other moderate nationalists asked whether the United States was ignorant of the brutalities Frenchmen had committed in Morocco and inquired, "Doesn't it understand that without opportunity the youth of Morocco will become fanatics?"

During the final phase of the struggle, the following open letter was addressed to "the freedom-loving people of the United States of America":

The soldiers of the Liberation Army of North Africa present their greetings to every freedom-loving American citizen.

Defenders of liberty! Your forefathers suffered the evils of colonialism. They struggled and spared no sacrifice in order to liberate the United States and to insure its progress until it became a world's super-power that propagates freedom and acts to check colonial despotism. The nations of North Africa are presently victims of the despotic French colonial yoke. They have long suffered misrule, terror, and injustice. Reports published by great American men and organizations are the best proof of this fact. The people of North Africa have taken a solemn vow to regain their complete freedom, no matter how much they must sacrifice to attain this aim and no matter how much in money and lives it may cost. The news about our joint resistance movement and its activities is merely the beginning of the struggle.

Your late President Franklin Delano Roosevelt promised on behalf of the United States that the freedom of our country would be guaranteed when World War II ended. This promise was given in acknowledgment of the undeniable sacrifices and services made by our people for the cause of democracy. Now you have strategic interests here, interests that can be safeguarded only if this country is free and independent. On many occasions, your official representatives in our country have announced the need to put an end to the French rule of terror. They asked for fulfillment of President Roosevelt's promise in order to safeguard the American strategic bases. But apparently certain American statemen still approve of the colonial mentality and think accordingly. They closed their ears and refused to listen to the demand for justice voiced by your own representatives in our country.

This is the situation in North Africa. We report it to freedom-loving Americans, exhorting them to intervene in order to end French violation of human rights. The United States must take a clear and unequivocal attitude toward our just cause so that we, in turn, can take an understanding attitude toward your interests in our country.

The North African Liberation Army

From 1951 until 1955, the Istiqlal maintained an active Office of Information and Documentation in New York, run by Balafrej and other nationalists. Their efforts to arouse public opinion were only slightly more successful than their fruitless attempts to influence the State Department, but they made many extremely useful individual contacts. Several American labor leaders, for example, gave considerable publicity to the nationalist cause, in addition to aiding the fledgling Moroccan labor movement, and several scholars and writers also publicized information on the Moroccan problem.

In contrast to the general apathy in the United States, a few American visitors to Morocco, and most of the Americans living in that country, were convinced of the justice of the Moroccan nationalist cause. Justice William O. Douglas, who visited Morocco in the summer of 1954, later reported, "Morocco presents colonialism at its worst. I predict that it will soon explode with a violence that will make Indochina look minor. France will call it a Communist-inspired uprising, but it will actually be nationalist in character." The Moroccan post of the American Legion issued a statement declaring, "We believe that not only the decline of our own position here, but the serious internal condition in Morocco, is attributable in large measure to the Department of State's failure to adhere to the principles of international law." The only American newspaper in Morocco attacked Protectorate policy so severely that the French tried (without success) to have the editor dismissed.

The sympathy of the American community in Morocco for the nationalist cause was bolstered by the fact that the period of terror had remarkably little effect on Americans: even during the major riots in the Port Lyautey medina in August, 1954, efforts were made to assure that no Americans were injured. (Perhaps a hundred American families living in this native quarter were thereafter evacuated into the European sector.) One American sailor later reported that, as he drove through the medina, rioters had fired on Frenchmen in the cars in front and behind him, but not at his car, which carried an American flag.

In September, 1954, several cars belonging to American military personnel and bearing the red military license plates were damaged by bombs and fire, and six American airmen in civilian clothes were slightly injured when a bomb was tossed into Rabat's fashionable Balima Hotel. During the Bastille Day riots in Casablanca in July, 1955, an export clothing warehouse belonging to an American businessman was burned, but none of the 2,500 Americans in

Casablanca were touched by the riots. Even in these exceptional cases, there was no indication that Americans or their property had been the targets of the attack; they were fortuitously in the wrong places at the wrong times. In any event, considering the possibilities, incidents such as these were rare. American business-men, nevertheless, suffered with their French and Moroccan coun-terparts from the rapidly deteriorating economic situation. One American soft-drink producer was even advised to stop selling his wares to Moroccan cafés because the beverage contained French sugar.

The noninvolvement of American military personnel in the violence was due not only to nationalist discretion, but also to the constant precautionary measures taken by their commanding offi-cers. Restrictions were imposed and relaxed, depending on con-ditions throughout the country or in the local areas; at the first sign of danger, medinas were placed off limits, and the men were required to wear uniforms at all times. During periods of wide-spread terrorism, all travel except that between homes and bases was prohibited. By June, 1955, when it was apparent that a show-down between the nationalists and the colons was imminent, all medinas were placed off bounds to American military personnel and remained so until after French recognition of Moroccan in-dependence. The restrictions imposed upon American personnel appeared at times too severe, but the officers considered them justified if they saved even a single life. As a result of this con-servative policy, American forces were involved in fewer incidents than in any other foreign country. Violations of any of these limitations were punishable by court martial. It was questionable, however, whether this sanction applied to American dependents or to civilians working on the bases in the light of two United States court decisions rendered during this period. The restrictions did not prevent some unfortunate incidents provoked *by* Ameri-cans, particularly in connection with drunken brawls, and traffic violations. Although servicemen were subject to Protectorate courts, these usually waived their jurisdiction in favor of American authorities.

Official American detachment from Moroccan affairs began to change with the Oued Zem incident. Immediately following that bloody August weekend, French authorities for the first time gave the Americans permission to fly the Stars and Stripes beside the Tricolor at the entrance to the military bases. The fear that the symbol of American freedom might inspire national unrest here gave way to the need for security. In addition, the United States voiced concern over French use of American equipment in the mop-up campaign that followed. Still, the State Department continued to act on the policy that maintenance of order in Morocco was a French responsibility and that it still had no program apart from hoping for the earliest possible restoration of peace and order.

The return of Mohammed V to his throne in November, 1955, brought this wish closer to fulfillment. The State Department immediately welcomed the Sultan's return, and the United States Minister in Tangier, Julius C. Holmes, delivered a personal greeting from President Eisenhower on behalf of the people of the United States, referring to the long friendship between the two countries. Holmes' visit to the palace was itself noteworthy, as such a gesture had never been made during the reign of the puppet Sultan, Moulay Ben Arafa. Mohammed V, in return, pledged continuation of American-Moroccan friendship and stated that Morocco still honored the 1789 treaty between the two states. In a special aside, he suggested to Mr. Holmes that the President come to Morocco to recuperate from his recent heart attack, noting that he would find a welcome as warm as the weather.

Pending the outcome of Franco-Moroccan negotiations, the State Department announced on January 2, 1956, that the United States would renounce its extraterritorial rights at an opportune moment, and it was quick to recognize Moroccan independence following the French declaration of March 2. Diplomatic ties developed slowly, though, as Washington wished to avoid the appearance of taking sides in the final negotiations between Morocco and France. However friendly its feelings, the United States was reluctant to negotiate with the Moroccans until France had completed all arrangements with the new state. Subsequent events made this continued hesitation difficult, but the United States steadfastly maintained that it had no intention of substituting American for French influence in Morocco.

Although the diplomatic accord between France and Morocco was signed in May, the United States did not open an embassy in Rabat until June. (Temporarily, the consulate in Rabat was raised to an embassy, while the legation in Tangier was downgraded to a consulate.) France, Spain, Great Britain, Egypt, and Tunisia had named their envoys before Washington acted. Finally, it was announced that Cavendish Cannon would be the first United States Ambassador to post-Protectorate Morocco. Rabat simultaneously nominated Dr. Mehdi Ben Aboud as the first Moroccan Ambassador to Washington, a move conforming to the practice of newly independent states in accrediting diplomats to the countries where they had served as nationalist representatives.

When Ambassador Cannon arrived in Rabat in September, he announced the termination of American consular jurisdiction in Morocco. This action affected 115 non-Americans who had received protégé status, as well as all American citizens. The declaration made it clear, however, that the United States did not intend to abandon its most-favored-nation status in matters of trade. Moroccans hailed the enlightened if limited concession, but Moroccan-American relations were soon clouded by far more important considerations.

The foremost of these issues was the status of the United States bases. Moroccans never forgot that the Americans' use of their land was due to an agreement with the French Protectorate concluded without the official knowledge even of their sovereign. The bases were regarded from the beginning as inconsistent with their independence and as courting danger by making Morocco a possible missile target in case the cold war turned hot. Furthermore, the conditions under which Moroccans were employed on the bases were not satisfactory: wages were a relatively minor consideration, since, although the 67-francs (19-cents) per hour minimum wage * was far below American standards, it was in line with the local labor market; but the politically explosive problem was that the French *intendant* (manager) system set out in the original base agreements, which permitted the French to hire and dismiss native employees and set their pay (the United States simply set the security standards, utilized the Moroccans' services, and handed over the pay checks), was continuing.

Before his return to Morocco, King Mohammed had promised that the Moroccan Government would come to a decision in regard to the bases. When Morocco signed the final diplomatic accord with France in May, 1956, she concurred in all agreements made by France on her behalf under the Protectorate, but a supplementary document excluded the Franco-American base agreement on the ground that it had not been made "on Morocco's behalf." Although Moroccan officials let it be understood that they wished the bases to remain, a series of misunderstandings soon altered this position.

One set of problems stemmed from labor agitation on the bases. The Moroccans who worked on the bases, like their compatriots,

* Only a few workers received this minimum wage. The average pay on the bases was 20,000 francs (about $60) a month in 1955.

had not been permitted to form a labor union under the Protectorate; but in December, 1955, a spokesman for the fledgling UMT had protested to Premier Bekkai about the "increase in anti-union repression on the bases" and deplored the "violation of Moroccan legislation by the administrative authorities of the American bases and the deliberate and senseless unilateral violations of labor contracts without guarantee of any indemnity under the false pretext of security." On December 31, a Union Syndicale des Bases Américaines was formed in affiliation with the UMT and held its first congress in Port Lyautey. Mohammed Bel Hadj El Hadi, general secretary of the new union, issued a statement defining its first demands: recognition of the union, reinstatement of employees arbitrarily discharged for union or political activity or under the pretext of security; creation of an employment agency, with participation by the union; promulgation by the Moroccan Government, after consultation with the union, of regulations to govern working conditions and pay of the civilian personnel on the bases; establishment of a promotion and reclassification board, in which workers' delegates would participate; institution of a board of discipline, with union representation; an immediate general wage increase of 5,000 francs ($14.30) a month; regulation of overtime; a family allowance for all employees; payment of sick leave, institution of a social security system, and creation of medico-social centers on the bases. Unfortunately, the union had an inflated view of American generosity. The requested salary increase alone would have amounted to a raise of 34 per cent for the lowest-paid workers and 17 per cent for the average and would have cost the Air Force $1 million a year.

In February, 1956, with union demands still unheeded, a delegation submitted protests to the designated Minister of Public Works, Douiri. It charged the Americans with racial discrimination in both employment and salaries, as well as with general "disdain for the dignity of Moroccans," and asked the Minister to intervene with French and American authorities to rectify these conditions. Douiri promised to do so, but no action was forthcoming, and inconclusive negotiations continued. In March, the union additionally asked for year-end bonuses, housing allowances, mutual insurance provisions, payments for occupational diseases, paid holidays, and benefits for discharged workers.

Finally, in April the union called a strike after last-minute discussions with an American committee had failed. The State Department favored a partial concession to the wage demands, but the armed forces objected on the ground that general salary increases might initiate an inflationary spiral. "We wish to follow and not lead the Moroccan economy," said the Civilian Director of the Seventeenth Air Force. When the armed services would grant no more than wage adjustments paralleling scales prevailing in Moroccan industry, the strike continued.

Picket lines set up at the bases prevented entry; even domestics failed to show up for work at American homes in town. Strikers held mass meetings to denounce indignities and discrimination at the bases; American authorities were alerted for possible violence. None occurred. The union's general secretary made it clear that the strike was not anti-American. "We do not want the Americans to leave; they have done a great deal for the country. But we are interested in our demands." Then, suddenly the union called off the strike after four days without guarantees of increased pay or major concessions. The bases' authorities agreed only to give the strikers their normal pay for the period they were absent, promised to commence formal negotiations through the French *intendant,* and agreed not to discriminate against any employee because of the strike. On the first day of work after the strike, tempers were short and several incidents almost caused another walkout. But, since the union had discovered it was unable to make headway by striking, it settled down to negotiations. On July 6, both sides accepted a two-year contract. It contained a no-strike clause and provided for wage increases that, with fringe benefits, reportedly amounted to less than 10 per cent of the total United States payroll in Morocco. Although political matters aroused the UMT against the bases on subsequent occasions, economic and social questions were never very troublesome thereafter.

At the time the American authorities achieved an accord with the UMT, however, they also encountered other difficulties with the Moroccan Government. Following an impetuous statement by Finance Minister Benjelloun, rumors circulated that Morocco would ask $430 million a year in base rental. Disturbed, the State Department replied by hinting that American bases under construction in Spain might render the Moroccan defenses obsolete. In July, 1956, the headquarters of the Seventeenth Air Force was moved from Rabat to Wheelus Field, Tripoli—a change attributed to Wheelus' central location in the command area, but the uncertainties of the Moroccan situation undoubtedly were important considerations.

Both the Sultan and Foreign Minister Balafrej attempted to stop the rumors dealing with the rental question. The Istiqlal's *al-Alam* adopted a more realistic bargaining position in calling for reversion of the bases to Morocco in ten years and the right to impose special conditions in accord with Moroccan interests in case of war. The Sultan was willing to permit the United States to use the bases for a specified period without financial return, although he pointed out that a voluntary offer of aid would be welcome. This recognized the American policy of not paying rent for overseas bases, but of providing the equivalent in parallel economic-aid agreements. Moroccan officials then insisted that any negotiations must be conducted between the United States and Morocco only. France, however, demanded that she be included in any talks in order to protect her rights and interests; moreover, she wished to conclude her military agreement with Morocco before the question of the bases was settled. Paris hinted to Washington that the State Department would save money by using France as a mediator; the Parisian daily *Combat*, reflecting French opinion, sneered at the United States as a sorcerer's apprentice and warned that it was about to be burned by the anticolonial fires it had started. Once again caught in the middle, the State Department gravitated toward the French position, causing Balafrej to suggest that the United States restrain its concern with France, which had shown no parallel concern for American interests in Morocco. The Foreign Minister's remark reflected his own lack of concern for America's NATO commitments, emphasizing the already obvious divergence between the basic objectives of American and Moroccan foreign policies.

In September, Secretary of the Air Force Donald A. Quarles paid a courtesy call on Ministers Balafrej and Guedira in the first official cabinet-level contact between the United States and Morocco. Quarles subsequently stated that the United States intended to keep its bases and expected in due course to reach an agreement with the Moroccan and French governments. But, whereas Washington was thinking in terms of defense arrangements between allies, mounting frictions with France were causing the Moroccans to think in terms of nonalliance, and the United States, as the ally of France, was to suffer from the growing wave of her anticolonialist neutralism.

Initial political pressure against the American bases was exerted by the UMT, which paradoxically had received its strongest foreign support from American labor unions. Moroccan dockers had long objected to unloading French troops and military supplies in Casablanca. In November, 1956, they further displayed their displeasure with foreign military intruders by refusing to unload an American ship that carried supplies for the bases. A month later, when

French military authorities rerouted their ships from Casablanca to the Port Lyautey naval base, irate Moroccans erected a barricade to block passage of French military vehicles. The French rolled out a few tanks and were prepared to destroy the barricade; but the potentially explosive situation was resolved when Moroccan authorities intervened to permit French passage. Minister Balafrej used the occasion to complain to the American Embassy about unloading French military supplies on bases occupied even jointly by Americans. Although the bases served as a guarantee of Moroccan security, he warned that they must not involve any interference with Moroccan affairs. When asked how Morocco could complain about bases whose existence she did not recognize, the Foreign Minister admitted that the bases did have *de facto* recognition but that the time had come to regularize their status.

After numerous informal exchanges among Moroccan, French, and American officials, negotiations finally began in May, 1957, between Moroccan and American representatives alone. Months passed without result; in December, in mutual desperation, the parties announced a temporary accord maintaining the *status quo* but recognizing Moroccan sovereignty. Although several modifications of the original agreement were made involving, among other things, import duties, it was obvious that the negotiations were still unable to produce an over-all solution that would simultaneously satisfy Washington's desire for continued use of the bases and Rabat's desire for their ultimate reversion to Morocco. An American pledge to evacuate troops and bases was demanded, not only for its own sake, but because it would set a useful precedent in discussing withdrawal with France and Spain.

The Moroccan Government, anxious to obtain substantial American aid and hopeful of lessening Washington's solidarity with Paris on such matters as Algeria, was not anxious to force a showdown that might alienate American good will. Rabat even rejected a Soviet note, sent by Marshal Bulganin, warning that countries harboring American bases must suffer in any future war. In February, 1958, when the Moroccan Government was already besieged with difficulties, a B–47 caught fire on the Sidi Slimane air strip, and the base was evacuated, allegedly as an exercise. Rumors immediately spread, however, that the plane had a nuclear bomb aboard, and American denials could not allay popular apprehension. The UMT loudly decried the atomic danger to Moroccans, and various political leaders in and out of the government, sensing a popular issue, began to demand that the United States abandon its bases. The news that the base at Nouasseur was to become a

Strategic Air Command installation heightened the agitation, although Americans explained that the change was purely an administrative matter. On several occasions, dockers again refused to unload American supply ships, aggravating the tension. The use of the air bases to transport American marines to Lebanon in July was the last straw.

In November, 1958, Mohammed V opened a final round of bargaining by demanding withdrawal of American troops. The United States promptly agreed in principle to pull out its forces, but asked a contract for continued use of the five bases for about seven years. Such a period presumably would have permitted American intercontinental ballistic missile sites and naval installations in Spain to become fully operational, minimizing the importance of the Moroccan bases. Moroccan spokesmen replied that a five-year period should be sufficient for liquidation of the bases. The King and many conservative elements would have preferred the United States to remain for both economic and security reasons, but even they insisted on American withdrawal because of its relationship to the French and Spanish troop question and its domestic political significance.

Finally, in December, 1959, Washington announced that military forces would be withdrawn from Morocco by the end of 1963 and that the Boulhaut base would be released in March, 1960. Morocco, in turn, agreed in principle to assume France's responsibility to guard the bases and also to recruit local labor on the installations. While the Moroccan bases had been important to the United States, they were then no longer essential to American defense and hardly worth the risk of antagonizing Morocco and, indirectly, other Arab and perhaps African countries. The agreement to withdraw was therefore a happy exception to the common fault of the Western nations of doing tomorrow what should have been done yesterday in the emerging areas of the modern world. Also and fortunately, the long period of negotiation permitted the United States to depart without courting serious political or strategic risks.

America's intentions to honor its commitment were evidenced in December, 1961, when Washington dispatched a ten-man survey team to cooperate with Rabat on conversion of the bases. The group recommended that Nouasseur become an international airport; Sidi Slimane an agricultural training school; Kenitra (Port Lyautey) a Moroccan Air Force base; and Benguerir a civilian aviation training school. Nevertheless, rumors circulated in Morocco that Washington was seeking to retain at least the Port

Lyautey base beyond 1963, and al-Fassi charged that the govern-ment was prepared to allow the United States to remain on the pretext of assisting in reconversion. The United States denied these reports and continued its efforts to meet the promised deadline. Al-though a few individuals in the Defense Department felt it de-sirable to retain at least one installation, the excessive cost of main-taining planes and equipment, added to the political hazards, even-tually outweighed their arguments.

Although the Moroccan Government had won a significant po-litical and diplomatic victory, it did not contemplate the departure of the Americans without misgiving. The bases had for many years been a significant factor in Morocco's economy.* Not only did the bases aid the Moroccan economy by offsetting the un-favorable balance of trade stimulated by the American businesses' imports, but they poured about $60 million a year into Morocco —$40 million that the government spent each year to maintain the bases, as well as another $20 million spent in Morocco by American personnel. This figure totaled more than a third of the entire Moroccan ordinary budget in the last few years of the Pro-tectorate and amounted to 5 per cent of the national income.

While the bases issue and its ramifications posed the most seri-ous threat to Moroccan-American amity, tensions over other mat-ters aggravated the basic incompatibility between America's anti-Communist policy and Morocco's neutralism for many years. Of even greater significance from the Moroccan viewpoint were the conflicting positions on Algeria. Conservative politicians and the palace at first hoped to see the struggle end before radical elements seized power and before republican winds gained the momentum

---

* Under the Protectorate, the American economic role in Morocco—centered about the business groups in Casablanca and Tangier, military and civilian government personnel and their dependents, and the American communica-tions network in Tangier—had grown enormously. Moroccan trade with the United States had risen from $100,000 a year in the mid-nineteenth century to $59 million in 1954 (the principal growth coming after World War II, as Morocco's need for the machinery and vehicles required in a modern economy increased). Despite obstructions in the form of import licenses, currency re-strictions, quota systems, international treaties, customs dues, and taxes, Amer-ican business operated successfully in Morocco, and, had France not en-forced limitations on trade (in violation of the Act of Algeciras), the commerce would have been even more extensive. These restrictions, as a matter of fact, had led to litigation in 1950 before the International Court at the Hague, as the United States alleged that French monetary regulations and imports con-trols not only jeopardized American interests in Morocco, but were arbitrary and unfair. The Court's decision, going against France, did little to stop the contested French practice.

to sweep across Morocco, even if this would involve a compromise on full independence. The leftists and many students, on the other hand, wished to see Algeria completely independent, partly out of genuine sympathy and partly to encourage social revolution in Morocco.

As Morocco's future in part depended on the outcome of the Algerian conflict, the government sought to induce the United States to take a positive role at least in encouraging France to end the war. However, following its precedents in Morocco and Tunisia, the United States proclaimed neutrality, while supporting France with military equipment and financial aid. The equipment was in most cases intended for NATO, but France seldom hesitated to appropriate it for her own use. Financial aid, particularly a grant of $600 million in 1958, kept France from being bankrupted by the Algerian struggle. Prior to 1958, the United States also sided with France in the United Nations on the Algerian issue, and the State Department refused to recognize the FLN provisional government established in September, 1958—on the ground that it did not exhibit such required qualifications as machinery of state, assent of the people, and capacity to fulfill obligations—although it only abstained on, and did not veto, a U.N. resolution calling for negotiations leading to Algerian independence. This general policy was occasionally criticized in the United States, notably by Senator John F. Kennedy, and aroused great antagonism in Morocco.

America's general Middle East policy was better received in Morocco than was her position on North Africa, but it likewise was seriously criticized on several occasions. In November, 1956, while the French press in Morocco bitterly attacked the American refusal to support France and England in the Suez crisis and called her an unfaithful ally, al-Alam gave cautious approval to Washington's position, although it also charged that Washington's refusal to help Egypt to build the Aswan Dam had occasioned the crisis. Al-Fassi frequently disagreed with the United States, although he could not readily be called anti-American.

The Kennedy Administration's avoidance of such actions, coupled with Morocco's diminishing involvement in Arab politics, greatly diminished criticism of America's role in the Middle East. Happier aspects of United States-Moroccan relations have been top-level and grass-roots exchanges, American aid, and numerous manifestations of the good will of the American people, exemplified by scholarships, shipments of relief to earthquake victims, and small but significant tokens of respect by members of the armed forces. When the then Crown Prince Hassan, with his sister Princess Lalla Aisha, went to Washington in 1956, he spoke cordially of Americans and their country. Later Moroccan visitors to the United States returned with generally favorable impressions, and a trickle of American visitors to Morocco, including athletes, labor leaders, teachers, and students, furthered friendly ties between the two peoples, which were also consolidated by a contingent of 130 Peace Corpsmen. However, probably the most dramatic and important exchanges occurred in March and November, 1957, and December, 1959. On the first occasion, Vice President Nixon stopped at Rabat at the beginning of a good-will tour of eight African states. An estimated 15,000 Moroccans turned out to cheer him as he drove from the airport to the palace and were particularly impressed when he stopped his car several times en route to descend to shake hands with enthusiastic welcomers. At the palace, the Vice President and the King discussed matters of mutual interest, and Mrs. Nixon was later received by the King in a private audience, an honor rarely accorded a foreign woman. Before leaving Rabat, the Vice President told a press conference that King Mohammed was a man destined greatly to influence the Muslim world. (The favorable impression left by Mr. Nixon was diluted by a French press report that quoted him as saying, "Morocco is a French country," when actually he had said "fringe" country, in reference to Morocco's exclusion from Eisenhower's Middle East policy. *Al-Alam* noted this distinction and was highly critical of this attempt to pollute the friendly atmosphere of the visit.) But many Frenchmen were irritated by the Vice President's visit and especially resented his discussion of the Algerian problem with Mohammed V. Mr. Nixon was reportedly convinced of the need to strengthen American ties with newly independent states of Africa, even to the detriment of the Franco-American alliance, as the only means of excluding Soviet influence from the continent.

In November, 1957, King Mohammed became the first Moroccan sovereign to visit the United States. While Moroccan government spokesmen emphasized that the trip was designed not to substitute friends but to multiply them, it was clear that Rabat regarded the United States as its alternative hope to a recalcitrant France. Mohammed V held several trump cards—the permission he might grant to allow the bases to stay, Morocco's strategic position, and his moderate and progressive attitude in the Arab world in general and Morocco in particular—and he intended to play them carefully to obtain American cooperation in a form that would not offend his subjects. The King was met by President Eisenhower at the airport and rode with him to the White House. Just prior to the state dinner scheduled for that night, President Eisenhower suffered his now famous heart attack, and their scheduled talks were canceled. Although the King met with the Secretary of State and the Vice President, the President's unfortunate illness clouded the entire visit. But two years later, at the conclusion of his eleven-nation tour in December, 1959, President Eisenhower visited Morocco, where he received an extremely enthusiastic welcome. Indicative of the President's personal popularity, perhaps as contrasted with some of his government's policies, the UMT quarreled bitterly with the government concerning the route to be taken by Eisenhower's car, desiring to change it so that he might see the impressive union hall in Casablanca. Eisenhower's arrival, accompanied by a State Department announcement concerning the future withdrawal of American forces, stirred hopes among Moroccan leaders that Washington was at last ready to treat African states as separate entities rather than as continuing European spheres of influence.

In March and April, 1963, King Hassan followed his father's precedent by making a state visit to Washington and a subsequent tour of the United States. While his official reception was warm, his personal extravagances, exemplified by the purchase of five Cadillacs, as well as an apparent disregard for his young wife and daughter, resulted in some criticism. However, the visit was successful, the more so as it squelched recurring rumors concerning an alleged desire by the United States to lease one of the military bases in Morocco.

By the end of August, the United States had relinquished all the bases except Nouasseur and Kenitra. Bats and pigeons had replaced B-47 bombers in the Nouasseur hangers, and only 600 Air Force personnel remained to dispose of the matériel. Finally, on December 16, the American flag was lowered on the last two sites. The military role of the United States in Morocco had come to an end, but it now plays other parts, as economic matters become increasingly important factors in the relationship between the two countries. Foremost in this regard are, of course, trade and aid.

A marked decline in the total value of American-Moroccan trade, which fell to a low of $46 million in 1957, had occurred just after Moroccan independence—due principally to the new tariff, the temporary curtailment of capital expansion, and the general decrease in Moroccan purchasing power. In 1964, Moroccan imports from the U.S. were valued at $50 million and exports at $5 million. Prospects for the future now seem bright, however, as Moroccan demand for American manufactured products and capital goods increases and as the United States imports greater quantities of Moroccan sardines and artisan products.

American aid to Morocco, linked as it is to the internal and external policies of both countries, has been subject to considerable criticism. At the same time, official circles in Rabat have gratefully acknowledged this aid, in view of Morocco's emphasis on economic and social improvements. Unfortunately, the sentiments of the leaders has often not been communicated to the people, again for political reasons.

In December, 1956, an ICA mission that visited Morocco for a preliminary study was asked for $36 million in direct monetary aid. The French Secretary of State for Foreign Affairs declared that American aid should be subject to consent by France; Washington finally agreed merely to supplement French assistance. With the temporary cessation of French Government aid after 1958, however, the United States became the primary supporter of Moroccan development.*

In addition to direct aid, American technical and special assistance programs supplied $126 million to Morocco between April 2, 1957, and June 30, 1961, under Mutual Security Program allocations. In 1960, the United States gave Rabat an additional $500,000 gift in arms, and in 1960 and 1961, it signed a $20-million military-aid agreement with Morocco, providing for training Moroccan soldiers and delivering equipment over a six-year period.

Regrettably, Moroccan suspicions of neocolonialism have made long-term plans for this aid difficult. Washington has also been criticized by Moroccan republicans for giving aid that might be construed as consolidating reactionary regimes. Despite such grievances, American financial aid has played an important role in Morocco's struggle to achieve a viable independent economy. Programs under the Mutual Security Act have been vital to agricultural development in such areas as drainage and irrigation, soil conservation, forestry, and locust control, which alone absorbed more than $60 million. In programs providing for social and industrial development, an equal expenditure has been devoted to construction of housing and roads and the training of specialized workers.

American reaction to the Soviet aid afforded Morocco has adversely affected United States-Moroccan relations. When the So-

* See above, chap. 6, pp. 161–62.

viet Union gave Morocco several MIG's in 1961, official and unofficial American observers were quick to criticize. Rabat adopted
an attitude of defiance, admonishing Washington to realize that
"allies who are bought will return only insults," and suggested
that the United States would gain more by economic and social
assistance than by military alliances. Although Washington denied
any intent to meddle in Moroccan internal affairs, the incident
was not immediately forgotten.

Another American response to "enemy" aid concerned Castro's
Cuba. As 75 per cent of United States credits to Morocco had
been used to buy 100,000 tons of sugar in Cuba (one-quarter of
Morocco's annual consumption), Washington proscribed further
use of dollar aid to buy Cuban sugar after 1961. In December,
1963, the United States Foreign Aid Act required that military
and economic assistance be withheld from countries engaging in
trade with Cuba. A note from the American Embassy in Rabat to
Moroccan authorities calling attention to this situation provoked
a sharp reaction. Guedira declared that Morocco's sovereignty
was being questioned and its policy of nonalignment put to the
test. Since Cuban sugar and Chinese tea are staples in the Moroccan diet and neither can be supplied by the U.S., it was not expected that this threat would be carried out. On February 14,
1964, however, after Moroccan merchant ships continued to trade
with Cuba, United States aid was in fact terminated.

The Moroccan Government unhappily concluded that it must
sacrifice principles to practical needs: given the deflated condition
of the budget and the need for American wheat to feed the hungry,
American aid was a vital necessity. Rabat therefore assured Washington that the trade with Cuba would be discontinued if another
source of sugar could be found. Washington agreed and restored
assistance in April. The Moroccan Government then concluded an
agreement for the delivery of 240,000 tons of sugar from South
America, Formosa, and South Africa through the facilities of two
Anglo-American companies. The re-establishment of American
aid was welcomed in some circles; however, it was denounced by
the Istiqlal press on the grounds that it would force Morocco's
budding merchant marine to rot in the harbors, would seriously
deplete Morocco's currency reserves, and was prejudicial to Moroccan sovereignty.

During the temporary suspension of aid, another small sore spot
developed when Guedira, in an interview with a Maghreb Arabe
Presse on February 20, announced that the United States had also
requested that Morocco stop shipping cobalt ore to China, since

the Communists could employ the cobalt for nuclear fission. However, the shipments to China were not large. Since the Moroccan ore contains only about 11 per cent cobalt, Morocco had difficulty finding any other customers. Defense Department officers were not too upset about the cobalt trade, since Morocco had yielded on the major issue of Cuba, and Washington has not pressed the matter further.

King Hassan's abandonment of an active neutralist foreign policy enhances the probability that American aid to Morocco and cordial relations will continue. However, Morocco needs more than financial and military aid from the United States; it requires understanding and encouragement. These qualities can be applied only through appreciation of the country's many political, economic, and social problems, and an ability to provide guidance where receptivity for such assistance exists, but exercising self-restraint where national pride requires that decisions be made and implemented in the absence of outside interference. The application of these principles requires a very high degree of empathy and patience, but the gain to be derived thereby is great by contrast with the effort involved.

Conclusion

MOROCCO HAS been independent for almost a decade, a period sufficiently long to force her citizens to accept independence as an irrevocable and unglamorous fact, long enough for her leaders to have second thoughts about what they have been doing and where they are heading, and long enough, certainly, for close observers *au-dessus de la mêlée* to form some tentative conclusions and prognoses.

An inventory in late 1965 reveals many undeniable accomplishments achieved since the chaotic days of early 1956. The first task of enforcing internal security and order has been met successfully with the aid of a strong military force. Minority communities now live in peace and relative prosperity. A constitutional form of government has been formalized. The often oppressive conformity of thought and deed demanded by a one-party state has been replaced by a variety of viewpoints, and followers are solicited by five major political organizations and two active trade-union associations. There have been no violent changes in government, and an intelligent young King both symbolizes and maintains national unity, continuity, and stability. The older generation can find comfort in the respect still accorded Islam and the tolerance of traditional ways of living; the younger can find encouragement in increased access to modern education and the growing opportunities in government, industry, and professions.

A flexible foreign policy has enabled Morocco simultaneously to include herself among the advocates of African liberation, gain at least superficial acceptance in revolutionary Arab circles, win the grudging respect of her potentially dangerous neighbor, Algeria, do business with Moscow and Peking, and obtain considerable aid from Paris and Washington. Morocco has progressed from a passive nonalignment first to a vocal Eastern-oriented neutralism and then to an open reliance upon Western bilateral and multi-lateral trade and aid; she has moved from national irredentism to radical nationalist African-bloc politics and then to a gradualist Pan-Africanism. All the while, she has managed to keep her diplomatic doors open, or at least ajar, to countries of every level of development, governments of every persuasion. The diversity of her outside contacts thus seem to match equally the varieties and contrasts within her borders, while the abrupt changes in direction often reflect the continuity of domestic trends.

An "in-depth" assessment, however, might reveal the Moroccan scene in a far less favorable light. Morocco's administrative unification is still incomplete and the authority of the central government is unquestioned only by common consent. Furthermore, internal political differences may yet erupt into violence if there is any change in the strong support of the monarchy by a loyal army leadership.

The evolution of responsible representative institutions has been slow, and the monarchy's full commitment to true constitutional principles is yet to be established. Accordingly, the locus of decision-making remains essentially where it was on the eve of independence: with the monarch, while the strength of the political parties lies more in their ability to obstruct the will of the monarch than in any positive capacity for forging and creating programs. Furthermore, the government has been reluctant to effect economic or social reforms except in response to political crises. Perhaps most important, occasional suppression of political opposition in the interest of maintaining a policy has prevented many persons potentially capable of making a valuable contribution from participating in politics or in the government.

Corruption and bureaucratic lethargy in the administration are serious problems that may be related in large part to the continuing lack of an educated and experienced cadre of civil servants. Meanwhile, debilitating conflicts over Arabization and Moroccanization of education dilute the benefits to be realized from the educational system.

In the area of foreign affairs, a genuine border settlement with Algeria is yet to be achieved, while the extension of Morocco's southern borders has brought few if any benefits to the annexed peoples and nothing to other Moroccans. The time and resources squandered on irredentism could better have been devoted to efforts to unify the populace in a concerted effort to rebuild Morocco within the boundaries of 1956. The strength of Morocco's political links to East and West is uncertain, and the new threads of Maghrib unity remain fragile. Financial and technical dependence on France continues almost undiminished.

In sum, the difficulties of the transition from the Protectorate to true and meaningful independence have continued and in some respects have intensified since 1956. King Hassan has clung to power through an estimable policy of moderation and negotiation. However valid these concepts, without accelerated reforms they remain inadequate to assure the evolutionary progress upon which the country's future depends.

The similarity of views entertained by de Gaulle and Hassan offers a basis for genuine *rapprochement* between France and Morocco. This has to some extent already come about, although internal politics in Morocco require Hassan not to publicize the new relationship. Nevertheless, the future of Morocco will be significantly influenced by this personal bond. If the young Moroccan monarch is able to accelerate the economy with French assistance, while at the same time furthering economic and social reforms, his own position will be stabilized and all Moroccans will be the beneficiaries. On the other hand, if Moroccan-French ties should again become strained, the consequent economic crisis would probably lead to renewed political instability and possibly the end of the monarchy. In such an event, the present uncertainties of Moroccan life would pale by comparison with the bitterness of the nation's consequent struggle for survival and viability.

Appendix A

Letter from George Washington to Sultan Muhammed bin Abdallah

City of New York, December 1, 1789

Great and Magnanimous Friend,

Since the date of the letter which the late Congress, by their President, addressed to Your Imperial Majesty, the United States of America have thought proper to change their government and institute a new one, agreeable to the Constitution, of which I have the honor, herewith, to enclose a copy. The time necessarily employed in the arduous task, and the disarrangements occasioned by so great though peaceable a revolution, will apologize, and account for Your Majesty's not having received those regularly advised marks of attention from the United States which the friendship and magnanimity of your conduct toward them afforded reason to expect.

The United States, having unanimously appointed me to supreme executive authority in this Nation, Your Majesty's letter of August 17, 1788, which by reason of the dissolution of the late-government, remained unanswered, has been delivered to me. I have also received the letters which Your Imperial Majesty has been so kind as to write, in favor of the United States, to the Bashaws of Tunis and Tripoli, and I present to you the sincere acknowledgments and thanks of the United States for this important mark of your friendship for them.

We greatly regret the hostile disposition of those regencies toward this nation, who have never injured them, is not to be removed, on terms in our power to comply with. Within our territories there are no mines, wither of gold or silver, and this young nation just recovering from the waste and desolation of a long war, have not, as yet, had time to acquire riches by agriculture and commerce. But our soil is bountiful, and our people industrious, and we have reason to flatter ourselves that we shall gradually become useful to our friends.

The encouragement which Your Majesty has been pleased, generously, to give to our commerce with your dominions, the punctuality with which you have caused the Treaty with us to be observed, and the just and generous measures taken in the case of Captain Proctor, make a deep impression on the United States and confirm their respect for and attachment to Your Imperial Majesty.

It gives me great pleasure to have the opportunity of assuring Your Majesty that, while I remain at the head of this nation, I shall not cease to promote every measure that may conduce to the friendship and harmony which so happily subsist between your Empire and them, and shall esteem myself happy in every occasion of convincing Your Majesty of the high sense (which in common with the whole nation) I entertain the magnamimity, wisdom and benevolence of Your Majesty.

May the Almighty bless Your Imperial Majesty, our Great and Magnanimous friend, with His constant guidance and protection.

George Washington

Declaration of the French Government on Morocco, September 12, 1955, Following the Discussions at Aix Les Bains *

The French Government, following consultations which have taken place over the last few weeks with representatives of the various trends of Moroccan public opinion, has decided to put into practice a co-ordinated plan designed to restore, between France and the Sherifian Empire, a climate of confidence permitting the development of Franco-Moroccan friendship.

The purpose of this plan is to establish a permanent union between the two states of France and Morocco and a community between their two peoples.

Such an objective can be achieved only in a climate of calm and order. It requires, moreover, the unreserved support of the most representative elements of Moroccan public opinion. And, last of all, it implies the swift modernization of the institutions of the Sherifian Empire.

Thus, France, faithful to her ideals of liberty and solidarity, intends to lead Morocco to the status of a sovereign and democratic state, and to maintain with it the permanent bonds of freely accepted interdependence.

She solemnly reaffirms on this occasion that her policy in Morocco is based upon the following principles:

* Text taken from Ambassade de France, Service de presse et d'information, *Moroccan Affairs*, No. 9, October 4, 1955.

1. Respect for the treaties concerning Morocco and for the recognized rights of the beneficiary powers.
2. Respect for Moroccan sovereignty and for the integrity of the Sherifian Empire.
3. Permanence of France's presence in Morocco, in the mutual interest of both countries and in the interest of the free world.
4. Recognition of the position and rights which the French community in Morocco has acquired as a result of its size and creative vitality, and of the essential role it must continue to play in the life of the country by benefiting, in particular, from a fair representation of its interests.

Moroccan Sovereignty

Faithful to the spirit and letter of the treaties, France intends to strengthen and promote Moroccan sovereignty, which she has undertaken to guarantee.

She notes that the growth of a modern Moroccan élite makes it possible today to entrust this élite with ever increasing responsibilities in the administration of public affairs. The Moroccan authorities must, therefore, exercise fully the attributes and powers which are rightfully theirs under the Treaty of Fez.

The French Government declares that it is ready to examine, with a representative Moroccan Government, the fields in which it would be possible to undertake by mutual agreement the reorganization and abolition of the present system of control, without the sound administration of public affairs, the protection of the legitimate interests of the populations and their security being in any way affected.

The Sherifian Throne

Anxious to safeguard, in accordance with the engagements it has entered into, the permanence and historic mission of the Sherifian throne, the French Government is ready to agree to any arrangements that may be made in order to solve, in a climate of peace and reconciliation, the crisis which has grievously divided Moroccan public opinion.

This solution, from which all spirit of revenge must be absent, will make it possible for the monarchy to remain, for all Moroccans, the symbol of their union and of their common faith in the destiny of the Sherifian Empire.

Constitution of a Moroccan Government

The Moroccan Government that is to be formed must be representative of the various trends of public opinion and of the different sections of the population. It will be, in principle, an all-Moroccan Government, but will include, to the extent and for the length of time which will appear necessary, the presence of French technicians.

In the immediate future, its task, within the framework of the Treaty of Fez, will be to administer public affairs, with respect for fundamental freedoms and the maintenance of acquired rights; to direct, without discrimination of any kind, the work of the Moroccan administration; and to devise the laws.

In addition, it will work out, in agreement with the French Government, then put into operation the modern democratic institutions with which Morocco is to be endowed.

It will also have the task of seeking, with the French Government, the new conditions, on the one hand for guaranteeing the rights and interests of France and of the French settlers in Morocco, and on the other hand for defining the permanent bonds which are to unite the two countries in the future.

Permanent Bonds Between France and Morocco

While acknowledging that a new definition of the permanent bonds between France and Morocco can only be worked out progressively, and will therefore entail some delays, the French Government declares itself prepared to deal with this problem and to resolve it in accordance with the following principles.

With France preserving, in the mutual interest of both countries, all the responsibilities entrusted to her in matters of defense and foreign affairs, the goal will be to build a modern edifice, freely discussed, defined, and accepted, and expressing in its common institutions the association between the two states and the community between the two peoples.

1. The association of the two states will involve:
   —a council consisting of delegations from each of the two Governments, and dealing with matters of common interest to the two states;
   —a high judicial body to deal with disputes concerning the functioning of the new system of association;
   —and, eventually, all other joint or complementary institutions.
2. The community between the two peoples must manifest itself, in particular, through the recognition of mutual rights in the various economic, political, administrative, and judicial spheres.

Justifiably proud of its traditions and its civilization, the Sherifian Empire, which, with the help of France and of the French people, has become receptive to modern life, is today anxious to continue this advance and to fulfill its aspirations. France will aid it to achieve this goal, in confidence, tolerance and harmony. With mutual respect for each other's dignity and personality, France and Morocco must together build an interdependent future on the indestructible foundations of friendship and brotherhood.

Throne Speech of Sidi Mohammed ben Youssef, November 18, 1955*

God alone be praised! To our dear and faithful people: on this blessed day, God is overwhelming us with His mercies in allowing us, after a painful separation, to return to our dear country and to the midst of our people, this people who have never ceased to wait for us as we have never lost hope of seeing them again, and who have generously repaid our fidelity toward them. Together, we have been subjected to a trial which, far from impairing our common will, has only succeeded in strengthening our faith in our destiny and in making us more than ever conscious of our rights and duties.

On this gala day, the twenty-eighth anniversary of our accession to the Throne of our glorious ancestors, we address to you, our people, according to our custom, our Speech from the Throne, recalling our past efforts and defining the objectives to be attained. You know our perseverance: we have always acted with a view to enabling Morocco to accede to a rank worthy of its wondrous past and of its important position in the modern world. Difficulties have not shaken us; obstacles have not made us retreat. We have never hesitated to proclaim the truth and to demand a change in the established regime in order to satisfy the will of our people and to fulfill their aspirations. Then a crisis arose and we had to face many perils. Almighty God, having judged us in that trial, willed that it should have a happy outcome. Once again the mosques were filled with the faithful, and on every hand prayers were offered for us and for our people. The sorrow of

* Text taken from Ambassade de France, Service de presse et d'information, *Moroccan Affairs*, No. 10, January, 1956.

separation has given way to rejoicing. Praise be to God, Who, in His infinite mercy, has taken away our afflictions!

We immediately took up our task again in accordance with the responsibilities that are ours, seeking advice from the most authoritative sources, following the course of reason and wisdom. While we were in France, we had talks full of cordiality and understanding with the French Government on the subject of Morocco. These talks resulted in agreement on essential principles.

It will be the task of the Government to be formed under our auspices to begin negotiations with the French Government. We rejoice in being able to announce the end of the regime of trusteeship and of the Protectorate and the coming of an era of freedom and independence.

The time has come to mobilize all the energies available for the construction of a new Morocco. This undertaking will demand a thoroughgoing transformation of the habits, the institutions, and the methods of government, as it will also imply an emancipation of the individual, assuring him the secure enjoyment of all his freedoms. Thus Morocco will succeed in attaining the independence that we have never ceased to claim not only as the natural right of all peoples without distinction, but also as the surest means of enabling them to benefit both from the evolution of the modern world and from the advantages of a democratic regime free from all racial discrimination and inspired by the Universal Declaration of Human Rights.

The independence to which our people aspire must not signify a weakening of our ties with France, for the friendship between our two countries is firmly rooted and has a long history. Furthermore, we have not lost sight of the fact that, thanks to this friendship and to French achievements in various domains, Morocco has been able to progress at a very rapid rate. We are counting on France's cooperation in inaugurating a new era of interdependence between our two countries.

Our first objective is the constitution of a responsible and representative Moroccan Government, truly expressive of the people's will. This Government will have three simultaneous tasks to fulfill:

1. The administration of public affairs.
2. The creation of democratic institutions resulting from free elections and founded on the principle of the separation of powers, within the framework of a constitutional monarchy granting to Moroccans of all faiths citizenship rights and the exercise of political and trade-union freedom. It stands to reason that Moroccan Jews have the same rights and duties as other Moroccans.
3. The third task of the future Moroccan Government will be to open negotiations with the French Government on the basis of the following considerations: the ideas of freedom and democracy have taken on such wide scope in the postwar world that the conscience of mankind no longer allows independence and

dignity to be the exclusive prerogative of a few peoples. Moreover, owing to the difficulties of the present-day world and to interdependent interests, all nations, in order to safeguard their heritage and ensure their security, must unite ever more securely and cooperate always more closely. That is why the Moroccan Government, in the course of the negotiations, must define the framework and the real meaning of the independence of our country and the new relations of interdependence between Morocco and France on the basis of their equality and with mutual respect for each other's sovereignty.

These new relations are not incompatible with the maintenance of our spiritual and cultural bonds with the other Arabic peoples. We should like to see the West take into consideration the needs and aspirations of these peoples and cooperate with them for the common welfare and happiness of mankind.

At the conclusion of these negotiations, the Protectorate regime will come to an end and Morocco will enter into a new era in which it will exercise its sovereignty in accordance with the new agreements and in a spirit of understanding and fruitful cooperation with the French people. Such are the fundamental political principles of which the Moroccan Government will have to work out the details with the French Government.

It is essential not to forget that Morocco has among its inhabitants a substantial number of French citizens who have contributed to its general development and more particularly to its economic prosperity. We have noted with satisfaction the understanding which most of them have shown for our people's aspirations to liberty and independence. We want them all to be reassured as to their future. We are ever ready to safeguard their interests, their rights and their personal status with due respect for Moroccan sovereignty. Our wish is to see Moroccans and Frenchmen working together for the prosperity of Morocco and the welfare of all with a view to consolidating their relations and safeguarding the friendship of our two countries.

Now that we have set forth our objectives, we call upon you to unite as brothers and to draw closer together so as to form a single unit. May the general interest and the defense of the rights of the Nation remain your constant preoccupation. We take this opportunity to express our gratitude to all those who have given evidence of their sympathy and their solidarity with us. We pray God to help us in our efforts to maintain the unity of the Nation, watch over its interests and ensure its happiness.

Appendix D

Joint Spanish-Moroccan Declaration and Protocol of April 7, 1956[*]

The Spanish Government and His Majesty Mohammed V, Sultan of Morocco, desirous of reaching a particularly friendly treaty, on a reciprocal basis, to strengthen their ties of friendship and to consolidate peace in the area in which their countries are situated, have agreed to issue the following declaration:

1. The Spanish Government and His Majesty Mohammed V, Sultan of Morocco, considering that the regime established in Morocco in 1912 no longer corresponds to present reality, declare that the agreement signed in Madrid on November 27, 1912, can no longer regulate Spanish-Moroccan relations.

2. Consequently, the Spanish Government recognizes Morocco's independence proclaimed by His Majesty Mohammed V, and Morocco's full sovereignty with all the attributes appertaining thereto, including those relating to foreign policy and the army.

The Spanish Government reaffirms its wish to respect the territorial unity of the empire, which is guaranteed by international treaties, and undertakes to adopt the necessary measures to render it effective.

The Spanish Government also undertakes to grant His Majesty the Sultan such aid and assistance considered necessary by mutual agreement, notably in matters of foreign relations and defense.

3. The purpose of the negotiations opened at Madrid between the Spanish Government and His Majesty Mohammed V, Sultan of Morocco, is to lead to new agreements between the two sovereign and

[*] Source: Morocco, Ministry of Foreign Affairs, *Morocco*, No. 1, 1957.

equal states, with the object of defining free cooperation in those spheres where their common interests are involved.

These agreements will guarantee, in the friendly spirit mentioned above, the freedoms and rights of Spanish nationals in Morocco and of Moroccans in Spain, of a private, economic, cultural, or social nature, on a basis of reciprocity and respect for the sovereignty of both countries.

4. The Spanish Government and His Majesty the Sultan agree that until such time as the aforementioned agreements enter into force, relations between Spain and Morocco shall be based upon the terms of the protocol annexed to the present declaration.

Protocol

1. Legislative power will be exercised in a sovereign manner by His Majesty the Sultan. The representative of Spain in Rabat will be advised of projected decrees of the Sultan that affect Spanish interests and will be allowed to make pertinent observations.

2. The powers exercised until now by the Spanish authorities in Morocco will be transferred to the Moroccan Government in conformity with formulas established by common agreement. The position of Spanish civil servants in Morocco will be maintained.

3. The Spanish Government will assist the Moroccan Government in organizing its own army. The Spanish Army will remain in Morocco during the period of transition.

4. Spanish currency shall remain in use pending the conclusion of a new agreement.

5. Visas and all administrative formalities required for passage of persons from one zone to the other are abolished.

6. The Spanish Government will continue to be responsible for the protection abroad of the interests of Moroccans native to the zone defined previously by the Convention of November 27, 1912, and residents abroad, until the Government of His Majesty the Sultan assumes this function.

Fundamental Law of June 2, 1961

His Majesty King Hassan II has promulgated a dahir making the codification of certain principles of Moroccan foreign and national policy the Fundamental Law of the Kingdom of Morocco.

Although this Fundamental Law can in no way be considered a constitution, it indubitably constitutes a new and important step toward a constitutional monarchy to which the late King Mohammed V and His Majesty King Hassan II have pledged themselves.

WHEREAS Our Sherifian Majesty, inspired both by the spirit of democracy that is found in the teachings of Islam and the principles that have always guided our revered Fathers' acts, has always worked toward establishing a constitutional monarchy, and

WHEREAS the proper management of the affairs of the state during the phase preceding the promulgation of a constitution requires that the country be led down that path effectively from now on, and

WHEREAS the coming of a better future requires Moroccans to exhibit self-denial and a spirit of sacrifice, therefore

His Majesty has decided to embody the following principles in a fundamental law of kingdom that will govern all governmental actions until a constitution has been promulgated and has become effective.

Article I. Morocco is an Arab and Muslim kingdom. It is on its way to becoming a constitutional monarchy that, with representative institutions, will allow the nation to choose proper ways to realize the national goals.

Art. II. Islam is the official religion of the state.

Art. III. Arabic is the official and national language of the country.

Art. IV. Within the limits of its true borders, Morocco is an entity, one and indivisible. It is a national duty to work toward the realization of territorial integrity and unity.

Art. V. The state must ensure the internal and external security of the country by all appropriate means.

Art. VI. Because the realization of national goals imperatively requires the unity of all subjects and the elimination of any obstacle of such a nature as to thwart this achievement, the state must preserve the unity of the nation and oppose everything that is likely to cause division within the national community.

Art. VII. Moroccans are equal; they share the same rights and the same duties.

Art. VIII. The state must protect personal dignity and the exercise of public and private liberties.

Art. IX. Every Moroccan has the right to equal justice. The state must ensure that this right is preserved through a separation of powers, the independence of the judicial body, and through democratic guarantees.

Art. X. There can be violation and penalty only in respect of a law enacted prior to the violation. Penalties apply only to the guilty party.

Art. XI. The state must protect individuals against the misappropriation of power, excess of power, abuse of power, and extortion, and it must deal rigorously with every attack on the basic foundations of the kingdom.

Art. XII. The aims of the economic institutions of the country must be the realization of social justice, the development of production, the raising of the living standard, and the Moroccanization of all national resources.

Art. XIII. The state will proceed with the mobilization of its nationals within the framework of the plans that have been, or will be, prepared so that the economic development of the country, as well as its demographic expansion and its social progress, will proceed under a rational plan and will correspond to a specific program with respect to goals and schedules for their realization.

Art. XIV. The state must provide education with an Arab and Islamic national orientation suited to the needs of the nation, including technical, professional, and scientific training.

Art. XV. In foreign affairs, Morocco's policy is one of nondependence, due to the conviction that this is the best way to contribute to world peace. She proclaims her bonds with the Bandung Principles; and her faithfulness to the League of Arab Nations, which she strives to strengthen, and to the Charter of the United Nations Organization.

Art. XVI. Morocco undertakes to apply both the Charter of the Casablanca Conference and the resolutions adopted by the latter regarding the promotion of African unity and the fight against racial discrimination and all forms of colonialism.

Art. XVII. The Fundamental Law will take effect 17 Hijja, 1380 (June 2, 1961).

The Constitution of 1962

The Kingdom of Morocco, a Sovereign State whose official language is Arabic, constitutes a part of the Great Maghrib.

As an African State, it has among its objectives the realization of the African unity.

Being aware of the necessity for incorporating its work within the frame of the international organizations of which it has become an active and dynamic member, the Kingdom of Morocco adheres fully to the principles, rights, and obligations emanating from the charters of such organizations, as it reaffirms its determination to further the cause of peace and security in the world.

CHAPTER I. GENERAL PROVISIONS

Article 1. Morocco shall have a social, democratic, and constitutional monarchy.

Art. 2. The sovereignty shall be that of the people, who shall exercise it directly, by means of referendum, or indirectly, through constitutional institutions.

Art. 3. While the political parties shall participate in the organization and representation of the citizens, there shall be no single-party regime in Morocco.

Art. 4. The law shall be the supreme expression of the will of the people, and all shall abide by it. The law shall have no retroactive effect.

Art. 5. All Moroccan citizens shall be equal before the law.

Art. 6. Islam shall be the official religion, while the State shall guarantee the freedom of worship for all.

Art. 7. The emblem of the Kingdom shall be a red flag with a five-pointed green star in the center.

The motto of the Kingdom shall be: GOD, COUNTRY, KING.

The Citizen's Political Rights

Article 8. Men and women shall enjoy equal rights. Any citizen of age and enjoying his or her civil and political rights shall be eligible to vote.

Art. 9. The Constitution shall guarantee to all citizens: freedom of movement through, and settlement in, all parts of the Kingdom; freedom of opinion; freedom of speech in all its forms; freedom of public meeting; freedom of association; and freedom to belong to any union or political group of their choice.

No limitation, except by law, shall be put to the application of these freedoms.

Art. 10. No one shall be arrested, imprisoned, or punished except under the circumstances and procedures prescribed by the law. The home shall be respected and shall be subject to search and inspection only under the conditions and procedures prescribed by the law.

Art. 11. Personal correspondence shall retain its secrecy.

Art. 12. Opportunities for government employment and public offices shall be uniformly open to all citizens.

The Citizen's Economic and Social Rights

Article 13. All citizens shall have equal rights in seeking education and employment.

Art. 14. The right to strike shall be guaranteed, and the conditions and forms of its use shall be regulated by an organic law.

Art. 15. The right to own property shall be guaranteed. The law shall put limitations to its extent and use, if so required by the socio-economical development planned for the country. There shall be no expropriation except when pronounced by law.

Art. 16. All the citizens shall participate in the defense of their country.

Art. 17. All citizens shall, according to their means, contribute to the public expenditures, which only the law shall enact and issue within the terms of the provisions of this Constitution.

Art. 18. All citizens shall bear in solidarity the costs resulting from disasters suffered by the nation.

CHAPTER II. MONARCHY

Article 19. The King, Amir al-Muminin [Leader of the Faithful], shall be the symbol of the unity of the country and guarantor of the perpetuation of the State, protector of the Faith and the Constitution. He shall be defender of the rights and liberties of each and every citizen, group, and organization, as he shall be guarantor of the territorial integrity of the Kingdom in all its rightful boundaries.

Art. 20. The Moroccan Crown and the constitutional rights thereof shall be inherited in direct male line and by order of primogeniture among the offspring of H. M. King Hassan II.

In the event that there are no direct linear descendants, the right of succession to the throne shall go to the oldest male in the collateral consanguinity.

Art. 21. The King shall be minor until he reaches the age of 18. During the state of minority, a Regency Council shall assume the authority and constitutional rights of the Crown.

The Regency Council shall be presided over by the oldest and closest male relative in the collateral line who shall have come of age at 21. The Council shall also include the Chief Justice, the Chairman of the Board of Directors of Moroccan Universities, and the Presidents of both Chambers of Parliament.

No Cabinet member shall hold office in the Regency Council.

The functioning of the Regency Council shall be regulated by organic law.

Art. 22. The King shall be entitled to a civil list.

Art. 23. The person of the King shall be sacred and inviolable.

Art. 24. The King shall appoint the Prime Minister and Cabinet members. Their services may be terminated either on his initiative or because of their resignation, individually or in a body.

Art. 25. The King shall preside over Cabinet meetings.

Art. 26. The King shall promulgate legislation, which may be submitted for a referendum vote or for a new reading, according to the terms of Chapter V.

Art. 27. The King shall have the right to dissolve the Chamber of Representatives by royal decree, in accordance with the conditions under Chapter V, Articles 77 and 79.

Art. 28. The King shall feel free to deliver addresses to Parliament or to the people. The content of such addresses, however, shall not be subject to parliamentary deliberations.

Art. 29. The King shall exercise his statutory power in areas explicitly assigned by the Constitution.

Royal decrees shall be endorsed by the Prime Minister, with the exception of those appearing under the terms of Articles 24, 35, 72, 77, 84, 91, 101.

Art. 30. The King shall be Commander in Chief of the Royal Armed Forces. He shall make civil and military appointments and shall reserve the right to delegate such power.

Art. 31. The King shall accredit ambassadors to foreign nations and international organizations, as ambassadors and representatives of foreign nations and international organizations shall be accredited to him.

The King shall sign and ratify treaties. He shall not, however, ratify treaties involving national expenses without full approval of Parliament.

Treaties incompatible with the provisions of the Constitution shall be approved in terms of the regulations laid down for the modification of the Constitution.

Art. 32. The King shall preside over the Supreme Council for National Reconstruction and Planning.

Art. 33. The King shall preside over the Supreme Court of Justice, and shall appoint magistrates according to the conditions laid down in Article 84.

Art. 34. The King shall hold the power of pardon.

Art. 35. Should the integrity of the national soil ever be threatened or should any event interrupt the course of action of the constitutional institutions, the King shall hold the right to declare, by decree, after consulting with Parliament and after delivering an address to the people, a state of national emergency. Therefore, notwithstanding all contrary provisions, the King shall assume the responsibility of taking necessary measures for the defense of the territorial integrity, and for the restoration of the normal functioning of the constitutional institutions.

The state of emergency shall be terminated by means of a procedure similar to that called for at the time of its declaration.

CHAPTER III. PARLIAMENT

Article 36. Parliament shall be composed of a Chamber of Representatives and a Chamber of Councilors.

Art. 37. Members of Parliament shall hold their mandate from the people. Their right to vote shall be personal and shall not be delegated.

Art. 38. No Member of Parliament shall be subject to prosecution, arrest, imprisonment, or trial because of expressing his opinion or casting his vote in the performance of his duties. During parliamentary sessions, no Member of Parliament shall be subject to prosecution or arrest for criminal or correctional reasons, without permission from his Chamber, except *flagrante delicto*. Outside parliamentary sessions, no Member of Parliament shall be subject to arrest without permission from the Board of his Chamber, except *flagrante delicto* or in the case of legal prosecution or a final sentence. The prosecution or arrest of a Member of Parliament shall be suspended if so requested by his Chamber.

Art. 39. Parliament shall hold two sessions a year, both of which shall be opened by the King. The first session shall begin on November 18 and the second on the last Friday in April.

The sessions may be closed by royal decree after at least two months.

Art. 40. Parliament may hold an extraordinary session either by request of one-third of the members of the Chamber of Representatives or by royal decree.

Art. 41. Cabinet members shall have access to both Chambers and their committees, as they shall have the right to designate their own assistants.

Art. 42. Parliamentary sessions shall be open to the public.

The minutes of these sessions shall be published in the *Official Bulletin*. Each Chamber shall have closed meetings upon request either of one-tenth of its members or of the Prime Minister.

Art. 43. Each Chamber shall lay down and ratify its own legislation by vote. Such legislation shall be effective only after approval by the Constitutional Board of the Supreme Court.

Art. 44. Representatives shall be elected by universal suffrage for a four-year term.

The number of Representatives and the manner of electing them on one hand, and the conditions of eligibilty on the other, shall be determined by organic law. The President and the members of the Board of the Chamber of Representatives shall be elected every year at the opening of the November session. Members of the Board shall be elected on the basis of proportional representation of the parties in Parliament.

Art. 45. Two-thirds of the Chamber of Councilors shall be comprised of members elected in each town and province by an electoral college consisting of town, province, and county councils. The other third shall consist of members elected by the Chambers of Commerce, Industry, and Arts and Crafts, and by delegates from union organizations. Only member-candidates of the electoral college, chambers, or unions shall be eligible.

Councilors shall be elected for a six-year term. Half of the seats shall be renewed every three years, and the seats subject to the first renewal shall be determined by drawing lots. The members shall be called Councilors of the Kingdom, and their number shall be determined by an organic law. Such a law shall also determine the conditions of eligibility and incompatibility.

Art. 46. The Chamber of Councilors shall hold its sessions at the same time as the Chamber of Representatives.

The Powers of Parliament

Article 47. Legislation shall be voted on by Parliament. Parliament may, by decree deliberated at a Cabinet meeting, authorize the Government to take measures generally compatible with the law for a limited period of time and for a definite purpose. Decrees shall become effective immediately after their publication but shall be submitted for sanction by Parliament at the expiration of the time allowed. Such a law shall become void in the event of the dissolution of the Chamber of Representatives.

Art. 48. In addition to the jurisdictions referred to in other articles of the Constitution, the following shall come under the legislative power:

— the individual and group rights enumerated under Chapter I of this constitution;
— the fundamental principles of the civil and criminal law;
— the judicial organization of the Kingdom;

—the fundamental guarantees granted civil and military public servants.

These provisions shall all be regulated by organic law.

Art. 49. Matters outside the legislative area shall come under the organic laws.

Art. 50. Bills in existence before the promulgation of this Constitution may be subject to possible modification by decree and upon approval by Parliament, should they come under the jurisdiction of the organic laws.

Art. 51. Declaration of a state of war shall have to be authorized by Parliament.

Art. 52. A state of martial law may be declared by ministerial decree for a period of thirty days, and may be extended by law only.

Art. 53. Financial legislation shall be passed by Parliament under the conditions laid down by organic law. The expenditures required for the execution of a project shall be voted on by Parliament only once, at the time of its sanction. The validity of this approval shall continue throughout the implementation of the project. The Government alone shall have the prerogative to introduce laws to modify the adopted project.

If, by December 31, the annual national budget has not been passed, the Government may by decree allocate the funds necessary for the operation of public services and corresponding to the appropriations made in the proposed budget.

Art. 54. Proposals and amendments advanced by Members of Parliament shall not be admissible when their adoption might cause a decrease in public resources, the creation of new public expenditures, or an increase in those already in force.

The Functioning of Parliamentary Institutions

Article 55. The Prime Minister as well as Members of Parliament shall have the power to draft laws.

Drafts of laws shall first of all be submitted to the Board of the Chamber of Representatives for study by the Chamber. Should a legislation project be voted down by the Chamber of Representatives after a first reading, the Government may approach the Chamber of Councilors.

Art. 56. The Government may reject any proposal or amendment irrelevant to the legislative realm. In case of disagreement, the Constitutional Board of the Supreme Court shall take action on it within a period of eight days, upon request of either Chamber of Parliament or the Government.

Art. 57. During the interval between parliamentary sessions, proposed legislation shall be submitted for study to the acting committees.

Art. 58. During the interval between parliamentary sessions, the Government may, in agreement with the acting committees, decree projects which shall be submitted for ratification when Parliament is in regular session.

Art. 59. The Board of each Chamber shall prepare an agenda listing for debate, by priority and in the order proposed by the Government, the legislative projects introduced by the Government and the proposed laws accepted by it.

One session a week shall be devoted, by priority, to questions asked by Members of Parliament and answers given by the Government.

Art. 60. Texts introduced by the Government shall be deliberated at the first reading.

When a text is submitted by either Chamber to the other, debate shall mainly concern it.

Art. 61. Members of Parliament and of the Government shall have the right to propose amendments. The Government may oppose the consideration of any amendment not submitted, prior to the opening of debate, to the committee in charge of this matter.

By request of the Government, the Chamber asked to handle the case shall take action on the bill, in whole or in part, by a single vote, holding only amendments proposed or accepted by the Government.

Art. 62. Every legislative project or proposal shall be examined successively by each Chamber in order that an identical text may be adopted.

Should a legislative project or a motion be voted down after two readings at each Chamber, or, in case of a Government-declared emergency, after one reading, the project or motion may be newly submitted to the Chamber of Representatives for approval or rejection by a two-thirds majority. In case of approval, the text shall be submitted to the King for final decision.

Art. 63. Organic laws shall be passed and amended under the following conditions: a legislative project or motion shall be submitted for debate and vote, by the first Chamber asked to handle it, only ten days after its transmittal. In such cases, the procedure outlined in Paragraph 2 of Article 62 shall not be applicable.

Organic laws shall not be promulgated before they are submitted for approval by the Constitutional Board of the Supreme Court.

CHAPTER IV. THE GOVERNMENT

Article 64. The Government shall be composed of the Prime Minister and the Cabinet.

Art. 65. The Government shall be responsible to the King and the Chamber of Representatives.

After the appointment of the Government by the King, the Prime Minister shall appear before both Chambers and present his proposed program.

Art. 66. The Government shall be responsible for the application of the law. All services shall be at its disposal.

Art. 67. The Prime Minister shall have the right to introduce bills, which may not be submitted to the Board of either Chamber before deliberation at Cabinet meetings.

Art. 68. The Prime Minister shall exercise such statutory powers as are not reserved by the Constitution to the King.

Bills introduced by the Prime Minister shall be endorsed by the Ministers responsible for their application.

Art. 69. The Prime Minister may delegate some of his powers to the Ministers.

CHAPTER V. RELATIONS BETWEEN THE POWERS

Relations Between the King and Parliament

Article 70. When a bill is submitted for the King's seal, the King may ask Parliament for a new reading.

Art. 71. A new reading shall be requested in a message endorsed by the Prime Minister.

Art. 72. The King may submit, by decree, any legislative project for approval by referendum.

Art. 73. No legislative project shall be submitted to a referendum before deliberation on it by both Chambers.

Art. 74. The results of the referendum shall be recognized by all.

Art. 75. When legislation is approved by referendum vote after being rejected by Parliament, the Chamber of Representatives shall be dissolved.

Art. 76. No legislative project or motion concerning the modification of the Constitution shall be promulgated before approval by referendum.

Art. 77. After consulting with the Chairman of the Constitutional Board of the Supreme Court and after delivering an address to the people, the King may decree the dissolution of the Chamber of Representatives.

Art. 78. The election of a new Chamber of Representatives shall take place no less than twenty and no more than forty days after the dissolution.

Art. 79. In the event of a dissolved Chamber of Representatives, the one succeeding shall not be dissolved before a year after its election.

Relations Between Parliament and the Government

Article 80. The Prime Minister may, after deliberation at Cabinet meetings, involve the responsibility of the Government before the Chamber of Representatives in connection with the proclamation of a general policy or the vote on a draft bill.

Confidence in the Government shall be withdrawn, and a bill rejected, only by a wide majority of the members of the Chamber of Representatives.

The vote shall be held three full days after the matter of confidence has been submitted.

In the event of a withdrawal of confidence, the Government shall resign in a body.

Art. 81. The Chamber of Representatives may raise an objection to the responsibility carried out by the Government, by adopting the motion of censure. Such a motion shall be accepted only when signed by at least one-tenth of the Chamber members.

The motion of censure shall be approved by the Chamber of Representatives only by vote of an absolute majority of its members. The vote shall take place only after three days after the motion has been submitted.

The vote for censure shall lead to the resignation in a body of the Government.

In the event of censure of the Government by the Chamber, no other motion of censure shall be accepted within a year.

CHAPTER VI. JUSTICE

Article 82. The judicial branch shall be independent from the legislative and the executive branches.

Art. 83. Justice shall be administered in the King's name.

Art. 84. Magistrates, whose names shall be submitted by the Supreme Council of Justice, shall be appointed by royal decree.

Art. 85. Magistrates of the Bench shall be irremovable.

Art. 86. The Supreme Council of Justice shall be presided over by the King. In addition to the President, it shall comprise:

—the Minister of Justice as the Vice President;
—the Chief Justice of the Supreme Court;
—the Attorney General to the Supreme Court;
—the President of the First Chamber of the Supreme Court;
—two representatives elected from among the magistrates of the Courts of Appeal;
—two representatives elected from among the magistrates of the district courts;
—and two representatives elected from among the magistrates of the Sadad [similar to the Court of the Justices of the Peace].

Art. 87. The Supreme Council of Justice shall look after the application of the provisions concerning the promotion and discipline of the magistrates.

CHAPTER VII. THE SUPREME COURTS OF JUSTICE

Article 88. Government members shall be responsible before the Supreme Court of Justice for any criminal act or violation committed while performing their duties.

Art. 89. The Chamber of Representatives may indict members of the Government and may commit them to trial before the Supreme Court of Justice.

Art. 90. Their case shall be decided on by a secret ballot and by a two-thirds majority of the members of the Chamber of Representatives, with the exception of those members called on to take part in conducting the prosecution and the investigation and pronouncing the sentence.

Art. 91. The Supreme Court of Justice shall be composed of members elected from both Chambers. Their number shall be equally represented.

The President of the Supreme Court of Justice shall be appointed by decree.

Art. 92. An organic law shall determine the number of the members of the Supreme Court of Justice, the method of their election and the parliamentary procedures to be adopted.

CHAPTER VIII. LOCAL COMMUNITIES

Article 93. The communities of the Kingdom—prefectures, provinces, and counties—shall be established by law.

Art. 94. They shall elect councils to run their affairs according to democratic principles and the provisions of the law.

Art. 95. In prefectures and provinces, the governors shall execute the decisions of the councils. They shall, moreover, be responsible for coordination between the various services and shall guarantee the application of the law.

CHAPTER IX. THE SUPREME COUNCIL FOR NATIONAL RECONSTRUCTION AND PLANNING

Article 96. A Supreme Council for National Reconstruction and Planning shall be founded.

Art. 97. The Supreme Council for National Reconstruction and Planning shall be presided over by the King. Its structure shall be determined by organic law.

Art. 98. The Supreme Council for National Reconstruction and Planning shall lay down planning projects and draw up the budgets necessary for their implementation.

Art. 99. Planning projects shall be submitted to Parliament for approval, after having been adopted at Cabinet meetings.

CHAPTER X. THE CONSTITUTIONAL BOARD OF THE SUPREME COURT

Article 100. A Constitutional Board shall be formed within the Supreme Court.

The Board shall be headed by the Chief Justice of the Supreme Court.

Art. 101. The Constitutional Board shall include, in addition to its Chairman:

—a magistrate from the Administrative Board of the Supreme Court

and a law professor from the School of Law, both of whom shall
be appointed by decree for a six-year term;

—two members elected, one by the President of the Chamber of
Representatives and the other by the President of the Chamber
of Councilors, at the beginning of a legislative term or after a
partial renewal.

Art. 102. The functioning and parliamentary procedures of the Constitutional Board shall be determined by organic law.

Art. 103. The Constitutional Board shall exercise the powers vested in it constitutionally. It shall, furthermore, enact rules regarding the elections of Members of Parliament and referendum procedures.

CHAPTER XI. REVISING THE CONSTITUTION

Article 104. The Prime Minister and Parliament shall alone have the right to propose a revision of the Constitution.

Art. 105. A proposed revision shall be drawn up by the Cabinet and shall be submitted to Parliament for deliberation.

Art. 106. The proposal for revision shall have to be adopted by a wide majority of the members of each Chamber.

Art. 107. A revision shall become final after approval by referendum.

Art. 108. The State system of monarchy, as well as the provisions made for the Islamic institutions, shall not be subject to any constitutional revision.

CHAPTER XII

Article 109. Parliament shall be inaugurated within a period between five and ten months after the date of promulgation of this Constitution.

For the inauguration of the other institutions founded by the Constitution, this period shall be extended to one year.

Art. 110. Until the inauguration of Parliament, His Majesty the King shall assume full authority in taking the legislative and statutory measures necessary for the installation of the constitutional institutions and the functioning of all public services.

Bibliography

ASHFORD, DOUGLAS. *Political Change in Morocco.* Princeton, N. J.: Princeton University Press, 1961.

AUBIN, EUGENE. *Morocco of Today.* London: Dent, 1906.

AYACHE, ALBERT. *Le Maroc: Bilan d'une colonisation.* Paris: Editions Sociales, 1956.

BARBOUR, NEVILL, ed. *A Survey of North West Africa.* 2d ed. London: Oxford University Press, 1962.

BARRAT, ROBERT. *Justice pour le Maroc.* Paris: Editions du Seuil, 1953.

BECHIR, MOSTAFA. *Hello Babbit! Voici le Maroc.* Cairo: Les Cahiers de l'Unité Arabe, 1954.

BENNOUNA, MEHDI. *Our Morocco.* Tetuán, 1951.

BERQUE, JACQUES. *Structures sociales du Haut-Atlas.* Paris: Presses universitaires de France, 1955.

———. *Le Maghreb entre deux guerres.* Paris: Editions du Seuil, 1962.*

BUTTIN, PAUL. *Le Drame du Maroc.* Paris: Editions du Cerf, 1955.

CATROUX, GEORGE. *Lyautey le Marocain.* Paris: Hachette, 1952.

COON, CARLETON. *Caravan: The Story of the Middle East.* Rev. ed. New York: Holt, 1958.

———. *Tribes of the Rif: Papers of the Peabody Museum.* Cambridge, Mass.: Harvard University Press, 1931.

DAY, GEORGES. *Les Affaires de la Tunisie et le Maroc devant les Nations Unies.* Paris: Padone, 1955.

DEMICIS, EDMONDO. *Morocco: Its People and Places.* Philadelphia: Henry T. Coates, 1897.

AL-FASSI, ALLAL. *The Independence Movements in Arab North Africa.*

* To be published in English translation under the title *French North Africa: The Maghrib Between Two Wars* by Frederick A. Praeger in 1966.

(Translated from Arabic by H. Z. Nuseibeh.) Washington: American Council of Learned Societies, 1954.

GORDON, DAVID C. *North Africa's French Legacy*. Cambridge, Mass.: Harvard University Press, 1962.

GRANDVAL, GILBERT. *Ma Mission au Maroc*. Paris: Plon, 1956.

GRAY, HENRY. *In Moorish Captivity*. London: Edward Arnold, 1899.

Guide de l'Industriel désirant s'établir au Maroc. Rabat: Ministry of Commerce, 1961.

GUILLAUME, GENERAL A. *Les Berbers marocains et la pacification de l'Atlas central*. Paris: Julliard, 1946.

HAHN, LORNA. *North Africa: Nationalism to Nationhood*. Washington, D.C.: Public Affairs Press, 1960.

HARRIS, WALTER BURTON. *Morocco That Was*. Edinburgh: William Blackwood and Sons, 1921.

JUIN, MARSHAL. *Le Maghreb en Feu*. Paris: Plon, 1957.

JULIEN, CHARLES-ANDRÉ. *L'Afrique du Nord en marche*. Paris: Julliard, 1952.
———. *Histoire de l'Afrique du Nord: Tunisie, Algérie, Maroc, de la conquête arabe à 1830*. 2 vols. Paris: Payot, 1952–53.

LACOUTURE, JEAN and SIMONNE. *Le Maroc à l'épreuve*. Paris: Editions du Seuil, 1958.

LANDAU, ROM. *Moroccan Drama, 1900–55*. London: Robert Hale; San Francisco: American Academy of Asian Studies, 1956.

LATOUR, PIERRE BOYER DE. *Vérités sur l'Afrique du Nord*. Paris: Plon, 1956.

LEARED, ARTHUR. *Morocco and the Moors*. New York: Scribner & Welford, 1876.

LEGEY, FRANÇOISE. *Folklore of Morocco*. London: Allen & Unwin, 1935.

LEPP, IGNACE. *Midi Sonne au Maroc*. Paris: Editions Montaigne, 1954.

LE TOURNEAU, ROGER. *Fez in the Age of the Marinides*. Norman, Okla.: University of Oklahoma Press, 1961.

LIEBESNY, H. J. *The Government of French North Africa*. Philadelphia: University of Pennsylvania Press, 1943.

LYAUTEY, LOUIS. *Paroles d'Action*. Paris: Colin, 1927.

MIKESELL, MARVIN W. *Northern Morocco: A Cultural Geography*. Berkeley, Calif.: University of California Press, 1961.

MONTAGNE, ROBERT. *Les Berbères et le Maghzen dans le sud du Maroc*. Paris: Alcan, 1930.
———. *La Naissance du prolétariat marocain*. Paris: Peyronnet, 1950.
———. *Révolution au Maroc*. Paris: France-Empire, 1953.

MOREL, EDMUND D. *Morocco in Diplomacy*, London: Smith, Elder, 1912.

Morocco. Rabat: U.S. AID Mission, 1963.

Morocco 1950. Rabat: Editions Africaines Perceval, 1950.

Morocco Under the Protectorate: An Analysis of Facts and Figures. New York: Istiqlal, 1953.

L'Oeuvre de la France au Maroc de 1912 à 1947. Rabat: Editions Africaines Perceval, 1948.

PARENT, PIERRE. *Causerie sur le Maroc 1951*. Toulouse: Imprimerie Régionale, 1951.

REZETTE, ROBERT. *Les partis politiques Marocains*. Paris: Colin, 1955.

ROBERT, JACQUES. *La Monarchie marocaine*. Paris: Librairie du droit et du jurisprudence.

STEVENS, EDMUND. *North African Powderkeg*. New York: Coward-McCann, 1955.

Tableau Economique du Maroc, 1915–1959. Rabat: Ministry of the National Economy, 1960.

The Truth About Morocco. New York: Moroccan Office of Information and Documentation, 1953.

WATERSTON, ALBERT. *Planning in Morocco*. Baltimore: Johns Hopkins Press, for the International Bank for Reconstruction and Development, 1962.

WELCH, GALBRAITH. *North African Prelude*. New York: Morrow, 1949.

ZARTMAN, I. WILLIAM. *Morocco: Problems of New Power*. New York: Atherton, 1964.

Index